Lecture Notes in Business Information Processing 578

LNBIP reports state-of-the-art results in areas related to business information systems and industrial application software development – timely, at a high level, and in both printed and electronic form.

The type of material published includes

- Proceedings (published in time for the respective event)
- Postproceedings (consisting of thoroughly revised and/or extended final papers)
- Other edited monographs (such as, for example, project reports or invited volumes)
- Tutorials (coherently integrated collections of lectures given at advanced courses, seminars, schools, etc.)
- Award-winning or exceptional theses

LNBIP is abstracted/indexed in DBLP, EI and Scopus. LNBIP volumes are also submitted for the inclusion in ISI Proceedings.

Alfredo Goldman · Sabrina Marczak ·
Graziela Simone Tonin · Dairton Bassi ·
Tiago Silva da Silva · Eva-Maria Schön ·
Michael Neumann · Andrea Pinna
Editors

Agile Processes in Software Engineering and Extreme Programming

27th International Conference
on Agile Software Development, XP 2026
São Paulo, Brazil, April 8–11, 2026
Proceedings

Springer

Editors
Alfredo Goldman
University of São Paulo
São Paulo, São Paulo, Brazil

Graziela Simone Tonin
INSPER
São Paulo, Brazil

Tiago Silva da Silva
Universidade Federal de São Paulo
Vila Clementino - São Paulo, São Paulo, Brazil

Michael Neumann
Hochschule Hannover
Hannover, Germany

Sabrina Marczak
Pontifical Catholic University of Rio Grande do Sul
Partenon - Porto Alegre, Rio Grande do Sul, Brazil

Dairton Bassi
Agile Trends
São Paulo, Brazil

Eva-Maria Schön
University of Applied Sciences Emden/Leer
Emden, Germany

Andrea Pinna
University of Cagliari
Cagliari, Italy

ISSN 1865-1348 ISSN 1865-1356 (electronic)
Lecture Notes in Business Information Processing
ISBN 978-3-032-22374-6 ISBN 978-3-032-22375-3 (eBook)
https://doi.org/10.1007/978-3-032-22375-3

This Springer imprint is published by the registered company Springer Nature Switzerland AG
The registered company address is: Gewerbestrasse 11, 6330 Cham, Switzerland

Preface

With great pleasure we introduce this volume of research proceedings of XP-2026, the 27th International Conference on Agile Software Development, held during April 8–11, 2026, at Insper, São Paulo, Brazil.

Over the years, XP conferences have played a pivotal role in fostering the successful evolution and widespread adoption of Agile practices by teams and organizations - not only within the software industry and academic settings, but also across a broader range of domains.

The theme for XP 2026 was "Expanding Agile: Transforming Today, Shaping a Sustainable and Inclusive Tomorrow", emphasizing the importance of flexibility, learning, and innovation in delivering sustainable value through Agile methodologies.

This volume of the XP 2026 conference proceedings showcases a wide range of research contributions in the field of Agile software development. The papers included explore a broad spectrum of topics such as Leadership and Culture, Business Agility, Data-Driven Agility and Transformations, Engineering, AI–Augmented Software Engineering, Product and Design, and AI in Agile Teams.

The review process was structured as follows: First, an initial screening process of all submissions was conducted by the Academic Program Chairs. There were four desk rejections, and the remaining 52 submissions underwent a thorough single-blind review process with 3 reviewers. Then, an additional layer of quality assurance was applied: six of the accepted papers were conditionally accepted, and the authors were required to submit a revised version, which was reviewed by the Academic Track Chairs with the support of individual reviewers. Based on this review process, 18 papers (16 full papers and 2 short papers) were accepted for presentation at the conference.

We sincerely thank the authors whose work is featured in this volume for advancing the discourse in Agile software development. Our gratitude also goes to the reviewers for their dedication and thoughtful feedback, which ensured the high quality of these papers. We further acknowledge the invaluable contributions of all speakers, sponsors, shepherds, chairs, and volunteers who helped bring this conference to life. A special thanks is extended to the XP Conference Steering Committee and the sponsor "Insper, of São Paulo, Brazil".

February 2026

Alfredo Goldman
Sabrina Marczak
Graziela Simone Tonin
Dairton Bassi
Tiago Silva da Silva
Eva-Maria Schön
Michael Neumann
Andrea Pinna

Organization

Conference Co-chairs

Alfredo Goldman	University of São Paulo, Brazil
Sabrina Marczak	Pontifical Catholic University of Rio Grande do Sul, Brazil
Graziela Simone Tonin	INSPER, Brazil
Dairton Bassi	Agile Trends, Brazil

Program Co-chairs

Tiago Silva da Silva	Federal University of São Paulo, Brazil
Eva-Maria Schön	University of Applied Sciences Emden/Leer, Germany

Publication Co-chairs

Michael Neumann	University of Applied Sciences & Arts Hannover, Germany
Andrea Pinna	University of Cagliari, Italy

Program Committee

Ademar Aguiar	University of Porto, Portugal
Scott Ambler	SA+A, Canada
Hubert Baumeister	Technical University of Denmark, Denmark
Till Becker	University of Applied Sciences Emden/Leer, Germany
Jan Bosch Chalmers	University of Technology, Sweden
Frank Buschmann	Siemens AG, Germany
Joelma Choma	Universidade Federale de São Carlos Sorocaba, Brazil
Madalina G. Ciobanu	Free University of Bozen-Bolzano, Italy
Filipe Correia	University of Porto, Portugal
Yael Dubinsky	Kinneret Academic College, Israel

Jutta Eckstein	Independent, Germany
Henry Edison	Blekinge Institute of Technology, Sweden
M.J. Escalona	University of Seville, Spain
Steven D. Fraser	Innoxec, USA
Juan Garbajosa	Technical University of Madrid, Spain
Alfredo Goldman	University of São Paulo, Brazil
Peggy Gregory	University of Glasgow, UK
Eduardo Guerra	Free University of Bozen-Bolzano, Italy
Tomas Gustavsson	Karlstads universitet, Sweden
Orit Hazzan	Technion - Israel Institute of Technology, Israel
Andreas Hinderks	University of Applied Sciences and Arts Hannover, Germany
Kiyoshi Honda	Osaka Institute of Technology, Japan
Victoria Jackson	University of California, Irvine, USA
Eriks Klotins	Blekinge Institute of Technology, Sweden
Fabio Kon	University of São Paulo, Brazil
Martin Kropp	University of Applied Sciences and Arts Northwestern Switzerland
Ville Leppänen	University of Turku, Finland
Lech Madeyski	Wrocław University of Science and Technology, Poland
Antonio Martini	University of Oslo, Norway
Frank Maurer	University of Calgary, Canada
Paulo Meirelles	University of São Paulo, Brazil
Jorge Melegati	University of Porto, Portugal
Tommi Mikkonen	Jyväskylä University, Finland
Alok Mishra	Atilim University, Turkey
Nils Brede Moe	SINTEF, Norway
Jürgen Münch	Reutlingen University, Germany
Michael Neumann	University of Applied Sciences and Arts Hannover, Germany
Anh Nguyen-Duc	University of South–Eastern Norway, Norway
Maria Paasivaara	LUT University, Finland and Aalto University, Finland
Adam Przybylek	University of Galway, Ireland
Mali Senapathi	Auckland University of Technology, New Zealand
Helen Sharp	Open University, UK
Darja Šmite	Blekinge Institute of Technology, Sweden
Christoph Johann Stettina	Leiden University / Centre for Innovation, Netherlands
Viktoria Stray	University of Oslo, Norway
Diane Strode	Open University, UK

Steering Committee

Sponsoring Organizations

Insper, Brazil
University of São Paulo, Brazil
Pontifical Catholic University of Rio Grande do Sul, Brazil
Federal University of São Paulo, Brazil
Agile Trends, Brazil

Contents

Engineering

AI Augmented Software Engineering

Product and Design

AI in Agile Teams

Leadership and Culture

Sustaining Agility: How Agile Coaches Ensure Changes Endure

Ehikioya Obode[1(✉)], Peggy Gregory[1], Derek Somerville[1], and Advait Deshpande[2]

[1] University of Glasgow, Glasgow, Scotland
e.obode.1@research.gla.ac.uk,
{Peggy.Gregory,Derek.Somerville}@glasgow.ac.uk
[2] The Open University, Milton Keynes, UK
advait.deshpande@open.ac.uk

Abstract. Agile coaches play a key role in supporting software teams and organisations during agile transformations, yet little is known about how they understand and design for the continuation of agility after their involvement ends. This study fills that research gap by examining how agile coaches perceive post-exit outcomes and describing the strategies they use to support endurance beyond their engagement. Drawing on sixteen semi-structured interviews with professional agile coaches across multiple organisations, we identify six interconnected themes that capture coaches' accounts of embedding routines, transferring ownership, and aligning agile values with organisational contexts. We synthesise these themes into the concept of sustainment work, referring to the professional and organisational efforts that coaches describe undertaking to support the continuation of agile ways of working beyond their direct involvement. This synthesis is represented in an empirically derived model comprising three interrelated domains: Embedding Practices, Enabling Ownership, and Aligning Culture. The model reflects how coaches conceptualise the relationship between their interventions, anticipated post-exit trajectories, and the endurance of agile practices, rather than providing evidence of long-term organisational outcomes. The paper contributes theoretically grounded insights into how agility is understood and approached by highlighting coaches' perceptions and intended sustainment strategies, as an ongoing organisational concern rather than a time-bound coaching intervention.

Keywords: Agile coaching · Sustainment work · Professional Identity · Institutional work · Organisational culture · Continuous improvement · Agile Transformation

1 Introduction

Agile coaches play an important role in helping software engineering teams and organisations adopt and transform towards agility in their ways of working. Their

A. Goldman et al. (Eds.): XP 2026, LNBIP 578, pp. 3–19, 2026.
https://doi.org/10.1007/978-3-032-22375-3_1

work typically involves facilitating collaboration, strengthening team independence, and guiding leaders in embedding a culture of continuous improvement [10,13,18]. However, agile coaching engagements are often temporary, especially when delivered by external or consultant coaches. This raises important but understudied questions about what happens after agile coaches leave, and how long-term effects are achieved.

Existing research highlights the benefits of agile coaching during engagements, including improved team morale, enhanced process improvement, and increased learning capability [16,21]. Research on agile transformation similarly highlights that adopting agile practices does not guarantee lasting change without cultural reinforcement and embedded practices [7]. Kalenda et al. [12] and Conboy et al. [6] in their studies on the challenges of implementing large-scale agile frameworks, further highlight that organisations frequently experience regression or superficial adoption when teams remain dependent on external expertise like agile coaches. Additionally, research studies investigating the structural and cultural factors that affect agile sustainability do not always examine how coaches work to embed those factors [1]. While research insights suggest that sustaining agility depends on internal ownership, cultural alignment, and the embedding of agile practices and routines within an organisation [6], there is limited detail about how coaches play a role in achieving that aim or how they intentionally work to ensure continuity.

Understanding how agile coaches perceive the impact of their work is essential. For organisations, it relates to sustaining agile ways of working and achieving a return on investment from coaching. For coaches, it is about their professional identity and credibility, and ensuring that their legacy extends beyond their tenure. For researchers, it sheds light on how temporary actors, such as agile coaches, contribute to the embedding of agile practices and approaches. This study addresses these issues through a qualitative study of sixteen experienced agile coaches, guided by two research questions: **RQ1:** *How do agile coaches perceive what happens after they leave a team or organisation?* **RQ2:** *How do agile coaches seek to ensure that the impact of their work endures after their engagement with a team or organisation ends?* To address our research questions, we draw on professional identity and identity-work concepts [2,11,22] alongside Institutional Theory [14,17]. Identity-work perspectives are useful because agile coaching is often a temporary, boundary-spanning role in which practitioners must negotiate credibility, responsibility, and withdrawal as teams move towards independence. Concepts from Institutional Theory complement this by helping to identify outcomes from coaching interventions, such as routines, artefacts, norms, and shared meanings, that need to be embedded before coaches exit.

2 Background and Related Work

2.1 Agile Coaching and Organisational Transformation

The role of agile coaching has evolved over the years from focusing on facilitating team-level change towards involvement in broader organisational transformation and cultural change [8,9]. Agile coaches often work across multiple software teams and mediate tensions between legacy organisational structures and new agile ways of working [20]. Previous research has investigated how agile coaches contribute to team development [13], cross-team coordination [21], and product ownership capability [19]. However, these studies focus on insights during the coaching period rather than after the agile coach has exited their coaching engagement. There is also little known about how agile coaches perceive what happens after they exit their coaching engagement or how they prepare software teams and organisations for continuity after their exit.

2.2 Professional Identity and Identity-Related Work

Research on professional identity examines how individuals construct, maintain, and adapt a sense of who they are as professionals within organisational and social contexts. This body of work emphasises that professional identity is not fixed, but continuously shaped through interaction, role expectations, and changing organisational conditions. A key concept of this literature is **identity work**, which refers to the cognitive and behavioural activities through which individuals make sense of their roles, negotiate expectations and articulate professional purpose [2,11,22] Closely related is the concept of **legitimation work**, which describes how individuals seek recognition, credibility, and acceptance from relevant stakeholders by demonstrating competence, aligning with organisational norms, and framing their contributions in ways that resonate with local expectations [22]. It involves demonstrating competence, navigating organisational norms, and aligning one's role with organisational expectations. Prior studies have used professional identity and identity-related perspectives to examine role emergence, professional boundary work, and contexts in which individuals must continually justify their value or redefine their role.

2.3 Institutional Theory

Institutional Theory (IT) provides a complementary lens, focusing on the cultural, normative, and structural forces shaping organisational behaviour. It explains how practices become established, routinised, and taken for granted within social systems. A core concept of IT is **institutional work**, which refers to the activities by which actors create, maintain, or disrupt institutions [14]. Institutional work includes embedding routines, creating shared culture, establishing governance mechanisms, and reinforcing norms. Institutional work has been used to examine organisational transformation and the institutionalisation of new practices, particularly where actors seek to make new behaviours durable.

The theoretical perspectives introduced above are used as sensitising concepts to inform interpretation, not as prescriptive frameworks or deductive lenses. This approach enables an in-depth exploration of how coaches reason about their role, legitimacy, and efforts to embed agile practices, while remaining grounded in participants' self-reported perceptions and experiences. Alternative frameworks such as organisational change models, communities of practice, or learning theories emphasise adoption, participation, or knowledge transfer, but offer limited explanatory power for the post-exit sustainment dynamics examined here. Combining identity-work and institutional perspectives allows us to link individual sensemaking with organisational embedding.

3 Research Method

The study employed a qualitative interview design using semi-structured interviews which were analysed using inductive thematic analysis [3].

3.1 Data Collection and Sampling

The semi-structured interview guide used open-ended questions to elicit detailed accounts of coaching work, perceived impact, and perceived outcomes after coaches' departure. Sample questions included: *"What happens after you leave a team or organisation?"* and *"How do you ensure your work has a lasting impact?"*. The interviews were conversational and while the interview guide indicates the starting questions, follow-up questions were asked based on participants' answers, and these varied from interview to interview. The University granted ethical approval for the study.

A purposive sampling approach was taken to identify participants with diverse coaching backgrounds and organisational contexts. Inclusion criteria were: (a) having completed agile coaching training or structured internal coaching development; and (b) holding current or recent practical experience as an agile coach in an organisational setting. Individuals whose work involved agile methods but who did not perform an explicit coaching role (e.g., developer or manager without coaching responsibilities) were excluded. Recruitment took place through local agile meetups, professional networks, and a conference attended by two of the authors. The sampling aim was to achieve variety over participant demographics and experience while taking into consideration pragmatic issues such as participant availability. The sample size was guided by analytic sufficiency. Following the concept of information power, the study prioritised the relevance and experience of participants and the depth of the interviews over a predefined number [15]. As analysis progressed, later interviews mainly added detail to existing themes rather than introducing new ones, indicating that the data were sufficient to address the research questions. This approach is consistent with qualitative guidance that cautions against fixed numerical rules for sample size and emphasises alignment with analytic purpose [4].

3.2 Sample Characteristics

Sixteen agile coaches participated in the study in total (see Table 1). They comprised nine women and seven men, representing six European countries and the United States, providing both gender and geographical diversity. Several coaches specialised in multiple agile frameworks, with Scrum and SAFe being the most prevalent. The participants had varied agile coaching experience, ranging from two to fourteen years. Participants' professional backgrounds fell into two broad categories: technical roles, such as software engineering and quality assurance, and business-oriented roles, including project management and business analysis. A majority of the participants (14) obtained recognised agile certifications during or before their transition; however, two coaches relied solely on internal agile coaching training. Professionally, 10 participants were permanent employees, and six acted as external consultants within the IT and financial services industries. Notably, two individuals brought extensive backgrounds in both technical and management roles to their coaching practice.

3.3 Interview Procedure

First, a pilot interview was conducted with an experienced agile coach using an initial version of the interview guide. The first and second authors independently reviewed and discussed the pilot transcript, refining the wording, order, and focus of questions to ensure alignment with the research questions and to improve clarity. A final interview guide was then created.

Interviews were conducted either face to face or via web conference, according to participants' preferences and availability. All interviews were audio-recorded with participants' informed consent and transcribed verbatim. Interviews lasted between 45 and 70 min, with an average duration of approximately 60 min. Participants' responses varied in the depth and breadth of examples and reflections they provided, but the combined dataset offered rich, multi-faceted accounts of coaching practice and perceived sustainment. After transcription, all personally identifiable information (e.g., names, specific organisations, and project details) was removed or pseudonymised to preserve confidentiality.

3.4 Data Analysis

Data were analysed using Braun and Clarke's six-phase inductive thematic analysis approach [3], supported by NVivo 14 for data management and coding. The first author initially checked each transcript against the corresponding audio recording to correct transcription errors and ensure accuracy. The transcripts were then read multiple times to ensure familiarity, and preliminary analytical memos were created. Coding proceeded inductively but was sensitised by the research questions. The first author conducted line-by-line coding of all transcripts in NVivo, generating a broad set of data-driven codes that captured salient features of the coaches' accounts. While RQ1 and RQ2 are analytically distinct, they are empirically intertwined. During analysis, we initially examined accounts of perceived post-exit outcomes independently from descriptions of sustainment strategies, before iteratively exploring how these accounts informed one another. Codes were iteratively collated into preliminary subthemes that represented patterns across participants. These subthemes were reviewed and refined through multiple team discussions, during which the authors compared interpretations, examined disconfirming cases, and returned to the raw data where

Table 1. Participant Demographics

ID	Gender	Employment	Method Specialism	Coaching (Yrs)	Sectors worked in	Country
P1	F	Contract	Scrum, Kanban, LeSS, SAFe	14	Telecoms; Banking; Oil & Gas; Automobile; Software; Printing	England
P2	F	Permanent	Scrum, SAFe	7	FinTech; Public Sector	Scotland
P3	M	Permanent	Scrum, SAFe	15	Financial Services; IT	Scotland
P4	F	Permanent	Scrum, Kanban	3	IT	Austria
P5	M	Contract	Scrum, SAFe, Spotify	6	Banking; Public Sector; Media; Automobile	Scotland
P6	F	Permanent	Kanban, Scrum	2	Public Sector	Scotland
P7	M	Permanent	Scrum, Lean	3	IT	Scotland
P8	F	Contract	Scrum, Kanban	6	Education	Germany
P9	M	Contract	Scrum, Kanban, SAFe, LeSS, Lean	14	Transport & Logistics; Pharmaceutical; Finance; FinTech; Consulting	Denmark
P10	F	Permanent	Scrum, Kanban, LeSS, SAFe, Systemic Coaching	8	IT; Medical; Logistics; Banking	Austria
P11	M	Permanent	SAFe	10	Public Sector; Pharmaceutical; Manufacturing; Food Retail	Switzerland
P12	F	Permanent	Scrum, LeSS, Kanban	5	Scientific	England
P13	F	Contract	Framework Agnostic	5	IT	Germany
P14	M	Permanent	Scrum	3	Banking; Telecoms	Austria
P15	F	Contract	Enterprise Scrum; Lean; Systems Thinking	17	Finance; Telecom; Startups; Insurance; Energy; Non-profit	USA
P16	M	Permanent	Scrum, SAFe	8	Automobile; Scientific; Banking; Consulting	Germany

necessary. Through this process, the subthemes were grouped into six overarching themes. At each step, decisions to merge, split, or retain subthemes were guided by clarity, internal coherence, and their ability to illuminate the research questions.

To support analytic triangulation, after manual analysis was complete, the anonymised transcripts were uploaded to AILYZE, an artificial intelligence driven qualitative analysis tool [5]. AILYZE was configured to generate an independent thematic overview of the dataset. The AILYZE-generated themes were then compared systematically with the manually developed themes. In several instances, the tool surfaced clusters that overlapped with the existing thematic structure (e.g., around building self sustaining teams or managing post-exit relationships), which increased confidence in these patterns. Where AILYZE suggested additional groupings or emphases, the team revisited the underlying data and discussed whether incorporating these would improve clarity and empirical grounding. Ultimately, differences were judged to be either already captured in subthemes or not sufficiently supported across cases, so no changes were made to the final thematic structure. The criteria for not modifying themes were (a) lack of robust support across multiple participants, (b) redundancy with existing subthemes. AILYZE thus served as a supplementary check and stimulus for reflexive discussion, rather than as a primary analytic tool.

3.5 Researcher Positionality

The authors' positionality as researchers and practitioners shaped the study. The first author has prior experience in agile coaching and consulting, which facilitated access to participants and informed the development of the interview guide, but also required reflexive attention to assumptions around good coaching practices. The other authors have backgrounds in software engineering and agile research. Throughout data collection and analysis, the team engaged in regular reflexive discussions to surface and bracket prior beliefs about agile coaching, sustainment, and organisational change, and to foreground participants' accounts.

3.6 Themes to Model Development

After completing the inductive thematic analysis, we moved from detailed themes to a higher-level synthesis aimed at understanding how coaches reason about the endurance of their work beyond their involvement. This step focused on integrating patterns across themes rather than generating additional themes. We conducted an iterative comparative review of the themes, examining how themes related to one another and what shared underlying concerns they reflected. For each theme, a brief analytic memo was produced summarising its core focus. These memos were compared to identify recurring concerns, overlaps, and tensions across the dataset. Through repeated reviews and revisiting the coded data, themes addressing similar underlying concerns were grouped into a smaller set of higher-level analytic groupings. These groupings, which we term domains, provided the organising structure for the conceptual model presented in Fig. 1. Identity work and legitimation work concepts from professional identity literature and institutional work concept from institutional theory were then used as sensitising concepts to inform the interpretation of these domains. Importantly, these concepts did not guide coding or domain construction, but supported the interpretation of the forms of work coaches described within each empirically derived domain, and situating the findings within existing research.

4 Findings

Our thematic analysis revealed six key themes that describe how agile coaches conceptualise the sustainment of agility beyond their direct involvement. Table 2 lists the six themes and their subthemes derived from the data analysis. They illustrate a spectrum of experiences and strategies through which agile coaches seek to ensure that agility endures. The findings show that the elements coaches focus on to achieve this involve deliberate attempts to embed autonomy, continuity, and cultural alignment. Each theme is presented in more detail below.

4.1 Building Self-sustaining Teams

The coaches described multiple practices aimed at reducing reliance on their ongoing presence. These included gradual handover of facilitation responsibilities, rotation of agile roles within teams, and co-creation of working agreements. While many coaches viewed self-redundancy as a marker of success, some noted that achieving this depended on team maturity and organisational support. For example, P13 explained that withdrawal was only feasible once teams demonstrated agile maturity. *"This is why I mentioned that, for me, my job is to guide the team to agile maturity. And if a team reaches maturity, then it's a good time for me to leave the team"*. while others described situations where premature exit risked dependency or regression. The strategy of building a self-sustaining team before the agile coach's exit captures how the coaches intentionally design themselves out of the team by shifting their role from being a facilitator of agility to an enabler of self-sustaining capability.

4.2 Post-exit Variability: From Sustainability to Regression

Accounts of what happens after a coach's departure were varied. Coaches noted that some teams maintained an agile mindset and practices and took pride in their independence. Others noted that teams stagnated or regressed from their agile practices and principles once the coach's support was withdrawn. Others also described uncertainty and limited visibility after their departure from a team or organisation, with some reporting that they rely on informal feedback or later observations to infer outcomes. This variability in outcomes was attributed to differences in leadership commitment to agile transformation, organisational stability, and cultural readiness. Regression was not always interpreted negatively, with some coaches seeing temporary setbacks as part of learning.

P10 noted, *"it's very hard to say what happens after I leave. I've worked with so many teams, and you know, some really have adopted agile practices on their own, whereas others have not"* P5 noted, *"If you look at the most common reason why digital transformations fail, in many cases they didn't even have any agile coaches, and or they maybe had agile coaches for six months and then withdrew them all, and then suddenly people just revert to their old ways of working"*. These

Table 2. Summary of Themes and Subthemes

Theme	Subthemes	Summary Description
BUILDING SELF-SUSTAINING TEAMS	*Maturing teams*	Coaches aim for redundancy by transferring autonomy, embedding agile values and rotating facilitation within teams
	Gradual handover	
	Distributed ownership	
	Values-led leadership	

continued

Table 2. continued

Theme	Subthemes	Summary Description
POST-EXIT VARIABILITY	*Sustained agile practice*	Teams follow diverse trajectories post-exit. Some teams sustain their agile practices, and others stagnate or regress depending on leadership and context
	Regression risk	
	Uncertainty after departure	
	Team reconfiguration	
MECHANISMS FOR CONTINUITY	*Deputies & succession*	Institutional artefacts (succession roles, documents, automation, dashboards) institutionalise agile routines beyond coach presence
	Documentation & guides	
	Automation & tooling	
	Feedback loops & metrics	
CULTURE OF CONTINUOUS IMPROVEMENT	*Training & agile frameworks*	Learning is embedded as a daily habit through education, small improvements, experimentation, and accountable follow-through
	Experimentation & adaptation	
	Transparency & feedback loops	
	Contextual and technological adaptation	
VALUE-ALIGNMENT OVER RITUAL	*Link to business outcomes*	Agility endures when aligned with real business value and kept lightweight and context-sensitive rather than ritualistic
	Contextual adaptation	
	Lightweight adaptive frameworks	
	Avoid ritualistic agility	
POST-EXIT RELATIONSHIPS & BOUNDARIES	*Light-touch follow-up*	Coaches balance informal post-exit contact with healthy detachment, through communities of practice and peer learning
	Professional detachment	
	External learning ecosystems	

accounts illustrate that coaches perceived post-exit outcomes as uncertain and context-dependent, often relying on indirect feedback or later observation.

4.3 Mechanisms for Continuity: Structures, Roles and Artefacts

Several coaches reported that they would try to establish specific institutional roles and artefacts to secure continuity, for example, succession roles, documentation, and automation. These artefacts or setups were created to outlive the coaches. Many discussed appointing a deputy within a team to shadow them to ensure the transfer of skills. They also created guide documents or formalised feedback loops and performance dashboards to maintain reflection cycles. Some relied on tooling and automation (e.g., DevOps pipelines, JIRA metrics) to institutionalise improvement routines, especially within software engineering teams. While some coaches described extensive use of documentation and automation, others noted that such mechanisms were constrained by organisational readiness or technical context

P11 described their approach to continuity in the following words: *"Documentation is key,... it's how we store all our tooling and techniques. Also, the ways of working and team agreements"*. These mechanisms represent the material and procedural imprint of agile coaching, which show evidence of how professional expertise becomes embedded within organisational systems.

4.4 Culture of Continuous Improvement

Several coaches described focusing on cultivating a habit of continuous learning. They emphasised the importance of helping teams reflect, experiment, and adapt. They highlighted the value of iterative improvements, supported the visibility of issues, and fostered team members' accountability. Experimentation, including the deliberate withdrawal of the coach, was used to test the resilience of teams. Continuous improvement was framed as the key cultural element that sustains agility within agile transformation programmes. Coaches linked continuous improvement to practices such as regular retrospectives, visible tracking of actions, and deliberate experimentation, describing these as ways to normalise learning rather than enforce compliance

P3 mentioned: *"The secret is training and small, small improvements. Every sprint, they should be tweaking something."* This theme illustrates how learning becomes internalised when teams own both reflection and action, turning agility into an enduring practice rather than a temporary project.

4.5 Value-Alignment over Ritual

Several coaches also advised against treating agile frameworks as ends in themselves. They argued that sustaining agility depends on connecting agile practices to real business value and organisational context. They also argued that simplifying agile frameworks, tailoring agile methods to organisational culture, and resisting ritualistic agility were seen as key to sustaining agility. They added that agility persists when it remains aligned to business outcomes.

P9 noted: *"I tell teams not to go blindly with frameworks, but to adapt to what fits their purpose and context"*. P9's view was reinforced by P13, who said, *"The lighter the process, the more likely it is to survive once you're gone."* Coaches described a shift from strict procedural adherence toward adapting agile practices to organisational goals.

4.6 Post-exit Relationships and Boundaries

Coaches described varied relationships with organisations after departure. Some maintained light-touch follow-ups or informal peer networks to monitor progress, while others viewed disengagement as professionally appropriate once contractual goals were met. A few of the coaches encouraged regular involvement in external agile learning communities and agile conferences as sources of renewal. These patterns show differing identity positions, ranging from sustained guardianship to purposeful detachment.

P12 highlighted*"I've moved on from quite a few teams, but I still have those relationships with the developers and encourage them to reach out if needed."* These accounts illustrate different approaches to post-exit contact and disengagement.

5 Discussion

The conceptual model in (Fig. 1) was created from our findings. The themes related to autonomy, role redundancy, and boundary-setting clustered around how coaches described transferring responsibility and capability to teams, which was synthesised as Enabling Ownership. Themes describing artefacts, routines, feedback mechanisms, and improvement systems clustered around how agile practices were stabilised beyond individual actors, which was synthesised as Embedding Practices. Themes related to value alignment, cultural acceptance, and post-exit variability clustered around the perceived legitimacy and stability of agility within the organisation, which was synthesised as Aligning Culture.

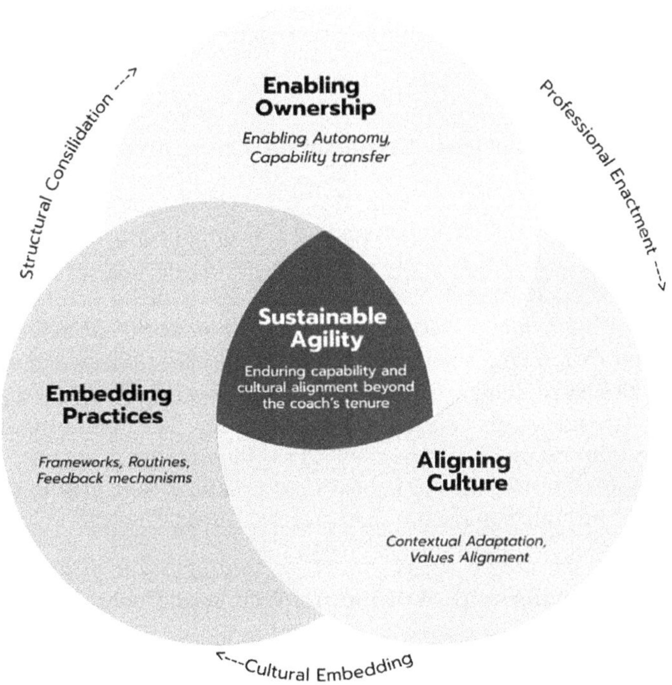

Fig. 1. Agile Coaching Sustainment Work Model.

Identity work and legitimation work concepts were used to interpret how coaches described negotiating role redundancy, authority, and withdrawal as teams moved toward autonomy. The institutional work concept was used to interpret how coaches described embedding routines, artefacts, and norms intended to persist beyond their involvement. The model addresses both research questions by integrating coaches' perceptions of what might happen when they leave with their plans for ensuring sustained agility. In relation to **RQ1,** it shows that coaches interpret what happens after their departure through recurring concerns about whether ownership has been transferred, practices are embedded, and agility is culturally aligned. In relation to **RQ2,** the model shows that coaches seek to ensure their work endures while still engaged by deliberately acting across these same concerns; enabling ownership through role handover for autonomy and capability transfer, embedding practices through frameworks, feedback mechanisms and routines, and aligning agile culture with organisational context and values in anticipation of exit. By bringing these together, the model captures how coaches' interpretations of post-exit situations and their sustainment strategies are reflexively connected. The cyclical structure reflects the reflexive relationship between coaches' interpretations of post-exit outcomes and the strategies they describe employing, rather than a linear or causal process. We use the term Sustainable Agility to refer to how coaches conceptualise the continuation of agile values, routines, and improvement practices after their departure, grounded in their accounts rather than as a claim about verified long-term outcomes.

5.1 Embedding Practices: Structuring Continuity Beyond Individuals

The themes *Mechanisms for Continuity* and *Culture of Continuous Improvement* describe how coaches seek to embed agile ways of working beyond individual roles via institutional work. Coaches reported introducing artefacts, routines, automation, feedback loops, and improvement frameworks intended to support continuity after exit. These accounts reflect how coaches understand sustainment as requiring practices that are repeatable and integrated into everyday work, rather than dependent on continued external support. This domain captures the structural dimension of sustainment work, illustrating how coaches describe translating their expertise into organisational practices that may persist beyond their presence, without evidencing institutionalisation directly.

5.2 Enabling Ownership: Autonomy, Exit and Post-exit Trajectories

The themes *Building Self-Sustaining Teams, Post-Exit Relationships and Boundaries, and Post-Exit Variability* highlight how coaches reason about the transfer of responsibility from themselves to teams and organisations. Coaches frequently framed professional success in terms of making themselves redundant through handing over facilitation roles, developing internal champions, and normalising self-organisation. Coaches also described varied post-exit trajectories, ranging from sustained autonomy to stagnation or regression. These variations were interpreted as reflecting differences in how effectively ownership had been transferred prior to exit, alongside contextual factors such as leadership support and team stability. Post-exit variability therefore, forms part of how coaches reason about ownership transfer rather than a separate outcome. Interpreted through identity and legitimation concepts, Enabling Ownership captures the relational dimension of sustainment work, encompassing both how coaches seek to enable autonomy and how they interpret what happens after they step back.

5.3 Aligning Culture: Making Agility Meaningful Rather Than Ritual

The theme *Value-Alignment over Ritual* highlights how coaches perceive cultural alignment as central to whether agility endures after their departure. Coaches described working to connect agile practices to organisational purpose, leadership language, and business priorities, emphasising that agility is more likely to persist when it is meaningful rather than performed mechanically. Aligning Culture captures how coaches reason about legitimacy and acceptance within organisational contexts. When such alignment was perceived as weak, coaches reported that teams were more likely to abandon agile practices after exit. Interpreted through the concept of identity work, coaches define and perform their role as enablers of autonomy; through legitimation work, they seek to transfer credibility and align agile values with organisational purpose; and through institutional work, they seek to embed these values within routines and structures that persist over time.

5.4 Integrating the Domains: Sustainment as Reflective Work

Together, the three domains illustrate how coaches conceptualise sustainment as ongoing work spanning structural, relational, and cultural concerns. The interaction of these concerns constitutes *sustainment work*, which describes how coaches reason about supporting continuity beyond their involvement.

Sustainment is thus understood not as a guaranteed outcome, but as a reflective process shaped by coaches' interpretations of prior engagements and their strategies for future ones. The model captures how coaches connect professional identity, organisational practices, and cultural meaning when reasoning about their role and their success.

5.5 Implications for Practice

Our findings highlight that agile coaches' approach to sustaining agility depends less on prolonged external support and more on how effectively they design for their own departure.

For agile coaches, results from this study highlight the importance of treating sustainment work as a part of each engagement rather than an afterthought.

Coaches can support endurance by planning for handover early, mentoring internal champions, and embedding agile routines, artefacts, and improvement practices into everyday work. Framing professional success in terms of reducing dependence on the coach helps shift focus from delivery to capability-building.

For organisations, the findings indicate that sustaining agility requires investment beyond the presence of individual coaches. Establishing internal coaching capabilities or recognised agile champion roles can help maintain continuity and legitimacy once external support ends. Leadership plays a critical role by reinforcing agile values in organisational language that resonates with business priorities and by treating coaching as a means of developing long-term capability rather than a short-term cost.

For teams, findings point to the value of peer learning and reflective practices in supporting independence. Practices such as rotating facilitation roles, regular retrospectives, and shared responsibility for improvement help teams internalise ownership and reduce reliance on external guidance. Agility is more likely to endure when teams take responsibility for learning and adaptation themselves.

Collectively, these implications suggest that effective coaching engagements are those that intentionally plan for their own redundancy. An agile coach's success at ensuring sustained agility is not about their continued presence. In this view, a coach's success is not defined by continued involvement, but by whether teams and organisations are better positioned to carry agile practices, values, and ways of working forward independently.

6 Conclusions

Findings show that coaches' knowledge of post-exit situations is partial and interpretive, shaped by experience and indirect feedback, and that this knowledge informs how they design for sustainment in future engagements. Sustainment is therefore framed as a matter of perception and professional judgement rather than a guaranteed organisational outcome. Addressing RQ1, coaches described varied post-exit trajectories, ranging from perceived sustained autonomy to stagnation or regression. These accounts reflect coaches' interpretations of organisational readiness, leadership support, and cultural maturity at the point of departure, highlighting sustainment as an ongoing and uncertain concern rather than a stable end state. In relation to RQ2, the study identifies deliberate strategies through which coaches seek to support continuity. We conceptualise these activities as sustainment work, encompassing efforts to transfer ownership, embed practices and artefacts, and align agile values with organisational contexts. Conceptually, these strategies reflect how coaches describe engaging in identity work, legitimation work, and institutional work as they reason about and design for sustainment beyond their involvement. The Agile Sustainment Work Model (Fig. 1) provides an empirically grounded synthesis of these findings. It illustrates how coaches conceptualise the interplay between ownership, practices, and cultural alignment when reasoning about anticipated post-exit trajectories, rather than evidencing long-term organisational effects. For practitioners, it highlights the importance of deliberate exit planning, distributed ownership, and cultural alignment. For researchers, it underscores the need for complementary perspectives and longitudinal work to examine how post-exit trajectories evolve beyond coaches' involvement.

6.1 Limitations and Future Work

This study has certain limitations that define the scope of its contributions, as is common with most qualitative research. First, the analysis is based on agile coaches' perceptions and reflections of post-exit dynamics rather than direct observation of organisational outcomes. The findings, therefore, highlight how agile coaches conceptualise and anticipate agility sustainment, rather than how it actually emerges after their exit. Second, the participant group reflects those willing and able to articulate their practices within interview settings. In addition, while the participants interviewed reflect diverse industry experience, it does not include perspectives from team members, leaders, or clients. Third, the study is cross-sectional, providing retrospective reflections rather than longitudinal evidence of change over time. These limitations also suggest fruitful directions for future research. Longitudinal and multi-stakeholder studies could examine how the mechanisms identified here (embedding practices, enabling ownership, and legitimising culture) play out in practice over extended periods. Comparative research across sectors and employment models (internal versus external coaches) may also reveal contextual differences in how identity and institutional work interact. Finally, the *Agile Coaching Sustainment Work Model* offers a conceptual foundation for studying the evolution of agility by examining how sustained practices adapt and regenerate in response to continuous transformation.

References

1. Barroca, L., Sharp, H., Deshpande, A., Gregory, P., Papadeas, S.: Sustaining agility: organizational change, factors and theoretical lenses. In: International Conference on Agile Software Development, pp. 115–131. Springer, Cham (2023)
2. Beech, N.: Liminality and the practices of identity reconstruction. Human Relat. **64**(2), 285–302 (2011). https://doi.org/10.1177/0018726710371235
3. Braun, V., Clarke, V.: Reflecting on reflexive thematic analysis. Qualit. Res. Sport Exercise Health **11**(4), 589–597 (2019)
4. Braun, V., Clarke, V.: Thematic Analysis: A Practical Guide. SAGE (2021)
5. Cameron, H.: Breaking up with nvivo: AI delivers faster, deeper, and better qualitative insights. In: Deeper, and Better Qualitative Insights (2025)
6. Conboy, K., Carroll, N.: Implementing large-scale agile frameworks: challenges and recommendations. IEEE Softw. **36**(2), 44–50 (2019). https://doi.org/10.1109/MS.2018.2884865
7. Denning, S.: The challenge of leadership in the age of agile. Learning Lead Leadership Organ. Dev. J. (2018). https://doi.org/10.1002/ltl.20371
8. Dingsøyr, T., Moe, N.B., Fægri, T.E., Seim, E.A.: Exploring software development at the very large-scale: a revelatory case study and research agenda for agile method adaptation. Empir. Softw. Eng. **23**(2), 765–797 (2018). https://doi.org/10.1007/s10664-017-9524-0

9. Gren, L., Torkar, R., Feldt, R.: Group development and group maturity when building agile teams: a qualitative and quantitative investigation at eight large companies. Empir. Softw. Eng. **20**(3), 734–772 (2015). https://doi.org/10.1007/s10664-014-9317-4
10. Hoda, R., Noble, J., Marshall, S.: Self-organizing roles on agile software development teams. IEEE Trans. Softw. Eng. **39**(3), 422–444 (2013). https://doi.org/10.1109/TSE.2012.30
11. Ibarra, H.: Provisional selves: experimenting with image and identity in professional adaptation. Adm. Sci. Q. **44**(4), 764–791 (1999). https://doi.org/10.2307/2667055
12. Kalenda, M., Hyna, P., Rossi, B.: Scaling agile in large organizations: practices, challenges, and success factors. J. Softw. Evolut. Process **30**(10), e1954 (2018). https://doi.org/10.1002/smr.1954
13. Klünder, J., Trommer, F., Prenner, N.: How agile coaches create an agile mindset in development teams: insights from an interview study. J. Softw. Evolut. Process **34**(2), e2380 (2022). https://doi.org/10.1002/smr.2380
14. Lawrence, T.B., Suddaby, R.: Institutions and institutional work. In: Clegg, S., Hardy, C., Lawrence, T.B., Nord, W.R. (eds.) The Sage Handbook of Organizational Institutionalism, pp. 215–254. Sage (2006)
15. Malterud, K., Siersma, V.D., Guassora, A.D.: Sample size in qualitative interview studies: guided by information power. Qual. Health Res. **26**(13), 1753–1760 (2016)
16. Obode, E., Gregory, P., Somerville, D., Deshpande, A.: Agile coaching research: a systematic mapping study. In: International Conference on Agile Software Development, pp. 19–36. Springer, Cham (2025)
17. Scott, W.R.: Institutions and Organizations: Ideas and Interests, 3 edn. Sage (2008)
18. Senapathi, M., Strode, D.: Challenges to sustaining agility: an exploratory case study. In: Proceedings of the 39th ACM/SIGAPP Symposium on Applied Computing, pp. 810–817 (2024)
19. Stettina, C.J., Hörz, J.: Agile portfolio management: an empirical perspective on the practice in use. Int. J. Project Manag. **33**(3), 437–448 (2015). https://doi.org/10.1016/j.ijproman.2014.08.001
20. Stray, V., Memon, B., Paruch, L.: A systematic literature review on agile coaching and the role of the agile coach. In: Proceedings of the International Conference on Product-Focused Software Process Improvement (PROFES), pp. 201–217. Springer, Heidelberg (2020). https://doi.org/10.1007/978-3-030-63432-7_14
21. Stray, V.G., Tkalich, A., Moe, N.B.: The agile coach role: coaching for agile performance impact. In: Proceedings of the Annual Hawaii International Conference on System Sciences (HICSS), pp. 6816–6825. University of Hawaii at Mānoa (2021). https://doi.org/10.24251/hicss.2021.817
22. Sveningsson, S., Alvesson, M.: Managing managerial identities: organizational fragmentation, discourse and identity struggle. Hum. Relat. **56**(10), 1163–1193 (2003). https://doi.org/10.1177/00187267035610001

From Fear to Reflection: Value Retrospectives to Enhance Value Creation in Agile Teams

Suvi Ihaksi(✉) and Maria Paasivaara

LUT University, Lahti, Finland
suvi.ihaksi@student.lut.fi, maria.paasivaara@lut.fi

Abstract. Although agile teams aim to maximize value, few studies have examined how teams collectively develop an understanding of value beyond the Product Owner's perspective. While Product Owners often define value priorities, team members' understanding of how daily work connects to business goals and broader organizational context often remains limited. To address this gap, this study introduces and evaluates a *value retrospective process*, a structured reflection on cost and value. Informed by Design Science Research principles, the process was jointly designed by the first author, acting as Agile Lead, and the company's finance function. The process was implemented across 61 cross-functional teams in a large Finnish conglomerate, and iteratively refined over two years. This study examines process design, organizational implementation, and participant experiences using semi-structured interviews. The findings show that participants initially perceived retrospectives as potentially judgmental or audit-like, but over time, these perceptions shifted toward psychologically safe, constructive dialogue. Value retrospectives supported increased awareness of costs and value, strengthened team-sponsor alignment, and prompted concrete improvement actions. This study contributes an empirically grounded process model and insights into how structured value reflection can support learning and alignment in agile teams.

Keywords: agile · cross-functional teams · value creation · retrospective · psychological safety · organizational learning

1 Introduction

Agile development emphasizes frequent feedback and continuous learning, yet many agile teams operate without a clear or shared understanding of the value they create. Prior research highlights this gap between intention and practice: while 84% of product owners report validating business value delivery, only 24% report actually measuring business value [1]. This suggests that value is often assessed informally rather than through explicit measurement. Although most agile frameworks, such as Scrum [2], SAFe [3], and LeSS [4], define explicit

A. Goldman et al. (Eds.): XP 2026, LNBIP 578, pp. 20–36, 2026.
https://doi.org/10.1007/978-3-032-22375-3_2

product-related roles with responsibility for prioritizing and maximizing value, they also emphasize that value is created and realized through collective efforts of cross-functional teams [5]. In enterprise settings, this shared responsibility is further complicated by diverse stakeholders, technical complexity, and layered decision-making, making it challenging for teams to reflect effectively on the costs and impacts of their work [6–8]. To address this gap, our research designed and introduced the concept of *the value retrospective* - a structured team reflection on cost and value. These sessions brought together team members, supporting roles (e.g. business controllers), and team sponsors i.e. management representatives to reflect on how work contributes to both local goals and enterprise priorities.

In our previous paper [9] we analyzed the documented outcomes of 61 team-level value retrospectives to understand how cross-functional agile teams articulate value to their organization, particularly towards top management. Building on these insights, the present study shifts focus from *what* types of value teams identify to *how* they experience and evolve their understanding of value creation through reflective practice. Specifically, we examine how the value retrospective process evolves over time, how individuals and teams experience it, and how teams perceive its influence on cost and value-related thinking and actions.

This study is informed by Design Science Research (DSR) principles [10]. The value retrospective process was jointly designed by the first author, acting in the organizational role of Agile Lead, and the finance function, and was continuously refined based on its use in practice. This study examines the introduction and evolution of a practically designed organizational process. In this study, the design science artifact is the value retrospective process, understood as a designed method supported by templates and facilitation practices.

We investigate the following research questions:

RQ1. *How do value retrospectives in cross-functional agile teams contribute to value creation at individual and team level?*
RQ2. *What changes in value creation practices or outcomes were realized between consecutive value retrospectives?*
RQ3. *How could the value retrospective process be improved?*

To address these research questions, we conducted a two-year longitudinal study in a large Finnish conglomerate. The following sections detail the conceptual background, the research design, and the findings that emerged from the participant experiences. This paper contributes an empirically evaluated process model for value retrospectives, along with insights into how such practices evolve over time and influence team learning, psychological safety, and strategic alignment.

2 Background and Related Work

Value in Agile and Software Engineering. The notion of value is central to agile development, yet it remains conceptually vague and operationally challenging. Value can be tangible or intangible [11] and is domain-dependent [8,12].

Agile frameworks emphasize maximizing customer and business value [2–4], but rarely specify how teams should define or evaluate it in practice. Earlier studies on software value [13,14] have proposed taxonomies describing diverse value dimensions - ranging from revenue and customer satisfaction to technical quality, time-to-market and team morale. While these contributions have advanced our understanding of what constitutes value in software-intensive organizations, they provide limited insight into how teams collectively interpret and enhance value within the team and with their sponsors.

Team-Level Sensemaking of Value and Costs. As shown in our previous study [9], teams interpret value through multiple lenses. This paper extends that insight by investigating how such understanding develops over time. Prior research, including our earlier study and work by Stettina et al. [15], reveals that value interpretations vary by team role and organizational level. Teams closer to customers tend to highlight external impact, while platform teams emphasize internal efficiency.

Organizations can enhance value understanding in various ways. Agile portfolio management [16–18] is often used in organizations applying SAFe. Objectives and Key Results (OKR) method [19,20] has recently gained traction [21], but interestingly one of the main difficulties in making them useful is insufficient understanding of objectives within the organization [22].

Retrospectives as Learning Mechanism. Retrospectives are a core agile practice, offering structured reflection for team learning and improvement [23]. While traditional retrospectives focus on team dynamics and processes [24], value retrospectives extend their utility to financial and strategic dimensions, promoting organization-wide alignment. Effective retrospectives depend on psychological safety, shared belief that the team is safe for interpersonal risk-taking [25], which supports open dialogue and innovation in agile contexts [26]. Financial topics can trigger defensiveness, fear or blame, making psychological safety especially important.

Value retrospectives in this study extend both the scope and stakes of traditional retrospectives. They require teams to examine not only how to work, but also what that work is worth. This raises new organizational learning questions about how reflective practices connect local and enterprise perspectives on value creation, as organizational learning emerges when individual learning is embedded in team and organizational routines [27].

3 Research Design

This study focuses on the design, implementation, and evaluation of a practical organizational process that supports cost and value reflection in agile teams. This study includes two parts:

- Value retrospective process design: creation and implementation of the value retrospective process within a large Finnish conglomerate.
- Qualitative interviews: exploring participants' lived experiences of the value retrospective process through semi-structured interviews.

3.1 Value Retrospective Process Design

Problem Context and Design Objectives. The value retrospective process was designed in a Finnish conglomerate as an organizational process to address the organization's challenge of strengthening value orientation and transparency within agile teams and between teams and management. The company applies its own agile model, drawing inspiration from multiple existing frameworks such as Scrum, the Spotify Model and the Product Operating Model [2,28,29]. The model is based on cross-functional teams that include business, technology, and customer expertise. Teams may define their detailed ways of working to best suit their purpose and needs, but they are required to follow common practices, such as using Objectives and Key Results (OKRs) for planning cycles, organizing regular demos and learning through retrospectives. While OKRs and regular retrospectives provided useful insights, there remained a need for an investment follow-up-like method tailored to agile teams.

A retrospective-inspired approach was chosen due to its established role in fostering team learning and iterative improvement. The value retrospective was grounded in the Retrospective Prime Directive [30]: "Regardless of what we discover, we understand and truly believe that everyone did the best job they could, given what they knew at the time, their skills and abilities, the resources available, and the situation at hand." This was accompanied by the principle that each expert's daily work and decisions affect team costs and value. The purpose was to foster data-informed and psychologically safe discussions of cost and value. The process (Fig. 1) was developed collaboratively by the Agile Lead and the finance function based on practitioner experience and introduced as a mandatory annual reflection practice, with the intention that teams could also apply it more frequently if deemed useful. During the process design, multiple sparring sessions were held with agile coaches, agile team members, leadership teams, and several C-level representatives. Before wider deployment, the value retrospective process was piloted by three voluntary teams, leading to significant improvements in the templates and other process artifacts, for example adding discussion on team purpose and scope as the first topic in the value retrospectives. At the time of the study, teams in the company worked on-site at least two days per week and jointly agreed on their remote and on-site arrangements. Accordingly, the value retrospective process was primarily designed as a face-to-face discussion, bringing team members and management around the same table.

The process aimed to enable both team-level and organizational learning by integrating financial awareness with agile reflection routines.

3.2 Qualitative Interviews on Participant Experience

Participant Selection. To investigate participants' lived experiences and perceived changes between consecutive retrospectives, semi-structured interviews were conducted. The interviewees had recently participated in a value retrospective, all but one having participated in two consecutive annual value retrospectives already. Purposeful sampling [31] ensured diversity of roles and viewpoints, including developers, product owners, business controllers, agile coaches, and sponsors. Table 1 summarizes the participant demographics and engagement with value retrospectives. To minimize bias, sampling decisions were reviewed collaboratively by both authors. Particular attention was paid to including participants with critical or reflective perspectives to ensure a balanced view of the process's impact and limitations.

Data Collection. Data were collected through semi-structured interviews as they offer insights into human actions, contexts, and historical information [32] and are ideal for enabling detailed responses and clarifications. The interviews were conducted by the first author in November 2025, with voluntary participation and informed consent. The interviews explored participants' reflections on the value retrospective process, perceived changes between rounds, and suggestions for improvement. The interview guide[1] included 25 general and 17 role-specific questions divided between 6 roles. The interview guide was reviewed by the second author, and questions were refined for neutrality and clarity. Interviews were conducted either on-site or remotely via Microsoft Teams, lasting between 30 and 56 min. Interviews were held in Finnish when it was the native language of both the interviewer and the participant, and in English otherwise. All interviews were audio recorded with consent and transcribed using Microsoft Teams Copilot, followed by manual proofreading and anonymization. Identifiers such as participant names, teams, and organizational units were replaced with pseudonyms. Participant quotes were translated by the first author, with accuracy ensured through contextual review of the full transcripts. The data includes company confidential information related to costs and value, and thus cannot be shared. Demographic attributes - including language, employment type, tenure, interview location, and duration - were imported into NVivo for analysis along with the transcripts Table 1.

Data Analysis. We adopted thematic analysis [33] with a hybrid deductive-inductive coding approach [34], suitable for Design Science evaluation where themes emerge both from research goals and empirical use contexts. An initial codebook was derived from the research questions, and it was iteratively developed through several rounds as new interviews were analyzed.

Reflexivity and Trustworthiness. The first author occupied an insider-researcher role [35], simultaneously serving as an Agile Lead in the case organization, responsible for design and implementation of the value retrospective

[1] Interview guide available at: https://doi.org/10.6084/m9.figshare.30767684.

Table 1. Participant demographics and engagement with value retrospectives

ID	Role	Tenure (months)	# Retros	Days since last	Interview	Duration (minutes)	Language
P1	Agile Coach	18	12	5	On-site	45	Finnish
P2	Team Lead	12	4	2	Remote	30	Finnish
P3	Product Owner	8	2	1	On-site	30	Finnish
P4	Business Controller	42	25	0	On-site	40	Finnish
P5	Designer	7	1	8	Remote	32	English
P6	Developer	36	2	8	Remote	36	English
P7	Product Owner	34	4	2	Remote	34	Finnish
P8	Process Specialist	32	2	7	Remote	30	Finnish
P9	Sponsor	34	10	0	On-site	56	Finnish
P10	Agile Master	38	5	0	On-site	50	Finnish

process. This dual position offered deep contextual understanding and access to rich data but also posed risks of bias - the "double-edged sword" of insiderness [36]. To strengthen research credibility, several mitigation steps were applied: The second author reviewed the interview guide, sample interview recording, related transcript and initial codebook. Sampling emphasized diversity and inclusion of critical voices. Multiple debriefing discussions were held between authors to question assumptions and interpretations.

The first author informed each participant prior to the interviews about the insider-researcher role, and explained in detail the research process, the data usage, confidentiality and the voluntary nature of participation.

4 Results

This section presents and evaluates the value retrospective process and its evolution through real-world use: how it was implemented and refined in a real-world setting across two implementation rounds. Insights of the initial implementation and subsequent feedback-driven improvements are complemented by qualitative findings from participant interviews conducted after Round 2.

4.1 Process Artifacts and Deployment

The value retrospective process was operationalized through the following supporting artifacts: (a) Value Retrospective concept introduction (Fig. 1), (b) team reflection template, (c) management-level summary template and instructions, (d) facilitator guide, and (e) MS Teams space for material storage. Together, these materials instantiated the value retrospective process and supported its consistent execution across 61 teams, supporting examination through real-world use. Agile coaches and business controllers collaboratively facilitated the initial rollout, and feedback was collected for refinement.

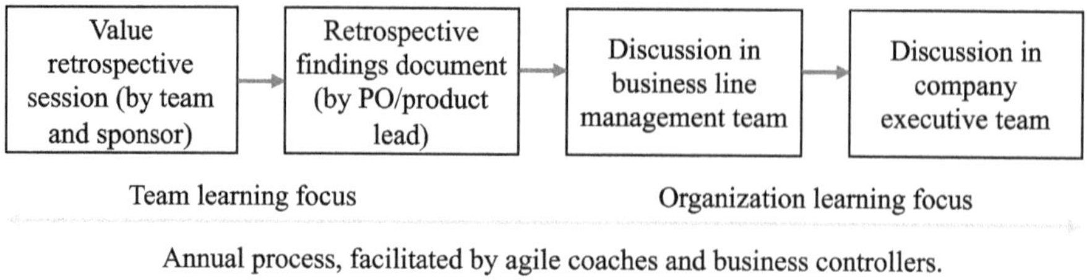

Fig. 1. Value retrospective overview.

4.2 Value Retrospectives - Round 1 Implementation

The first round of value retrospectives was conducted between October 2024 and March 2025 across 61 agile cross-functional teams. Value retrospectives were typically two-hour sessions facilitated by agile coaches with participation from team members, sponsors, and business controllers. While primarily planned as on-site sessions, some were conducted in hybrid mode without changes to the agenda structure. Some participants mentioned that on first round the time allocated for cost deep-dive was exceeded, but on second round more time was spent on understanding value.

Each retrospective followed a seven-step structure (see Table 2), covering introductions, review of cost and value data, joint reflection, and identification of improvement actions. Discussions were documented directly in the team's reflection template, and team-level summaries were later consolidated into a management-level synthesis. The consolidated report included quantitative metrics, qualitative insights, and aggregated observations per business area.

The subsequent sections report how teams experienced the process, how the retrospectives evolved between rounds, and how participants assessed and proposed improvements.

4.3 RQ1. How Do Value Retrospectives Contribute to Value Creation at Individual and Team Levels?

The analysis revealed that value retrospectives supported reflection and learning across individual, team, and organizational levels. However, this process was not straightforward: early reactions were characterized by doubt, confusion, and even fear about the purpose of the exercise. Only after the first round did retrospectives evolve into constructive, psychologically safe dialogues on cost and value.

Individual Level: from Suspicions to Active Dialogue. Before the first value retrospective, many participants were concerned that the session might resemble an inquisition or cost audit, suspecting it to be a blaming game or even fearing layoffs. These reactions shaped improvements to process design and facilitation. For example, specific guidance was created for top management

Table 2. Value Retrospective Agenda—Round 1

Topic & Duration	Content • Guiding Questions
Intro to Value Retro (10 min)	Participant introductions. Reminding of the retrospective's purpose. Agenda walkthrough. • What is our team's purpose and scope of responsibility?
Costs Deep-Dive (20 min)	Review of financial data prepared by Product Owner and business controller. Guiding questions: • What is the team total cost? What is the balance between development and operations? What is the internal vs. external resource cost ratio? Are there significant non-personnel costs? How is the team funded?
Value Deep-Dive (20 min)	Exploration of delivered value based on participant input. Guiding questions: • What strategic value has the team delivered? What measurable financial benefits were realized? What qualitative or intangible benefits emerged?
Cost-Value Discussion (20 min)	Joint reflection on cost-value relationship and lessons learned. Example questions: • Are our objectives ambitious enough? Are the metrics we use fit-for-purpose? What priority conflicts arose and how were they resolved? What did we learn and want to change?
Main Messages to Management (15 min)	Formulation of 2–4 key messages for the executive team. • What cost- or value-related topics should leadership know? Any other critical messages we want to raise?
Next Steps & Actions (15 min)	Defining concrete improvement actions and follow-up ownership. • What will we develop further? How and where will we track progress?
Buffer (10 min)	Time reserve for overruns or emergent discussions.
Total duration	**110 min**

about what to expect and how to behave when seeing the value retrospective outcomes. This quote of an agile coach demonstrates the participant feelings:

> *"To be honest, I have to say I was positively surprised. I remember when the coaching team first practiced this exercise themselves, it made me feel a bit skeptical — wondering how it would work, and whether the measurement would work. I was also worried about how people would react once we started talking about investment, money, and costs. But when we actually started doing it, I realized that it turned out to be really effective and successful." (P1, Agile Coach)*

By the second round, participants reported that *"now that we have experience that this was not roasting"* (P3) they felt they could speak openly even with a Vice President present. Still, the sponsor offered a more cautious reflection, recognizing that psychological safety remains fragile:

> *"Even though the retrospective is supposed to be a safe space, I personally see the world as cold enough that most people — and I believe the Product Owners understands this too — will still think: 'We'd better come up with some really good answers if we want this team (and the funding) to keep going." (P9, Sponsor)*

Individuals described a new awareness of costs and the broader impact of their work, sometimes for the first time in their careers. One participant described an eye-opening moment of realizing their financial impact:

> *"The savings we achieved simply by refining a process and no longer sending customers material they immediately discard when using the mobile service. Moments like these gave us tangible proof — and real confidence — that the decisions we make as a team truly affect the bottom line." (P8, Process Specialist)*

Participants especially appreciated the opportunity to examine their work from a broader organizational perspective, through a dedicated discussion together with the team sponsors. One participant described it as *"outside-in look"* (P6), while another appreciated the chance *"to be seen and heard despite being far from decision-making"* (P4).

The process encouraged reflection beyond regular role boundaries. An agile coach and agile master described expanding their role from methods coaching to value creation coaching. A business controller described "*connecting the dots from the numbers that I crunch to actual business and customer value*" (P4).

Team Level: Alignment and Measuring the Unmeasurable. At the team level, the retrospectives triggered reflection on purpose, direction, and collective contribution. Discussions clarified expectations and strengthened alignment between the team and its sponsor, and *"gave kind of direction to our team"* (P5). One team, for example, discovered that they and their sponsor had different interpretations of the product's goal, sponsor seeing it more sales-focused, and team more customer experience -focused. The value retrospective surfaced and resolved this misalignment: "*This was a good checkpoint for our team's value promise.*" (P7)

Many participants had never seen the actual costs of their work, and this transparency was both surprising and empowering:

> *"We just had more of a sense of the costs. It was quite a surprise to see the numbers up on the screen of how much money is involved in running the team." (P6, Developer)*

For non-customer-facing teams, articulating value remained difficult. Teams responsible for infrastructure, data, or internal services often found their impact less tangible. One analytics team described its value as *"helping business make wiser decisions*" (P10), which is not easily captured in numerical metrics. Some teams found it helpful to reframe value hypothetically - "*What would happen if our team did not exist?*" (P7) - as a way to surface their hidden contributions.

Organizational Level: The Role of Sponsors. Sponsor participation was crucial. Facilitators noted that active engagement reinforced purpose, while absence limited impact.

> *"Some [sponsors] were very active and encouraging and brought business inputs to our teams, and gave concrete feedback from the end users of our services. Some were less active, but still encouraging (...) I felt like not all sponsors knew what it is they are participating in and how important it is." (P2, Business Controller)*

Teams with strong sponsor engagement reported more constructive dialogue and better alignment between the team and management. Conversely, teams without sponsor presence struggled to articulate their value in enterprise terms. Interestingly, IT and platform teams demonstrated strong cost literacy but struggled more with expressing value, while customer-facing teams often experienced the opposite.

Teams valued the sponsor participation which provided the opportunity for rare face-to-face discussion that was fully dedicated to their specific topics.

> *"There might be some problems or blockers in the way of value creation—issues that the team has talked about for years, and then they suddenly come up as a surprise. It turns out they're actually very easy and quick to fix, as long as the right people sit at the right table. For me, it's been surprising that such things have come up, even though we operate in agile model where, in principle, management is quite close to the teams—yet it still hasn't always been quite enough" (P4, Business Controller)*

4.4 RQ2: What Changes in Value Creation Practices or Outcomes Were Realized Between Consecutive Value Retrospectives?

Beyond the changes in team understanding and behaviour, the organization itself learned from the first-round experiences. The process was iteratively refined based on feedback from facilitators, team members, and sponsors.

Evolution of the Value Retrospective Process Between Rounds. Table 3 summarizes multi-source feedback from Round 1 that led to conceptual and practical improvements for the next iteration. These refinements resulted in a clearer, more structured process that enhanced usefulness while preserving familiarity.

Table 3. Summary of Feedback and Implemented Improvements for Round 2

Source	Key Feedback	Improvements
Executive Team (discussions)	Requested clearer split of operational vs. development costs, better timing with company's budgeting cycle, and stronger evidence of value to funding entities.	Added explicit cost-split guidelines and a dedicated *Value to Funding Entities* section in the management summary. Adjusted the overall schedule based on the company budgeting timeline.
Agile Teams/Coaches (discussion documented in Miro board)	Process clarity, value creation, cost transparency, and enabling conditions needed improvement.	Redesigned team value-retrospective template: better flow, rephrased questions, higher consistency.
Business Controllers (face-to-face meeting)	Inconsistent cost collection and categorisation, alignment between team and management summaries.	Standardised cost sub-categories and strengthened linkage between team-level data and executive summaries.
External Developers (face-to-face meeting)	Improved sense of contribution to the case company goals when allowed to participate.	Encouraged agile teams to include external developers in the discussions.

Cost-Impacting Findings and New Focus on Value. Several teams implemented cost-saving actions directly inspired by the value retrospectives. In one case, reviewing cost data revealed a legacy system that was consuming 18% of the team's budget. After a critical discussion between the team and the sponsor in the value retrospective, the joint decision was to prioritize the work needed to discontinue and replace this system, leading to multi-million-euro savings.

> *"Earlier, the plan was to retire it somewhere towards the end of the decade. But once the costs hit us in the face, the decision was made if not around the value retrospective table, almost immediately after, and we expect the system to be shut down by the end of the year." (P10, Agile Master)*

Teams also described value becoming more tangible, as sponsors provided feedback in monetary terms.

Comparing the two rounds of retrospectives revealed a clear shift from participant caution to engagement, and from awareness to action. The first round was dominated by cost discussions and careful observation. The second round, in contrast, featured more confident and creative dialogue about value, trade-offs, and possibilities. The tone of discussions also evolved. By the second round, participants requested bolder questions. For example, a question initially phrased as *"What if you had 20% more or 20% less budget?"* was replaced with "What if your team's budget was doubled or tripled?" This shift encouraged aspirational thinking and *"painting the dreams"(P8)*, with participants acknowledging that *"we would never have dared to voice them if we hadn't been explicitly asked"(P4)*.

4.5 RQ3: How Could the Value Retrospective Process Be Further Improved?

Round 2 interviewees offered additional suggestions for making the process more systematic and participatory, and to modify the guiding questions to provoke bolder thinking. Content and question design were the most common area for improvement. Participants suggested refining or tailoring the guiding questions to team maturity and context and to focus the discussion on fewer questions. Some found the current questions too abstract, while others wanted more future-oriented questions that trigger wider discussions and thinking about strategy and customer impact.

> *"We switched to bolder questions like What if your team suddenly doubled or tripled? Suddenly people started coming up with ideas they hadn't considered before. Sometimes, after a short discussion, we realized that some crazy ideas were actually feasible and we could implement them anyway. These moments stretch the team's thinking and lead to surprising growth and innovation." (P9, Sponsor)*

Interviewees highlighted the need to increase developer engagement during the sessions. This was brought from two viewpoints: how to encourage them to be more active during discussions, and how to structure the process so that Product Owners will not hijack the discussion as they have done most of the preparation.

Clarity of purpose and preparation were common themes. Some teams entered the first retrospective with little understanding of what it was about or what data would be used. Although guidelines and templates existed, they were not always applied consistently.

Facilitators had intentionally kept the preparation light, but participants recommended striking a better balance between efficiency and readiness. Some participants worried about POs spending too much time in preparation of data, while others wanted more data to be available before the value retrospective to be able to prepare and reflect meaningfully during the session.

Finally, the interview question regarding the opportunity to share learnings across teams divided the participant opinions: typically the team members did not see a big need or value in sharing value retrospective insights across teams, while team sponsors and team supporting roles identified topics that would support cross-team learning and team-sponsor dialogue if shared effectively.

5 Discussion

The value retrospective process was perceived to improve agile teams' understanding of value. Similarly to [15], also our research concluded that understanding of value differs on different levels in the organization. Focused discussions on team purpose, cost and value and extended participation by team sponsors and business controllers makes it possible to address issues beyond team's scope, opposite to team-only focus observed by Lehtinen et al. [24].

While teams see their outputs, the value retrospectives helped them gain broader context and clarify their purpose. The value networks, as described by Allee [11] were visible also in the value retrospective discussions: sometimes the value takes multiple steps to realize as customer value (e.g. analytics team and platform team). It may also take multiple forms (customer satisfaction, efficiency savings, etc.), depending on the team purpose, similar to the prior software engineering value taxonomies [13,14].

Our findings confirm prior research [25] on the role of psychological safety in enabling open and rich dialogue. Notably, the shift observed between retrospective rounds highlights the importance of repeated, well-facilitated reflection to build trust.

Value retrospectives were new for most people, and some participants compared them to what they called regular retrospectives [23]. Retrospectives are mostly used for reflecting on ways of working, but based on our research similar thinking can be applied to costs and value. Most teams used the combination of annual value retrospectives with 2–3 month OKRs (Objectives and Key Results) [19,20] when asked how they measure their success. Participants viewed the yearly cadence good for company-wide implementation, but suggested the team-level cadence to be determined through practice.

5.1 Threats to Validity

We assess threats to validity following guidelines by Runeson and Höst [37], with additional consideration for design-oriented research principles such as relevance, rigor, and artifact evaluation [10].

Construct Validity. This study focuses on a novel process artifact, the value retrospective, designed to enhance value reflection in agile teams. Construct validity is supported through careful artifact definition, including templates, facilitation structures, and framing principles. To mitigate bias from the first author's insider role, the second author reviewed the interview guide, sample transcripts, and codebook. Participant diversity and inclusion of critical voices helped ensure a balanced understanding of the process impact.

Internal Validity. Observed changes in the perceptions and practices may have been influenced by external factors (e.g. organizational shifts). However, the two-round implementation and triangulation across roles support a contextual and interpretive understanding of how participants experienced the effects of the value retrospective process. The qualitative interviews helped reveal how participants themselves linked observed changes to the value retrospective process. This supports evaluating the practical usefulness of the process, as emphasized in Design Science.

External Validity. Although the process was implemented in 61 teams, the interviews during Round 2 involved only ten participants from two business areas. While purposeful sampling captured diverse roles, wider sampling would provide additional insights.

Reliability. Reliability was addressed through transparent and systematic research procedures. All interviews were recorded, transcribed and coded using a documented codebook and qualitative analysis tools. The first author led the analysis, with the second author providing critical review of the interview guide, sample transcripts, and coding decisions. Due to organizational confidentiality, the raw data cannot be shared; however, detailed descriptions of the process, instruments, and analytical steps are provided to enable analytical and procedural replication in similar contexts.

6 Conclusions

This study explored and refined a value retrospective process, structured reflections on cost and value, to strengthen shared understanding, cost awareness, and organizational learning in cross-functional agile teams. Through a two-year longitudinal study, we observed how teams initially approached the process with caution, but gradually developed psychological safety, enabling honest and constructive dialogue. Additionally, we observed that the teams identified concrete measures to improve value and cost, especially after seeing the actual costs of their systems and processes. Rather than proving increases in delivered value, the contribution of this study lies in making cost and value discussable, visible, and actionable within agile teams and their sponsors. Value retrospectives also helped the teams clarify and validate their purpose. In line with design-oriented research principles [10], this paper contributes an empirically grounded and evaluated process model for structured value reflection grounded in real-world implementation, refined through feedback, and aligned with established Design Science principles of utility, relevance, and artifact rigor.

Future work should explore how this process scales across varied team types, and how it ties up with other management structures and executive-level needs. Also, studying value retrospective process in a hybrid or remote setting would provide interesting new insights.

Acknowledgements. We warmly thank all interviewees for their time, insights, and openness in sharing their experiences. AI tools (ChatGPT, ScholarGPT) were used for language polishing and formatting support.

References

1. van Daalen, E., van Solingen, R.: The current state of operationalizing value by Dutch product owners in agile software development. In: Agile Processes in Software Engineering and Extreme Programming. Lecture Notes in Computer Science, vol. 512, pp. 89–106. Springer, Cham (2024)
2. Scrum.org: The Scrum guide. Online (2020). Accessed 2025
3. Scaled Agile, Inc.: Scaled Agile Framework. Online (2025). Accessed 2025
4. LeSS Company B.V.: Large-Scale Scrum Framework. Online (2025). Accessed 2025
5. Hofman, M., Grela, G., Oronowicz, M.: Impact of shared leadership quality on agile team productivity and project results. Proj. Manag. J. **54**(3), 285–305 (2023)
6. Steegh, R., Van De Voorde, K., Paauwe, J.: Understanding how agile teams reach effectiveness: a systematic literature review to take stock and look forward. Hum. Resour. Manag. Rev. **35**(1), 101056 (2025)
7. Delisle, J., Marnewick, C., Romero-Torres, A.: Exploring temporal dimensions of benefits realisation management in agile IT environments. Int. J. Inf. Syst. Proj. Manag. **13**(4), 1–17 (2025)
8. Chong, E., Handscomb, C., Maj, T., Markenday, R., Morse, L., West, D.: In pursuit of value - not work (2022)
9. Ihaksi, S., Paasivaara, M., Hyrynsalmi, S.: From customer proximity to enterprise goals: how agile teams perceive and articulate value. Accepted for publication (forthcoming) (2026)
10. Hevner, A.R., March, S.T., Park, J., Ram, S.: Design science in information systems research. MIS Q. **28**(1), 75–105 (2004)
11. Allee, V.: The value evolution. J. Intellect. Cap. **1**(1), 17–32 (2000)
12. Porter, M.E.: Competitive Advantage. The Free Press (1998)
13. Khurum, M., Gorschek, T., Wilson, M.: The software value map – an exhaustive collection of value aspects for the development of software intensive products. J. Softw. Evol. Process **25**(7), 711–741 (2013)
14. Alahyari, H., Berntsson Svensson, R., Gorschek, T.: A study of value in agile software development organizations. J. Syst. Softw. **125**, 271–288 (2017)
15. Stettina, C.J., van Els, V., Croonenberg, J., Visser, J.: The impact of agile transformations on organizational performance. In: Agile Processes in Software Engineering and Extreme Programming. Lecture Notes in Computer Science. Springer, Cham (2021)
16. Vähäniitty, J.: Towards agile product and portfolio management. Aalto University (2012). ISSN: 1799-4942 (electronic)
17. Stettina, C.J., Hörz, J.: Agile portfolio management: an empirical perspective on the practice in use. Int. J. Project Manage. **33**(1), 140–152 (2015)
18. Bechtel, J., Kaufmann, C., Kock, A.: Agile projects in non-agile portfolios: how project portfolio contingencies constrain agile projects' teamwork quality. IEEE Trans. Eng. Manage. **69**(6), 3514–3528 (2022)
19. Doerr, J.: Measure What Matters: How Google, Bono, and the Gates Foundation Rock the World with OKRs. Portfolio Penguin, New York, NY (2018)
20. Wowerath, C.: Engaging the entire organization: how OKRs enhance integrative strategy implementation. J. Bus. Strategy **11**, 1–19 (2025)
21. Stray, V., Gundelsby, J.H., Ulfsnes, R., Brede Moe, N.: How agile teams make objectives and key results (OKRs) work. In: Proceedings of the International Conference on Software and System Processes and International Conference on Global Software Engineering. ICSSP 2022, New York, NY, USA, pp. 104–109. Association for Computing Machinery (2022)

22. Jonathan, M., et al.: Unlocking the OKR framework: insights into benefits and barriers for an effective implementation in practice. In: Software Engineering and Advanced Applications. SEAA 2025. Lecture Notes in Computer Science, vol. 16082. Springer, Cham (2026)
23. Derby, E., Larsen, D.: Agile retrospectives: making good teams great. The pragmatic programmers. Pragmatic Bookshelf, Raleigh, N.C (2006)
24. Lehtinen, T.O.A., Itkonen, J., Lassenius, C.: Recurring opinions or productive improvements–what agile teams actually discuss in retrospectives. Empirical Softw. Eng. Int. J. **22**(5), 2409–2452 (2017)
25. Edmondson, A.: Psychological safety and learning behavior in work teams. Adm. Sci. Q. **44**(2), 350–383 (1999)
26. Ahmad, M.O.: Strengthening large-scale agile teams: the interplay of high-quality relationships, psychological safety, and learning from failures. J. Softw. Evol. Process **37**(1) (2025)
27. Levitt, B., March, J.G.: Organizational learning. Ann. Rev. Sociol. **14**(1), 319–340 (1988)
28. Kniberg, H.: Spotify engineering culture (part 2)
29. Cagan, M.: Inspired: How to Create Tech Products Customers Love, 2nd edn. Wiley (2018)
30. Kerth, N.L.: Project Retrospectives: A Handbook for Team Reviews. Addison-Wesley (2013)
31. Hoda, R.: Qualitative Research with Socio-Technical Grounded Theory: A Practical Guide to Qualitative Data Analysis and Theory Development in the Digital World, 1st edn. Springer (2024)
32. Yin, R.K.: Case study research and applications (2018)
33. Braun, V., Clarke, V.: Using thematic analysis in psychology. Qual. Res. Psychol. **3**(2), 77–101 (2006)
34. Feraday, J., Muir-Cochrane, E.: Demonstrating rigor using thematic analysis: a hybrid approach of inductive and deductive coding and theme development. Int. J. Qual. Methods **5**(1), 80–92 (2006)
35. Brannick, T., Coghlan, D.: In defense of being "native": the case for insider academic research. Organ. Res. Methods **10**(1), 59–74 (2007)
36. Mercer, J.: The challenges of insider research in educational institutions: wielding a double-edged sword and resolving delicate dilemmas. Oxf. Rev. Educ. **33**(1), 1–17 (2007)
37. Runeson, P., Höst, M.: Guidelines for conducting and reporting case study research in software engineering. Empir. Softw. Eng. **14**, 131–164 (2009)

Business Agility

Decision-Making and Team Autonomy in Large-Scale Agile Software Development: An Analysis of Scaling Frameworks

Lucas Rocha[1(✉)], Fabiana Mendes[1], Maria Paasivaara[2], and Casper Lassenius[1]

[1] Aalto University, Espoo, Finland
{lucas.rocha,fabiana.mendes,casper.lassenius}@aalto.fi
[2] Lappeenranta-Lahti University of Technology, Lahti, Finland
maria.paasivaara@lut.fi

Abstract. Team autonomy—the extent to which teams can make decisions—is a central tenet of agile development. When scaling agile, technical and coordination challenges necessitate restricting autonomy. While greater autonomy is often considered better, the reasons for, and the extent to which, autonomy is, or should be, restricted in large-scale agile development remain poorly understood. In this paper, we address this gap by analyzing large-scale agile frameworks using decision-making theory. Applying inductive thematic analysis to the primary documents of scaling frameworks, we identify and categorize their decisions and related decision-making elements by decision-maker, decision type, decision-making style, decision timing, and affected artifacts. This research contributes to decision-making knowledge by providing a systematic categorization of decision points in large-scale agile development. For practitioners, the resulting classification helps identify key decision points, define roles and responsibilities, and plan team autonomy in large-scale agile.

Keywords: team autonomy · large-scale agile software development · scaling frameworks · SAFe · LeSS · Nexus · Spotify · Scrum at Scale

1 Introduction

Agile software development relies on autonomous teams, i.e., self-managing teams that take responsibility for their own work [6]. For single agile teams working closely with the customer, high levels of autonomy are often considered beneficial [12]. However, when agile development is scaled to multiple interdependent teams, full autonomy may no longer be optimal or even feasible [13]. Scaled agile approaches must therefore balance organizational control and standardization with the desire for team autonomy to find an appropriate "sweet spot" [13].

In this paper, we focus on *decision-making autonomy*, a central dimension of team autonomy: the extent to which teams have authority and responsibility

A. Goldman et al. (Eds.): XP 2026, LNBIP 578, pp. 39–55, 2026.
https://doi.org/10.1007/978-3-032-22375-3_3

over decisions that shape their work. While team autonomy may also include freedom in execution and self-management, we think focusing on decision rights provides a concrete, fine-grained lens for analyzing how autonomy is structured and constrained.

Decision-making can be understood as the process of making a series of choices to address complex problems [2]. By examining which decisions teams are allowed to make, and under what constraints or escalation structures, we gain insight into the decision-making aspect of autonomy in agile organizations.

Despite the central role of autonomy in agile development, relatively little research has examined how autonomy is structured and constrained in large-scale settings [10,13]. While agile methods emphasize autonomous teams, there is, to our knowledge, a lack of detailed studies investigating (a) how major scaling frameworks explicitly allocate or limit decision-making authority, and (b) how much autonomy teams actually exercise in practice within such frameworks.

In this paper, we address the first of these gaps by offering a systematic comparison of leading agile scaling frameworks through the lens of decision-making autonomy. Our analysis provides a more fine-grained account of how autonomy is prescribed across frameworks than has previously been available, and establishes a conceptual foundation for future empirical studies of team autonomy *in vivo*.

2 Background and Related Work

Agile software development relies on autonomous teams delivering working software. This is explicitly stated or implied in agile methodologies. For example, in the Scrum Guide, which presents Scrum as a framework for small teams: *"Scrum teams are...self-managing, meaning they internally decide who does what, when, and how"* [19]; and Lean software development states that *"empowering people, encouraging teamwork, and moving decision-making to the lowest possible level are fundamental to any lean implementation"* [15]. Throughout this paper, when we refer to Scrum as defined Scrum Guide [19].

Team autonomy refers to the degree of freedom granted to teams and is widely studied outside the field of software engineering [1,6]. One often-used definition defines autonomous teams as *"employees that typically perform highly related or interdependent jobs, who are identified and identifiable as a social unit in an organization, and who are given significant authority and responsibility for many aspects of their work, such as planning, scheduling, and assigning tasks to members, and making decisions with economic consequence."* [5]

While higher autonomy can lead to better performance, this is not necessarily the case when scaling to many interdependent teams [13]. Granting too much autonomy can create issues, e.g., with coordination [1]. Empirical studies have shown that autonomy often is reduced in practice [7,12].

Previous studies on large-scale agile software development have examined autonomy only at a high level of abstraction, focusing on general structures, rather than on concrete decision points and how specific decisions are made in practice [3]. We suggest creating such a view through the lens of decision-making. We propose that the Vroom-Yetton decision model [22], which categorizes decision-making styles by the level of stakeholder involvement, can be used to understand team autonomy. Originally developed in the field of business management, the model has been widely used in that area, and also in software engineering [11].

Some studies on decision-making and agile software development exist. E.g., one study [4] examined the correlation between 32 decisions made in Scrum sprints and the level at which these decisions were made, tactical or strategic. The study highlights six decision-making challenges faced by Agile teams, ranging from internal team problems (such as members not taking ownership of decisions) to external ones (such as conflicting customer priorities). Although the study compares Scrum with the decisions made, it does not focus on scaling frameworks; e.g., coordination and integration challenges are not even mentioned.

Another paper [14] studied the decision-making process in communities of practice (CoPs) in a LeSS-based development organization. The authors emphasized the shift of decision-making autonomy from management to teams, but did not provide details on the specifics of the decisions, who is responsible for them, or when they should be made.

A comparison of the levels of autonomy across the main scaling frameworks is provided in [13], but it covers only SAFe, LeSS, and Spotify and is at a very high level, not examining specific decisions, decision-making styles, or decision-makers.

3 Research Method

This research aims to **understand how decision autonomy is defined and how decisions are distributed among stakeholders in large-scale agile frameworks**. To reach this goal, we seek to answer the following research questions (RQ):

RQ 1. What are the differences and similarities at the team level in decision autonomy across the large-scale agile frameworks?
RQ 2. What are the differences and similarities at the team of teams level in decision autonomy across the large-scale agile frameworks?

To keep the effort manageable, we opted to include only the most widely known frameworks in our study, as well as Scrum [19] as a baseline, since many frameworks focus on scaling or adding practices to it. Of the available scaling frameworks, we selected Nexus [18], Scrum@Scale (S@S) [20], the "Spotify Model" [9], LeSS [21], and SAFe [17], which are the most commonly adopted ones [16], except for internal frameworks, which would be impractical to consider in this study.

For all frameworks, we relied on the most recent version of the framework's official documentation available at the time of data collection (June 2025). Next, we decided on how to identify decisions in that material. We had two cases: a) a sentence explicitly describes a decision by using the word decision or a related synonym, and b) the decision is implicit.

For implicit decisions, we employed Klein's recognition-primed decision-making model as a conceptual lens. The model characterizes decisions based on four aspects: plausible goals, relevant cues, expectancies, and actions. [8]

In practice, plausible goals and actions were identifiable in most cases, as the documentation typically specifies the scope of a decision and the set of possible actions. Relevant cues and expectancies were less frequently observable, as they often involve individual judgment or situational assessment, which would require empirical case studies rather than prescriptive framework documentation. An example of an implicit decision is the statement *"[The Product Owner] may do the above work or may delegate..."* [19, p. 7], which implies a delegation decision. In summary, inductive thematic analysis was initially used to identify decision points, while the recognition-primed decision-making model was used to interpret implicit decisions.

For each decision found in the document, we decided to extract the following: (a) *Decision description:* a brief description of the decision identified in the text; (b) *Role (who):* the decision-maker, either an individual or a group; (c)*Event (when)*: the moment in the agile process when the decision occurs; and (d) *Decision-Making Style:* degree of stakeholders participation in decision making [22].

The categorization of the decision-making style is based on the Vroom-Yetton model, which has been widely used in different fields, with the book [22] cited more than 7300 times according to Google Scholar in February 2026. In the context of Software Engineering, there are, e.g., studies that explore the correlation between decision-making style and the decision-maker's personality traits [11], corroborating the broad applicability of the model.

The Vroom-Yetton model [22] defines five decision-making styles, ranging from the most autocratic to the most participative. In this paper, we reduce these into three distinct styles: (1) **autocratic**, where one individual is responsible for deciding without consulting anyone else; (2) **consultative**, where one person decides after gathering input from some or all stakeholders; and (3) **group consensus**, where a decision is made collectively by a group of individuals who reach an agreement.

The original model differentiates between consultative decisions based on the number of participants involved—whether it is one individual or an entire group. In our coding, we captured both the decision-maker and the participants in consultative decisions, allowing this information to be retrieved from the coded data.

Three people conducted the research: one coder and two reviewers. The coder is a junior researcher, while both reviewers are experienced researchers, one has extensive knowledge of large-scale agile frameworks, while the other is an expert in decision-making.

We conducted coding in several iterations, during which decisions were coded. At the end of each iteration, agreement was ensured through review meetings, when the coder and two reviewers met, and the coder presented the results, and the reviewers validated the work and suggested changes as needed. It was also an opportunity to discuss the need for data aggregation or the creation of new coding categories. At the end, both reviewers independently reviewed all codes, and any disagreements were resolved in joint meetings. Thus, the result reflects the consensus of all three researchers.

In the final phase, the team aggregated and visualized the coded data to create the foundation for further analysis. The decisions were summarized and organized by relevance. Additionally, we used pivot tables and visual summaries to identify patterns across different scaling frameworks, support interpretation, and efficiently address all research questions.

4 Team-Level Decision Autonomy (RQ1)

In this section, we present the results at the team level, organized around four main activities of the agile team-level process: planning, execution, synchronization, review, and retrospective. Scrum is included as a baseline for comparing the scaling frameworks. All notes and comments in this section were derived through thematic analysis.

Table 1 summarizes the decisions at the team level. In each cell, we have coded the decision-maker (e.g., T for Team) and the decision-making style (e.g., A for autocratic decisions). A dash means that the framework lacks information. We assigned an ID to each decision, which will be referenced in the text. In each cell, multiple entries separated by semicolons indicate that the same decision can be made by different decision-makers or using different decision-making styles across the framework. Due to space limitations, we highlight some interesting differences but cannot discuss each decision in detail.

Table 1. Decision-Making at the Team Level

Decide on (the)...	Scrum	Nexus	Spotify	S@S	LeSS	**SAFe**
Iteration Planning						
SP1. invitations to iteration planning	T(G)	T(G)	-	-	T(G)	T(G)
SP2. team workflow	T(G)	T(G)	T(G)	T(G)	T(G)	T(G)
SP3. product backlog	PO (ACG)	PO(AC)	PO(AC)	PO (ACG)	PO(AC)	PO(AC)
SP4. product goal	PO (ACG)	-	-	-	-	PO(G)
SP5. iteration goal	T(G)	T(G)	-	-	PO(AC); T(G)	PO(AC); T(G)
SP6. next MVP increment	-	-	-	-	PO(AC)	PO(G)
SP7. product backlog breakdown	T(CG)	T(G)	-	PO(AC)	T(G)	T(G)
SP8. how to execute and coordinate the work	T(G)	T(G)	T(G)	T(G)	T(G)	T(G)
SP9. acceptance criteria	-	-	-	-	-	PO(A)
SP10. release content	-	-	-	PO(G)	PO(AC)	T(G)
SP11. release timing	-	-	-	PO(G)	PO(AC)	T(G)
SP12. release methods	-	-	-	-	PO(AC)	T(G)
SP13. capacity allocation	-	-	-	-	-	PO(G); T(G)

(*continued*)

Table 1. (*continued*)

Decide on (the)...	Scrum	Nexus	Spotify	S@S	LeSS	**SAFe**
Execution						
Ex1. team member tasks	T(G)	-	I(ACG)	-	T(G)	T(G)
Ex2. adjusting the product backlog	PO(ACG); T(G)	PO(ACG); T(G)	-	-	PO(ACG); T(G)	PO(ACG); T(G)
Ex3. cancelling the Sprint	PO(A)	PO(A)	-	-	PO(A); T(G)	-
Ex4. event collaboration	SM(ACG)	-	-	-	-	-
Ex5. definition of done	T(G)	T(G)	-	T(G)	T(G)	T(G)
Ex6. stories to implement	-	-	-	-	-	T(G)
Ex7. adjusting the sprint backlog	T(G)	-	-	-	-	T(G)
Ex8. modifying product assets	-	-	-	-	-	I(ACG)
Syncronization						
Syn1. techniques to use	T(G)	-	T(G)	-	T(G)	T(G)
Syn2. how to conduct the Daily Scrum	-	-	-	-	T(G)	-
Syn3. meetings after the Daily Scrum	-	-	-	-	T(G)	-
Syn4. how to hold the coordination sync meeting	-	-	I(A); PO(A); T(A)	-	-	T(G)
Review & Retrospective						
RR1. sprint achievements	T(G)	-	-	-	PO(ACG); T(G)	T(G)
RR2. what to do next	T(G)	-	-	-	PO(ACG); T(G)	T(G)
RR3. improvement items	T(G)	-	-	-	-	T(G)
RR4. improving coordination	-	-	-	-	T(G)	-
RR5. retrospective format	-	-	-	-	-	I(A); T(G)

4.1 Iteration Planning

Team-level iteration planning is conducted by the whole team, including the product owner. In addition, Scrum, Nexus, LeSS, and SAFe state that the team can invite additional people to provide input as needed (SP1, Table 1). In large-scale development, these are often representatives of other development teams.

When scaling agile, a team-of-teams-level planning event often precedes team-level planning, focusing and restricting the team's autonomy, e.g., by allocating certain backlog items to the teams. On the other hand, all scaled frameworks give the team some leeway in defining their workflow (SP2), with the Nexus, S@S, and LeSS frameworks closely following Scrum, whereas in Spotify and SAFe, the team can decide whether to follow Scrum or Kanban.

The product backlog is the responsibility of the Product Owner (PO), and the decision-making style for backlog content and prioritization is up to them (SP3), as they have complete autonomy. The models recognize that backlog decisions can be made either autocratically or consultatively. The exceptions are Scrum and S@S, since the PO can delegate backlog work to other team members, more closely resembling consensus-based decision-making.

In Scrum, the PO can delegate the definition of the product goal (SP4) to another team member. Decision autonomy over the product goal is reduced in scaled frameworks, such as SAFe, where the PO must consult stakeholders and business owners outside the team. The Scrum Team typically defines the iteration goal (SP5) in most frameworks, but in LeSS and SAFe, the PO can initially decide it on their own.

In LeSS and SAFe, the PO is further responsible for deciding the Minimum Viable Product (MVP) (SP6). In both frameworks, the PO serves as the decision-maker, and the Scrum Master can help assess business value, acting in a consultative capacity. However, in LeSS, the MVP definition occurs at the portfolio level, so several scaled groups are involved, not just the PO of a single team.

Iteration planning results in a prioritized iteration backlog based on the product backlog. Developers usually have autonomy to break down these product backlog items (SP7) in a consultative or consensus-based manner with the group, and they are also responsible for sizing. Most frameworks suggest that the iteration backlog should be defined by the developers or the Scrum Team (PO included), whereas in S@S, each PO is solely responsible for their sprint backlog.

Each team also determines how they execute and coordinate their work (SP8): they create and refine backlog items, turn them into stories, and decide which stories to implement. In this way, the responsibility for stories lies entirely with the teams, since they need to create, select, task, and estimate, although approval is always by the PO. In SAFe, the PO defines acceptance criteria (SP9) for an iteration, whereas other frameworks either provide no information about acceptance criteria or explicitly state that it is not recommended (e.g., LeSS).

Decisions related to product release, such as the content (SP10), the release date (SP11), and the methods adopted for the releases (SP12)—such as doing interim releases (LeSS)—are usually made by the PO. The PO has complete autonomy over the product release, as long as it agrees with the teams on the items to be completed by the release date, thereby contributing to independence among teams. In S@S, the PO makes a decision together with the PO team, requiring consensus. In LeSS, the PO can make the decision alone or consult with other POs from requirement areas (e.g., LeSS Huge [21]). Finally, in SAFe, there are exceptions: releases occur only during PI planning (teams-of-teams level), and an individual team can also decide on its release process, as long as it aligns with the scaled levels.

Finally, SAFe recognizes decisions on capacity allocation (SP13), in which the team establishes the time and resources available for the sprint jointly with the PO and the system architect.

4.2 Execution

Scrum clearly defines how a sprint should occur. The Scrum Team has a high level of autonomy, since they must decide on the activities its members will execute (Ex1), and can even decide whether to split into smaller Scrum Teams. Both LeSS and SAFe reflect this autonomy in decision-making regarding activities, though the suggestion to split into smaller Scrum Teams is only a recommendation in those frameworks.

Spotify provides an exception, as it also assigns purely individual decisions during hack days. These decisions could be associated with the entire set of decision-making styles, since developers can make them autocratically (alone or by gathering information from others), consultatively (checking with individuals or groups on how hack days will be run), or as a group, if they want to improve collaboration.

During planning, only the PO controlled the product backlog. However, during execution, developers can also adjust the backlog through group consensus (Ex2). Still, they do not have complete control over the iteration: in general, only the PO can decide to cancel it (Ex3), for example, when the iteration goal becomes obsolete. In LeSS, there is an exception: the development team also has autonomy to terminate the sprint before schedule, not only the PO. Either of these roles can act as a decision-maker. The Scrum Master role is only active in SAFe regarding decisions and autonomy, as they can decide how to collaborate during events (Ex4), which is not explicitly stated in other frameworks.

Between iterations, it is necessary to create a definition of done. This is determined by both the PO and the Development Team (Ex5), so consensus between them is required.

Finally, SAFe differs from most frameworks, since the iteration backlog can be adjusted by the team during the sprint (Ex7). The backlog is usually discussed during team synchronization, but it is not mandatory. Most frameworks do not address team-level sprint backlog adjustments; they handle them at a higher level.

In this way, SAFe follows the principle of collective ownership, which allows any team member to modify relevant product assets (Ex8). This level of individual autonomy is rarely observed in most frameworks (e.g., Spotify restricts this to hack days).

4.3 Synchronization

During synchronization events, frameworks that include Syn1 show consensus that developers need to select, as a group, which development and coordination techniques to use during the project (Syn1), such as selecting development tools and granting them full decision-making autonomy.

Regarding meetings, in LeSS, the whole development team can decide how to conduct the team's Daily Scrum (Syn2), and can even send extra individuals to observe other teams' Daily Scrum. The team can also choose to hold additional meetings after the Daily Scrum (Syn3).

On the other hand, in SAFe, each team decides on how to hold their coordination sync meetings (Syn4), called Team Sync. For instance, in Spotify, this type of meeting is ad-hoc, whereas in SAFe and other frameworks, it can be a cadence-based event. Note that Nexus and S@S did not present decisions regarding the synchronization stage at the team level, as both frameworks, as complements to Scrum, focus on events at their scaled levels (team of teams).

4.4 Review and Retrospective

In most frameworks, during the review event, the team and stakeholders review and collaborate on what was done in the sprint (RR1) and what to do next (RR2) as a group, but at the team level, only Scrum, LeSS, and SAFe address these issues as decisions. LeSS stands out in this regard, allowing the PO to decide these points in advance and make them public to the team and stakeholders only then.

As a result of these meetings, Scrum and SAFe explicitly discuss when to address the improvement items (RR3). The Scrum Team decides when to address improvement items and how to improve them, and can even add new improvement items to the backlog for the next sprint. In SAFe, each team holds its own iteration retrospective and iteration review, during which they can agree on how to improve for the next sprint, with stakeholder consensus.

Concerning retrospective events, LeSS has a particular feature: at the team level, each team runs its own retrospective, as in one-team Scrum. There is also a scaled version of this event—the overall retrospective —, where people from all development teams come together to decide how to improve coordination during the sprint (RR4), and everyone must give their consensus. On the other hand, reviews usually occur only at the team-of-teams level, involving all teams.

As discussed in planning, a significant difference in SAFe concerns acceptance criteria. While other frameworks do not address the PO accepting the work done by teams—and LeSS even criticizes doing so—in SAFe, the PO has autonomy to decide on acceptance criteria and can do so by engaging with the teams.

In SAFe, the team usually decides on the retrospective format. However, there is an alternative to this practice: rotating individuals who make decisions in a completely autocratic manner. During the iteration review, teams can also adjust their iteration backlog, as discussed in the execution event. Again, as frameworks focused on expanding Scrum to higher organizational levels, Nexus and S@S do not present team-level decisions for these events. The Spotify document, in turn, does not include any section on reviews and retrospectives.

5 Team of Teams Level Decision Autonomy (RQ2)

This section explores decision autonomy at the team-of-teams level. We have organized the sections around four main events: planning, execution, synchronization, and review and retrospective. All comments in this section were derived through thematic analysis. Table 2 summarizes the elements involved at the team-of-teams level.

Table 2. Decision-Making at the Team of Teams Level

Decide on (the)...	Nexus	Spotify	S@S	LeSS	SAFe
Planning					
SP12. scaled backlog	SPO(G); Ts(G)	-	SPO(AC)	-	SPO(G)
SP13. scaled goal	SPO(CG); Ts(C G)	-	-	-	-
SP14. tasks to work on	-	SPO(ACG)	-	SPO(ACG)	SPO(G)
SP15. content and the optimal time for the product	-	-	SPO(G)	SPO(ACG)	SPO(G)
SP16. common backlog	-	-	SPO(AC)	-	-
SP17. which team will work on each item of the backlog	-	-	SPO(G)	SPO(ACG); Ts(CG)	SPO(G)
SP18. decomposing backlog into stories	-	-	-	-	Ts(G)
SP19. team of teams backlog	-	-	-	-	SPO(ACG)
SP20. mission and vision	-	-	-	-	SPO(C)
SP21. product scope	-	-	-	-	SPO(C)
SP22. whether the PI objectives fulfill the business needs	-	-	-	-	BOs(C)
SP23. release content	-	-	-	-	SPO(G); BOs(G); Ts(G)
SP24. release timing	-	-	-	-	SPO(G); BOs(G); Ts(G)
SP25. release methods	-	-	-	-	SPO(G); Ts(G)
Execution					
Ex9. decomposing the product backlog	Ts(G)	-	-	PO(CG)	-
Ex10. update the backlog	Ts(G)	-	-	PO(CG)	-
Ex11. definition of done	Ts(G)	-	SPO(G); SMs(G)	-	Ts(G)
Ex12. product delivery	-	-	Ts(G)	-	-
Syncronization					
Syn5. when sync event will happen	-	Ts(G); SPO(G); SMs(G)	-	-	-
Syn6. who will attend the sync event	-	-	Ts(ACG)	-	-
Syn7. team reallocation	-	-	-	SPO(ACG)	-
Syn8. content of the sync event	-	-	-	-	Ts(G)
Review & Retrospective					
RR6 improvement items	Ts(G)	-	SMs(G)	Ts(CG)	Ts(G)
RR7 how to improve	Ts(G)	-	SPO(G); SMs(G)	Ts(CG)	Ts(G)
RR8 what to do in the next	Ts(G)	-	Ts(G)	Ts(CG)	Ts(G)

5.1 Planning

During planning, Nexus proposes that representatives from each Scrum Team and the Product Owner define four artifacts: the Nexus sprint backlog, the Nexus sprint goal, the sprint goal, and the sprint backlog (SP12 and SP13, Table 2). Since the artifacts from both team and team-of-teams levels are produced in this event, Nexus could replace the individual sprint planning event for teams, or not. Also, autonomy is diminished compared to Scrum, as all Scrum Teams must understand the product backlog, and dependencies should be detected and minimized.

In Spotify, each squad member can be an active part in planning and choose which tasks to work on (SP14), even in a team of teams. In this way, autonomy is the primary focus at Spotify. In contrast, in S@S, there is a significant difference: all POs (the Product Owner Team) decide on the product's content and the optimal time for the product. So there is a group consensus decision on the backlog (SP15). Also, each PO decides the sprint backlog, unlike the developers in Scrum or the Scrum Team in SAFe. Not crucial to our scope, but there is a significant backlog (common backlog) defined by the Scaled Product Owner (SP16).

As mentioned before, the first part of planning in LeSS is tied to the team-of-teams level. Usually, the whole development team—and in some cases only representatives, often with the help of the Product Owner—has to decide which team will deliver which product backlog items initially (SP17). This means they can even swap items between themselves, with full autonomy to decide what they want to work on and how to distribute them. On the other hand, following the same idea as in different frameworks, the Product Owner is the only one responsible for prioritizing the product backlog items.

At the team-of-teams level, SAFe holds a PI Planning event where teams can decide how to decompose backlog items into stories (SP18). As a result, they would have the PI Objectives, and in other frameworks, teams may generate the sprint backlog following the same idea. At this level, everything decided by a team is a consensus, such as iteration goals and Work-in-Progress limits.

Following the PO idea in Scrum, the role that acts as a PO at the team-of-teams level in SAFe is Product Management (Scaled Product Owner), which could be a single person (autocratic or consultative) or a group. They can also decide on the items and the priority of the Agile Release Train (ART) (team of teams) backlog (SP19), and the MVP, just like stated in LeSS, but at a scaled level.

Since scaled frameworks require more coordination between teams, Product Management is responsible for defining the mission and vision (SP20) by collecting input from stakeholders, system architects, business owners, customers, POs, and teams. Product Management, as a decision-maker, also collaborates with the release train engineer (consultant) to define and adjust the product's scope (SP21). Following the same idea as in the acceptance criteria, teams must consult with business owners to determine whether the PI objectives meet business needs, and then make an approval decision (SP22).

Finally, SAFe complements the product release decisions discussed at the team level regarding content (SP23), date (SP24), and method (SP25). A key difference between SAFe and LeSS is that agile teams can release directly to the customer. Teams have more autonomy once release decisions, such as routine deployments and primary release timings, are not restricted by the PO. These take place at a scaled level during the PI Planning event and involve both individual teams and scaled roles (scaled POs, business owners, architects).

5.2 Execution

In Nexus, all Scrum Teams participate in the Cross-Team refinement event (Ex9). The product backlog is decomposed to make the dependencies transparent, identified across teams, and removed or mitigated. This type of scaled decision reduces autonomy even further than a team-level task allocation decision, because all Scrum Teams must participate.

The high-level object Nexus sprint backlog (Nexus sprint goal added by the product backlog items from all Scrum Teams) is updated by all Scrum Teams (Ex10). All Scrum Teams define their Definition of Done (Ex11)—a general one—by consensus, which consequently results in a loss of team autonomy. However, each Scrum Team can choose to apply a more stringent definition of done than the general one, it gives teams more independence.

In S@S, all Scrum Teams decide how the product is delivered (Ex12), ensuring total group consensus. The definition of done is determined by the Product Owner Team and the Scrum of Scrums Master, so it is more restrictive than Nexus, with less autonomy for the team and greater focus on the PO and the Scrum of Scrums Master.

In LeSS, the Product Owner remains responsible for the composition of the Product Backlog and its items, and for managing it by adjusting and selecting items to refine (an overall product backlog refinement). Although it is a purely autocratic decision, it is stated that these decisions are made after collecting feedback from teams. This means the Product Owner acts as a decision-maker while consulting with the teams. In this way, the PO can decide alone or in consensus, so it varies from consultative to group consensus. On the other hand, in SAFe, the PI initially covers the entire ART, but each team can adjust the PI (the first and subsequent iteration plans), giving teams more autonomy.

5.3 Synchronization

As stated in other frameworks, in Spotify, people can adjust the product backlog at the team-of-teams level to meet the scope and eliminate problematic dependencies. The problem is that the Spotify document does not specifically state who is responsible for this decision. Scrum of Scrums, on the other hand, happens on demand (Syn5) so that anyone can convene, but participants (coaches, squad members, PO, the whole squad) must agree to participate as a group.

In S@S, Scrum Team representatives can decide who will attend the scaled Daily Scrum (Syn6), but anyone or any team may attend as needed. In this situation, all decision-making styles are possible, since they can decide solely who is essential for this meeting (autocratic), consult with others (consultative), or reach a consensus (agree on who is necessary).

In team of teams, LeSS includes a coordination event focused on the Product Owners, where they meet to decide on team reallocation (Syn7). As stated in the LeSS document, this decision can be made using any decision-making style, but since it occurs in a coordination meeting, it is most likely to be a group consensus.

The Daily Scrum can also be used for coordination between teams by having people from other teams observe. These observers are referred to in the LeSS document as Scouts. At the team-of-teams level, decisions are made solely based on group consensus. There is also a synchronization event in SAFe between teams called System Demo, with content and participants determined by teams and stakeholders (Syn8).

5.4 Review and Retrospective

As discussed before, there are team-level events that are replaced by events in the team-of-teams scope. Nexus Sprint Review, for instance, replaces individual Scrum Team sprint reviews, having the whole Nexus (team of teams) and stakeholders as participants.

Following this idea, S@S offers something unique: a scaled retrospective where the Scrum Masters from each team decide on the improvement items (RR6) and how to improve for the next sprint (RR7). This event is similar to the team-level retrospective across various frameworks, but this time, the decision-makers are the Scrum Masters, rather than the Scrum Teams. However, it still reflects group consensus. The same applies to Nexus and SAFe, but the decision-makers are teams of teams, such as the Nexus and the ART, respectively.

LeSS introduces a different approach to decision-making compared to most other frameworks: the community decides how to improve the next sprint (RR8), collaborating with all development teams, customers, stakeholders, and the PO. This collaboration is similar to what happens in SAFe, with Communities of Practice (CoPs). In this way, the PO in LeSS cannot decide on its own, as in other frameworks (e.g., SAFe), where stakeholders and the PO jointly decide. These decisions cannot be purely autocratic, since the PO collects feedback from teams and, thereafter, can only decide based on the information, consult people or teams, or reach group consensus.

At a scaled level in SAFe, there is an event called Inspect and Adapt, where the teams of teams decide on the nature of sprint problems and what to do about them, which could reduce autonomy. Improvement items are also defined here to compose the ART backlog by the whole ART. At the end of the Program Iteration (PI), teams decide together what to do in the following PI during the Innovation and Planning Iteration, with total group consensus.

6 Discussion

We investigated team autonomy in large-scale agile frameworks through analyzing how decisions are distributed among stakeholders on two levels: the team level (RQ1) and the teams-of-teams level (RQ2).

In general, when comparing the frameworks, SAFe exhibits lower diversity in decision styles, suggesting that the model is more restrictive in the level of autonomy it allows, consistent with previous studies [13,16]. SAFe also has more extensive documentation, which may contribute to its more defined level of decision autonomy.

The range of decision styles allowed during the execution phase is limited to a single style, regardless of whether it's at the team level or the team-of-teams level. In contrast, the planning phase typically allows for multiple decision styles. The variety of decision styles allowed indicates greater autonomy during the planning phase and less during the execution phase. This makes sense because during execution, development is ongoing, and changes resulting from a decision might be more challenging to implement. Whereas, during sprint and product configuration, changes can be easily made based on decisions.

Autonomy at the Team Level. At the team level, decision autonomy refers to how much teams can decide regarding their activities during a sprint. In the frameworks, most team-level decisions occur during sprint planning, such as defining sprint activities, the methods to be used for this, and resolving potential conflicts with the product scope. Not surprisingly, the scaling frameworks limit autonomy compared to Scrum. This is mainly due to the need for inter-team coordination. As an example, the team in Scrum decides on the Sprint Goal [19]. In Nexus, representatives from the Scrum Teams and the Product Owner collaboratively decide on the sprint goal [18]. In LeSS, the Product Owner can establish the sprint goal in advance, although the Development Team may make subsequent changes [21].

Autonomy at the Team-of-Teams Level. At the team-of-teams level, different frameworks prescribe different levels of autonomy. For instance, in Nexus, representatives from each Scrum team, along with the Product Owner, are responsible for deciding on the sprint backlog. Meanwhile, in S@S, all Product Owners collectively make the decision, whereas in SAFe, this is the responsibility of Scrum Teams. Similarly, in Nexus, Scrum Teams representatives decide about the definition of done, while in S@S the decision is made by consensus between the Product Owner and the Scrum of Scrum Master. As with the team level, at the team-of-teams level, the planning phase typically involves more decisions than other phases, which is logical because this is when all product and sprint settings are defined.

7 Limitations and Validity

We used the methodology proposed in [23] to assess the study's limitations and threats to validity. Concerning construct validity, the main threat lies in how we define "decision", especially when we use the recognition-primed decision-making model to address implicit decisions. Despite the inherent subjectivity of qualitative analysis, each identified decision was reviewed by three researchers to mitigate misinterpretation. During the stage of selecting appropriate documents to represent the frameworks, potential biases may arise regarding internal validity. To mitigate this, we chose only official, up-to-date documents.

Regarding external and conclusion validity, selecting the best-known large-scale agile frameworks and presenting the results in tables may risk overgeneralizing similarities or inferred relationships among frameworks, potentially overlooking contextual differences. To mitigate this threat, we carefully aggregated the data and provided detailed visualizations to ensure that multiple observations, rather than isolated cases, support the patterns observed.

8 Conclusions

This paper aimed to understand how decision autonomy is allocated and how decisions are distributed among stakeholders in large-scale agile frameworks. To reach this goal, we applied inductive thematic analysis to the primary documents of the main scaling frameworks to identify and categorize their decision-making elements by decision-maker, decision type, decision-making style, decision timing, and affected artifacts.

As a result, we presented a decision-level analysis of team autonomy in large-scale agile software development, considering the team and team-of-teams levels. By analyzing the levels and comparing them, we could show that scaling frameworks restrict autonomy compared to single-team development. Future empirical studies should complement this theoretical analysis with real-world data on how team autonomy is implemented in practice in large-scale agile software development.

References

1. Boss, V., Dahlander, L., Ihl, C., Jayaraman, R.: Organizing entrepreneurial teams: a field experiment on autonomy over choosing teams and ideas. Organ. Sci. **34**(6, SI), 2097–2118 (2023)
2. Burge, J.E., Carroll, J.M., McCall, R., Mistrik, I.: Decision-making in software engineering. In: Rationale-Based Software Engineering, pp. 67–76. Springer, Heidelberg (2008). https://doi.org/10.1007/978-3-540-77583-6_5
3. Dikert, K., Paasivaara, M., Lassenius, C.: Challenges and success factors for large-scale agile transformations: a systematic literature review. J. Syst. Softw. **119**, 87–108 (2016)
4. Drury, M., Conboy, K., Power, K.: Obstacles to decision making in Agile software development teams. J. Syst. Softw. **85**(6), 1239–1254 (2012)
5. Guzzo, R.A., Dickson, M.W.: Teams in organizations: recent research on performance and effectiveness. Annu. Rev. Psychol. **47**(1), 307–338 (1996)
6. Hackman, J.R.: The psychology of self-management in organizations. In: Pallack, M.S., Perloff, R.O. (eds.) Psychology and Work: Productivity, Change, and Employment. American Psychological Association, Washington, DC (1986)

7. Hodgson, D., Briand, L.: Controlling the uncontrollable: 'Agile' teams and illusions of autonomy in creative work. Work Employ Soc. **27**(2), 308–325 (2013)
8. Klein, G.: Naturalistic decision making. Hum. Fact. **50**(3), 456–460 (2008)
9. Kniberg, H., Ivarsson, A.: Scaling Agile @ Spotify with Tribes, Squads, Chapters & Guilds (2012)
10. Lassenius, C., Dingsøyr, T.: Towards a taxonomy for autonomy in large-scale agile software development. In: 2025 IEEE/ACM 18th International Conference on Cooperative and Human Aspects of Software Engineering (CHASE), pp. 96–101 (2025)
11. Mendes, F., Mendes, E., Salleh, N., Oivo, M.: Insights on the relationship between decision-making style and personality in software engineering. Inf. Softw. Technol. **136**, 106586 (2021)
12. Moe, N.B., Dingsøyr, T., Dybå, T.: Overcoming barriers to self-management in software teams. IEEE Softw. **26**(6), 20–26 (2009)
13. Moe, N.B., Šmite, D., Paasivaara, M., Lassenius, C.: Finding the sweet spot for organizational control and team autonomy in large-scale agile software development. Empir. Softw. Eng. **26**(5), 101 (2021)
14. Paasivaara, M., Lassenius, C.: Empower your agile organization: community-based decision making in large-scale agile development at Ericsson. IEEE Softw. **36**(2), 64–69 (2019)
15. Poppendieck, M., Cusumano, M.: Lean software development: a tutorial. IEEE Softw. **29**(5), 26–32 (2012)
16. Putta, A., Uludağ, O., Hong, S.L., Paasivaara, M., Lassenius, C.: Why do organizations adopt agile scaling frameworks? A survey of practitioners. In: Proceedings of the 15th ACM/IEEE International Symposium on Empirical Software Engineering and Measurement (ESEM), ESEM '21, October 2021, pp. 1–12. Association for Computing Machinery, New York, NY, USA (2021)
17. Scaled Agile, Inc.: Scaled Agile Framework (2025)
18. Schwaber, K., Scrum.org: The Nexus Guide (2021)
19. Schwaber, K., Sutherland, J.: The Scrum Guide (2020)
20. Sutherland, J., Scrum Inc.: The Scrum@Scale Guide (2022)
21. The LeSS Company B.V.: The LeSS Framework (2025)
22. Vroom, V.H., Yetton, P.W.: Leadership and Decision-Making. University of Pittsburgh Press (1973)
23. Wohlin, C., Runeson, P., Höst, M., Ohlsson, M.C., Regnell, B., Wesslén, A.: Experimentation in Software Engineering. Springer, Heidelberg (2024). https://doi.org/10.1007/978-3-662-69306-3

From Tensions to Solutions: Managing Paradoxes in Large-Scale Agile

Nina Haugland Andersen[1(✉)], Nils Brede Moe[1], Astri Barbala[1], Rasmus Ulfsnes[1], Cansu Kilit[3], Hatice Fidan[3], and Viktoria Stray[1,2]

[1] SINTEF, Trondheim, Norway
{Nina.H.Andersen,Nils.B.Moe,Astri.Barbala,Rasmus.Ulfsnes}@sintef.no
[2] University of Oslo, Oslo, Norway
Viktoria.Stray@uio.no
[3] Vend, Oslo, Norway
{Cansu.Kilit,Hatice.Fidan}@vend.com

Abstract. Agile at scale introduces persistent tensions as organizations attempt to balance autonomy, coordination, and control across teams and layers. Some tensions are paradoxes, which are persistent contradictions in which both sides matter. Drawing on a qualitative case study of MarketCorp, a multinational marketplace company, we explore how paradoxes manifest in a large-scale agile context and how leaders respond. Interviews with 15 top managers and reflective conversations with 60 employees reveal three paradoxes: centralization vs. autonomy, internal vs. external focus, and product vs. project approaches. We explored two approaches for designing facilitated dialogue around paradoxes in leadership teams. The study highlights the importance of recognizing, normalizing, and collaboratively managing paradoxes and offers practical guidance for large-scale agile organizations, demonstrating that paradoxes can provide a valuable focus for continuous improvement and strengthen agile learning practices.

Keywords: Paradox · Paradoxical Cognition · Leadership · Qualitative Case Study · Platform Organization · Large-scale agile · Autonomous Teams

1 Introduction

Since the advent of the Agile Manifesto, technology organizations have increasingly sought to apply agile principles at scale. A growing body of research explores the challenges of scaling agile [7,16,20], and several prescriptive frameworks, such as LeSS, SAFe and the Spotify model have emerged to address the operational challenges of agile in the large. Yet, regardless of the model chosen, organizations continue to experience persistent tensions that arise from the interplay between agile principles and organizational realities [14]. For example, as companies scale agile methods, they must balance team autonomy with

A. Goldman et al. (Eds.): XP 2026, LNBIP 578, pp. 56–72, 2026.
https://doi.org/10.1007/978-3-032-22375-3_4

organizational control [18], as agile methodologies promote self-managing teams while large organizations simultaneously require alignment with strategic goals, standardized processes, and the management of cross-team dependencies [4,10]. Another example is navigating delivery pressure, which forces team members to balance meeting deadlines with maintaining sustainable, high-quality work practices [13]. In the organizational literature, such enduring tensions are conceptualized as paradoxes, defined as "contradictory yet interrelated elements that persist over time" [24]. Paradoxes appear central to the lived experience of large-scale agile organizations, and they remain regardless of the framework or scaling model in use. We argue that practitioners and leaders need to be vigilant about how they frame these paradoxical tensions. For many, this requires a reframing: rather than treating paradoxes as problems to eliminate, they must be understood as dynamics that arise, evolve, and persist over time.

Paradox theory offers a useful lens for understanding these dynamics. According to paradox theory, paradoxes cannot be "solved" but must be actively managed, making it crucial for practitioners and leaders to learn how to navigate these competing demands effectively [24]. Mismanaged paradoxes can lead to negative outcomes such as chaos, conflict, and organizational decline, as shown in a review of paradox literature [21]. This perspective highlights why certain tensions in large-scale agile resist simple trade-offs or fixes and underscores the need for dynamic, ongoing management of contradictions, such as balancing speed with stability or team autonomy with organizational control [10,24]. Given that paradoxes are influential in large-scale agile environments [10], yet remain under-explored in empirical agile research, we focus on understanding how paradoxes manifest in practice and how they can be productively managed. In this single-case study of a multinational company engaged in ongoing efforts to sustain and deepen its agility, we aim to answer the following research questions:

RQ1: *How do paradoxes manifest in large-scale agile organizations?*

RQ2: *How can agile practitioners and leaders manage paradoxes?*

Drawing on a real-world industry case, our study contributes insights into paradoxes that emerge in large-scale agile organizations and how practitioners can manage them. Beyond these contributions, we propose integrating paradoxes as an explicit theme in agile practices, such as retrospectives, and highlight how their persistent nature aligns with agile's emphasis on continuous reflection and learning for improved effectiveness [3].

2 Background

2.1 The Nature and Impact of Paradoxes in Organizations

To deepen the conceptual grounding introduced above, we draw on paradox theory, which frames paradoxes as one distinct category of organizational tensions. Smith and Lewis [24] define paradoxes as "contradictory yet interrelated elements that exist simultaneously and persist over time" (p. 382), and argue that they require organizations to attend to competing demands simultaneously. They further distinguish paradoxes from related concepts: *dilemmas*, which involve choosing between competing options, and *dialectics*, which can be resolved through integration. Importantly, they highlight that tensions are not static; they can evolve over time and shift from one form to another.

Organizational life is full of such paradoxes. For instance, in post-pandemic worklife, software developers often seek flexibility while employers are opting for structured return-to-office mandates, illustrating how contradictory demands coexist and shape organizational dynamics [15,22]. Similar challenges emerge in agile contexts, for example Strode et al. [26] identified paradoxes in their study of organizations transforming to agility.

As these paradoxes surface, organizations need to respond, and sometimes they do so constructively, sometimes harmfully [24]. Such responsiveness matters because paradoxes are deeply embedded in organizational systems, not merely operational issues [14]. Their emergence often prompts organizations to seek ways to balance competing demands. For example, Hyrynsalmi et al. [11] show how hybrid work reduced spontaneous interactions, creating a tension between employees' desire for flexibility and the organization's need for collaboration, prompting deliberate efforts to facilitate informal connections.

Paradoxes thus provide an important lens for navigating organizational complexity, and the way organizations handle them has significant implications for long-term agility. Putnam et al. [17] outline various responses to organizational tensions, including paradoxes, not all of which lead to desired outcomes. For example, defensive reactions may foster individual burnout, prioritizing one pole over the other can reduce synergy and increase stress, and paralysis may arise when actors feel "damned if you do and damned if you don't". Likewise, Schad et al. [21], in their review of paradox research in management science, summarize a range of organizational consequences associated with paradoxes and their management. Negative outcomes include ambivalence, chaos, collapse, conflict, and organizational decline, while positive outcomes include creativity, learning, sustainability, and superior long-term performance. Taken together, this underscores that ongoing paradox management is valuable and necessary.

2.2 Paradoxes Influence Large-Scale Agile

Prior research has documented several paradoxes influencing large-scale agile organizations. One illustrative example is the paradox of *team autonomy vs. organizational alignment*. The adoption of agile methods, with their emphasis on flexibility and collaboration, has expanded from single projects to entire organizations [1,8,9], giving rise to organizational tensions such as balancing local autonomy with global coordination and control [4]. Moe et al. [14] describe how balancing team autonomy and inter-team coordination is critical, and that misalignment or overly strong control mechanisms can reduce the effectiveness of autonomous teams. The case of Spotify offers one example of how designed mechanisms can balance this, by enabling decentralized decision-making while maintaining alignment [23]. Another example is the paradox of *long-term planning vs. short-term delivery*. Agile favors adaptability and short feedback loops, yet large organizations require long-term roadmaps and investment planning to ensure direction and stability [7]. Balancing flexibility with predictability creates a persistent paradox. Finally, there is the paradox of *old vs. new practices*. During agile transformations, legacy structures and plan-driven methods are often maintained in parallel with new agile ways of working [7]. Rather than a clean transition, the transformation becomes a hybrid state where conflicting logics need to be managed. Rolland et al. [19] argue that successful scaling of agile practices often depends on integrating elements from both paradigms.

In the context of large-scale agile, unresolved paradoxes may manifest as delayed transformations, frustrated teams, or conflicting initiatives that drain energy. For instance, overemphasis on control may suppress innovation, while too much team autonomy can lead to misalignment with strategic goals [7]. This highlights the importance of managing paradoxes in such environments.

2.3 Responding to Paradoxes by Facilitating Dialogue

Prior research outlines several ways organizations may respond to paradoxes [17,21]. Smith and Lewis [24] emphasize that managing paradoxes is an ongoing process, captured in their cyclical dynamic equilibrium model, in which organizations work to engage opposing poles simultaneously and sustainably. Effective responses require awareness of the paradoxes at play [24] as well as critical reflexivity and collective consciousness [17]. In large-scale agile environments, this implies that leadership teams must recognize the paradoxes at play and create space for reflective dialogue to deepen their understanding and selecting appropriate strategies to manage the paradoxes. As a brief illustration, Paasivaara et al. [16] show how Ericsson used open dialogue to navigate the tension between experimentation and strategic alignment during agile transformation.

Facilitating dialogues about identifying and managing paradoxes requires careful support. Below is a summary of advice to pracitioners based on two accounts from the paradox literature.

Lüscher and Lewis **[12]:**

1. **Use interventive questioning.** Conduct sparring sessions (structured interactive sessions) using purposeful, reflective questions to advance understanding and support managing paradox.
2. **Towards a workable certainty.** The goal is not to resolve paradoxes but to move towards a workable certainty enabling change.
3. **Identify polarities, explore both/and options.** Start by articulating a messy issue and narrow it to a specific problem. Then identify polarities, before exploring both/and options.
4. **Encourage experimentation.** Challenge simplistic solutions to motivate ongoing experimentation.

Danneels and Viaene **[6]:**

1. **Use a neutral facilitator.** Preferably one with company knowledge.

2. **Mindful wording and balancing poles.** Paradox work might be sensitive; use familiar organizational language and phrase paradoxes in a balanced way to ensure acceptance.
3. **Prioritize strategically important paradoxes.** Focus time and resources on the paradoxes that are strategically important to address.
4. **Challenge assumptions by adopting the other's viewpoint.** Pull people out of their entrenched perspectives to make them look at problems from the other's point of view.
5. **Let paradoxes guide decision-making.** Ask what (future) strategic choices need to be made for each pole of the paradox.
6. **Periodically map progress.** For example by visualizing both poles as two equally important tracks.

Based on these accounts, we argue that paradox work is an iterative, collaborative process that benefits from thoughtful support, surfacing multiple perspectives, careful navigation of sensitivities, and channeling insights into productive and meaningful paths forward. Moreover, a clear approach to paradox-based strategic dialogues can increase leaders' confidence, aligning with Lüscher and Lewis's [12] observation that working through paradox reduces anxiety and enables more effective responses.

3 Methodology

Next we present MarketCorp and why this case is a good fit for studying paradoxes in a large-scale agile, then we present our method.

3.1 MarketCorp

MarketCorp is a multinational digital marketplace company with several thousand employees and a strong Nordic presence. Historically, it emphasized horizontal optimization, leveraging synergies across business areas and shared technology platforms. This supported cross-company alignment, but also introduced high internal complexity and interdependencies that slowed product development and reduced organizational responsiveness. Recognizing these constraints, MarketCorp has now embarked on a transformation of the company. They are aiming to transform into a fully agile company with a product development model that is structured around long-lived, cross-functional product teams described as the "fundamental unit" of delivery. Each team includes developers, product managers, designers, analysts, and engineering managers, and is responsible for the full lifecycle of specific user-facing services. To scale agility, product teams were organized into Areas, which share customer journeys or business domains. Each Area encompasses several teams (typically 3–7), guided by an Area leadership group responsible for strategy, priorities, and coordination. Areas are further embedded into Verticals (each representing a specific domain), which connect teams to company-wide goals and business strategies through shared Objectives and Key Results (OKRs) and regular planning cadences. At the time of this study, the organizational structure was becoming more fluid, with teams and leadership shifting in response to changing priorities.

MarketCorp is currently a mature agile company within the parts of the organization where agile ways of working have already been established. It emphasizes "aligned autonomy"; teams are expected to move quickly and make independent decisions while staying anchored to shared goals and strategic direction. Principles such as "action over perfection", "outcome over output", and "fall in love with the problem" reflect a strong culture of continuous learning and customer focus. At the same time, the ongoing transformation seeks to extend and integrate this mature agile practice across the entire enterprise, moving to a fully agile organization. This coexistence of established agile maturity and a broader enterprise-wide transformation clarifies that the organization is both agile today and still working to scale agility consistently across all units. These conditions also suggest the potential for inherent tensions between speed and alignment, and autonomy and coordination, which makes MarketCorp highly relevant for studying paradoxes in large-scale agile development.

3.2 Method

Data Collection and Analysis: The study began with a broad exploration of how members of top management perceived the ongoing transformation. All top leaders were invited to interviews via email, and between 25 June and 6 September 2024 we conducted 15 interviews with individuals occupying key leadership roles across the organization. The interview sample included Chief Technology Officers (CTO) and Chief Product Officers (CPO), as well as individuals with overarching managerial responsibilities. This composition ensured that a wide range of leadership perspectives was captured. The interviews were recorded and most lasted 50–60 min. Our interview centered on the transformation, and examples of questions were: *"How has the transformation gone?"*, *"What are the challenges/barriers today?"*, and *"How is the work being done to get everyone to move in the same direction?"*. Initial interview analysis, supported by dialogue with the company, indicated the presence of paradoxical tensions. This insight prompted a systematic re-investigation of the interview data.

Alongside this, MarketCorp sought to establish common ways of working across the organization. To support this effort, insights were collected from employees about the current situation, existing gaps, and the desired future state. Around sixty employees participated in 36 reflective conversations, held individually or in small role-based groups, between 29 November 2024 and 27 January 2025. Participants were identified through a review of organizational charts to ensure representation across roles, teams, and units, enabling the inclusion of diverse perspectives and experiences. Each conversation addressed three key questions related to desired ways of working and the factors that enable or constrain them. One facilitator led the conversation while another took notes. All notes were then reviewed and synthesized into a summary. AI tools supported this process, but all outputs were manually checked to ensure accuracy and anonymization. The conversations surfaced several tensions shaping daily work practices. These tensions are described in the summary, which we have included in our analysis to validate and enrich findings from the leader interviews.

To conduct the re-analysis, we followed Braun and Clarke's (2006) principles of thematic analysis [5]. Using NVivo, we systematically and semantically coded all segments of the transcribed interviews that referred to organizational tensions, as well as the summary of employee conversations. At the coding stage, we labeled each segment with a brief descriptive statement summarizing its content. Codes representing similar tensions were grouped together. From these tensions, we applied Smith and Lewis's (2011) framework [24] to identify which qualified as paradoxes. Consistent with that framework, we classified as paradoxes those tensions informants portrayed as ongoing and interdependent. This process resulted in three paradoxes with sufficient empirical support. These are presented in the Results section. Parts of the interview findings have also been reported in a previous paper focusing on large-scale continuous software engineering [2].

Approaches for Facilitating Dialogue Among Leaders: Throughout the study, organizational tensions, particularly paradoxes, emerged as influential and warranted leadership attention. In response, we designed two facilitation approaches for dialogue (described in the Results section) and reflected on the design of the approaches in light of relevant theory and feedback from the company. Our analysis draws on meeting summaries, work notes, and organizational documents. The focus was on understanding how the design of the facilitation approaches functioned, rather than on conducting a comprehensive assessment of their effectiveness or outcomes.

4 Results

We begin by presenting the paradoxes that influenced MarketCorp, followed by initiatives designed to raise awareness and foster dialogue about these paradoxes at the leadership level.

4.1 Paradoxes

Our analysis revealed three paradoxes that influence MarketCorp (see Table 1 for an overview). Centralization vs. autonomy emerged as the dominant paradox, supported by both leaders and employees. The other two paradoxes appeared more unevenly across stakeholder groups and can therefore be considered secondary but still consequential. The paradoxes are described below.

The most notable paradox was **centralization vs. autonomy**, mentioned in 13 out of 15 leader interviews and strongly supported by insights from the conversations with the employees. At its core, this paradox reflects tensions between creating common foundations, such as technology infrastructure, cultural identity, and strategic direction, and the desire for local specificity and autonomy for agile teams and their verticals. One prominent aspect relates to *organizational*

Table 1. Overview of paradoxes.

Paradox	Keywords	No. Leader Interviews	Highlighted by Employees
Centralization vs. Autonomy	– Corporate culture vs. regional and brand cultures – Central priorities vs. unit-specific priorities – Horizontal technical solutions vs. unit-specific solutions	13	Largely
Internal focus vs. External focus	– Market vs. internal affairs – Business and products vs. technology	10	Small extent
Product approach vs. Project approach	– Clash between product-driven and project-driven parts of the company	2	Largely

culture: while there is an ambition to build a unified identity, deeply rooted local, national and brand cultures persist. This can leave people trying to foster several cultures at once. As expressed by one leader: *"In my vertical we work to create a sense of belonging and culture (...), [but] we are also part of a bigger collective with many dependencies"* (I05), which this individual linked to the necessity of having common ways of working across the entire company.

Another aspect concerned how *priorities* were set across the organization. The company faces an ongoing need to balance competing priorities, and this creates tensions between decisions made centrally and those made within individual units. The company intends for each vertical to define and prioritize its own goals; however, the leadership team must still make overarching decisions that influence unit-level priorities and economics. This creates what one leader described as a *"tug-of-war between cost synergies across the organization and letting the vertical decide for itself"* (I1). Team autonomy tends to diminish when demands from the central organization increase or become overly specific. As summarized in the accounts from employees: when top management dictates specific solutions, teams feel they lack autonomy within their scope of control.

Finally, the centralization vs. autonomy paradox also relates to *technology*. The company is establishing a core technology unit responsible for developing a common platform and shared technological solutions across the organization. This approach aims to avoid duplication, where each unit would otherwise need to build and maintain its own solutions for similar functions (leveraging economies of scale). However, the reality is complex: differences between verticals require adaptations and tailoring to meet unit-specific needs. Consequently, the organization must balance how far the common platform serves all units versus what tasks individual units should still own. Employees expressed differing views on how the core unit can best support the verticals, and this tension seems to persist, like indicated by this leader: *"the platform [is] not really giving [the verticals] the degrees of freedom that they need"* (I13).

The paradox of **internal vs. external focus** appears to be influential. This was mentioned in 10 leader interviews, but received only a minor focus from the employees. This paradox is about the organization needing to balance attention between *internal priorities and market demands*, yet doing both effectively at the same time is challenging. For example, one leader (I5) remarked that internal matters have recently taken much of the attention, often at the expense of focus on the market and customers. Yet the organization must balance delivering value to external stakeholders with establishing effective ways of working, supporting employees, and developing new structures and solutions.

Another influential issue lies in balancing being *business-/product-driven and technology-driven*. The company's strong focus on the new platform has raised concerns that the user perspective receives less attention than it should, and the employees also pointed to limited commercial awareness in the strategic outlook. Although the aim is to realize the benefits of shared technological solutions while creating user value, maintaining progress on both fronts is difficult. As one leader (I8) noted: platform migration offers little short-term user value, yet pausing business development is not an option. As a result, technology and business priorities often compete, and shared resources are tied to the transformation.

The final paradox concerns working with **a product vs. a project approach**. This only came up in two leader interviews, but was strongly supported by the employees. Leaders described a *divide between different parts of the organization*: central functions and the technology unit are seen as bureaucratic, procedural, and less agile compared to other areas. Employees echoed this, noting that functions such as strategy, finance, sales, and marketing typically work in a project-driven way, whereas agile product teams follow a product-led approach. This mismatch creates collaboration challenges. Employees also described a culture of seeking approval rather than iterating and learning, where leaders differ in how much they encourage ownership and experimentation. These factors make it harder for teams that want to adopt a genuine product approach to do so.

4.2 Approaches for Facilitating Dialogue About Paradoxes

This study examines two approaches to facilitating dialogue about paradoxes at the leadership level, shown in Fig. 1 and presented next.

Approach One: Silent Meeting and Taking a Stance to Spark Discussion: The purpose of this meeting was to seek feedback from senior leaders on their positions regarding organizational tensions to guide ongoing work of establishing common ways of working. To achieve this, a memo structured around questions highlighting key tensions was prepared. The memo was based on insights from the reflective conversations with employees, and each question included a title and contextual information, making the juxtaposed poles and their ripple effects clear. It is important to note that this memo presented organizational tensions without attempting to distinguish paradoxes from other tensions, thus it includes both tensions that are paradoxical and tensions that are not.

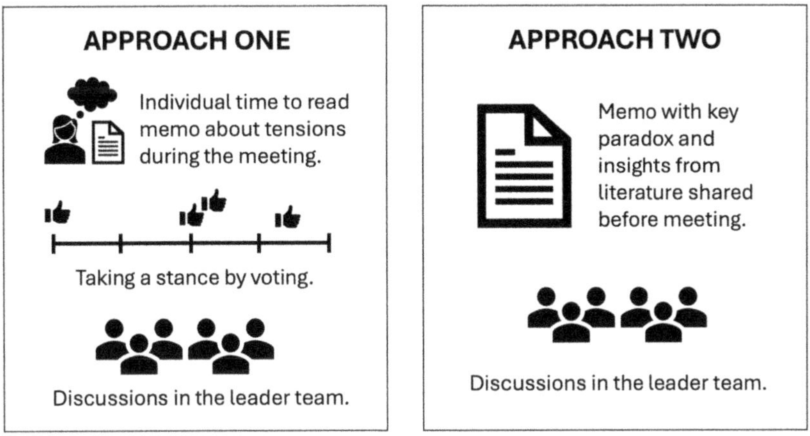

Fig. 1. Overview of the two approaches to facilitate dialogue.

Senior leaders were then invited to a one-hour long meeting, split in two parts. During the first 30 min, participants read the memo, added comments and discussion topics, and individually indicated their position by placing a visual vote on a scale between the two poles of each tension (see Fig. 2 for an example). The second half was dedicated to moderated discussion. The aim of working with tensions and taking a stance was to provoke healthy debate and clarify different positions.

The outcome of the meeting was pointers from the leaders on how to balance tensions. For example, a written summary noted that leaders wished to *"keep a clear focus on typical product management, but include (agile) project ways of working as a tool in the toolbox for collaborations that involve many dependencies"* and that they would *"continue to iterate on [a solution] to ensure cross-unit collaboration works well"*. Beyond these pointers, the session also appeared to raise awareness of the paradoxical nature of some tensions. One facilitator reflected that a particular tension *"revealed itself as a paradox rather than a trade off - not something we need to choose between but something we need to balance based on our context"*. This suggests that the approach not only stimulated dialogue but also helped shift thinking.

Approach Two: Paradox Theory and Research to Spark Discussion: This approach also centered on a memo as the starting point for dialogue. The memo described, based on initial analysis from the leader interviews, the paradox of centralization vs. autonomy that was strongly influencing the company. Moreover, the memo included general insights from the paradox literature [24], such as paradoxes being a natural part of organizations, that they are persistent in nature, and that paradoxes need to be continuously managed (they are not "something that needs to be fixed").

As a part of the process of developing the memo, we consulted with one of the managers at MarketCorp. This collaboration proved valuable, as the man-

Self-organized collaboration & emerging processes		← Scale of extremes →			Defined structures, process, tool
1 0	2 0	3 0	4 0	5 0	6 0

Fig. 2. Participants visually indicated their position by placing a vote on the scale between the two poles. In this example, the starting point for the scale was a question about how structured the collaboration guidance should be when working across the verticals and the core technology unit.

ager contextualized the research insights within recent company developments. He explained that: *"(...) the company had matured - now this paradox is referred to as 'being one integrated company' vs 'being verticalised'. Thus, this is wording that leaders immediately will recognize"*. After consulting with him, the memo used language even more familiar to the leaders and reframed the paradox to align with the company's current focus on operating as a large-scale agile organization, rather than "the transformation" emphasized during the interviews.

The memo content was later shared with the leadership team during a top-level gathering, and we have since learned that the company continues to address this paradox of centralization versus autonomy. Their operating model, describing the mechanisms for operating as one integrated company, now explicitly states that: *"Our challenge is to constantly balance what is best for our unit with what is best for the whole. When we strike that balance, we get the best of both worlds; strong, autonomous verticals and the power, speed, and leverage that come from being one integrated organisation"*.

5 Discussion

In the following section, we address our research questions by first examining how paradoxes manifest within MarketCorp (RQ1), and then exploring how agile practitioners and leaders can manage paradoxes (RQ2).

5.1 Large-Scale Agile: A Paradox in Practice

Our analysis revealed three influential paradoxes at MarketCorp, and these were manifesting across multiple dimensions of the organization, including culture, technology, ways of working, and strategic priorities. This echoes prior research stating that tensions are present in large-scale agile companies [7,14] as well as encountered during agile transitions [26].

The most influential paradox was centralization versus autonomy, mentioned in most leader interviews and strongly supported by the accounts of the employees, corroborating findings by Moe et al. [14]. This paradox manifested across culture, priorities, and technology, indicating that it is deeply embedded in multiple organizational dimensions. Practitioners in large-scale agile environments should therefore remain vigilant and actively manage this tension. Its persistence is, however, unsurprising considering that large-scale agile combines contradictory principles: team-level self-management central to "agile" and goal alignment and coordination essential for "large-scale" [4,10]. As noted by the manager involved in developing the memo, the paradox of centralization vs. autonomy endured beyond the initial transformation, reflecting inherent tensions that naturally arise in large organizations adopting agile ways of working. For example, such organizations require long-term roadmaps to ensure stability and direction [7], which contrasts with agile principles emphasizing flexibility [8,9]. These enduring tensions underscore the need for *continuous* dialogue that constructively address this paradox to foster sustainable solutions.

Moreover, our study suggests that, alongside the paradox of centralization vs. autonomy, other paradoxes often coexist. In our study, internal versus external focus and product versus process approaches simultaneously influenced the organization, making paradox management a complex endeavor. Tracking how paradoxes evolve over time is useful [6], as they may shift in nature or transform into other types of tensions [24]. This is a particularly interesting point in the case of MarketCorp. The company is currently undergoing a major transformation, which raises the question of whether the paradoxes identified in this study are tied to the transformation itself or whether they will persist once it is complete. The available data does not allow us to determine how these paradoxes will unfold in the future; however, Strode et al. [26] argue that paradoxes are tensions that are likely to persist throughout transformation and beyond (p. 3579). In our case, it is reasonable to expect that the paradox of centralization versus autonomy will remain, as it is rooted in the organization's large-scale structure rather than in the transformation process. The balance between internal and external focus is also likely to represent an enduring challenge, although its expression may evolve over time (for example, shifting from the current emphasis on integrating the new technology platform to other future priorities). Finally, the current clash between product and project approaches may diminish if the organization becomes fully agile, but may persist if parts of the organization continue to work in a project-oriented manner.

5.2 Managing Paradoxes Through Dialogue

Effectively identifying, working through, and managing paradoxes requires collaborative effort and sustained dialogue [6,12,24]. Organizations must foster constructive conversations around tensions, not only to determine which are truly paradoxical, but also to explore strategies for addressing them. Facilitating ongoing dialogue is therefore essential for enabling the iterative, experimental work of managing paradoxical tensions and supporting leaders and practitioners in responding productively to competing demands. Prior research suggests that agile coaches often take on facilitative responsibilities at both team and organizational levels, supporting reflection, alignment, and decision making when tensions persist over time [25].

As part of this study, we carried out two approaches designed to foster dialogue within large-scale agile leadership teams. Viewed through the lens of paradox theory [6,12], both approaches share important strengths: they maintain neutrality, use company-specific language, identify polarities, incorporate multiple internal perspectives, and present opposing viewpoints without favoring either side. However, they differ in how they stimulate engagement and frame paradoxes. The first approach actively encourages discussion among top management by posing provocative questions and visualizing diverse viewpoints. In contrast, the second approach introduces literature-based insights on paradoxes, helping normalize organizational tensions and promote "both-and" thinking, thereby supporting exploration of solutions for navigating competing demands.

We argue that our work involves three valuable process choices that are worth foregrounding. *First*, in both approaches, a written memo based on interviews played a central role in initiating dialogue. Danneels and Viaene [6] emphasize the importance of mindful wording and reusing organizational language when describing paradoxes. We add to this by showing that opposing forces can be effectively identified and described based on speaking to multiple organizational members. This suggests that presentations grounded in employees' voices can serve as a powerful starting point for dialogue about paradoxes. *Second*, the structure of our first approach offers a useful way of designing meetings focused on paradoxes. Participants were first given time to read a memo outlining relevant paradoxes and were then asked to indicate which poles they considered most important by visually marking their position on a scale. This process provides a structured yet inclusive way to surface diverse perspectives and creates a strong foundation for meaningful discussion. It may help participants move beyond entrenched positions, a key principle in paradox discussions [6]. *Third*, one of our memos drew on paradox literature to help the leadership team understand that paradoxes are normal, persistent, and demand continuous management [24]. We argue that normalizing paradoxes in this way contributes to a constructive space for open dialogue and encourages exploration of "both-and" solutions.

Despite these promising characteristics, both approaches have limitations. Productive dialogue about organizational tensions should encourage experimentation with different solutions for dealing with paradoxical tensions [12], track how paradoxes evolve over time [6] and cultivating a dynamic equilibrium [24]. While our approaches laid the foundation for fostering experimentation and finding sustainable solutions (e.g., by providing useful pointers from leaders), the explicit facilitation of concrete follow-up actions were missing, making them more of an initial step than a comprehensive solution. To fully support paradox management, future efforts must adopt a more holistic design that combines dialogue with mechanisms for ongoing learning and adaptation.

5.3 Implications for Practice

The practical implications from this study can be summarized as eight pieces of advice to practitioners who wish to facilitate dialogue about paradoxes. The advice draws on paradox theory [6,12] and the discussion above:

1. **Create spaces for collective dialogue**, as managing paradoxes is a collaborative process and requires sharing diverse viewpoints.
2. **Dedicate time to identify which tensions are truly paradoxical.**
3. **Describe paradoxes carefully and neutrally.** Use data-driven insights, company-specific language, and balanced framing of opposing poles.
4. **Normalize paradoxes as a natural part of organizational life**, emphasizing that they require ongoing attention rather than one-time fixes.
5. **Use techniques to advance dialogue**, such as interventive questions, individual reading for deeper insight, or visualizing different perspectives.
6. **Encourage experimentation with responses to paradoxes**, recognizing that there are no universal solutions and approaches must be adapted to the organization and the specific paradoxes.
7. **Track progress over time** to understand how paradoxes evolve and whether your responses are working well.
8. **Treat paradoxes as strategically significant**, allowing them to inform decision-making and guide priorities.

In a broader perspective, we argue that the enduring nature of paradoxes makes them a productive focus for continuous improvement in large-scale agile settings. They also align well with agile's emphasis on continuous reflection and learning for improved effectiveness [3]. Consequently, practitioners working at scale may benefit from incorporating structured paradox dialogues into their agile routines, for example, as part of retrospective sessions.

6 Conclusion, Limitations, and Future Research

This qualitative study of a multinational digital marketplace company examined paradoxical tensions in a large-scale agile organization and how practitioners and leaders can manage them. We found that multiple paradoxes simultaneously influence the organization, and that the paradox of centralization and autonomy appears to be inherent in large-scale agile environments. Our study also highlights that careful facilitation of collective dialogue is crucial for managing paradoxes. They cannot be resolved through one-off efforts; they require ongoing organizational engagement, experimentation, reflection, and learning. As part of the study, we explored two approaches for facilitating dialogue among company leaders and offer practical advice based on our experiences and assessment of these approaches.

This study has two main limitations. *First*, data were collected at a single point in time, and the facilitation approaches were applied to initiate dialogue rather than to follow its development. As a result, we cannot speak to how paradoxes evolve or are managed over time. Given that persistence is a defining characteristic of paradoxes [24], this may have obscured important temporal dynamics. We see this as a valuable avenue for future research and encourage longitudinal designs that capture how paradoxes unfold and how organizations continually address them.

Second, we did not systematically collect data on leaders' perceptions or on the detailed content of the discussions associated with the two facilitation approaches, nor did we document in detail how the workshop in the second approach unfolded in practice. Consequently, our analysis focuses on the initial design of the facilitation approaches, and a formal evaluation of their effectiveness is absent. While this was a deliberate choice that positions the study as an initial, design-oriented step aimed at surfacing design principles and practical considerations, it also means that the study does not provide a full account of how the approaches played out in practice. We therefore call for future research to build a more comprehensive evidence base for facilitating dialogue around paradoxes, including systematic examination of participant experiences and interaction dynamics.

Acknowledgements. We would like to thank the research participants for their time and for sharing their experiences and reflections, as well as the company for an inspiring collaboration. This research was co-funded by the Research Council of Norway (grant number 346563).

Disclosure of Interests. The authors have no competing interests to declare that are relevant to the content of this article.

References

1. Barbala, A., Berntzen, M., Moe, N.B.: Social capital in large-scale agile software product management: a multi-case study. Inf. Softw. Technol. 107841 (2025)
2. Barbala, A., Ulfsnes, R., Moe, N.B., Andersen, N.H., Emmerhoff, J.: Large-scale continuous software engineering: exploring three dimensions of transformation. In: Proceedings of the 29th International Conference on Evaluation and Assessment in Software Engineering, pp. 283–293 (2025)
3. Beck, K., et al.: Manifesto for agile software development (2001). https://agilemanifesto.org/. Accessed 19 Jan 2026
4. Berntzen, M., Stray, V., Moe, N.B., Hoda, R.: Responding to change over time: a longitudinal case study on changes in coordination mechanisms in large-scale agile. Empir. Softw. Eng. **28**(5), 114 (2023)
5. Braun, V., Clarke, V.: Using thematic analysis in psychology. Qual. Res. Psychol. **3**(2), 77–101 (2006)
6. Danneels, L., Viaene, S.: Identifying digital transformation paradoxes: a design perspective. Bus. Inf. Syst. Eng. 1–18 (2022)
7. Dikert, K., Paasivaara, M., Lassenius, C.: Challenges and success factors for large-scale agile transformations: a systematic literature review. J. Syst. Softw. **119**, 87–108 (2016)
8. Dingsøyr, T., Bjørnson, F.O., Schrof, J., Sporsem, T.: A longitudinal explanatory case study of coordination in a very large development programme: the impact of transitioning from a first- to a second-generation large-scale agile development method. Empir. Softw. Eng. **28**(1), 1 (2022)
9. Edison, H., Wang, X., Conboy, K.: Comparing methods for large-scale agile software development: a systematic literature review. IEEE Trans. Software Eng. **48**(8), 2709–2731 (2021)

10. Horlach, B., Drechsler, A.: It's not easy being agile: unpacking paradoxes in agile environments. In: International Conference on Agile Software Development, pp. 182–189. Springer (2020)
11. Hyrynsalmi, S.M., Broomandi, F., Salman, I., Paasivaara, M.: Fostering a sense of belonging in hybrid work within agile software development. In: International Conference on Agile Software Development, pp. 37–51. Springer (2025)
12. Lüscher, L.S., Lewis, M.W.: Organizational change and managerial sensemaking: working through paradox. Acad. Manag. J. **51**(2), 221–240 (2008)
13. Meckenstock, J.N., Wallmichrath, V.: Adapt and overcome-how agile practitioners adapt to issues that impede the delivery of value: an interview study. In: International Conference on Agile Software Development, pp. 245–264. Springer (2025)
14. Moe, N.B., Šmite, D., Paasivaara, M., Lassenius, C.: Finding the sweet spot for organizational control and team autonomy in large-scale agile software development. Empir. Softw. Eng. **26**(5), 101 (2021)
15. Moe, N.B., Stray, V., Šmite, D., Mikalsen, M.: Attractive workplaces: what are engineers looking for? IEEE Softw. **40**(5), 85–93 (2023)
16. Paasivaara, M., Behm, B., Lassenius, C., Hallikainen, M.: Large-scale agile transformation at ericsson: a case study. Empirical Softw. Eng. **23** (2018)
17. Putnam, L.L., Fairhurst, G.T., Banghart, S.: Contradictions, dialectics, and paradoxes in organizations: a constitutive approach. Acad. Manag. Ann. **10**(1), 65–171 (2016)
18. Ravn, J.E., Moe, N.B., Stray, V., Seim, E.A.: Team autonomy and digital transformation. AI Soc. **37**(2), 701–710 (2022)
19. Rolland, K.H., Fitzgerald, B., Dingsøyr, T., Stol, K.J.: Acrobats and safety nets: problematizing large-scale agile software development. ACM Trans. Softw. Eng. Methodol. **33**(2), 1–45 (2023)
20. Russo, D.: The agile success model: a mixed-methods study of a large-scale agile transformation. ACM Trans. Softw. Eng. Methodol. (TOSEM) **30**(4), 1–46 (2021)
21. Schad, J., Lewis, M.W., Raisch, S., Smith, W.K.: Paradox research in management science: looking back to move forward. Acad. Manag. Ann. **10**(1), 5–64 (2016)
22. Smite, D., et al.: Who "Controls" Where Work Shall Be Done? State of Practice in Post-Pandemic Remote Work Regulation. arXiv preprint arXiv:2505.15743 (2025)
23. Šmite, D., Moe, N.B., Floryan, M., Gonzalez-Huerta, J., Dorner, M., Sablis, A.: Decentralized decision-making and scaled autonomy at spotify. J. Syst. Softw. **200**, 111649 (2023)
24. Smith, W.K., Lewis, M.W.: Toward a theory of paradox: a dynamic equilibrium model of organizing. Acad. Manag. Rev. **36**(2), 381–403 (2011)
25. Stray, V., Tkalich, A., Moe, N.B.: The agile coach role: coaching for agile performance impact. In: Proceedings of the 54th Hawaii International Conference on System Sciences, pp. 6816–6825. AIS Electronic Library (2021)
26. Strode, D.E., Sharp, H., Barroca, L., Gregory, P., Taylor, K.: Tensions in organizations transforming to agility. IEEE Trans. Eng. Manage. **69**(6), 3572–3583 (2022)

What Shapes Hybrid Work Preferences and Behaviors in Agile Software Engineering?

Fateme Broomandi[1(✉)], Emily Laue Christensen[2], and Maria Paasivaara[1,3]

[1] LUT University, Mukkulankatu 19, 15210 Lahti, Finland
{fateme.broomandi,maria.paasivaara}@lut.fi
[2] IT University of Copenhagen, Rued Langgaards Vej 7, 2300 Copenhagen S, Denmark
emic@itu.dk
[3] Aalto University, Otakaari 1B, 02150 Espoo, Finland
maria.paasivaara@aalto.fi

Abstract. Hybrid work has become the norm post pandemic, yet organizing it effectively in agile software engineering requires understanding how individual and contextual factors shape preferences and behaviors. This study surveyed 65 agile practitioners to explore these influences. Respondents generally preferred flexible office attendance policies, but not full-time remote work. Larger teams expressed interest in agreed on presence at the office, while small or medium size teams leaned slightly more toward individual choice. Social interaction was a strong reason to come to the office, and most respondents viewed in-person meetings as highly beneficial for social and problem-solving activities. In virtual meetings, camera use was guided mainly by social presence and visibility, while multitasking activities were mostly meeting-supportive and work related, with managers and agile leaders reporting slightly higher levels of multitasking and significantly higher levels of camera use.

Keywords: Hybrid work · agile software engineering · survey

1 Introduction

Hybrid work, defined as a setting in which *"some team members work mostly or completely from home, others mostly or completely from the traditional office, and others in some combination of the two"* [9], has gained popularity post-pandemic and is likely to remain a long-term norm in software engineering (e.g., [20,26]). Prior research shows that organizational adaptation to hybrid work and work-setting issues remain central to research agendas in agile software engineering [5]. Nevertheless, many organizations continue to struggle with developing effective hybrid work strategies and policies [5].

A. Goldman et al. (Eds.): XP 2026, LNBIP 578, pp. 73–89, 2026.
https://doi.org/10.1007/978-3-032-22375-3_5

These observations point to a gap in understanding the drivers of employees' work-related preferences and behaviors in hybrid settings [15]. Since hybrid work policies influence everyday work practices [26], gaining a clearer picture of these factors is important for developing organizational approaches that align with individual needs and support agile ways of working. The significance of understanding these factors is particularly pronounced in agile software development, where collaboration and frequent interaction are central [17] and where preferences may vary across individuals and contexts [15]. Motivated by this gap, we investigate the following research question:

RQ: *What individual and contextual factors influence hybrid work preferences and behaviors in agile software engineering?*

To address this question, we use an exploratory research design based on an online survey and analyze 65 responses using descriptive statistics. We focus on how individual factors (i.e., gender, tenure, childcare responsibilities, and commute time) and contextual factors (i.e., role, team size, and team distribution) shape hybrid work preferences and behaviors. In this study, preferences refer to favored ways of organizing and performing hybrid work, including policies for office presence, team co-presence agreements, and attendance office across different types of agile meetings. The behaviors examined concern camera use and multitasking in virtual meetings (i.e., meetings conducted online in digitally mediated environments [14]).

2 Related Work

Prior research has examined the motivators behind employees' work location preferences within the context of hybrid work in agile software engineering (e.g., [15,25]). These studies highlight that similar underlying considerations, such as work–life balance and personal well-being, can lead to divergent preferences depending on individual circumstances. For example, while some employees report improved work–life balance and concentration when they work from home (WFH), others find the office environment more conducive to focused work and maintaining boundaries between work and personal life [15]. This variation underscores the importance of examining not only the broad motivators but also the individual and contextual factors that shape employees preferences and behaviors in hybrid work.

As shown in Table 1, related studies have examined individual and contextual factors that influence work location preferences in hybrid work within agile software engineering environments. Existing research has focused primarily on preferences regarding where work is carried out, emphasizing the previously mentioned individual factors and contextual factors. Although these contributions provide valuable insights into individual work location preferences, they offer only limited understanding of the factors that shape preferences for team agreements concerning office presence. Similarly, while research on camera use and multitasking behaviors during virtual meetings has identified influential factors and underlying motivations (e.g., [4,6]), this work has largely been conducted outside agile and hybrid work contexts.

Furthermore, much of the prior work was conducted during the Covid-19 pandemic (e.g., [1,11]) or during the early phase of post-pandemic hybrid work (e.g., [3,27]). As hybrid work becomes more stabilized and intentional, there is a need to revisit these influencing factors in more mature post-pandemic settings.

Table 1. Themes and main findings in prior research

Theme	Main findings
Individual factors influencing work location preferences	Commute time is the strongest predictor of WFH, with longer commutes associated with higher remote-work frequency [7,18,26].
	Age and tenure influence office attendance, with older employees showing a stronger preference for office work [7,18,26].
	Gender effects are minimal, with women working remotely slightly more often without statistical significance [7].
Contextual factors influencing work location preferences	Organizational role shapes work location choice, with managers generally less likely to WFH than non-managerial engineers [7,26,30].
	Meeting type affects location decisions: status meetings are often held virtually to preserve office time for collaboration [27], while planning and retrospectives are frequently preferred in the office [30], although some studies report preferences for conducting these practices remotely [19].
Camera use during virtual meetings	Keeping cameras on improves communication by showing body language [1–3].
	Cameras are turned off due to multitasking, social conformity, discomfort with visibility, and passive participation roles [4].
Multitasking during virtual meetings	Multitasking is widespread in virtual meetings and primarily involves meeting-supportive and work-related activities [4].
	Multitasking is shaped by intrinsic meeting characteristics, such as size, length, timing, and type [6].

To address these gaps, our study extends prior research by examining additional work-related preferences and behaviors relevant to hybrid work in agile software engineering environments. These include preferences for team agreements regarding office presence, and camera use and multitasking behaviors in virtual meetings. Our study also considers a broader range of individual and contextual factors, such as the presence of children in the household, team size, and team distribution.

3 Research Design

This study adopts an exploratory research design and uses a cross-sectional online survey [28] to investigate the factors that influence individuals' hybrid work preferences and behaviors in agile software engineering. The survey method was selected because it enables systematic and standardized data collection [12], is well suited for describing trends and opinions within a population [10], and is appropriate for identifying influencing factors in software engineering contexts [28]. The survey combined closed and open-ended questions and drew on validated instruments from prior studies on remote work in software development (e.g., [23]) and large-scale agile settings [22]. Its design was further informed by insights from related empirical research (e.g., [4,6,24]). The questionnaire consisted of demographic information and five thematic sections: office presence and policies, meetings (including camera use and multitasking behaviors), productivity, well-being, and future hopes for hybrid work. For this study, we analyzed only the responses to seven closed-ended questions related to hybrid work policies, team agreements about office presence, future hopes for hybrid work, and meeting practices, along with demographic data. These topics were selected because they directly address hybrid work preferences and behaviors central to our research question. The survey instrument was created in LimeSurvey and was pilot-tested and reviewed by two senior researchers with expertise in survey design to ensure alignment with best practices.

To collect responses, we employed a non-probabilistic convenience sampling approach, in which data were obtained anonymously from individuals who were willing and available to participate [21]. The survey was initially distributed at the 25th International Conference on Agile Software Development (XP 2024) on June 4 via a QR code and through the conference Slack channel. The survey was subsequently advertised on LinkedIn through two posts published in July. Data collection remained open until September 20, 2024. In total, 65 complete responses were obtained and retained for analysis. The survey questionnaire and data collected are available in the supplementary materials[1] All respondents provided informed consent and confirmed in the questionnaire that they were software practitioners working with agile methods in hybrid work settings. Their demographics are shown in Table 2. When multiple roles were reported, the highest-responsibility role was assigned.

Descriptive statistics, including frequencies and percentages, were used to summarize the responses, following the reporting guidelines of Kitchenham et al. [16]. This approach is well suited for identifying and presenting patterns in data without relying on the distributional assumptions required for larger samples. Inferential analyses were not conducted, as the study aimed to provide an exploratory overview of trends rather than statistical generalization, and the sample size was insufficient to support reliable inferential testing.

[1] Supplementary materials: https://doi.org/10.6084/m9.figshare.30734513.

Table 2. Demographics of the 65 survey respondents

Gender	43 men (66%) | 18 women (28%) | 1 non-binary (1%) | 3 non-disclosed (5%)
Children in home	44 without children (68%) | 21 with children (32%)
Country	31 from Finland (48%) | 12 from Denmark (19%) | 6 from India (9%) | 4 from Italy (6%) | 12 from other countries (18%)
Commute time	30 with up to 30 min (47%) | 31 with more than 30 min (47%) | 4 with no commute (6%)
Tenure	38 seniors with 10> years (58%) | 27 juniors/mid-levels with <10 years (42%)
Role	20 managers (31%) | 16 team members (25%) | 15 agile leaders (23%) | 14 specialists (21%)
Team size	37 in small or medium with up to 9 members (57%) | 25 in large with at least 10 members (38%) | 3 not in team (5%)
Team distribution	32 in same country, different city (49%) | 23 in different country (36%) | 10 in same city (15%)

3.1 Threats to Validity

Several measures were taken to mitigate validity threats [28], though some limitations remain. Misinterpretation of concepts and self-report bias threaten *construct validity*. To address these risks, we grounded survey items in prior literature, provided definitions in the questionnaire, pilot-tested the instrument, and ensured anonymity to reduce social-desirability bias. We included only respondents with confirmed agile and hybrid work experience, and although the recruitment routes differed, the shared inclusion criteria likely minimized major differences. Nevertheless, some constructs were still operationalized narrowly. Care responsibilities were assessed only through items about children and pets, excluding other dependencies (e.g., elder care). Reasons for camera use in virtual meetings were captured through predefined options without an open-ended 'other reasons' field, potentially limiting the identification of additional or context-specific motivations. Although both current and preferred team agreements were collected, these measures were not designed for direct comparison, as current agreements were measured with a single-choice question, whereas preferred agreements allowed multiple selections, limiting conclusions about misalignment between existing agreements and individual preferences.

Regarding *internal validity*, the exploratory, cross-sectional survey design supports descriptive but not causal interpretation. Temporal order cannot be established, and unmeasured factors such as team maturity and leadership style may influence responses. Concerning *external validity*, generalizability is constrained by convenience sampling and the characteristics of the respondent pool. Distribution via LinkedIn within Nordic networks yielded responses primarily from Nordic countries and predominantly from men, reflecting the gender composition of software professionals. WFH is more common in the Nordic countries than in much of Europe, often linked to high digitalization and trust, which may shape hybrid work preferences [13]. Additionally, recruitment channels were not recorded, preventing descriptive comparison across routes. To support transferability, we report contextual characteristics in detail and present findings as indicative rather than representative. Finally, limited sample size and uneven subgroup distributions constrain *conclusion validity*. We therefore we avoid inferential claims and report counts alongside percentages to ensure transparency.

4 Results

In this section, we report what individual and contextual factors influence preferences for hybrid work policies, team agreements, and meeting practices, including camera use and multitasking behaviors in virtual meetings, as shown in our results.

4.1 Hybrid Work Policies and Team Agreements

Current and Preferred Hybrid Work Policies. The respondents' current and preferred hybrid work policies are shown in Fig. 1. While 27 respondents were working under a *fully flexible* policy, an even larger group (n = 36) preferred this policy. In contrast, 13 respondents were currently working under a *remote-first* policy, but only 6 preferred this policy. Differences between current and preferred *semi-fixed* policies, requiring two to three office days per week, were minimal. Likewise, preferences for both *fully-fixed* policies which mandate specific office days, and for *office-first* policies, which designate the office as the primary work location, were very low and closely aligned with current polices.

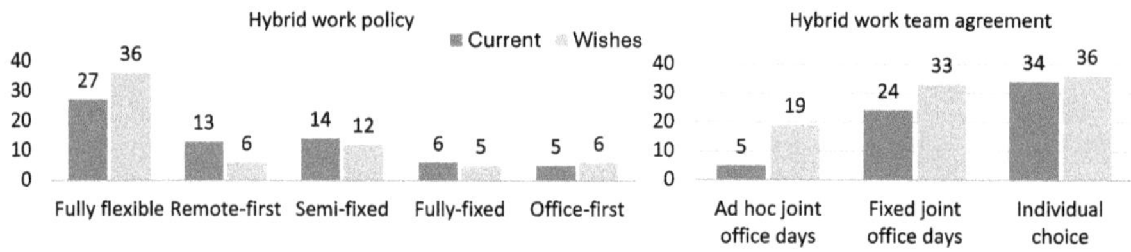

Fig. 1. Current and preferred hybrid work policies and team agreements.

Individual Factors Influencing Policy Preferences. The individual factors influencing hybrid work policy preferences are summarized in Fig. 2. Overall, patterns remained broadly consistent, with fully flexible policies dominating across all categories. Regarding *tenure*, among the 38 senior practitioners, 25 preferred remote-first or fully flexible policies, compared to 17 of the 27 junior or mid-level practitioners who reported similar preferences. *Commute time* did not meaningfully influence policy preferences. Respondents with longer and shorter commutes showed very similar patterns across all hybrid work policy preferences. A closer examination of the data revealed that 21 of the 30 respondents with commutes

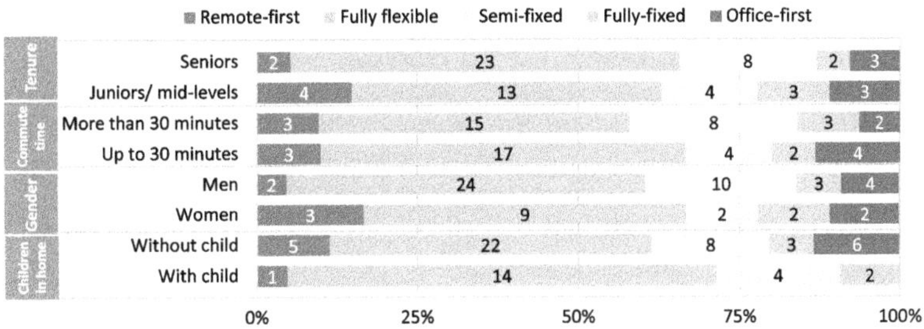

Fig. 2. Hybrid work policy preferences segmented by individual factors.

under 30 min worked in teams distributed across different cities or countries. This suggests that the perceived benefit of office attendance is tied more to opportunities for physical team co-presence and collaboration than to the length of the commute itself.

Gender differences were relatively small: of the 43 men, 24 preferred fully flexible policies, compared to 9 of the 18 women, who nevertheless reported slightly higher preferences for remote-first policies, suggesting only minor gender-related variation. Family situation showed a clearer effect: among respondents with *children in the home* (n = 21), 14 favored fully flexible policies over semi-fixed or fully-fixed options, and none selected office-first, indicating that child caregiving responsibilities may shape preferences toward greater autonomy. Overall, these results highlight how individual factors can shape what agile practitioners view as the best hybrid work policy.

Current and Preferred Team Agreements. Overall, many respondents expressed a desire for more agreed on team office presence, as shown in Fig. 1. Notably, 19 respondents preferred *ad hoc joint office days*, while only 5 currently had this team agreement. Likewise, more respondents preferred *fixed joint office days* with their team (n = 33), than was the current agreement (n = 24). In contrast, responses about individual choice were largely similar.

Contextual Factors Influencing Team Agreement Preferences. Figure 3 illustrates how preferred hybrid work team agreements vary across different roles, team sizes, and team distributions. Regarding the *role*, managers and leaders reported a slightly higher preference for agreed on team office days (n = 30), specifically fixed and ad hoc joint office days, compared with team members and specialists (n = 22). In contrast, team members and specialists reported a stronger preference for individual choice. As for *team size*, members of small or medium-sized teams with up to nine members reported a preference for individual choice (n = 24), whereas members of larger teams with more than ten members (n = 11) reported a slightly higher preference for fixed office days. Finally, regarding *team distribution*, teams that were distributed across countries tended to favor individual choice, while teams located in the same country, particularly those in the same city, were more likely to prefer fixed or ad hoc joint office days.

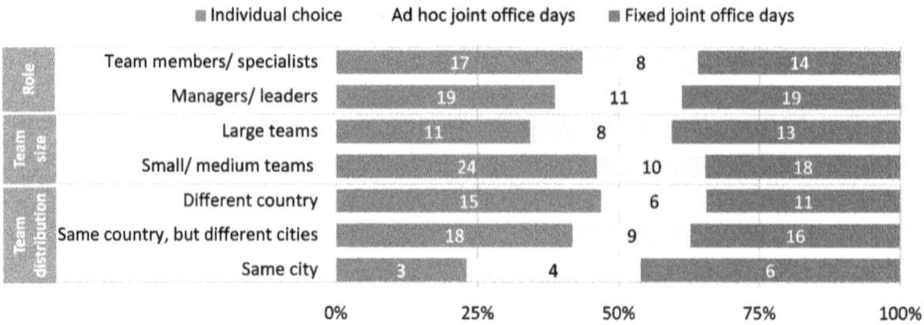

Fig. 3. Team work agreement preferences segmented by contextual factors.

4.2 Meeting Practices

Office Attendance for Agile Meetings. Respondents' perceptions of which agile meetings benefit most from having all attendees together at the office are shown in Fig. 4, excluding responses from individuals who did not attend the respective meeting type. *Social get-togethers* were perceived as the most beneficial to have with all attendees present in the office, with 59 of 65 respondents rating them as extremely or very beneficial. *Brainstorming* followed closely (n = 42), underscoring the value of in-person interaction for creative and discussion-oriented meetings. *Planning meetings* and *retrospectives* fell in the middle range, with about half of the respondents indicating that these activities were extremely or very beneficial to conduct in person (34 and 31, respectively). Likewise, *technical* and *backlog refinement* meetings received mixed perceptions, with 25 and 21 respondents rating them as extremely or very beneficial to hold in person. In contrast, *sprint reviews*, *information-sharing*, and *daily meetings* were more frequently perceived as not benefiting from having all attendees together at the office, with 17, 16, and 21 responses, respectively.

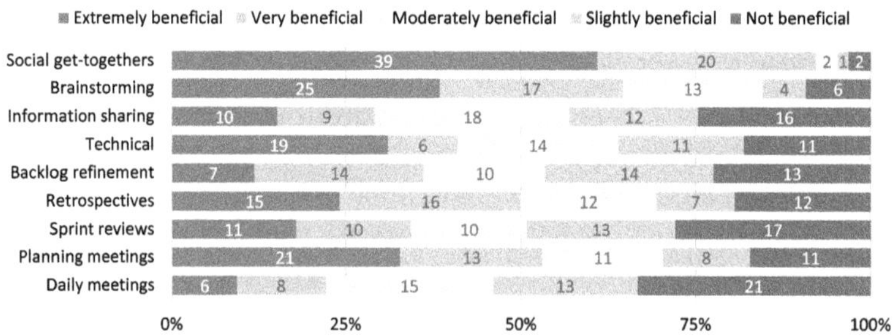

Fig. 4. Perceived degree to which meetings benefit from having all attendees together at the office.

Multitasking Activities Performed During Virtual Meetings. The reported frequency of multitasking activities performed during virtual meetings is shown in Fig. 5. The most common activity was meeting-supportive, i.e.,

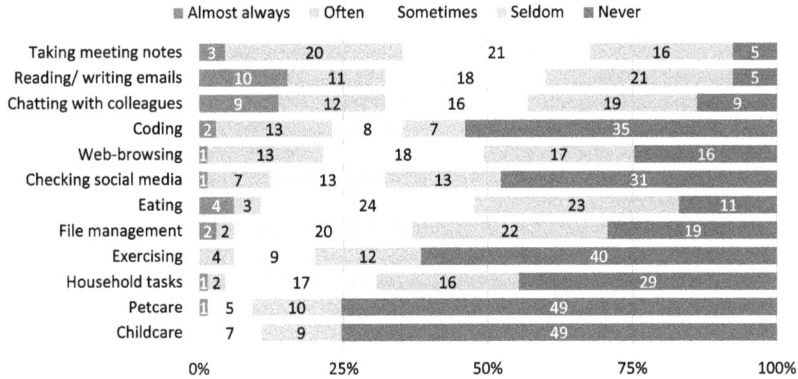

Fig. 5. Multitasking activities performed during virtual meetings.

taking meeting notes, followed by other work-related activities, i.e., reading or writing emails, and chatting with colleagues. These activities were performed almost always or often by between 23 and 21 respondents. Additionally, while coding was performed less frequently, 15 respondents still reported almost always or often conducting this work-related activity. Daily or practical activities were also conducted, albeit less frequently. Web browsing, checking social media, eating, file organization/cleaning, exercising, and performing household tasks were reported as almost always or often conducted during virtual meetings by between 14 and 3 respondents. Finally, activities involving pet and child care were the least frequent, with only one respondent almost always conducting petcare, while between 58 and 59 respondents seldom or never carried out these two activities. Taken together, the responses show that, although a subset of participants frequently engaged in specific work-related multitasking, most activities were performed infrequently, indicating that multitasking was not a widespread behavior among respondents.

Gender-Based Multitasking. As shown in Fig. 6, women and men differed in how frequently they reported multitasking during virtual meetings. On average, women reported multitasking slightly more often than men across most activities, including taking meeting notes, checking social media, performing household tasks, childcare, petcare, and eating. In contrast, men were more likely to multitask by coding during virtual meetings. Further examination revealed that 13 of the 18 women in our sample held managerial roles, which may account for their lower reported frequency of coding relative to men. Other activities, such as web browsing and chatting with colleagues, were reported at similar levels across both genders.

Role-Based Multitasking. Respondents in different roles also reported differing work-related multitasking frequencies during virtual meetings, as depicted in Fig. 7. Managers and agile leaders reported slightly higher multitasking frequencies across nearly all work-related activities compared with team members

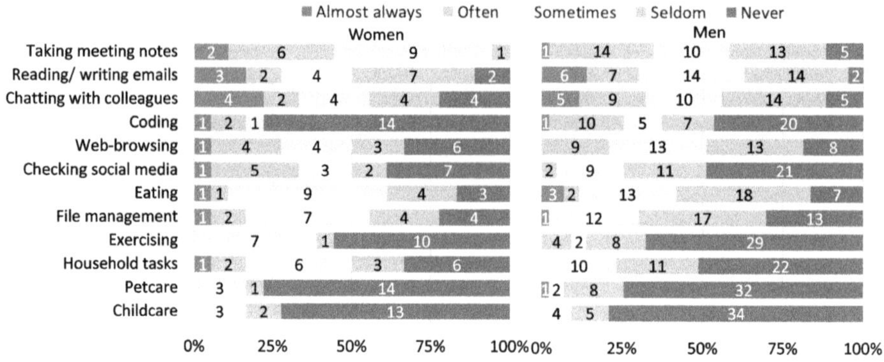

Fig. 6. Gender-based multitasking during virtual meetings.

and specialists, particularly for reading and writing emails, chatting with colleagues, and taking meeting notes. In contrast, team members and specialists reported greater engagement in task-related multitasking, especially coding and note-taking.

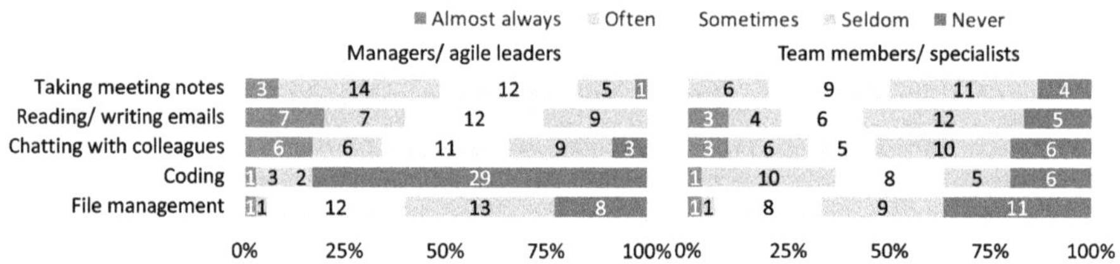

Fig. 7. Role-based multitasking during virtual meetings.

Using Cameras During Virtual Meetings. Respondents' self-reported reasons for turning their cameras on or off during virtual meetings are shown in Fig. 8. The most common reasons for turning *cameras on* were socially oriented, namely: to maintain or improve relationships, being a key speaker, showing engagement, setting an example for others, and being in line with other meeting attendees (reported by between 39 and 51 respondents). Reasons related to the social context of the meeting also showed moderate relevance: not knowing other participants in the meeting ($n = 29$) and team agreement ($n = 28$), suggesting that some respondents viewed camera use as a way to support group dynamics or meet shared expectations.

Between 30 and 39 respondents marked three reasons as *not relevant* for their decision, i.e., team agreement, self-consciousness about appearance, and company policy, indicating that these considerations generally played a limited role in decisions about camera use. In contrast, between 25 and 49 respondents

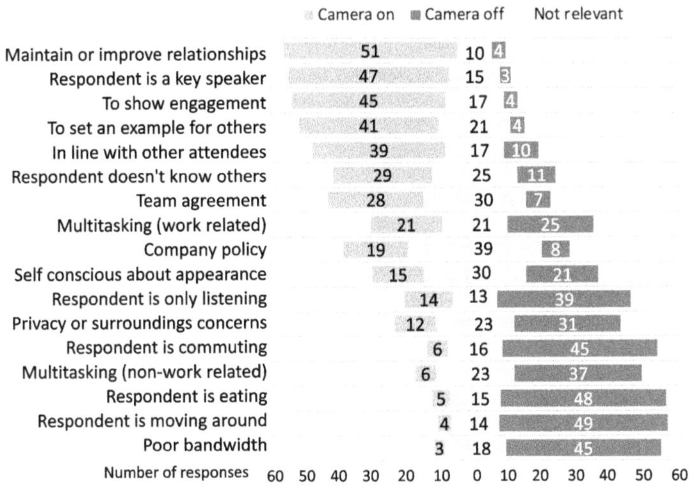

Fig. 8. Reasons for turning cameras on or off in virtual meetings.

reported keeping their *cameras off* due to situational or personal factors: multitasking for work, being concerned about privacy or surroundings, multitasking for non-work reasons, only listening, poor bandwidth, commuting, eating, and moving around.

Role-Based Camera Use. Additional role-based analysis revealed that managers and agile leaders were far more likely to turn their *cameras on*, compared to team members and specialists. As shown in Fig. 9, the most common reason for turning cameras on, namely to maintain or improve relationships, was reported by 32 of the 35 managers and agile leaders (91%), in contrast with 19 of the 30 team members and specialists (63%). Overall, managers' and agile leaders' camera-on behavior was primarily linked to leadership, visibility, and engagement-related reasons, whereas team members' and specialists' camera-off behavior was mainly associated with listener-oriented participation, multitasking, and practical constraints.

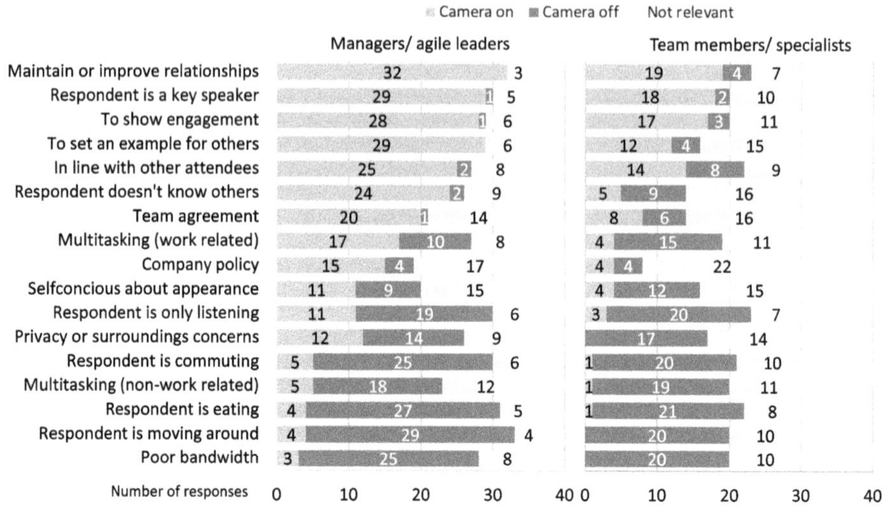

Fig. 9. Role-based camera usage in virtual meetings.

5 Discussion

In this section, we discuss our results in relation to our research question and prior work, highlight the key takeaways, report the implications for practice, and suggest directions for future research.

Tenure and Childcare Influenced Policy Preferences. Overall, although respondents expressed a desire for greater policy flexibility, they did not show a strong preference for remote-first policies, suggesting that agile practitioners value autonomy in choosing their place of work while still recognizing the benefits of maintaining some degree of office presence. Similarly, earlier findings indicate that while autonomy is valued, many agile software engineers choose office work [19,26,29], and some worked on-site more than half the week [7], highlighting the continued importance of in-person work. However, senior practitioners in our study showed a slightly stronger preference for fully flexible policies than junior and mid-level practitioners. This aligns with prior research indicating that younger engineers often preferred more office presence for socialization and learning, whereas senior practitioners, being more independent and sometimes balancing family responsibilities, preferred flexibility [7,26]. However, Moe et al. [18] reported the opposite pattern, suggesting that age and tenure may shape preferences differently across organizational contexts.

Respondents with children favored fully flexible policies, with none preferring office-first policies, underscoring the influence of childcare responsibilities on hybrid work preferences. Gender differences were minimal: women showed a slightly stronger preference for remote-first policies, but the effect was small and not tied to childcare factors in our sample. This aligns with prior work showing limited gender effects on work location preferences [7,18,26]. However, because most of the women in our sample held managerial roles, and managers tend to prefer working at the office [30], this suggests that individual and contextual factors such as gender, tenure, and role may interact in important ways.

In-person Team Collaboration Outweighed Commute Duration. Unlike previous studies reporting that employees with long commutes tend to prefer more flexible policies [7,26,29], our results show no meaningful differences between those with shorter and longer commutes. A likely explanation is that many respondents with short commutes worked in geographically distributed teams, limiting the value of going to the office regardless of travel time. Prior studies (e.g., [25,29]) consistently show that opportunities for in-person collaboration are a primary driver of office attendance. Our findings reinforce this insight by indicating that such collaborative benefits matter more to agile practitioners than commute duration.

Managerial Roles Favored Agreed Office Attendance. We found that managers and leaders were slightly more supportive of agreed office days than team members or specialists. This finding aligns with previous research reporting that managers prefer office attendance more than team members for Scrum events [30], and are less likely to work remotely because their perceived availability is increased through office presence [7]. In contrast, the stronger preference for individual choice among team members and specialists may reflect the more task-oriented and independent nature of their work [29]. Together, these results suggest a consistent pattern in which managerial roles place greater value on physical co-presence.

Team Distribution and Size Shaped Preferences for Office Attendance Agreements. Teams located in the same city were more open to agreed office days, possibly because coordinated in-person collaboration was more feasible, while internationally distributed teams preferred individual choice. Members of small or medium-sized teams also leaned slightly more toward individual choice for office presence, whereas larger teams favored fixed agreements, likely due to greater coordination needs and communication overhead [31]. However, this difference was modest. To our knowledge, prior research has not examined these contextual factors within hybrid work in agile settings, highlighting a clear opportunity for further investigation.

Meeting Type Influenced Preferences for Office Attendance. Our results show that office attendance was valued most for social get-togethers and brainstorming meetings, where socialization, solving problems, and ideation benefit from in-person collaboration [19,25]. Prior studies report similar patterns, identifying social interaction as a major driver of office attendance [15,25,29], and recommending that social events [19] and discussion-heavy meetings [8] take place at the office. Together, this underscores that the primary value of shared office time lies in supporting social connection and collaborative problem-solving. Routine meetings, such as daily stand-ups and information-sharing sessions, were viewed as less dependent on in-person presence. This aligns with research showing that information-sharing meetings work well virtually [8] and that status-reporting meetings are best kept online to preserve office time for spontaneous collaboration [27]. Planning, retrospective, backlog refinement, and technical meetings occupied a middle ground: respondents saw office attendance as beneficial, but did not consider it essential. This contrasts with studies suggesting that these meetings clearly benefit from being held in person [1,30]. One explanation may be that, after several years of hybrid work, teams have adapted their planning and reflection practices to virtual formats, developing practices and shared understanding that allow these meetings to function effectively virtually.

Role, Gender, and Personal Circumstances Shaped Multitasking Behaviors. Consistent with prior work identifying common multitasking activities in virtual meetings [4], respondents in our study frequently engaged in note-taking, a meeting-supportive activity, along with other work-related activities such as emailing, and messaging colleagues. Multitasking not related to work was far less common. Gender, role, and personal circumstances shaped these behaviors: women reported slightly more multitasking overall, especially household and care-related tasks. Managers and agile leaders also multitasked slightly more, most often performing communication-focused activities, whereas team members and specialists multitasked less, and tended to engage in more technical tasks, such as coding. These patterns indicate that multitasking in virtual meetings a structured behavior shaped by both contextual and individual factors such as role-related and gendered responsibilities, as well as personal circumstances.

Role Shaped Behaviors Around Camera Use. Our findings show that respondents primarily turned cameras on to maintain or improve relationships, show engagement, or when speaking. Cameras were turned off mainly due to situational or personal factors such as moving, eating, commuting, or bandwidth limitations. This aligns with Balogova and Brumby [4], who found that cameras are often disabled to accommodate parallel activities such as eating. These patterns indicate that visibility [2] and social presence, and social context, are key motivations for camera use in meetings. Moreover, our results show that managers and agile leaders are more likely to keep their cameras on, compared with team members and specialists.

Key Takeaways. Overall, our study contributes evidence that tenure seniority influence preferences for policy flexibility more strongly than gender, and that in-person collaboration, not commute time, remains the key motivator for office attendance. Our results show that managers value agreed office days more than team members, and that team size and geographical distribution shape preferences for co-presence agreements, an area not addressed in earlier research. Additionally, we extend knowledge on meeting practices by showing that social and brainstorming activities drive office attendance, while more routine meetings are increasingly effective virtually. Finally, our findings reveal that camera use in virtual meetings is shaped by social factors, while role expectations, gendered responsibilities, and personal circumstances influence multitasking behaviors. Together, these insights deepen understanding of how agile practitioners navigate hybrid work and identify factors that organizations should consider when designing policies and practices.

Implications for Practice. In agile software engineering, hybrid work policies should be designed to provide enough flexibility while enabling purposeful in-person interaction. Teams should explicitly coordinate office attendance around meetings that benefit most from co-presence, such as social and problem-solving activities. Because meeting-supportive multitasking was most common activity performed, it is important to distinguish between types of multitasking rather than treating them uniformly, as these differences can shape engagement and meeting effectiveness. Likewise, camera use in virtual meetings should be guided by social presence needs and situational constraints rather than treated as a uniform expectation across roles or contexts.

Future Research Directions. As an exploratory study, these findings motivate further research with larger and more diverse samples. Future work could examine the extent to which WFH is suitable across different companies and contexts, and investigate the reasons for employees' preferred work policies and team agreements, particularly the influence of team size. Broader, globally distributed samples would help assess whether these patterns generalize and guide organizations in improving hybrid work strategies and policies.

Acknowledgments. This research has been supported by the Finnish Work Environment Fund, under grant #240172 and the Kempower Electric Mobility Research Center. We thank Iflaah Salman, Sonja M. Hyrynsalmi, and Paolo Tell for survey design support, and Dron Khanna and Stefano Vincenti for promoting the study during data collection.

References

1. Ågren, P., Knoph, E., Berntsson Svensson, R.: Agile software development one year into the covid-19 pandemic. Empirical Softw. Eng. **27**(6), 121 (2022)
2. Lisboa de Andrade, A.S., Luz de Quadros, E.L., Oliveira Fortes, L., Prikladnicki, R.: Developing a collaborative recommendations guide for hybrid software development: a focus group study. In: Proceedings of the XXIII Brazilian Symposium on Software Quality. SBQS 2024, pp. 39–48 (2024)
3. Bablo, J., Marcinkowski, B., Przybylek, A.: Overcoming challenges of virtual scrum teams: lessons learned through an action research study. In: Agile Processes in Software Engineering and Extreme Programming, XP 2023, pp. 34–49. Springer, Cham (2023)
4. Balogova, K., Brumby, D.: How do you zoom?: a survey study of how users configure video-conference tools for online meetings. In: Proceedings of the 1st Annual Meeting of the Symposium on Human-Computer Interaction for Work. CHIWORK 2022, pp. 1–7 (2022)
5. Broomandi, F., Paasivaara, M., Christensen, E.L., Hyrynsalmi, S., Khanna, D.: Hybrid work in agile software engineering: current research and future directions. In: Agile Processes in Software Engineering and Extreme Programming - Workshops. XP 2025, pp. 53–67. Springer, Cham (2025)

6. Cao, H., et al.: Large scale analysis of multitasking behavior during remote meetings. In: Proceedings of the 2021 CHI Conference on Human Factors in Computing Systems, CHI 2021, pp. 1–13 (2021)
7. Chatzipetrou, P., Šmite, D., Tkalich, A., Moe, N.B., Klotins, E.: Interest in working remotely: is gender a factor? In: International Conference on Product-Focused Software Process Improvement. PROFES 2024, pp. 156–171. Springer, Cham (2024)
8. Christensen, E.L., Paasivaara, M., Salman, I.: Hybrid work in agile software development: recurring meetings. In: 2025 IEEE/ACM 18th International Conference on Cooperative and Human Aspects of Software Engineering. CHASE 2025, pp. 120–130. IEEE (2025)
9. Conboy, K., Moe, N.B., Stray, V., Gundelsby, J.H.: The future of hybrid software development: challenging current assumptions. IEEE Softw. **40**(02), 26–33 (2023)
10. Creswell, J.W., Creswell, J.D.: Research Design: Qualitative, Quantitative, and Mixed Methods Approaches, 5th edn. Sage Publications, Thousand Oaks, CA (2018)
11. Ford, D., et al.: A tale of two cities: software developers working from home during the covid-19 pandemic. ACM Trans. Softw. Eng. Methodol. **31**(2), 1–37 (2021)
12. Fowler, F.J.: Survey Research Methods, 5th edn. Sage Publications, Thousand Oaks, CA (2014)
13. Gill, A., Hensvik, L.E., Skans, O.N.: Why are nordic workers so remote?: potential causes and (some) indirect labor market consequences. Technical report, National Bureau of Economic Research (2025)
14. Heath, C., Luff, P., Sellen, A.: Reconsidering the virtual workplace: flexible support for collaborative activity. In: Proceedings of the Fourth European Conference on Computer-Supported Cooperative Work. ECSCW 1995, pp. 83–99. Springer, Dordrecht (1995)
15. Kemell, K.K., Saarikallio, M.: Hybrid work practices and strategies in software engineering-emerging software developer experiences. IEEE Access **11**, 112861–112876 (2023)
16. Kitchenham, B.A., et al.: Preliminary guidelines for empirical research in software engineering. IEEE Trans. Softw. Eng. **28**(8), 721–734 (2002)
17. Moe, N.B., Dingsøyr, T., Rolland, K.: To schedule or not to schedule? An investigation of meetings as an inter-team coordination mechanism in large-scale agile software development. Int. J. Inf. Syst. Proj. Manag. **6**(3), 45–59 (2018)
18. Moe, N.B., Ulsaker, S., Šmite, D., Hildrum, J.M., Ay, F.C.: Understanding the difference between office presence and co-presence in team member interactions. In: Proceedings of the 57th Hawaii International Conference on System Sciences. HICSS 2024. University of Hawai'i at Manoa (2024)
19. Neumann, M., et al.: What remains from covid-19? Agile software development in hybrid work organization: a single case study. In: 2022 10th International Conference in Software Engineering Research and Innovation, pp. 29–38. IEEE (2022)
20. Ozkaya, I.: The future of software engineering work. IEEE Softw. **38**(05), 3–6 (2021)
21. Pfleeger, S.L., Kitchenham, B.A.: Principles of survey research, part 5: populations and samples. Softw. Eng. **27**(5), 17–20 (2002)
22. Putta, A., Uludağ, Ö., Hong, S.L., Paasivaara, M., Lassenius, C.: Why do organizations adopt agile scaling frameworks? A survey of practitioners. In: Proceedings of the 15th ACM/IEEE International Symposium on Empirical Software Engineering and Measurement. ESEM 2021, pp. 1–12 (2021)

23. Ralph, P., et al.: Pandemic programming: how covid-19 affects software developers and how their organizations can help. Empirical Softw. Eng. **25**(6), 4927–4961 (2020)
24. Šmite, D., Christensen, E.L., Tell, P., Russo, D.: The future workplace: characterizing the spectrum of hybrid work arrangements for software teams. IEEE Softw. **40**(2), 34–41 (2022)
25. Šmite, D., Klotins, E., Moe, N.B.: What attracts employees to work on site in times of increased remote working? IEEE Softw. **42**(1), 100–109 (2024)
26. Šmite, D., Moe, N.B., Hildrum, J., Gonzalez-Huerta, J., Mendez, D.: Work-from-home is here to stay: call for flexibility in post-pandemic work policies. J. Syst. Softw. **195**, 111552 (2023)
27. Sporsem, T., Moe, N.B.: Coordination strategies when working from anywhere: a case study of two agile teams. In: Agile Processes in Software Engineering and Extreme Programming. XP 2022, pp. 52–61. Springer, Cham (2022)
28. Wohlin, C., Runeson, P., Höst, M., Ohlsson, M.C., Regnell, B., Wesslén, A.: Experimentation in Software Engineering, 2nd edn. Springer, Heidelberg (2024)
29. Zaidman, N., Van Dijk, D.: Why do software developers like working from the office? Inf. Softw. Technol. **179**, 107647 (2025)
30. Zaidman, N., Van-Dijk, D., Bouskila-Yam, O., Gazit, L.: Where is the best location to conduct scrum meetings? A quantitative and qualitative analysis of developers' perspectives. Behav. Inf. Technol. **44**(18), 1–18 (2025)
31. Zia, A., Arshad, W., Mahmood, W.: Preference in using agile development with larger team size. Int. J. Adv. Comput. Sci. Appl. **9**(7), 116–123 (2018)

Data-Driven Agility and Transformations

The Agile Mindset and Its Impact on Job Satisfaction, Goal Orientation and Change Resistance – A Scale Development and Validation

Karen Eilers[1(✉)], Christoph Peters[2], and Ulrich Bretschneider[3]

[1] BSP Business and Law School, Am Kaiserkai 1, 20457 Hamburg, Germany
karen.eilers@bsp-campus-hamburg.de
[2] University of the Bundeswehr Munich, Werner-Heisenberg-Weg 393GEB, 85579 Neubiberg, Germany
christoph.peters@unibw.de
[3] Universität Kassel, Pfannkuchstraße 1, 34121 Kassel, Germany
bretschneider@uni-kassel.de

Abstract. To cope with ongoing change, an increasing number of companies view agile approaches as fundamental for remaining competitive in dynamic environments. However, realizing the outcomes associated with agility requires not only the implementation of agile practices but also employees who possess an agile mindset. Although scholarly understanding of the agile mindset has increased in recent years, a validated measurement instrument for individuals is still lacking. This paper addresses this research gap by following the validation procedure proposed by MacKenzie, Podsakoff, Podsakoff [1]. Based on a systematic review of existing conceptualizations of the agile mindset, we empirically developed a scale and specified a corresponding measurement model. To quantitatively evaluate and validate the model, we analyzed data from four independent samples (content validity: n = 184; pretest: n = 500; validation: n = 202; cross-validation: n = 218). As a result, we validate a four-dimensional conceptualization of the agile mindset comprising the attitude toward learning, collaborative exchange, empowered self-guidance, and customer co-creation. Furthermore, we demonstrate that the agile mindset is correlated with key individual outcomes: job satisfaction, goal orientation, and reduced resistance to change and thereby reinforcing its relevance. In addition to its theoretical contribution, this study provides practical value by offering an economically efficient instrument for measuring the agile mindset.

Keywords: Agile Mindset · Scale Development · Agility · Scale Validation

1 Introduction

Today's business environment is characterized by increasing dynamism, challenging organizations to cope with continuous change. In response, many organizations view agility as a fundamental capability for remaining competitive [2, 3]. Agility can be

A. Goldman et al. (Eds.): XP 2026, LNBIP 578, pp. 93–108, 2026.
https://doi.org/10.1007/978-3-032-22375-3_6

defined as "sensing and responding to change" [4] and has its roots in software development and information systems (IS) [5]. It is typically introduced with the goal of maintaining or improving organizational performance [6]. Prior research has shown that agility can positively influence various outcomes in IS and beyond, such as organizational performance and job satisfaction [3, 7]. However, not every agile transformation or project achieves these outcomes. A lacking agile mindset has been identified as a key reason for failed agile transformation efforts [3, 8]. In such cases, organizations often revert to traditional ways of working, employees experience stress and team pressure [9], and "emerging business opportunities fall by the wayside or, even worse, into the hands of more agile competitors" [10]. The agile mindset has been recognized as a relevant human-centered success factor for agility in both theory and practice [3, 8, 11, 12]. Although many papers highlight its relevance [8, 13] and initial conceptualizations of the agile mindset exist at different levels [6, 11, 14], quantitative approaches to measure and investigate the agile mindset remain limited. This lack of validated instruments implies that actions, methods, and tools intended to strengthen the agile mindset are often implemented without knowing the existing level of the agile mindset, and the effectiveness of such efforts cannot be evaluated. To advance theory by examining relationships with other relevant constructs, valid measurement instruments are required. Instruments that do not meet established quality criteria risk producing misleading results. Although a first agile mindset scale was developed by Eilers, Peters, Leimeister [6], it does not meet all required quality standards for scale validation, and the authors explicitly call for further refinement. The need for research that aligns existing conceptualizations, establishes a common foundation, and enables the agile mindset to be measured therefore becomes evident. Practitioners in particular lack a tangible and clear understanding of the extent of the agile mindset in their organizations.

Our research addresses these challenges. Building on the initial conceptualization and empirical work of Eilers, Peters, Leimeister [6], we further developed and validated their agile mindset scale. To do so, we followed the state-of-the-art recommendations for instrument development and validation proposed by MacKenzie, Podsakoff, Podsakoff [1]. By applying their ten-step procedure, we developed a validated instrument that provides a springboard for further research and supports employees, leaders, and people development departments in agile working contexts in strengthening agility and thereby contributing to overall performance goals.

2 Theoretical Background: Agile Mindset

Miler, Gaida [15] define the agile mindset as "a specific attitude towards the team and other people as well as a proactive and open mind of the individual." The concept of mindset originates in cognitive psychology and refers to the cognitive evaluation processes that shape how individuals perceive and interpret new situations. In other words, a mindset reflects the perspective from which individuals view the world [16].

Most conceptualizations of the agile mindset describe it as a form of attitude [15, 17]. From a psychological standpoint, attitudes are more specific than mindsets, as they refer to an individual's evaluation of a particular object or behavior, including its degree of favor or disfavor [18]. Extant literature suggests that the agile mindset influences individual behavior. Several theoretical models explain the relationship between attitudes and behavior (e.g., TAM [19]), and following these theoretical insights, the agile mindset is assumed to positively affect pro-agile behavior [6, 20]. Consequently, the agile mindset is considered an essential element in developing an agile workforce. Eilers, Peters, Leimeister [6] provide insights into its stability: attitudes develop through experiences and learning processes resulting from interactions with the environment. They can change over time when individuals encounter new experiences that lead them to form revised attitudes toward a specific object [21].

3 Scale Development

To develop a scale for measuring the agile mindset, we followed the ten-step procedure for construct conceptualization, measurement development, and instrument validation proposed by MacKenzie, Podsakoff, Podsakoff [1]. Their framework synthesizes established methodological guidelines from information systems research [22, 23] and integrates additional insights from behavioral research. This makes it particularly suitable for developing a human-centered construct such as the agile mindset.

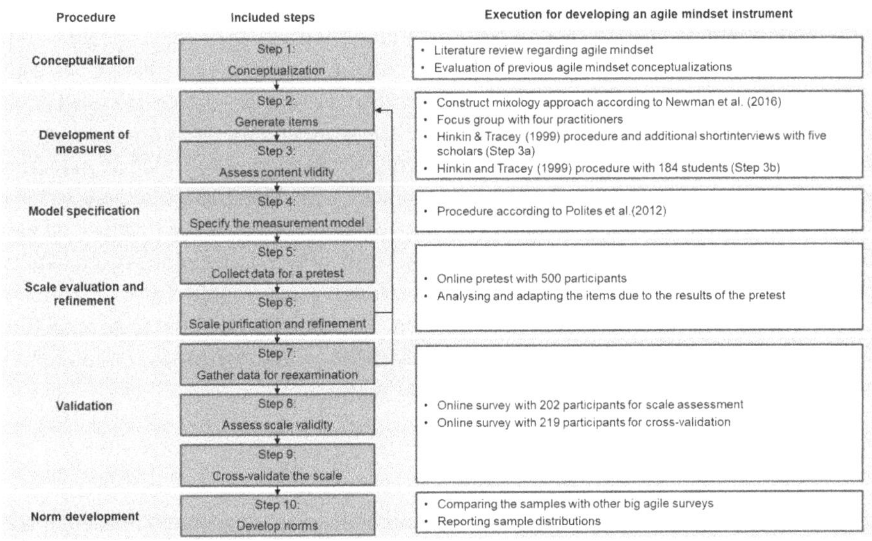

Fig. 1. Scale Development Process (adapted from MacKenzie, Podsakoff, Podsakoff [1])

Figure 1 provides an overview of the ten steps and illustrates how we applied them in the development of the agile mindset scale. In the following, we summarize the key recommendations of the procedure and outline how each step was executed. For the first four steps, we relied on the dataset reported in Eilers, Peters, Leimeister [6], and subsequently refined and validated the scale using two additional datasets.

3.1 Conceptualization (Step 1)

The first step contains the conceptualization of the construct. Only if the conceptualization is clear, it is possible to develop a valid scale, investigate a construct specifically, finding relations to other constructs, and taking goal-oriented activities to handle it in practice [1, 24]. To evaluate a conceptualization for scale development it is recommend to review the literature regarding previous results [1]. Eilers, Peters, Leimeister [6] carefully screened previous conceptualizations and evaluate them regarding their appropriateness for scale development. They further evaluate how the construct is described in regards to its conceptual theme including the dimensionality [25], necessary and sufficient attributes which describe the construct [1, 26] as well as stability of the construct. Finally, they consider how the construct behaves to other constructs [1, 26].

Eilers, Peters, Leimeister [6] conducted a systematic review of previous conceptualizations and evaluated their suitability for scale development. They examined how the agile mindset is described in terms of its conceptual theme, including its dimensionality (e.g., relationships between dimensions and the focal construct) [25], its necessary and sufficient defining attributes [1, 26], and the stability of the construct over time and across situations. Furthermore, they considered how the construct relates to other constructs, including potential antecedents and outcomes [1, 26]. Based on their systematic review and additional interviews, the authors developed a four-dimensional conceptualization of the agile mindset. It comprises a positive attitude toward: 1.) *Learning Spirit* – the degree to which an individual values openness and the search for new approaches when working in complex environments; 2.) *Collaborative Exchange* – the degree to which an individual values transparency and knowledge sharing for collaborative problem-solving in complex environments; 3.) *Customer Co-creation* – the degree to which an individual values customer orientation and direct engagement with customers to create value in complex environments; and 4.) *Empowered Self-guidance* – the degree to which an individual values self-reflection, autonomous organization of work, and taking responsibility for one's work processes [6]. This conceptualization has been applied and supported in several subsequent studies [27, 28] and has even been transferred to the team level [29]. We therefore adopted this established conceptualization and used it as the foundation for further developing and improving the initial scale.

3.2 Generate Items (Step 2)

Based on the construct conceptualization, the second step is to generate items that adequately represent the construct's conceptual domain. Newman, Harrison, Carpenter, Rariden [30] proposes the construct mixology approach, which highlights that new theoretical constructs are often conceptualized and operationalized by combining content from established constructs. This approach offers several advantages, such as handling theoretical redundancies transparently, reducing conceptual overlap, and improving parsimony and measurement efficiency [30].

Eilers, Peters, Leimeister [6] identified 79 conceptually related ("orbiting") constructs. During our investigations, we expanded this number by identifying six additional orbiting constructs. The constructs most closely related to the agile mindset included scales such as workforce agility [31], self-determination as part of psychological empowerment [32], customer orientation [33], learning orientation [34], and work-related curiosity [35]. Following the recommendations of DeVellis [22], MacKenzie, Podsakoff, Podsakoff [1], Eilers, Peters, Leimeister [6] adapted relevant items from these related constructs to reflect the conceptual domain of the agile mindset. Drawing on three sources—scales of related constructs, expert workshops, and literature on the agile mindset—they developed an initial item pool consisting of 52 items. These items are available in the online repository [36].

3.3 Condensate and Assessing the Content Validity of Items (Step 3a)

The developed items must be assessed for content validity, which refers to "the extent to which a specific set of items reflects a content domain [of a construct]" [22]. MacKenzie, Podsakoff, Podsakoff [1] recommend the procedure of Hinkin, Tracey [37] for evaluating content validity. However, this procedure is associated with substantial cognitive effort for participants, particularly when a large number of items are involved [38]. Applying the procedure to all 52 items would therefore impose a high cognitive burden and risk compromising data quality. Consequently, we adapted the strategy. First, we conducted a face validity check with practitioners, during which the initial 52 items were reviewed and condensed. Based on this assessment, 28 items were identified as adequately capturing the agile mindset. In a second step, we evaluated the reduced item set quantitatively using a version of the approach of Hinkin, Tracey [37]. Five scholars were asked to rate the fit of each item to each of the four dimension definitions on a 7-point Likert scale. To compensate for the small expert sample and to gain deeper insights into item interpretation, follow-up interviews of 10–30 min were conducted. These interviews helped identify and resolve minor misunderstandings and further examine the alignment between items and dimensions. The quantitative analysis compared the average fit rating of each item across all four dimensions. All items received the highest average rating on their corresponding dimension, indicating a strong conceptual fit.

3.4 Measurement Model Specification (Step 4)

After establishing content validity, the measurement model must be specified [1, 38]. For multidimensional constructs, Jarvis, MacKenzie, Podsakoff [39] provide guidelines for model specification. First, researchers should consider the construct domain and the underlying theoretical assumptions, which typically involves reviewing relevant literature. Second, theory-driven decisions must be made regarding the nature of the construct's facets—specifically, whether the construct should be represented by a single set of items or is composed of multiple Dimension. Third, researchers must specify the directionality of the relationships among items, dimensions, and the overall construct [40]. The agile mindset is conceptualized as a superordinate construct in which the four dimensions reflect the higher-order construct, and each dimension is in turn reflected by a set of items. Based on empirical findings and supported by theory from related constructs the agile mindset is best modeled as a reflective first-order and reflective second-order construct. The four dimensions emerged inductively from the data as distinct yet interrelated facets of the agile mindset. Items within a given dimension are interchangeable and collectively reflect that dimension. Such reflective–reflective multidimensional measurement models are common in social science, psychology, and IS research [40] and align with the theoretical understanding of the agile mindset as an attitudinal construct composed of multiple related facets.

3.5 Conduct Pretest Data Collection (Step 5)

To conduct a pretest, MacKenzie, Podsakoff, Podsakoff [1] provide specific recommendations for data collection. The process should consider three central aspects: 1.) Representativeness of the sample, as the psychometric properties of instruments may vary across populations that differ in age, education, work environment, or experience; 2.) Adequate sample size, since an exploratory factor analysis (EFA) is required to examine the dimensionality and initial psychometric properties of the instrument; and 3.) Inclusion of alternative scales, meaning that measures of the focal construct, conceptually related constructs, and theoretically relevant constructs should be incorporated [1].

For data collection, Eilers, Peters, Leimeister [6] recruited a sample in cooperation with a market research institute. Participants were screened to ensure they were of legal age, employed, and had experience with agile work. We used this raw dataset as the basis for further improving and validating the scale. After removing careless responders, the final pretest sample comprised $n = 500$ participants. The sample included individuals from different sectors, organizational sizes, levels of agile work experience, age groups, and genders. The survey additionally incorporated scales for workforce agility and psychological empowerment, representing conceptually related constructs. In this way, all three characteristics recommended in the beginning [1] were addressed.

3.6 Scale Purification and Refinement (Step 6)

In this step, the scale must be evaluated in terms of discriminant, convergent, and nomological validity [1, 23]. According to MacKenzie, Podsakoff, Podsakoff [1], four aspects must be considered when assessing the measurement model: 1.) overall goodness of fit, 2.) validity of the indicator sets at the construct level, 3.) reliability of the indicator sets at the construct level, and 4.) individual indicator validity and reliability (see the online repository Table 1 [41] for details).

To evaluate the scale, we used SPSS and AMOS. As an initial step, we conducted an exploratory factor analysis (EFA) to examine individual indicator properties. Prior to running the EFA, we inspected the correlation matrix to ensure that items intended to capture the same dimension were significantly correlated ($p < .001$). We applied a Varimax rotation and eliminated items that exhibited insufficient loadings or substantial cross-loadings [1, 42]. Throughout this process, we carefully evaluated whether the remaining items continued to align with the conceptualization of the agile mindset. The purification process resulted in a set of 11 items. A scree plot analysis supported a four-factor structure of the agile mindset. One factor exhibited an eigenvalue below 1 (attitude toward collaborative exchange = .83). Most squared multiple correlations exceeded .50; however, items CE_1 (.35) and LS_1 (.35), as well as the dimension attitude toward collaborative exchange (.43), fell below this threshold. We assessed overall model fit using Chi-square, which yielded $\chi^2(40) = 111.25$, $p < .001$. The ratio of Chi-square to degrees of freedom was 2.78, indicating acceptable fit. Given the sensitivity of Chi-square to sample size, we also examined incremental and absolute fit indices. Both the Comparative Fit Index (CFI = .96) and the Root Mean Square Error of Approximation (RMSEA = .06) indicated satisfactory model fit. To evaluate construct validity and reliability, we calculated the average variance extracted (AVE) for all first-order constructs. Most dimensions met the recommended threshold of .50 [1], with the exception of attitude toward collaborative exchange (AVE = .43). Internal consistency was assessed using Cronbach's α (for Learning Spirit, Customer Co-creation, and Empowered Self-guidance) and the Spearman–Brown coefficient (for Collaborative Exchange). Cronbach's α values were acceptable (CCC = .83; LS = .75; ES = .81) [43], while the Spearman–Brown coefficient for attitude toward collaborative exchange did not reach the recommended threshold (.59) (see online repository Table 2 [41] for a overview). Given these issues, we refrained from examining the nomological network at this stage. Instead, we refined the scale based on the empirical insights gained and revised the items for subsequent testing. Furthermore, we adopted a consistent item syntax reflecting personal preference, beginning each item with "I like to…". Such item phrasing is already used in attitude research (e.g., [44, 45]).

3.7 Assessing Content Validity of the Adapted Items (Step 3 b)

Because the items were revised based on the findings from the scale purification step, it was necessary to reassess their content validity. For this purpose, participants with strong cognitive abilities and familiarity with the subject matter are recommended [37, 46]. We therefore recruited 184 students enrolled in an agile project management course, who met these criteria. To reduce cognitive burden, participants were randomly assigned to two subsamples, with each subsample receiving half of the items for evaluation. Participants rated the extent to which each item corresponded to each of the four agile mindset dimensions on a 5-point scale (1 = "not at all" to 5 = "completely"). Items were presented in random order to avoid sequence effects.

After screening for language proficiency, speeding behavior, and attention, the final dataset comprised 131 participants (subsample 1: n = 68; subsample 2: n = 63). In line with Hinkin, Tracey [37] and Schriesheim, Powers, Scandura, Gardiner, Lankau [46], we first examined item intercorrelations and found significant relationships between items. We then conducted an exploratory factor analysis with Varimax rotation. Prior to extraction, data adequacy was verified via Bartlett's test of sphericity (sample 1: $\chi^2(36) = 208.25$, $p < .001$; sample 2: $\chi^2(45) = 206.73$, $p < .001$) and the Kaiser–Meyer–Olkin measure (sample 1: KMO = .66; sample 2: KMO = .71), indicating suitability for factor analysis [47]. Items with low factor loadings or problematic cross-loadings were removed, resulting in a set of 19 items (6 for Customer Co-creation; 4 for Collaborative Exchange; 4 for Learning Spirit; 6 for Empowered Self-guidance) (see online repository Table 3 and Table 4 [41] for factor loadings). The retained items explained 77.92% of the variance in subsample 1 and 74.38% in subsample 2. Although one factor showed an eigenvalue below 1 in both samples (sample 1: LS = .91; sample 2: CE = .87), the scree plot supported a four-factor solution consistent with the theoretical model. Given the well-documented limitations of the eigenvalue-greater-than-one rule, the theoretically grounded four-factor structure was retained [37]. Descriptive analyses showed that each item exhibited the highest mean rating for its theoretically assigned dimension. To further assess distinctiveness, we conducted Friedman tests with pairwise post-hoc comparisons (Dunn–Bonferroni). For 17 of the 19 items, the assigned dimension differed significantly from each of the three alternative dimensions. For two items—LS_1 ("I like to test new approaches in order to gain knowledge from them") and CE_2 ("I like to approach others to generate and discuss solutions when I encounter difficulties")—one of the three comparisons did not reach statistical significance (LS_1: $z = -0.25$, $p = .26$, $p\_corr = 1.00$; CE_2: $z = 0.23$, $p = .32$, $p\_corr = 1.00$). Given the overall strong pattern of item–dimension alignment, both items were retained for further evaluation. Overall, the descriptive analyses, exploratory factor analyses, and non-parametric tests provide evidence for satisfactory content validity of the revised scale.

3.8 Conduct New Sample Data Collection (Step 7)

After purifying the agile mindset scale, it must be validated using an independent sample [1]. The objective of this step is to "evaluate whether responses to the scale behave as one would expect if they were valid indicators of the focal construct" [1]. For reflective indicators, MacKenzie, Podsakoff, Podsakoff [1] recommend two techniques: 1.) Assessing differences in scale scores across theoretically relevant groups, following approaches commonly applied in attitude-scale validation [48]; and 2.) Examining relationships between the focal construct and theoretically related constructs, that is, evaluating its position within a nomological network.

To conduct this validation, we collected data from 202 participants via Prolific. The sample size meets the recommended criteria for scale validation [1]. Participants were prescreened to be between 18 and 65 years old, employed either full-time or part-time, and working in an agile context. To avoid language-related issues, only native English speakers from the UK were recruited. Participants who failed two attention checks were removed. The survey gathered demographic and contextual information, including sector, organizational size, agile work experience, and age. To examine convergent and discriminant validity within the nomological network, we included workforce agility [31] as a closely related behavioral construct. Based on prior research and Person–Job Fit theory [49], we expected that individuals with a higher extent of agile mindset should perform better in complex environments than individuals with lower levels. Accordingly, we incorporated goal orientation and job satisfaction as outcome variables, both of which correlate with individual performance [50]. Furthermore, we included resistance to change [51] as a theoretically negative outcome of the agile mindset. All constructs were measured on a seven-point Likert scale (1 = strongly disagree; 7 = strongly agree).

3.9 Assess Scale Validity (Step 8)

Our evaluation of the conceptualization suggested that employees with greater experience in agile work tend to exhibit a higher agile mindset. This aligns with prior findings that attitudes may change through repeated exposure and external influences [52]. Based on this theoretical expectation, we compared scale scores between groups differing in agile work experience as an initial validity check. To establish nomological validity, we examined the three individual-level outcomes that are conceptually linked to performance in dynamic environments: job satisfaction, goal orientation, and resistance to change. We expected that individuals scoring high on the agile mindset would report greater job satisfaction, consistent with findings that agile work environments enhance satisfaction and motivation [7]. Likewise, we anticipated that the agile mindset would be positively associated with goal orientation, an antecedent of individual performance [53]. Finally, because employees with a more agile mindset should respond more constructively to change, we expected a negative association with resistance to change, in line with prior findings that cognitive rigidity impedes adaptation [51]. Before assessing these relationships, we re-evaluated the measurement model of the agile mindset. The model yielded $\chi^2(50) = 88.05$, $p < .001$, with a χ^2/df ratio of 1.76, indicating acceptable fit. Additional fit indices further supported the model (CFI = .97, RMSEA = .06, SRMR = .04). All dimensions showed satisfactory average variance extracted (AVE $\geq$ .50), and all regression weights were significant. Reliability coefficients (Cronbach's α = .73–.84; depending on dimension) confirmed internal consistency [43] (see as well online repository Table 5 for an overview [41]).

Table 1. Items of the Agile Mindset Scale.

Customer co-creation		Collaborative exchange	
Item No.	I like to	Item No.	I like to
CCC_1	…involve my customers from the beginning	CE_1	…address problems openly with others
CCC_2	…determine my customers' needs in direct interactions	CE_2	…approach others to generate and discuss solutions when I encounter difficulties
CCC_3	…exchange with the customer often	CE_3	…share my thoughts if someone asks me for advice
Learning spirit		Empowered self-guidance	
Item No.	I like to	Item No.	I like to
LS_1	…test new approaches in order to gain knowledge from them	ES_1	…take responsibility for myself and my actions
LS_2	…try new things at work to learn from them	ES_2	…choose by myself how to proceed at work
LS_3	…draw insights from new situations in order to learn from them	ES_3	…take responsibility for my work results

To test whether agile mindset scores vary by agile work experience, we computed a correlation between the agile mindset score and participants' tenure in agile work. The correlation was small but significant (Spearman's $\rho = .18$, $p = .01$), suggesting that the agile mindset may develop over time. We then compared groups with low (< 1 year, $n = 45$) and high (5–10 years, $n = 32$) agile work experience using a Mann–Whitney U test.

Results indicated that participants with greater experience scored significantly higher on the agile mindset (p = .007). Next, we estimated a measurement model including the agile mindset and the three outcome variables (job satisfaction, goal orientation, and resistance to change). The model demonstrated acceptable fit: $\chi^2(203) = 353.93$, p = .01, $\chi^2/df = 1.74$, CFI = .93, RMSEA = .06. All parameter estimates were significant. Figure 2 illustrates the resulting nomological network. To assess discriminant validity, we examined the intercorrelations among constructs, which should remain below .71 [1]. Correlations ranged from −.32** to .62** (see online repository Table 6 [41]), thereby supporting discriminant validity. Furthermore, common method bias is unlikely to be problematic, as the first factor accounted for only 33.7% of the variance.

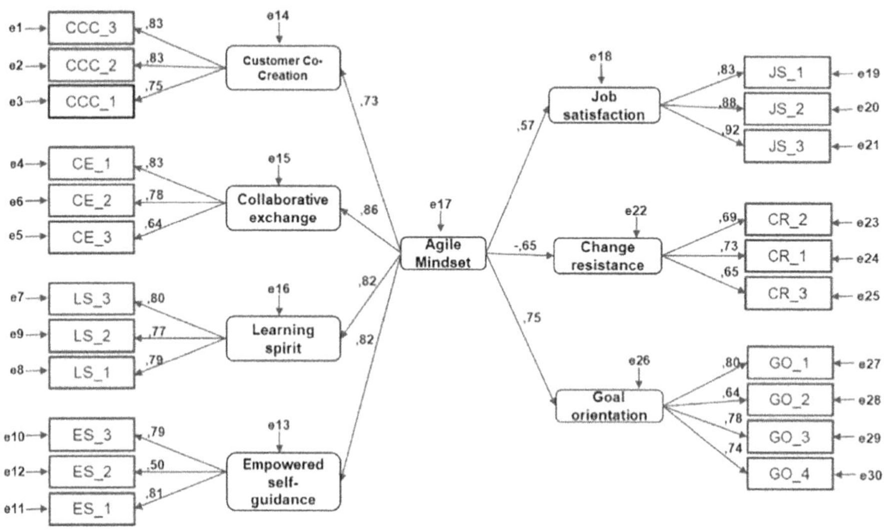

Fig. 2. The Agile Mindset in a Nomological Network with Job Satisfaction, Goal Orientation and Change Resistance

3.10 Cross Validate the Scale (Step 9)

After validating the scale, the next step is to cross-validate it using a further independent sample to evaluate the stability of the instrument. To do so, we collected a new dataset via Prolific, applying the same prescreening criteria as in the previous study. Using the same platform also allowed us to exclude participants who had taken part in the earlier data collection. After data cleaning, the final sample consisted of 219 respondents. Consistent with our prior assumptions, we expected that individuals with higher agile mindset scores would exhibit higher levels of goal orientation [54, 55] and job satisfaction [50], as well as lower resistance to change [51]. To assess the measurement model, we followed the evaluation procedure described in Step 8 and examined Chi-square, CFI, RMSEA, and SRMR [1]. We also assessed convergent validity (AVE), internal consistency (Cronbach's α) [43], regression weights, and squared multiple correlations in line with the criteria proposed by Fornell, Larcker [42]. Analyses were conducted using SPSS and AMOS. The results support the reliability and validity of the developed scale. The overall model showed $\chi 2(203) = 285.49$, $p < .001$, with a $\chi 2/df$ ratio of 1.40, indicating excellent fit. Additional fit indices confirmed this assessment (CFI = .97; RMSEA = .04; SRMR = .056). All regression weights were significant. Cronbach's α values ranged from .72 to .93 across the constructs, indicating strong internal consistency. AVE values were above the recommended threshold of .50 for all constructs except resistance to change, which showed a borderline value (.47). Intercorrelations among constructs did not exceed .71, thereby showing enough discriminant validity [1] (see online repository Table 7 and Table 8 for details [41]).

3.11 Develop Norms for the Scale (Step 10)

To enable meaningful interpretation of individual scores, the final step in the scale development process is the establishment of norms. Although "few scales reported in the field of management information systems have well-established norms" [1], reporting score distributions provides valuable context and supports interpretation. Ideally, the distribution of a representative population sample should be known for this purpose [1, 22, 56]. Moreover, the sample used for norm development should be sufficiently large to ensure stability and generalizability [1, 56]. Because obtaining large, representative samples of the general population is difficult we follow the approach of Hoehle, Venkatesh [38] and compare our quantitative samples with established large-scale agile surveys. Specifically, we contrasted the demographic characteristics of our two employee samples with those of The Future Organization Report [3], which includes 517 participants from Germany, Austria, and Switzerland, and with a large international Agile State of the Art survey comprising 1121 participants, 83% of whom are from Western cultures [57]. The comparison indicates that the demographic distribution of our samples is largely similar to those in these broader agile workforce studies. This supports the assumption that our samples reasonably represent employees working in agile environments. Furthermore, prior research emphasizes that developing norms requires sufficiently large samples to demonstrate stability and generalizability [1, 38]. In total, our scale was evaluated across more than 1,000 participants: 184 students in the content validity assessment and three separate samples of 500, 202, and 219 employees for pretesting, validation, and cross-validation. In addition, nine academic experts and practitioners evaluated the instrument qualitatively. Taken together, this extensive data basis provides a robust foundation for generating meaningful and interpretable norms for the agile mindset scale.

4 Contribution to Theory and Practice

This research makes several contributions to theory. First, we address a central gap in the literature by providing a validated instrument to quantitatively measure the agile mindset at the individual level. This enables researchers to empirically examine theoretical relationships involving the agile mindset and to use the instrument when testing models in which the construct plays a role. The validated scale allows for efficient and standardized measurement, thereby supporting cumulative research and facilitating comparisons across studies. Second, by analyzing the agile mindset within a nomological network—including job satisfaction, goal orientation, and resistance to change—we extend the theoretical understanding of how attitudes toward agile work relate to relevant individual outcomes in IS research. Our study thereby expands nomological knowledge on agility at the individual level and provides a common conceptual and empirical basis for future work on attitudes in complex and dynamic environments. Third, the instrument offers a foundation for developing new theoretical frameworks. Researchers can build upon the validated dimensions to examine antecedents, mediators, moderators, and outcomes of the agile mindset. This supports a more human-centered perspective on agility, a field that is increasingly recognized as critical for organizational success. Finally, our findings highlight the particular relevance of employees' attitudes for successful agile work. While prior studies predominantly focused on agile behavior, personality traits, or motivation, our work aligns with the growing interest in attitudinal aspects of agile work [3, 12, 14]. Previous qualitative insights indicated that the agile mindset contributes to sustained agile use [20], organizational performance [6], team effectiveness [15], and overall agile success [11, 12]. However, robust empirical evidence regarding individual outcomes has been scarce. Our study fills this gap by demonstrating that a higher agile mindset is associated with increased job satisfaction and goal orientation, and reduced resistance to change.

This research also provides important implications for practitioners. First, our work clarifies the previously diffuse concept of the agile mindset and offers a validated and clearly defined instrument for assessing it. This clarity enables meaningful discussions about the agile mindset and supports practitioners in distinguishing its core dimensions. Second, the agile mindset scale provides employees with insights into their own mindset and allows leaders and people development departments to assess the status quo within their teams or organizations. This information can guide the design of targeted interventions aimed at strengthening specific dimensions of the agile mindset. Third, the instrument enables evidence-based development activities. Organizations can use the scale periodically to monitor changes over time, evaluate the effectiveness of interventions, and link improvements in agile mindset dimensions to agile performance goals. This enables more nuanced and data-driven decisions regarding training priorities, team development, and organizational change initiatives.

5 Limitations and Future Research

Like all research, our study is subject to several limitations. First, the agile mindset scale is a self-report instrument. Self-report data can be affected by common method variance (CMV) and social desirability bias [26]. To address these concerns, we followed established procedural remedies during the design of our study [26] and conducted Harman's single-factor test [58]. The results suggest that CMV is unlikely to pose a substantial threat. Nevertheless, future research should consider collecting data from multiple sources to further reduce potential bias. In line with this, we do not recommend using the scale as a recruitment or employment testing tool. Second, due to the practical context of our study, we were not able to assess performance using directly observable behavioral indicators. Including objective performance data in future studies would provide additional insights and strengthen the explanatory power of the agile mindset in organizational settings. Longitudinal studies would also be valuable for examining the developmental trajectory of the agile mindset and evaluating the effectiveness of interventions designed to foster it. Third, our samples consisted primarily of participants from European or Western cultural contexts. As cultural norms can influence attitudes and behaviors, the generalizability of our findings to other cultural environments may be limited. We therefore encourage future research to investigate the agile mindset across diverse cultural settings and organizational contexts.

References

1. MacKenzie, S.B., Podsakoff, P.M., Podsakoff, N.P.: Construct measurement and validation procedures in MIS and behavioral research: integrating new and existing techniques. Manage. Inf. Syst. Q. (MISQ) **35**, 293–334 (2011). https://doi.org/10.2307/23044045
2. Alt, R., Leimeister, J.M., Priemuth, T., et al.: Software-defined business. Bus. Inf. Syst. Eng. **62**, 609–621 (2020). https://doi.org/10.1007/s12599-020-00669-6
3. Peters, C., Simmert, B., Eilers, K., et al.: Future Organization Report 2020. Institute of Information Systems, University of St.Gallen; Campana & Schott Business Services GmbH, St.Gallen, Switzerland and Frankfurt, Germany (2020)
4. Tallon, P.P., Queiroz, M., Coltman, T., et al.: Information technology and the search for organizational agility: a systematic review with future research possibilities. J. Strateg. Inf. Syst. **28**, 218–237 (2019). https://doi.org/10.1016/j.jsis.2018.12.002
5. Coyle, S., Conboy, K., Wang, X., et al.: People over process: key challenges in agile development. IEEE Softw. **28**, 48–57 (2010). https://doi.org/10.1109/MS.2010.132
6. Eilers, K., Peters, C., Leimeister, J.M.: Why the agile mindset matters. Technol. Forecast. Soc. Chang. **179**, 1–14 (2022). https://doi.org/10.1016/j.techfore.2022.121650
7. Tripp, J.F., Riemenschneider, C., Thatcher, J.B.: Job satisfaction in agile development teams: agile development as work redesign. J. Assoc. Inf. Syst. **17**, 267–307 (2016). https://doi.org/10.17705/1jais.00426
8. Dikert, K., Paasivaara, M., Lassenius, C.: Challenges and success factors for large-scale agile transformations: a systematic literature review. J. Syst. Softw. **119**, 87–108 (2016). https://doi.org/10.1016/j.jss.2016.06.013
9. Annosi, M.C., Magnusson, M., Martini, A., et al.: Social conduct, learning and innovation: an abductive study of the dark side of agile software development. Creat. Innov. Manage. **25**, 515–535 (2016). https://doi.org/10.1111/caim.12172
10. Sull, D., Spinosa, C.: Promise-based management: the essence of execution. Harv. Bus. Rev. **85**, 79–86 (2007)
11. Mordi, A., Schoop, M.: Making it tangible: creating a definition of the agile mindset. In: European Conference on Information Systems n.v.: 1–17 (2020)
12. van Manen, H., van Vliet, H.: Organization-wide agile expansion requires an organization-wide agile mindset. In: Product-Focused Software Process Improvement. PROFES 2014. LNCS, pp. 48–62 (2014)
13. van Hoek, R.I., Harrison, A., Christopher, M.: Measuring agile capabilities in the supply chain. Int. J. Oper. Prod. Manag. **21**, 126–148 (2001). https://doi.org/10.1108/01443570110358495
14. Denning, S.: How to make the whole organization "agile." Strategy Leadersh. **44**, 10–17 (2016). https://doi.org/10.1108/SL-06-2016-0043
15. Miler, J., Gaida, P.: On the agile mindset of an effective team: an industrial opinion survey. In: Proceedings of Federated Conference on Computer Science and Information Systems, pp. 841–849 (2019). https://doi.org/10.15439/2019F198

16. Armstrong, H.: Understanding mindshift learning: the transition to object-oriented development. MIS Q. **31**, 453 (2007). https://doi.org/10.2307/25148803
17. Ozkan, N., Gök, M.Ş., Köse, B.Ö.: Towards a better understanding of agile mindset by using principles of agile methods. In: Proceedings of the Federated Conference on Computer Science and Information Systems (FedCSIS), pp. 721–730 (2020). https://doi.org/10.15439/2020F46
18. Eagly, A.H., Chaiken, S.: The Psychology of Attitudes. Harcourt Brace Jovanovich College Publishers, Fort Worth (1993)
19. Davis, F.D.: Perceived usefulness, perceived ease of use, and user acceptance of information technology. MISQ **13**, 319–340 (1989). https://doi.org/10.2307/249008
20. Senapathi, M., Srinivasan, A.: Sustained agile usage: a systematic literature review. In: International Conference on Evaluation and Assessment in Software Engineering n.v.: 119–124 (2013). https://doi.org/10.1145/2460999.2461016
21. Schwarz, N.: Attitude construction: evaluation in context. Soc. Cogn. **25**, 638–656 (2007). https://doi.org/10.1521/soco.2007.25.5.638
22. DeVellis, R.F.: Scale Development: Theory and Applications, 4th edn. Applied Social Research Methods. Sage, Los Angeles (2017)
23. Straub, D.W.: Validating instruments in MIS research. Manag. Inf. Syst. Q. **13**, 147–169 (1989). https://doi.org/10.2307/248922
24. Wacker, J.G.: A theory of formal conceptual definitions: developing theory-building measurement instruments. J. Oper. Manag. **22**, 629–650 (2004). https://doi.org/10.1016/j.jom.2004.08.002
25. MacKenzie, S.B.: The dangers of poor construct conceptualization. J. Acad. Mark. Sci. **31**, 323–326 (2003). https://doi.org/10.1177/0092070303031003011
26. Podsakoff, P.M., MacKenzie, S.B., Lee, J.-Y., et al.: Common method biases in behavioral research: a critical review of the literature and recommended remedies. J. Appl. Psychol. **88**, 879–903 (2003). https://doi.org/10.1037/0021-9010.88.5.879
27. Augner, T., Schermuly, C.C.: Beyond a buzzword: the agile mindset as a new research construct in organizational psychology. J. Manag. Psychol. **40**, 274–288 (2025). https://doi.org/10.1108/JMP-04-2024-0261
28. Geffers, K., Bretschneider, U., Eilers, K.: Conceptualizing the Agile Mindset in Agile Software Development Teams. Wirtschaftsinformatik 2024 Proceedings (2024)
29. Verwijs, C., Eilers, K.: How A Team-Level Agile Mindset Shapes Team Effectiveness | by Christiaan Verwijs | The Liberators | Medium (2025). https://medium.com/the-liberators/how-a-team-level-agile-mindset-shapes-team-effectiveness-880f9b2b8f89. Accessed 06 Feb 2026
30. Newman, D.A., Harrison, D.A., Carpenter, N.C., et al.: Construct mixology: forming new management constructs by combining old ones. Acad. Manag. Ann. **10**, 943–995 (2016). https://doi.org/10.5465/19416520.2016.1161965
31. Breu, K., Hemingway, C.J., Strathern, M., et al.: Workforce agility: the new employee strategy for the knowledge economy. J. Inf. Technol. **17**, 21–31 (2002). https://doi.org/10.1080/02683960110132070
32. Spreitzer, G.M.: Psychological empowerment in the workplace: dimensions, measurement, and validation. Acad. Manag. J. **38**, 1442–1465 (1995). https://doi.org/10.5465/256865
33. Saxe, R., Weitz, B.A.: The SOCO scale: a measure of the customer orientation of salespeople. J. Mark. Res. **19**, 343–351 (1982). https://doi.org/10.1177/002224378201900307
34. Santhanam, R., Sasidharan, S., Webster, J.: Using self-regulatory learning to enhance E-learning-based information technology training. Inf. Syst. Res. **19**, 26–47 (2008). https://doi.org/10.1287/isre.1070.0141
35. Mussel, P., Spengler, M., Litman, J.A., et al.: Development and validation of the German work-related curiosity scale. Eur. J. Psychol. Assess. **28**, 109–117 (2012). https://doi.org/10.1027/1015-5759/a000098

36. Eilers, K.: Why The Agile Mindset Matters, Mendeley, V1 (2022). https://doi.org/10.17632/5KJY43868M.1
37. Hinkin, T.R., Tracey, B.J.: An analysis of variance approach to content validation. Organ. Res. Methods **2**, 175–186 (1999). https://doi.org/10.1177/109442819922004
38. Hoehle, H., Venkatesh, V.: Mobile application usability: conceptualization and instrument development. Manage. Inf. Syst. Q. (MISQ) **39**, 435–472 (2015). https://doi.org/10.25300/MISQ/2015/39.2.08
39. Jarvis, C.B., MacKenzie, S.B., Podsakoff, P.M.: A critical review of construct indicators and measurement model misspecification in marketing and consumer research. J. Consum. Res. **30**, 199–218 (2003). https://doi.org/10.1086/376806
40. Polites, G.L., Roberts, N., Thatcher, J.: Conceptualizing models using multidimensional constructs: a review and guidelines for their use. Eur. J. Inf. Syst. **21**, 22–48 (2012). https://doi.org/10.1057/ejis.2011.10
41. Eilers, K., Peters, C., Bretschneider, U., [Online Repository] Eilers, et al.: Agile Mindset Scale Development, Mendeley Data, V1 (2026). https://doi.org/10.17632/58t4tbhdfj.110.17632/58t4tbhdfj.1
42. Fornell, C., Larcker, D.F.: Evaluating structural equation models with unobservable variables and measurement error. J. Mark. Res. **18**, 39–50 (1981). https://doi.org/10.1177/002224378101800104
43. Cronbach, L.J.: Coefficient alpha and the internal structure of tests. Psychometrika **16**, 297–334 (1951). https://doi.org/10.1007/BF02310555
44. Labroo, A.A., Nielsen, J.H.: Half the thrill is in the chase: twisted inferences from embodied cognitions and brand evaluation. J. Consum. Res. **37**, 143–158 (2010). https://doi.org/10.1086/649908
45. Harmon-Jones, E., Harmon-Jones, C., Amodio, D.M., et al.: Attitudes toward emotions. J. Pers. Soc. Psychol. **101**, 1332–1350 (2011). https://doi.org/10.1037/a0024951
46. Schriesheim, C., Powers, K.J., Scandura, T.A., et al.: Improving construct measurement in management research: comments and a quantitative approach for assessing the theoretical content adequacy of paper-and-pencil survey-type instruments. J. Manag. **19**, 385–417 (1993). https://doi.org/10.1016/0149-2063(93)90058-U
47. Worthington, R.L., Whittaker, T.A.: Scale development research: a content analysis and recommendations for best practices. Couns. Psychol. **34**, 806–838 (2006). https://doi.org/10.1037/h0087233
48. Thurstone, L.L., Chave, E.: The Measurement of Attitudes. University of Chicago Press, Chicago (1929)
49. Kristof-Brown, A.L., Zimmermann, R.D., Johnson, E.C.: Consequences of individuals´ fit at work: a meta-analysis of person-job, person-organization, person-group, and person supervisor fit. Pers. Psychol. **58**, 281–342 (2005). https://doi.org/10.1111/j.1744-6570.2005.00672.x
50. Judge, T.A., Bono, J.E., Erez, A., et al.: Core self-evaluations and job and life satisfaction: the role of self-concordance and goal attainment. J. Appl. Psychol. **90**, 257–268 (2005). https://doi.org/10.1037/0021-9010.90.2.257
51. Oreg, S.: Resistance to change: developing an individual differences measure. J. Appl. Psychol. **88**, 680–693 (2003). https://doi.org/10.1037/0021-9010.88.4.680
52. Krönung, J., Eckhardt, A.: What determines user attitudes in IS research?: A meta-analytic structural equation modeling approach. J. Inf. Technol. Theory Appl. (JITTA) **18**, 34–65 (2017)
53. Porath, C.L., Bateman, T.S.: Self-regulation: from goal orientation to job performance. J. Appl. Psychol. **91**, 185–192 (2006). https://doi.org/10.1037/0021-9010.91.1.185

54. Button, S.B., Mathieu, J.E., Zajac, D.M.: Goal orientation in organizational research: a conceptual and empirical foundation. Organ. Behav. Hum. Decis. Process. **67**, 26–48 (1996). https://doi.org/10.1006/obhd.1996.0063
55. Janssen, O., van Yperen, N.W.: Employees' goal orientations, the quality of leader-member exchange, and the outcomes of job performance and job satisfaction. Acad. Manag. J. **47**, 368–384 (2004). https://doi.org/10.5465/20159587
56. Urbina, S.: Essentials of Psychological Testing. Wiley, Hoboken (2014)
57. Digital.ai: 14th annual state of agile report (2020). https://digital.ai/catalyst-blog/the-14th-annual-state-of-agile-report. Accessed 09 Jan 2022
58. Podsakoff: Self-reports in organizational research: problems and prospects. J. Manage. **12**, 531 (1986)

The Future of Experimentation: A Research Agenda Based on Practitioners' Reflections

Nils Stotz, Kevin Anderson(✉), and Paul Drews

Leuphana University Lüneburg, Lüneburg, Germany
nils.stotz@stud.leuphana.de, kevin@experimentationjobs.com, paul.drews@leuphana.de

Abstract. Experimentation has become a cornerstone of agile, evidence-driven software development. To explore how it may evolve in the coming decade, we collected qualitative data from 58 experts across the global experimentation community. Using an inductive thematic analysis inspired by the Gioia methodology, we identified six interrelated trends that capture how practitioners envision the future of experimentation: AI-augmented workflows, segment-level personalization, platformization and warehouse-native architectures, expansion beyond web contexts, rigor at scale, and cultural capability building. These trends highlight experimentation's evolution from a technical testing practice toward a socio-technical learning system. Building on these insights, the paper outlines a practice-inspired research agenda for the next decade of evidence-based product development.

Keywords: Continuous Experimentation · A/B Testing · Product Development

1 Introduction

Continuous Experimentation enables agile, evidence-driven teams to reduce uncertainty, validate assumptions, and make product decisions grounded in data. In agile software development, experimentation operationalizes fast feedback loops by empirically validating assumptions in running systems, complementing iterative delivery with evidence-based learning. Over the past decade, organizations have increasingly treated experimentation not as a peripheral testing technique, but as a strategic capability embedded in the software delivery lifecycle [2,3]. Large-scale technology companies have led this transformation by operationalizing online controlled experiments—popularly known as A/B tests—at massive scale. These experiments inform design, feature prioritization, and business strategy in near real time [1,4,5].

Simultaneously, the rise of Artificial Intelligence (AI) has introduced new possibilities for scaling and optimizing experimentation. AI techniques—from

A. Goldman et al. (Eds.): XP 2026, LNBIP 578, pp. 109–117, 2026.
https://doi.org/10.1007/978-3-032-22375-3_7

multi-armed bandits and contextual personalization to natural language processing and causal inference—are increasingly being applied to design, prioritize, and analyze experiments [8,19]. While some organizations use AI to automate statistical computations or recommend experiment variants, others envision intelligent platforms that proactively identify learning opportunities. These developments point to a future in which AI augments the experimentation lifecycle end-to-end, assisting human decision-makers without replacing them [1].

Despite this momentum, significant gaps remain in the scholarly literature. While prior studies have outlined the architecture of experimentation platforms [14], organizational challenges to adoption [15,16], and statistical pitfalls in A/B testing [18], few have synthesized how practitioners envision the next generation of experimentation systems. In particular, the integration of AI, the pursuit of greater statistical rigor, and the cultural reconfiguration required to scale experimentation remain underexplored.

This study addresses that gap by presenting an expert-informed research agenda for the future of experimentation. Drawing on qualitative input from 58 practitioners, we identify key trends shaping the field over the next five to ten years. These include AI-assisted experimentation, segment-level personalization, platform consolidation, governance mechanisms, and the cultural and organizational conditions required to support large-scale, trustworthy experimentation. By mapping these developments to current literature, we aim to support both researchers and practitioners in understanding how experimentation may evolve—and how to shape that evolution responsibly.

Accordingly, this study addresses the following research question:

RQ: How do experienced experimentation practitioners envision the evolution of continuous experimentation over the next five to ten years, particularly in light of increasing automation and AI integration?

2 Background

Continuous experimentation (CE) refers to the systematic testing of hypotheses through controlled changes to a product or system to observe their impact on user behavior or business outcomes. Rooted in the scientific method, CE has become a central mechanism for learning in modern software engineering. It enables organizations to validate ideas empirically, reduce uncertainty in product development, and align decision-making with real-world data [1,2].

Research on CE has examined its technical, methodological, and organizational foundations. From a technical standpoint, experimentation platforms play a critical role in automating the assignment of users to variants, logging behavior, computing metrics, and ensuring the reproducibility and trustworthiness of results [13,14]. Prior work on large-scale experimentation platforms emphasizes the need for scalability, reliability, and governance in platform design [1,4]. Recent architectural patterns also reflect a shift toward "warehouse-native" experimentation, where data infrastructure and experimentation systems are tightly integrated to support cross-team experimentation at scale [12].

At the methodological level, researchers have stressed the importance of statistical rigor in CE. Misinterpretation of experiment results—due to issues like insufficient power, metric misuse, or interference effects—can undermine decision quality [18]. Studies have proposed safeguards such as pre-registration, guardrail metrics, and robust stopping rules to mitigate these risks [1]. The introduction of AI techniques into experimentation adds further complexity: while methods like contextual bandits can personalize treatments and accelerate learning, they also challenge traditional statistical assumptions and increase the need for interpretable, causal reasoning [8].

Organizationally, CE adoption demands more than tools and metrics. It requires a cultural shift toward hypothesis-driven thinking, transparency, and psychological safety. Empirical studies across startups and large enterprises highlight that successful experimentation programs depend on factors such as leadership support, cross-functional collaboration, and shared understanding of success metrics [15–17]. Organizations that fail to address these socio-technical dynamics often struggle to move beyond superficial experimentation practices.

3 Method

3.1 Data Collection

We assembled a qualitative dataset of written reflections from 58 recognized practitioners in product experimentation, including platform owners, product leaders, and consultants. Participants were sourced via the professional network of *ExperimentationJobs.com*. One co-author contacted potential contributors on LinkedIn between July 2023 and November 2025, inviting brief, open-ended reflections on how experimentation may evolve over the next five to ten years and how Artificial Intelligence (AI) could shape that trajectory.

All contributions were provided voluntarily as short written statements; no synchronous interviews were conducted. We consolidated responses into a structured spreadsheet for analysis, preserving respondent wording and basic metadata (role, organization type). The written format ensured consistent capture across contributors and facilitated cross-case comparison at scale.

3.2 Data Analysis

The analysis followed a qualitative, inductive approach inspired by the Gioia methodology, which emphasizes systematic concept development and transparency from data to theory [20]. All 58 written responses were compiled into a single spreadsheet and treated as analytical units. Both authors independently read the material multiple times to gain a holistic understanding and noted recurring patterns and surprising statements.

In the first coding cycle, first-order concepts were derived using participants' own language whenever possible (e.g., "AI-assisted experimentation," "platform consolidation," "cultural adoption"). These were iteratively grouped into broader second-order themes through constant comparison and discussion until conceptual clarity was reached. This process yielded six aggregate dimensions representing shared practitioner perspectives such as AI-augmented workflows and rigor at scale.

Throughout coding, the evolving codebook was documented to maintain traceability. Disagreements between authors were resolved through discussion to ensure interpretive reliability. The resulting data structure preserves a transparent link from raw statements to conceptual insights, forming the foundation of the findings presented in the next section.

4 Findings

This section presents the results of our qualitative analysis of expert perspectives on the future of experimentation and the integration of Artificial Intelligence (AI) into experimentation practices. Drawing on 58 semi-structured interviews, we identified six central future-oriented trends that capture shared expectations and tensions regarding the evolution of experimentation. Each trend represents a cluster of related ideas that appeared consistently across participants' statements. While the first subsection summarizes these empirical trends, the second develops a forward-looking research agenda derived from them.

4.1 Trends Identified in the Data

Our analysis surfaced six interrelated trends describing how experts expect experimentation to evolve across technology, methods, and organization.

T1: AI-Augmented Experimentation Across the Lifecycle. Experts expect AI to assist hypothesis generation, design, QA, analysis, and insight communication. Anticipated benefits include speed, consistency, and surfacing non-obvious signals; corresponding needs include verification, transparency, and robust guardrails.

T2: From Average Effects to Segment-Level Insights and Personalization. Practitioners foresee a shift from single average treatment effects toward heterogeneous treatment effects across segments and contexts. This raises requirements for richer data, careful multiple-comparison control, and maintenance-aware thresholds for deploying personalization.

T3: Platformization and Warehouse-Native Experimentation. Respondents expect consolidation of tools and tighter coupling with the modern data stack. Warehouse-native patterns (shared assignment, exposure, and metric computation over central models) are viewed as foundations for scale, reproducibility, and governance.

T4: Expansion Beyond Web and App Contexts. Experimentation is framed as a general decision-making approach spanning product strategy, marketing, logistics, and operations. Methodological adaptations are needed for small samples, interference, delayed effects, and quasi-experimental designs.

T5: Rigor at Scale. Scaling throughput increases the premium on statistical power, variance reduction, sequential controls, and causal reasoning. Automation must not substitute for principled design and interpretation; trustworthiness remains the primary objective.

T6: Culture and Capability Building. Sustained impact depends on culture, incentives, and cross-functional literacy. As execution accelerates, bottlenecks shift to interpretation and decision-making, requiring shared ownership, psychological safety, and clearly governed metrics.

4.2 Research Agenda

Building on these trends (T1–T6), we outline six corresponding research directions (R1–R6). To avoid presenting practitioner expectations in isolation, each direction reflects where related work already exists and where gaps remain.

R1: Advancing Understanding of AI Integration Across the Experimentation Lifecycle. Recent work has begun exploring AI-supported experiment design and analysis, especially around adaptive optimization and automation [8,22]. However, questions of human–AI collaboration, interpretability, and governance remain largely unaddressed. Research is needed on how AI can accelerate experimentation without undermining trust or replacing human judgment.

R2: Investigating Heterogeneous Treatment Effects and their Responsible Operationalization. There is growing academic interest in methods for segment-level effects and data-driven personalization [1]. Yet most work focuses on statistical detection rather than sustainable operationalization. Scholars should study how teams can avoid overfitting, balance maintenance costs, and integrate causal machine learning responsibly when using heterogeneity in decision-making.

R3: Designing and Evaluating Platform and Warehouse-Native Architectures for Experimentation. While platform architectures have been documented extensively [13,14], the recent shift toward warehouse-native systems is driven primarily by industry practice and remains underexplored in research. This creates an opportunity to examine governance, interoperability, and transparency in tightly coupled data–experimentation architectures.

R4: Adapting and Assessing Experimentation Methods in New Domains. Although experimentation is expanding beyond web interfaces, academic work in non-digital or operational domains remains sparse. Existing studies on experimentation in embedded systems and B2B settings [6,7] offer a starting point, but broader methodological adaptation is needed for contexts with small samples, interference, or long feedback cycles.

R5: Safeguarding Rigor in High-Throughput Experimentation Environments. Rigor at scale is a recurring theme in current literature, particularly concerning power, false positives, and interference [18]. New statistical work also highlights how high experiment volumes increase false positives and proposes scalable correction strategies [21]. Future research should identify scalable statistical techniques—variance reduction, sequential controls, causal modeling—that maintain validity as organizations increase velocity and breadth of experimentation.

R6: Explaining and Enabling Experimentation Culture and Capabilities. Research has shown that organizational structures and cultural conditions strongly influence experimentation outcomes [15–17]. Yet little work examines how these socio-technical factors evolve under increasing automation and scale. Studies are needed on incentives, literacy, and cross-functional governance models that enable experimentation to function as a continuous learning system.

5 Discussion and Conclusion

5.1 Research Contributions

This study contributes to a deeper understanding of how experimentation as a socio-technical practice is evolving and which developments practitioners consider most influential for its future. Based on empirical insights from 58 experts, the paper synthesizes expectations regarding technological advances, methodological shifts, and organizational transformations that are likely to shape experimentation over the next decade.

The findings expand the existing body of knowledge by offering a comprehensive, practice-based view of experimentation's future. Rather than treating experimentation as a purely technical process, the analysis illustrates its evolution as a socio-technical system that connects infrastructure, statistical rigor, and organizational culture. This perspective complements earlier empirical studies that underscored the socio-technical barriers to continuous experimentation, including organizational resistance, siloed data ownership, and lack of statistical literacy [15–17].

Through six empirically derived trends, the study highlights practitioner expectations that align with, extend, or challenge existing research—from AI-assisted workflows and heterogeneous treatment effects to platform consolidation and cultural adoption. This framework enriches prior conceptual models such as the RIGHT framework for continuous experimentation [10], and extends earlier taxonomies that focused predominantly on platform architectures and process roles [13,14]. By synthesizing expert perspectives with state-of-the-art literature, the study identifies both areas of continuity and emerging gaps, offering a forward-looking schema that captures experimentation's evolving purpose, scale, and scope in contemporary software engineering.

In addition, the research agenda proposed here bridges academic inquiry and industry practice. It outlines open questions about the human–AI division of labor, the operationalization of rigor at scale, and the organizational mechanisms that sustain experimentation as a continuous learning system. These questions align with recent calls to integrate AI into experimentation workflows without undermining interpretability or accountability [8,19], and to embed experimentation within broader organizational governance frameworks [1,12].

5.2 Limitations

This study is exploratory and qualitative in nature. Its insights reflect the perspectives of experienced practitioners and are therefore interpretive rather than statistically generalizable. The sample consists of practitioners already active in the experimentation community, which introduces a selection bias toward organizations and individuals favorable to experimentation practices. Consequently, the findings capture informed expectations rather than representative views of the broader software development population.

The findings reflect expectations at a specific point in time and both the pace of AI development and the maturity of experimentation practices are likely to evolve rapidly. Future work could revisit these trends longitudinally, contrast expert perspectives with those of non-specialist practitioners. A full paper building on this work could extend the dataset, integrate mixed-method approaches and develop a more comprehensive theoretical model explaining how technological, methodological and organizational developments jointly shape the evolution of experimentation.

References

1. Kohavi, R., Tang, D., Xu, Y.: Trustworthy Online Controlled Experiments: A Practical Guide to A/B Testing. Cambridge University Press (2020). https://doi.org/10.1017/9781108653985
2. Fitzgerald, B., Stol, K.-J.: Continuous software engineering: a roadmap and agenda. J. Syst. Softw. **123**, 176–189 (2017). https://doi.org/10.1016/j.jss.2015.06.063
3. Bosch, J.: Building products as innovation experiment systems. In: Proceedings of 3rd International Conference on Software Business (ICSOB), pp. 27–39 (2012). https://doi.org/10.1007/978-3-642-30746-1_3
4. Tang, D., Agarwal, A., O'Brien, D., Meyer, M.: Overlapping experiment infrastructure: more, better, faster experimentation. In: Proceedings 16th ACM SIGKDD International Conference on Knowledge Discovery and Data Mining (KDD), pp. 17–26 (2010). https://doi.org/10.1145/1835804.1835810
5. Feitelson, D.G., Frachtenberg, E., Beck, K.L.: Development and deployment at Facebook. IEEE Internet Comput. **17**(4), 8–17 (2013). https://doi.org/10.1109/MIC.2013.25
6. Rissanen, O., Münch, J.: Continuous experimentation in the B2B domain: a case study. In: Proceedings of 2nd International Workshop on Rapid Continuous Software Engineering (RCoSE), pp. 12–18 (2015). https://doi.org/10.1109/RCoSE.2015.10

7. Mattos, D.I., Bosch, J., Olsson, H.H.: Challenges and strategies for undertaking continuous experimentation in embedded systems: industry and research perspectives. In: Proceedings of 19th International Conference on Agile Processes in Software Engineering and Extreme Programming (XP), pp. 277–292 (2018). https://doi.org/10.1007/978-3-319-91602-6_20
8. Ros, R., Hammar, M.: Data-driven software design with constraint-oriented multivariate bandit optimization (COMBO). Empirical Softw. Eng. **25**(5), 3841–3872 (2020). https://doi.org/10.1007/s10664-020-09856-1
9. Fagerholm, F., Guinea, A.S., Mäenpää, H., Münch, J.: Building blocks for continuous experimentation. In: Proceedings of 1st International Workshop on Rapid Continuous Software Engineering (RCoSE), pp. 26–35 (2014). https://doi.org/10.1145/2593812.2593816
10. Fagerholm, F., Guinea, A.S., Mäenpää, H., Münch, J.: The RIGHT model for continuous experimentation. J. Syst. Softw.**123**, 292–305 (2017). https://doi.org/10.1016/j.jss.2016.03.034
11. Auer, F., Felderer, M.: Current state of research on continuous experimentation: a systematic mapping study. In: Proceedings of 44th Euromicro Conference on Software Engineering and Advanced Applications (SEAA), pp. 335–344 (2018). https://doi.org/10.1109/SEAA.2018.00062
12. Auer, F., Ros, R., Kaltenbrunner, L., Runeson, P., Felderer, M.: Controlled experimentation in continuous experimentation: knowledge and challenges. Inf. Softw. Technol. **134**, 106551 (2021). https://doi.org/10.1016/j.infsof.2021.106551
13. Kevic, K., Murphy, B., Williams, L., Beckmann, J.: Characterizing experimentation in continuous deployment: a case study on Bing. In: Proceedings of 39th International Conference on Software Engineering: Software Engineering in Practice Track (ICSE-SEIP), pp. 123–132 (2017). https://doi.org/10.1109/ICSE-SEIP.2017.19
14. Gupta, S., Ulanova, L., Bhardwaj, S., Dmitriev, P., Raff, P., Fabijan, A.: The anatomy of a large-scale experimentation platform. In: IEEE International Conference on Software Architecture (ICSA) (2018). https://doi.org/10.1109/ICSA.2018.00009
15. Schermann, G., Cito, J., Leitner, P., Zdun, U., Gall, H.C.: "We're doing it live": a multi-method empirical study on continuous experimentation. Inf. Softw. Technol. **99**, 41–57 (2018). https://doi.org/10.1016/j.infsof.2018.02.010
16. Yaman, S.G., et al.: Introducing continuous experimentation in large software-intensive product and service organizations. J. Syst. Softw. **133**, 195–211 (2017). https://doi.org/10.1016/j.jss.2017.07.009
17. Melegati, J., Edison, H., Wang, X., Abrahamsson, P.: XPro: a model to explain the limited adoption and implementation of experimentation in software startups. IEEE Trans. Softw. Eng. **48**(6), 1929–1946 (2022). https://doi.org/10.1109/TSE.2020.3042610
18. Quin, F., Weyns, D., Galster, M., Costa Silva, C.C.: A/B testing: a systematic literature review. J. Syst. Softw. **211**, 112011 (2024). https://doi.org/10.1016/j.jss.2024.112011
19. Schermann, G., Leitner, P.: Search-based scheduling of experiments in continuous deployment. In: Proceedings of 34th IEEE International Conference on Software Maintenance and Evolution (ICSME), pp. 485–495 (2018). https://doi.org/10.1109/ICSME.2018.00059
20. Gioia, D.A., Corley, K.G., Hamilton, A.L.: Seeking qualitative rigor in inductive research: notes on the Gioia methodology. Organ. Res. Methods **16**(1), 15–31 (2013). https://doi.org/10.1177/1094428112452151

21. Kohavi, R., Chen, N.: False positives in A/B tests. In: Proceedings of 30th ACM SIGKDD Conference on Knowledge Discovery and Data Mining (KDD '24), pp. 5240–5250 (2024). https://doi.org/10.1145/3637528.3671631
22. Stotz, N., Drews, P.: Use cases for artificial intelligence in the product experimentation lifecycle. In: Product-Focused Software Process Improvement (PROFES 2024), pp. 289–304. Springer, Heidelberg (2025). https://doi.org/10.1007/978-3-031-78386-9_19

Engineering

Evaluating the Consequences of Process Adjustment Patterns for Handling Software Architecture Uncertainties

André Paris[1], Fábio Fagundes Silveira[3](✉), Jorge Melegati[4], and Eduardo Guerra[2]

[1] Institute of Research of São Paulo, São Paulo, Brazil
andreparis.comp@gmail.com
[2] Free University of Bozen-Bolzano, Bolzano, Italy
eduardo.guerra@unibz.it
[3] Federal University of São Paulo, São José dos Campos, Brazil
fsilveira@unifesp.br
[4] INESC TEC, Faculty of Engineering, University of Porto, Porto, Portugal
melegati@fe.up.pt

Abstract. Architectural uncertainties arising from incomplete or unclear information pose significant challenges when making architectural decisions in Agile teams. Based on a limited number of case studies that employed a technique called ArchHypo, four patterns were identified that propose small adjustments in the development process to handle architectural uncertainties: Protective Guideline, Bring the Specialist, Plan for Preparation, and Quality Checkpoint. Although the patterns derived from these experiences can be useful in real projects, their applicability and consequences were based on limited evidence and specific scenarios. To address this issue, this paper presents an interview study with experienced software architects and engineers to gather further information on the application of these patterns. The research method employed semi-structured interviews to gather the experiences of professionals with the target practices, and thematic analysis was used to assess their recurrence, applicability, and consequences. The findings confirmed that most professionals recognized those practices in real projects and their suitability as actions in uncertainty management. Moreover, new positive and negative consequences, not previously documented in the patterns, were identified. As a result, this work contributes to the field by providing guidance to professionals on how to better evaluate the trade-offs of those patterns when applied to architecture uncertainty management.

Keywords: Hypotheses engineering · Software architecture · Handling uncertainty · Guideline · Programming · Development Process

A. Goldman et al. (Eds.): XP 2026, LNBIP 578, pp. 121–136, 2026.
https://doi.org/10.1007/978-3-032-22375-3_8

1 Introduction

While embracing changes is a key principle in Agile software development, it is challenging to apply this principle to software architecture. While functional changes are typically more limited to a specific part of the software, architectural changes can be broad and impact the entire system. While practices like TDD, refactoring, and clean code can make the code ready for functional changes, in several cases, they are not enough to address broader software architecture changes, such as those related to scalability or security. A recent study provided evidence that confirmed that changes in requirements related to architectural quality attributes happen frequently in later project stages [19].

A recent technique, named ArchHypo [16], proposed the identification and management of architectural uncertainties as an approach to handle possible changes in the software architecture. The first step is to identify points where essential information is lacking in software requirements and software components necessary for making architectural decisions. Based on that, actions to reduce the change impact and the uncertainty can be taken by the team to find a better moment in which a decision could be made. This approach aligns with Agile principles because it enables iterative development of the software architecture. ArchHypo utilizes the principles of hypothesis engineering and was developed based on a set of patterns [9,20] that target Agile architecture practices.

This initial set of patterns was complemented by additional practices that were identified in case studies [16,17]. What was initially called "*development guidelines*" in the case studies context, was later documented in four patterns: Paris et al. [14]: (a) adding constraints to programming tasks (Protective Guideline) [14]: (a) adding constraints to programming tasks (PROTECTIVE GUIDELINE); (b) adding steps before an activity (PLAN FOR PREPARATION); (c) including the participation of people with certain expertise when a given condition arises (BRING THE SPECIALIST); and (d) adding a verification step after a task is completed (QUALITY CHECKPOINT). While some of these patterns might sound like more general practices, they were documented in the context of architectural uncertainty management, considering, for instance, forces and consequences that are specific to this context.

However, these patterns were based on limited evidence, as they were derived from their usage in only a few projects. As a result, some important consequences that were not relevant to these specific projects may not have been documented. This fact can impair a professional's ability to evaluate the trade-offs associated with implementing each of them. Moreover, additional evidence regarding the recurrence of such practices can provide greater confidence in their implementation, confirming that they are indeed patterns [2].

Focused on this limitation, the primary aim of this paper is to assess the recurrence of these patterns as established practices, confirm their applicability in managing uncertainties, and explore the positive and negative consequences arising from their implementation. The research method used semi-structured interviews with software development professionals, particularly those with experience in software architecture. The interview questions aim to assess the effectiveness of the target patterns in handling architectural uncertainty and other consequences that may arise from it.

Building on the documented patterns presented in [14], this work contributes to the field of agile architecture by providing additional evidence and information regarding the consequences of these patterns. Based on these results, practitioners can better evaluate the trade-offs of their usage, considering the experience of professionals across a wide range of software projects.

The remainder of this paper is organized as follows. Section 2 reviews agile architecture and the ArchHypo technique, detailing its relevance. Section 3 summarizes the four process-adjustment patterns. Section 4 details the research method, covering participant selection and data analysis. Section 5 presents our results and discussion, focusing on pattern recognition and the new consequences that have been identified. Finally, Sect. 6 provides the conclusion and direction for future work.

2 Agile Architecture

The evolution of software development practices, particularly within the Agile movement, has introduced concepts such as Agile Architecture and Continuous Architecture [7,8]. An analysis assessing works that utilize these terms [12], based on their common characteristics, suggested that they can be treated as synonyms. Within this context, software architecture design in agile projects, also referred to as agile software architecture, plays a pivotal role in the success of software development [4]. Unlike traditional approaches, where the architecture is defined upfront and rigidly adhered to, agile projects adopt a more dynamic approach, recognizing that the architecture must evolve and adapt over time.

In the agile framework, architectural decisions are made iteratively and incrementally, consistent with the agile principles of adaptability and collaboration [4]. Agile teams are encouraged to explore various options as development progresses, aiming to establish an architecture that addresses current requirements while remaining adaptable for future enhancements.

ArchHypo is a technique based on hypothesis engineering that proposes an architecture design based on uncertainty management [16,17]. It addresses the challenges posed by incomplete or evolving information that can impact architectural decisions. Unlike traditional approaches, which focus on the documented requirements, ArchHypo explicitly identifies and manages uncertainties that can affect the design and evolution of software architectures. It is based on hypothesis engineering, where uncertainties are documented as hypotheses and handled throughout the software development lifecycle. It provides a more systematic way to postpone architecture decisions [16], which is one of the pillars of continuous architecture [8].

ArchHypo is based on the fact that uncertainties become more manageable when made explicit. Once these uncertainties are documented as hypotheses, the team should create a technical plan that may include one or more actions aimed at: (a) definitively confirming or refuting the hypothesis; (b) reducing the degree of uncertainty; (c) mitigating its potential consequences; or (d) defining criteria for postponing its resolution. ArchHypo provides a systematic approach for Agile teams to structure their decision-making process around these uncertainties, ensuring that architecture decisions are made at the most suitable moment, considering explicitly factors that remain uncertain. This technique builds upon the Agile architecture pattern FIND WHERE IT HURTS [9], which suggests that the architectural design should focus on areas that are critical for that project. ArchHypo suggests that these critical areas are those whose hypotheses were classified as having high impact and high uncertainty.

A crucial aspect of this technique is the development of the technical plan. For instance, software analytics patterns [3] can help diminish uncertainty, while a flexible solution can limit potential effects. It is essential to emphasize that the objective is not to resolve every hypothesis immediately, as uncertainty is intrinsic to software projects, but rather to manage them to determine the appropriate moment for making architectural decisions [22]. ArchHypo adheres to the notion that effective solutions arise from combining technical knowledge with creativity [11,13]. Thus, although the documented patterns provide a collection of practices for addressing architectural hypotheses, teams should not feel constrained by them and are encouraged to seek creative alternatives as well. From these alternatives, the patterns described in the next section emerged.

3 Process Adjustments Patterns for Handling Uncertainties

This section briefly presents the patterns described in Paris et al. [14] that the study presented in this paper targets. They were identified through case studies [16,17] that employed the ArchHypo technique, as well as through others that adopted practices to handle uncertainty. These patterns can be applied even without an explicit method for managing architectural uncertainty. Moreover, since patterns are recurrent solutions that arise from practice, they might be applied even without an explicit awareness.

What is particular about the patterns presented by [14] is that they are associated with small adjustments in the development process that can be employed to manage uncertainties impacting software architecture. In general, these adjustments introduce mechanisms that enable the collection of more information or mitigate the impact of changes, providing strategies to handle the architectural evolution. An outline of the patterns is provided below:

PROTECTIVE GUIDELINE addresses the issue of programming practices being adopted without full awareness, which can potentially limit future architectural decisions. The solution involves establishing clear programming guidelines that align with long-term architectural goals and maintaining flexibility to support future architectural decisions.

BRING THE SPECIALIST focuses on minimizing uncertainties in the development of architectural features by involving individuals with the necessary expertise in a particular technology or domain. Addresses challenges arising from a lack of specific knowledge or expertise within the development team.

Plan for Preparation tackles recurrent uncertainties during specific architectural activities by introducing preparatory actions to gather relevant information beforehand. This approach helps reduce uncertainty and minimize surprises that can arise in production.

Quality Checkpoint introduces a verification step to ensure the desired quality of a software development artifact, such as a class or document. Ensuring quality at the artifact level helps reduce architectural uncertainty about this quality across the overall software.

These patterns share a common context: their use in managing uncertainties related to software architecture. It is important to note that, although some of these solutions can also be applied in other contexts, the target patterns document their applicability, with the respective forces and consequences, to this specific context. This paper also focuses only on their use for architectural uncertainty management.

4 Research Method

To explore the effectiveness of patterns in managing uncertainty in software architecture, this study was guided by the following two research questions:

- RQ1: Are the proposed patterns recognized practices by the professionals?
- RQ2: What consequences have professionals identified when applying the target patterns?

To answer these research questions, the study consisted of an interview-based study [15] based on semi-structured interviews [18]. By adopting this approach, we aim to gain insight into participants' perceptions and experiences with the proposed patterns. The interviews were conducted as the data collection method [1,6], with questions designed to explore the effectiveness, consequences, and applicability of the patterns in real-world scenarios. The responses were transcribed, coded, and categorized following an inductive thematic analysis approach [5]. This iterative process ensured that emerging themes and insights were grounded in the participants' data, contributing to the refinement of the patterns.

Interviews Execution: Between October and November 2024, we conducted nine semi-structured interviews with software development professionals, guided by a semi-structured interview protocol. Depending on the participant's choice, the interviews were held in Portuguese, English, or Spanish and lasted approximately 60 min. Furthermore, a pilot interview was conducted with participant P1, whose feedback was used to improve the interview protocol. Since the content remained unchanged, we included P1's answers in the study.

Interview Approach: The interview began with an explanation of the research purpose and obtaining the participant's consent to participate. After that, for each pattern, we used the following protocol: (a) it was presented and explained, followed by two illustrative examples; (b) we confirmed with the participant his understanding of the pattern; (c) we asked the participant if he recognize the pattern and already applied it (RQ1); (d) we asked the positive and negative consequences in the patterns usage, including the reducing an uncertainty level and its impact (RQ2). Following the semi-structured approach, when the participant mentioned something relevant, additional questions were asked to further explore it. During the interview, we made clear that the patterns should be considered only in the target context of software architecture uncertainties. To ensure participants understood the patterns and were referring to these solutions in this context, we asked them to report their specific experience with the pattern application.

Participants: To properly evaluate the patterns, we selected professionals for interviews, considering their experience in software development and architectural decision-making processes. We employed purposive (or expert) sampling, targeting individuals in senior roles and with extensive experience in software development. The participants were recruited primarily through the authors' professional networks and academic contacts, ensuring a pool of recognized experts in software architecture. Inclusion criteria ensured that participants possessed the requisite knowledge to evaluate the patterns, including at least eight years in a relevant technical role (e.g., software architecture or technical leadership) and familiarity with agile or iterative development projects. Of the 10 people selected for the study, 9 agreed to participate in the study.

Data Analysis: The interview sessions were recorded with the participants' prior authorization and transcribed by Microsoft Teams. To analyze these transcripts, we followed an inductive coding scheme. This approach was chosen to explore participants' perspectives on the software development process, with a particular focus on their experiences regarding the consequences of implementing each pattern. So, with transcriptions, the analysis began with a thorough reading of them to become deeply familiar with the data. Specific text segments were then identified, labeled, and converted into initial codes [5]. We reviewed the transcripts multiple times to improve accuracy and ensure consistency and alignment with the context of the participants' statements.

The relationship between the identified codes and the pattern consequences was established through a systematic comparative analysis. For each pattern, the generated codes were compared against the consequences previously documented in the patterns [14]. In the results, we separated the codes that matched existing consequences from those that represented new findings.

Finally, to assess the saturation of the thematic analysis, we employed the information threshold method [10]. This method proposes collecting data into chunks, e.g., a defined number of interviews, called runs, and stopping data collection when the proportion of new codes obtained in a run over the codes obtained in the first run, called the base, is below a certain threshold. As suggested by the authors, we considered a threshold of 5% of the new codes in a step. We conducted five interviews to create the base, and each run consisted of an additional two interviews. The threshold was achieved in the second run after nine interviews.

5 Results and Discussion

This section presents the analysis of the data collected through the semi-structured interviews with professionals in software development[1].

Participant's Profile. Table 1 presents the profile of the participants in the study. The participants fit the required experience to participate in the study, with 8 out of 9 rating themselves as Advanced or Specialist. Their diverse roles and backgrounds (finance, healthcare, outsourcing, and academia, across five different countries) ensure a broad set of practical insights regarding architectural uncertainty management.

Table 1. Participant Roles, Business Segments, Countries, and Self-Reported Expertise Levels.

ID	Primary Role	Business Segment	Country	Years Exp.	Expertise Level
P1	Senior Software Architect	Finance	USA	10–15	Advanced
P2	C-level Executive	Entertainment	Mexico	>15	Specialist
P3	Product Manager	Outsourcing	USA	10–15	Advanced
P4	Software Engineer	Healthcare	Germany	10–15	Advanced
P5	Senior Software Architect	Academia	UK	10–15	Advanced
P6	Software Engineer	Finance	Mexico	10–15	Advanced
P7	Software Engineer	Healthcare	Italy	>15	Specialist
P8	Product Manager	Entertainment	USA	10–15	Intermediate
P9	Senior Software Architect	Outsourcing	Mexico	10–15	Advanced

Code Saturation. Each quote was carefully interpreted in its context to refine the coding process. This iterative approach yielded the identification of 21 distinct codes from the analyzed transcripts. We evaluated the theoretical saturation according to the information threshold method [10]. Table 2 shows the number of new codes in each interview. The first five interviews served as the basis for determining the point of saturation. In the next run, two additional interviews were conducted (P6 and P7), which added a number of codes above our threshold. Therefore, another round of interviews with P8 and P9 was conducted, and the percentage was below 5%, which was the threshold for theoretical

[1] A replication package is available at Zenodo: https://zenodo.org/records/18342558.

saturation. We considered this criterion as a reference to ensure that sufficient data had been gathered and analyzed, and that no significant insights would emerge from additional interviews.

Table 2. Code Saturation Tracking per Participant Interview Using the Information Threshold Method.

Participant	New codes	Percent of new codes added
P1	19	100%
P2	10	34.48%
P3	8	21.62%
P4	7	15.91%
P5	0	0%
P6	3	6.38%
P7	3	6.00%
P8	2	3.85%
P9	2	3.70%

5.1 Pattern Recognition and Recurrence

In this section, we answer RQ1: *Are the proposed patterns recognized practices by the professionals?*. In summary, the analysis of the interviews revealed that all four patterns were recognized by most participants. The next paragraphs describe the results for each pattern.

PROTECTIVE GUIDELINE was recognized by eight out of the nine participants. For example, P7 said: "*It's about controlling things and ensuring that things don't go off track*", explaining how it applied similar guiding principles to prevent uncertainty in their projects. Similarly, P4 said: "*By implementing this approach, we can identify and request to fix the vulnerability*", referring to how they had proactively used strategies like those suggested in the PROTECTIVE GUIDELINE, such as identifying potential threats to a current uncertainty and addressing them before they escalate.

BRING THE SPECIALIST was recognized by seven out of the nine participants. For example, P3 mentioned: "*When you bring in someone who understands the uncertainty you're facing, they have the expertise to fix it*", reflecting that they had used a similar approach to solve specific uncertainties by involving specialists. Similarly, P6 explained: "*Having a specialist onboard can help identify the core of the problem and prevent mistakes*", showing their recognition of the value and experience of involving experts when the team lacks that knowledge.

PLAN FOR PREPARATION was recognized by seven out of the nine participants. For example, P3 said: "*It's a way to eliminate uncertainty because you can experiment with the solution, gradually reducing uncertainties as you refine your concepts*". This sentence reflects the PLAN FOR PREPARATION approach, where early experimentation and gathering information help reduce uncertainty. On the other hand, P7 expressed a concern based on his experience with this practice: "*Spending too much time into preparation can delay the process*", pointing out the trade-off that preparation could take away from actual development if it is overdone.

Quality Checkpoint was recognized by eight out of the nine participants. For example, P2 said: "*Having Quality Checkpoint s throughout the project helps ensure that we don't go too far off track*", indicating his experience in applying this practice. In addition, P8 pointed out that "*It's important to maintain quality, but too many checkpoints can slow things down and create additional overhead*". This point suggests that while Quality Checkpoint is recognized as an important practice, it should be implemented in a few key areas where it adds the most value, highlighting the relevance of documenting its trade-offs.

Answering RQ1, the patterns presented in this study were recognized as recurrent practices among the participants. It is worth highlighting that, since these patterns were only recently documented, our analysis did not consider recognition by the pattern name, but rather by the application of the pattern solution in their past experiences. This result confirms that these patterns reflect well-established and recurring practices that can be applied in managing architectural uncertainty. Moreover, it highlights the value in documenting these practices as patterns with well-defined trade-offs, thereby creating awareness among new professionals and formalizing knowledge among experienced ones.

5.2 Pattern Consequences

This section answers RQ2 by presenting the positive and negative consequences of each target pattern. For each pattern, a table (from Tables 3, 4, 5 and 6) summarizes the identified consequences. A '+' prefix indicates a **benefit (positive consequence)**, and a '–' prefix indicates a **challenge or trade-off (negative consequence)**. The **left column** lists consequences that were present in the original pattern documentation and were confirmed by the interviews, while the **right column** lists **new findings** identified in this study that were not originally in the pattern descriptions. After each code presented in the tables, a number in parentheses shows the number of occurrences that it has in the interviews.

The Protective Guideline was identified as highly effective in reducing uncertainty and promoting code standardization, but it also introduced certain trade-offs. As **P1** mentioned, "*This can be restrictive because there will always be new professionals entering as juniors who may not understand those guidelines*", talking about the increase of the architectural complexity which might create a barrier for new professionals. Participants also mentioned the possibility of technology restrictions caused by a guideline limiting the tools and resources they could use, as **P2** commented: "*Too many guidelines can lock down development. You can't evolve if you stick to old rules*". However, they also argued that this could be beneficial for the project, as **P4** said "*we have to control, this is the final resource to maintain a standard to achieve a certain level of quality or avoid some type of error*", saying that control with restrictions is necessary to ensure quality and avoid errors.

From an agile perspective, these trade-offs highlight a tension between maintaining architectural health (through standardization) and maximizing development flow (by preventing unnecessary complexity or technical restrictions that inhibit rapid evolution). Based on the practitioners' interviews, it is recommended to balance the immediate reduction of uncertainty against the future costs of increased architectural complexity when applying this pattern.

While the pattern claims that the reduction of the impact is its main goal, the majority of the participants considered that the reduction in uncertainty was more relevant, arguing "*This is much more on the developers hands*", said by **P4**, and "*A technical guy could implement this, because if you don't have him/her with clarity, you'll have nothing*", said by **P5**. These two quotes reflect the fact that it is challenging to ensure that developers will follow the guidelines properly. The consequences that arise from the interviews are presented in Table 3.

Table 3. Consequences of the PROTECTIVE GUIDELINE Pattern: Confirmed vs Newly Emerged.

Confirmed by the study (existing)	Emerged from the study (new)
+ Cost reduction for new members (2)	– Architectural complexity increased (4)
+ Ensures quality (1)	– Introduction of rework flow (1)
+ Improvement of documentations (1)	– Risk of over-preparation (2)
+ Productivity increased (2)	– Technology restrictions (4)
+ Standardization of the code (5)	+ Avoid issues of internal specialization (1)
+ Uncertainty's impact reduction (3)	– Barrier for new professionals (4)
	+ Creates controlled environment (1)
	– Difficulty to promote team engagement (5)
	+ Increase team maturity (1)
	– Project cost increased (2)
	– Project time increased (3)
	+ Uncertainty's reduction (5)
	+ Potential uncertainty's impact reduction (2)

BRING THE SPECIALIST was highlighted, as expected, for reducing uncertainty, avoiding issues of internal specialization, increasing team maturity, and productivity. **P1** highlighted: "*It helps reduce uncertainty because when you bring in someone who understands the uncertainty you're facing, they have the expertise*". Additionally, **P4** emphasized: "*Having a specialist in the business helps identify the impact of the software, ensuring that the planned goals are being met and reducing uncertainty*".

The participants noted that dedicating an internal member to a specialized role can consume project time and, if not done correctly, may lead to a negative effect, as **P4** pointed out in the statement:"*You can specialize someone, considering the time and resource that you have (...) I think that will increase the uncertainty and impact*". Besides, the participants emphasized another important point, the knowledge transferred from the specialist to team may help the team increase the maturity and will save research time of an internal specialization would require, as said by **P1** and **P3**, "*At the moment when you bring* *a specialist you have a huge opportunity to learn with him/her*" and "*These are well-known process (for an expert), so you'll gain velocity*", respectively. Table 4 presents the codes related to this pattern.

Table 4. Consequences of the BRING THE SPECIALIST Pattern: Interview Confirmations New Findings.

Confirmed by the study (existing)	Emerged from the study (new)
+ Avoid issues of internal specialization (6)	– Difficulty to promote team engagement (3)
+ Creates a controlled environment (1)	+ Potential uncertainty's impact reduction (2)
– Dependence of external specialist (4)	+ Uncertainty's impact reduction (2)
+ Ensures quality (1)	
+ Increase team maturity (5)	
+ Productivity increased (5)	
– Project cost increased (6)	
– Project time increased (2)	
+ Uncertainty reduction (8)	

PLAN FOR PREPARATION was valued, as documented in the original pattern, for its role in reducing uncertainty, allowing teams to anticipate and prepare for challenges, and increasing team productivity. **P1** said: "*By doing this, you significantly reduce uncertainty because you are studying the subject in depth and documenting it*". Moreover, **P3** commented: "*The positive is that you identify the issue before you start implementing. By doing this research before we do any activities, this is going to avoid and make sure that we are not doing any effort that is not necessary*", in the context of avoiding wasted effort on unnecessary activities.

On the other hand, the negative consequences included increased project time and others, such as the risk of over-preparation. **P3** expressed: "*We often focus too much on preparation, which can delay the process*". **P4** also noted: "*This is a cultural paradigm, trying to prepare too much might never get you anywhere*". The risk of over-preparation is a direct threat to agile principles, as it can make the process overly cumbersome. Considering this potential consequence, teams should continuously evaluate the applicability of this pattern to avoid unnecessary additional tasks. Table 5 highlights the consequences mentioned in the interviews.

QUALITY CHECKPOINT was identified as a practice for ensuring quality and mitigating the impact of uncertainty. While the original pattern documentation emphasized impact reduction, the study findings showed that most participants mentioned that its primary effect is reducing the uncertainty itself. **P1** emphasized: "*The QUALITY CHECKPOINT can help reduce the impact because you ensure that no functionality is broken after making changes*". Similarly, **P2** remarked: "*This approach significantly reduces uncertainty by confirming that everything works as expected, avoiding any negative impact*".

Additionally, four participants mentioned the increase in project costs and time, as well as the introduction of the rework flow. **P3** said: "*The obvious*

Table 5. Consequences of the Plan for Preparation Pattern: Existing vs Interview-Identified Effects.

Confirmed by the study (existing)	Emerged from the study (new)
+ Creates controlled environment (2)	+ Cost reduction for new members (1)
− Difficulty to promote team engagement (1)	+ Potential uncertainty's impact reduction (2)
+ Ensures quality (1)	− Risk of over-preparation (3)
+ Improvement of documentations (4)	+ Uncertainty's impact reduction (1)
+ Increase team maturity (1)	
+ Productivity increased (4)	
− Project cost increased (2)	
− Project time increased (6)	
+ Uncertainty reduction (9)	

negative point is that you always do the work twice. You have to adjust the tests.", and **P9** "*It demands more time, but ensures that everything works well in the end*". **P2** added: "*Honestly, I don't see a negative impact. I think it takes time and investment to have this structure, but depending on the criticality of your functionality, you may lose a user forever*". Furthermore, the participants mentioned other new consequences, such as the technical level required to create tests being a barrier for new professionals, and, at the same time, the possibility of increasing the team's maturity through learning how to create the tests. Table 6 presents the results that emerged from the interviews.

Table 6. Consequences of the Quality Checkpoint Pattern: Previously Documented vs Newly Emerged Themes.

Confirmed by the study (existing)	Emerged from the study (new)
+ Creates controlled environment (1)	− Barrier for new professionals (2)
+ Ensures quality (9)	− Difficulty to promote team engagement (1)
− Project cost increased (6)	+ Increase team maturity (2)
− Project time increased (4)	+ Introduction of rework flow (4)
	+ Productivity increased (2)
	+ Uncertainty's impact reduction (9)

Results Summary. Based on the interview, we were able to identify the following number of consequences for each pattern: Protective Guideline (13 new, 6 existing), Bring the Specialist (3 new, 9 existing), Plan for Preparation (4 new, 9 existing), and Quality Checkpoint (6 new, 4 existing). The confirmation of the pattern consequences is a significant result because it provides empirical evidence to support what was documented in the pattern based on limited evidence. Moreover, the new consequences that emerged in the interview are an important contribution, as they will enable professionals to consider a more comprehensive set of trade-offs when implementing the pattern. That will provide better conditions to make a more informed decision.

5.3 Threats to Validity

In this study, ***internal validity*** could be threatened by factors such as bias in participant selection, the subjective nature of interviews, or uncontrolled influences during data collection. Since we applied a purposive sample using the authors' professional networks, the participants may share similar perspectives or backgrounds. To mitigate that threat, we invited participants with professional experience in different countries and segments. However, this sample strategy led to a gender bias, since all the participants in the study were male. We recognize this as an important limitation of this work, which should be considered when assessing its results and addressed in future work.

To mitigate these, a thorough participant selection process was employed based on their experience and familiarity with software architecture design. Additionally, the semi-structured interviews allowed responses to be focused on the research questions, while minimizing external influences.

Threats to ***external validity*** concern the generalization of results to industrial practice [21]. In this study, the results are based on interviews with nine software architects; therefore, the generalizability of the findings to a broader population of software professionals may be limited. To mitigate this threat, participants were selected to represent a diverse range of industries and geographic regions, thereby providing some level of diversity. Moreover, we used the information threshold method [10] to assess code saturation.

Threats to ***construct validity*** are concerned with whether the treatment (method) accurately reflects the cause and whether the outcome accurately reflects the effect [21]. In this study, the treatment involved presenting patterns to manage architectural uncertainty, and the outcome was the participants' recognition and application of these patterns. One potential threat to construct validity is the possibility that participants did not fully understand the patterns as described in the interviews. Additionally, this approach could lead to confirmation bias, since the effort to explain the pattern might make participants more likely to confirm its use. To address this, explanations were provided in the participants' preferred language, making clear that we were looking for reports based on their experience and focused on dealing with software architecture uncertainties. The participants were encouraged to explain the practice in their own words and relate the patterns to their own experiences, allowing an assessment of whether the patterns were understood and could be applied to those experiences.

Finally, threats to ***conclusion validity*** are related to issues that may affect the analysis of the experiment's results, such as sample size selection, statistical test selection, and caution in the implementation and analysis of the experiment [21]. One potential threat to conclusion validity in this study is the small sample size, which limits the ability to detect statistically significant effects and increases the risk of bias. Another threat is the risk of overinterpretation in evaluating the consequences, since participants might point to consequences based on their reasoning rather than their experience. To mitigate these threats, the study involved only highly qualified participants, as their experience provides a more reliable basis for understanding the patterns. We also consider that this experience gives them the capability to assess the consequences of applying the patterns for handling architectural uncertainty, even if they did not have the experience in applying it. In these cases, the participants also presented the reasoning to support their statements.

6 Conclusion

Managing architectural uncertainty is a common challenge in software development, particularly when non-functional requirements change frequently [19]. This paper focuses on four patterns [14]—PROTECTIVE GUIDELINE, BRING THE SPECIALIST, PLAN FOR PREPARATION, and QUALITY CHECKPOINT—that focus on reducing uncertainty and its impacts and were identified by the experience of applying these patterns in some projects. These patterns were identified based on limited evidence, which might raise questions like: "*Are they really recurrent solutions to be called patterns?*" and *Were all patterns' important positive and negative consequences documented?*".

Based on semi-structured interviews with experienced professionals, the findings confirmed that these patterns resonate with standard practices in the field, thereby empirically validating their practical relevance (RQ1). Beyond the original outcomes, practitioners highlighted how applying these adjustments also directly reduces uncertainty itself, not just its impact. These insights demonstrate the potential of these adjustments to bring clarity and focus to the complexities of agile projects, especially when applying techniques to manage software architecture uncertainties, such as ArchHypo [16].

Another primary contribution of this study is the comprehensive, empirically derived set of consequences (RQ2) that refine the documented patterns. For practitioners, this research reveals crucial trade-offs that are important to consider when implementing the pattern. Examples of such consequences are increased project costs and timelines, creation of onboarding barriers, and the risk of unnecessary burden due to over-preparation. These factors should be balanced with the effect that they have on the uncertainty management. This refined understanding ensures the patterns can be applied responsibly in dynamic development environments.

For practitioners, this study provides additional evidence on practices that can be employed to manage architectural uncertainty. These four particular patterns highlight that the actions to reduce uncertainty or its impact should not be limited to the technical domain, and small adjustments in the development process can also be a relevant alternative. For researchers, these findings suggest opportunities for further exploration, such as evaluating the effect of these patterns in case studies and proposing specific approaches for their implementation.

Future research could investigate how organizational cultures and team structures influence the effectiveness and applicability of these patterns across industries and project contexts. Other efforts could also identify and document patterns that leverage process adjustments to manage software architecture uncertainty.

Acknowledgments. The authors would like to thank the São Paulo Research Foundation (FAPESP) – grant 2023/14646-1 – for financial support.

References

1. Braun, V., Clarke, V.: Using thematic analysis in psychology. Qual. Res. Psychol. **3**(2), 77–101 (2006)
2. Buschmann, F., Henney, K., Schmidt, D.C.: Pattern-Oriented Software Architecture, on Patterns and Pattern Languages. John wiley & sons, Hoboken (2007)
3. Choma, J., da Silva, T.S., Guerra, E.M.: Pattern Language for Lightweight and Interactive Software Analytics Process, pp. 162–189. Springer, Heidelberg (2025). ISBN 978-3-662-70810-1
4. Cockburn, A.: Agile Software Development: The Cooperative Game. Addison-Wesley Professional, Boston (2008)
5. Creswell, J.W.: Research Design: Qualitative, Quantitative, and Mixed Methods Approaches, 4th edn. Sage Publications (2013)
6. Cruzes, D.S., Dybå, T.: Recommended steps for thematic synthesis in software engineering. In: International Symposium on Empirical Software Engineering and Measurement, pp. 275–284. IEEE (2011)
7. Dragicević, Z., Bošnjak, S.: Agile architecture in the digital era: trends and practices. Strat. Manag. **24**(2), 12–33 (2019)
8. Erder, M., Pureur, P.: Continuous Architecture: Sustainable Architecture in an Agile and Cloud-centric World. Morgan Kaufmann, Burlington (2015)
9. Guerra, E., Wirfs-Brock, R., Yoder, J.: Patterns for initial architectural design on agile projects. In: 4th Asian Conference on Pattern Languages of Programs (AsianPLoP), pp. 1, 3, 5 (2015)
10. Guest, G., Namey, E., Chen, M.: Saturation in qualitative research: theoretical foundations and practical applications. Qual. Health Res. **30**(6), 846–856 (2020)
11. Gutbrod, R., Wiele, C.: The Software Dilemma: Balancing Creativity and Control on the Path to Sustainable Software. Springer, Cham (2012)
12. Holmes, B., Nicolaescu, A.: Continuous architecting: just another buzzword. In: Full-Scale Software Engineering/The Art of Software Testing, pp. 1–6 (2017)
13. Mohanani, R., Ram, P., Lasisi, A., Ralph, P., Turhan, B.: Perceptions of creativity in software engineering research and practice. In: 2017 43rd Euromicro Conference on Software Engineering and Advanced Applications (SEAA), pp. 210–217 (2017)
14. Paris, A., Guerra, E., Silveira, F., Silva, K.: Patterns for small adjustments in the development process to deal with architectural uncertainties. In: Proceedings of the 29th European Conference on Pattern Languages of Programs, People, and Practices, EuroPLoP '24. Association for Computing Machinery, New York (2024). ISBN 9798400716836
15. Ralph, P., et al.: Empirical standards for software engineering research (2021)
16. Silva, K., Melegati, J., Silveira, F., Wang, X., Ferreira, M., Guerra, E.: Archhypo: managing software architecture uncertainty using hypotheses engineering. IEEE Trans. Softw. Eng. 1–19 (2024)
17. Silva, K., Melegati, J., Wang, X., Ferreira, M., Guerra, E.: Using hypotheses to manage technical uncertainty and architecture evolution in a software start-up. IEEE Softw. **41**(4), 7–13 (2024)
18. Thomas, J., Harden, A.: Methods for the thematic synthesis of qualitative research in systematic reviews. BMC Med. Res. Methodol. **8**(1), 1–10 (2008)

19. Viviani, L., Guerra, E., Melegati, J., Wang, X.: An empirical study about the instability and uncertainty of non-functional requirements. In: Agile Processes in Software Engineering and Extreme Programming: 24th International Conference on Agile Software Development, XP 2023, Amsterdam, The Netherlands, 13–16 June 2023, Proceedings, vol. 475, p. 77. Springer, Cham (2023)
20. Wirfs-Brock, R., Yoder, J., Guerra, E.: Patterns to develop and evolve architecture during an agile software project. In: Proceedings of the 22nd Conference on Pattern Languages of Programs (2015)
21. Wohlin, C., Runeson, P., Höst, M., Ohlsson, M., Regnell, B., Wesslén, A.: Experimentation in Software Engineering. Springer, Germany (2012)
22. Woods, E., Erder, M., Pureur, P.: Continuous Architecture in Practice: Software Architecture in the Age of Agility and DevOps. Addison-Wesley Professional, Boston (2021)

TD-Suite: All Batteries Included Framework for Technical Debt Classification

Karthik Shivashankar(✉) and Antonio Martini

Department of Informatics, University of Oslo, Oslo, Norway
karths@uio.no

Abstract. In Agile software development, maintaining velocity requires the continuous management of Technical Debt (TD). However, the rapid iteration cycles inherent to Agile often obscure debt accumulation, making manual identification in issue trackers prohibitively expensive. To address this, we present TD-Suite, a comprehensive framework engineered to automate the classification of technical debt. It leverages state-of-the-art transformer models to analyze textual artifacts, such as developer discussions in issue reports, where subtle indicators of debt often lie hidden. TD-Suite provides a seamless end-to-end pipeline suitable for Agile ML Engineering, managing everything from initial data ingestion and rigorous preprocessing to model training, thorough evaluation, and final inference. It supports both binary classification (debt or no debt) and granular categorization—identifying code, architecture, design, or documentation debt—enabling Agile teams to formulate targeted refactoring strategies. To ensure robustness on real-world, imbalanced datasets, TD-Suite incorporates k-fold cross-validation, early stopping, and class weighting strategies. The framework explicitly integrates the tracking and reporting of carbon emissions associated with model training. Furthermore, it features a user-friendly Gradio web interface within a Docker container, simplifying integration into DevOps pipelines and democratizing access for practitioners without deep ML expertise.

1 Introduction

The effective management of Technical Debt (TD) stands as a critical enabler of sustained agility in modern software development. Agile methodologies fundamentally rely on the principle of iterative development and responsiveness to change. However, the accumulated cost of future rework—stemming from expedient, short-term design choices—exerts a significant burden on team velocity and software quality [7]. This phenomenon, metaphorically termed Technical Debt, is not merely a coding concern but a systemic risk that affects architectural stability, documentation quality, and test coverage. As software systems evolve through continuous integration and deployment (CI/CD) pipelines, the manual identification of TD through conventional code reviews and architectural audits

A. Goldman et al. (Eds.): XP 2026, LNBIP 578, pp. 137–151, 2026.
https://doi.org/10.1007/978-3-032-22375-3_9

becomes a bottleneck, hindering the rapid feedback loops that Agile teams rely upon [38].

The challenge is exacerbated in large-scale projects where debt is not explicitly documented in code comments (Self-Admitted Technical Debt or SATD) but is instead buried within the unstructured text of issue trackers, pull request discussions, and commit messages. Identifying these "hidden" debts requires parsing the natural language of developers, a task that static analysis tools are ill-equipped to handle [24]. Consequently, the Agile workflow requires automated, intelligent approaches to make debt visible and manageable without slowing down the development lifecycle.

Recent advancements in machine learning, specifically transformer-based language models like BERT, RoBERTa [12,25], and DeBERTaV3 [17,32], offer promising avenues for automating the detection of TD in software artifacts. These models possess the semantic understanding necessary to distinguish between a feature request and Technical Debt. However, a gap persists between these theoretical advancements and their widespread adoption in industrial Agile environments. Existing tools often lack the seamless integration required for DevOps workflows or require specialized AI expertise that may not be present in all Agile cross-functional teams [13]. Furthermore, the environmental impact of training these large language models is often overlooked, presenting a contradiction to the sustainability goals of modern software engineering.

This paper introduces TD-Suite, a robust framework designed to support Agile process by automating TD classification and 13 distinct types of TD identified in the ontology by Alves et al. [5] from source trackers like GitHub and Jira. The 13 distinct types of Technical Debt are: **Architecture, Build, Code, Defect, Design, Documentation, Infrastructure, People, Process, Requirement, Service, Automation, and Test Debt**. TD-Suite contributes to the field by offering: (1) A modular architecture supporting binary and multi-type debt categorization (code, design, documentation and architecture) to inform backlog prioritization; (2) An automated data processing pipeline compatible with diverse data sources; (3) An advanced training system with cross-validation and imbalance handling to ensure reliability; and (4) Accessible deployment options via Docker and Gradio, facilitating integration into Agile toolchains. Crucially, TD-Suite also integrates carbon emission tracking to decide which model is environmental sustainable.

2 Background

2.1 Transformers for Text Classification

Natural Language Processing (NLP) has undergone a paradigm shift, increasingly relying on machine learning approaches rather than traditional rule-based methods [21] for fundamental tasks like text classification [1]. In this domain, unstructured text is automatically mapped to predefined categorical labels, powering diverse applications ranging from commercial spam filtering [34] and consumer sentiment analysis [28] to niche domain-specific tasks. Within the software engineering domain specifically, this approach is instrumental in identifying Technical Debt (TD) within artifacts such as commit messages, code comments, or issue descriptions [27] by training models on manually curated and labeled examples. However, traditional neural architectures often struggled with the inherent ambiguity of natural language [4] and the computational bottlenecks associated with large data volumes. The introduction of the Transformer architecture marked a significant advancement, overcoming the sequential processing limitations of Recurrent Neural Networks (RNNs) and Long Short-Term Memory (LSTM) networks.

Transformers utilize a self-attention mechanism [42] to effectively weigh the importance of different words relative to one another, capturing long-range contextual dependencies regardless of their distance in the sequence. This capability is particularly vital in software documentation, where technical jargon and references often require broad context for correct interpretation. This architectural innovation facilitated the creation of large Pre-trained Language Models (PLMs) such as BERT [12], which utilize bidirectional training to learn general language understanding from vast, unlabelled text corpora. These powerful PLMs, often democratized through open-source platforms like Hugging Face [44], act as a robust foundation that can be efficiently fine-tuned on smaller, task-specific datasets (e.g., TD-annotated labelled text). This transfer learning approach allows researchers to achieve state-of-the-art performance in classification and other downstream NLP applications [8,18] without the need to train massive models from scratch.

3 Related Work

The systematic detection and classification of technical debt within software projects has been an active research area for over a decade, evolving significantly with advances in software analysis and machine learning [38]. Initial efforts predominantly relied on static code analysis tools and predefined rule-based systems [41], focusing on identifying coding standard violations, detecting specific code smells (e.g., long methods, large classes), or calculating complexity metrics (e.g., cyclomatic complexity). While valuable for localized structural issues, these early methods often lacked contextual understanding, struggled to differentiate intentional design from genuine debt, generated numerous findings requiring manual filtering, and were largely confined to source code analysis, neglecting other crucial information sources like documentation. Consequently, they provided an incomplete picture, often failing to capture systemic or non-code-related debt forms like architectural mismatches or inadequate testing [16].

As machine learning matured, researchers explored its application to technical debt identification, moving beyond simple rule matching [19]. Traditional models like Support Vector Machines (SVMs), Naive Bayes, and Random Forests were trained on labeled datasets (code snippets, commit messages) to predict debt presence or type. These methods improved over static analysis by learning patterns, yet often relied on handcrafted features from text or code metrics, potentially missing complex semantic nuances indicative of certain debt types. Their effectiveness heavily depended on the quality and representativeness of the feature engineering [24,40].

The advent of deep learning, particularly transformer models like BERT and its variants [12], shifted the paradigm in natural language processing and subsequently influenced software engineering research [14].

Research into automated Technical Debt (TD) and Self-Admitted Technical Debt (SATD) identification has progressed from early Natural Language Processing (NLP) techniques for classifying SATD types [26] and N-gram based approaches [43], to exploring word embeddings like Word2Vec [15]. Deep Learning models were subsequently applied, including Convolutional Neural Networks (CNNs) for SATD detection in Infrastructure as Code [31] and alongside Recurrent Neural Networks (RNNs) for analyzing SATD removal [45]. LSTMs were also utilized for SATD type classification [33], and various studies compared traditional ML with DL models like CNNs, RNNs, and LSTMs [3,23,40].Âă

More recently, Transformer architectures have demonstrated strong results; BERT was found effective for TD detection in R package reviews [20], while Transformers have been applied to classify TD [37] and identify TD types [35] in issue trackers, with recent reviews corroborating BERT's effectiveness [29]. This body of work relies on curated datasets derived from sources such as Apache projects [22], R package reviews and code comments [10], and ML software [30].

Surveying the current landscape reveals a fragmented tool ecosystem [2]. Existing solutions often specialize: some in static analysis for code-level debt, others in architectural metrics, and others using NLP on issue trackers or documentation. Few tools offer a holistic approach identifying and classifying multiple debt types (code, design, documentation, test, etc.) in one integrated platform. This fragmentation challenges teams seeking a comprehensive view of project health [35].

Furthermore, critical limitations persist. A primary issue is lacking comprehensive coverage, with most tools targeting only a subset of the technical debt spectrum. Integrating multiple specialized tools is often complex, burdensome, and hinders adoption [13]. Evaluation practices vary considerably; non-standardized datasets and metrics make reliable comparison of tools difficult. Finally, the computational resources and environmental impact (e.g., carbon emissions) of sophisticated models are often overlooked aspects gaining importance for sustainable software development.

4 TD-Suite Framework

The TD-Suite framework is architecturally designed for modularity and extensibility, balancing classification performance with resource efficiency. As illustrated in Fig. 1, the system is organized into interconnected components that manage the technical debt classification workflow from data ingestion to model inference.

The Data Management layer functions as the foundation, handling the ingestion and validation of diverse data formats, including CSVs and Hugging

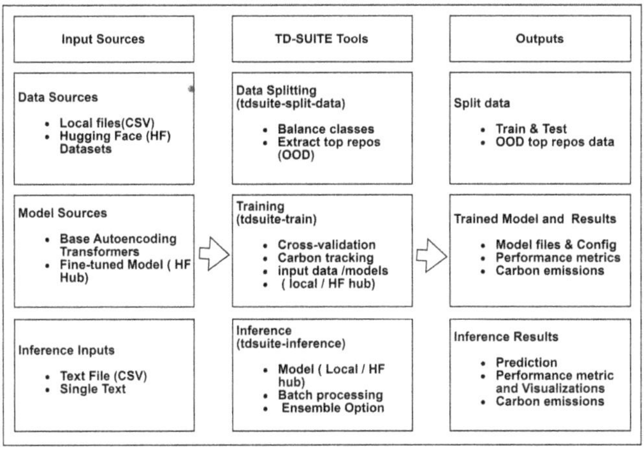

Fig. 1. TD-Suite High level Architecture

Face Datasets. This component manages preprocessing pipelines—encompassing cleaning, normalization, and tokenization—and executes data splitting strategies to prepare optimized dataset objects [11]. Following preparation, the Training Pipeline orchestrates model optimization using the Hugging Face Trainer API [39]. To ensure robustness, this pipeline supports k-fold cross-validation, early stopping to prevent overfitting, and class weighting to address imbalanced data. Crucially, it integrates tracking for computational resource usage and carbon emissions, promoting sustainable model development [6].

Finally, the Inference Engine facilitates the efficient application of trained models. Optimized for scalability, it supports batch processing to classify large volumes of text, handling the full lifecycle of loading checkpoints, preprocessing input, and formatting predictions with confidence scores. The design supports potential extensions for ensemble methods [35]. We have open-sourced this package with comprehensive documentation and evaluation[1].

5 Results

To assess the capabilities of the TD-Suite framework, we executed a comprehensive set of experiments quantifying performance on technical debt classification tasks using SATD GitHub issue datasets [35]. The evaluation measured efficiency and robustness across multiple representative transformer architectures using standardized metrics.

5.1 Experimental Setup

Our evaluation relied on the balanced TD Datasets provided by Shivashankar et al. [35], which encompass diverse debt types such as Code, Documentation,

[1] https://github.com/KarthikShivasankar/text_classification.

Testing, and Architecture, ensuring equal representation of positive and negative classes. We selected four transformer architectures representing the performance-efficiency spectrum: BERT-base-uncased, RoBERTa-base [12,25], the lightweight DistilRoBERTa-base-uncased, and DeBERtav3-base [17,32].

Consistent hyperparameters were applied across experiments: a maximum sequence length of 512 tokens, a batch size of 32, a learning rate of 2e-5, and a training duration of 3 epochs with a 500-step warmup phase. Performance was assessed using accuracy, precision, recall, F1-score, and Matthews's Correlation Coefficient (MCC) on a reserved test set containing data from projects unseen during training. We emphasize MCC as a statistically reliable metric for binary classification [9]:

$$MCC = \frac{TP \cdot TN - FP \cdot FN}{\sqrt{(TP + FP) \cdot (TP + FN) \cdot (TN + FP) \cdot (TN + FN)}}$$

MCC provides a balanced evaluation ranging from -1 to 1, where a score greater than 0 indicates performance better than random chance.

5.2 Data Availability

The replication package is publicly available at Zenodo[2]. The source code and documentation are hosted on GitHub Link. Additionally, the specific models and datasets used are available in Hugging Face collections Link: TD-suite Model Collections Link and TD-suite Dataset Collections Link.

5.3 Performance Metrics Obtained from TD-Suite Framework

Table 1. Comparison of Performance Metrics

Metric	BERT	RoBERTa	DistilRoBERTa	DeBERTaV3
Accuracy	0.8831	0.8827	0.8857	0.8983
Precision	0.9174	0.8254	0.8389	0.8635
Recall	0.8013	0.9236	0.9099	0.9078
F1 Score	0.8554	0.8717	0.8730	0.8851
MCC	0.7630	0.7684	0.7716	0.7947

Table 1 presents a comparison of the performance metrics for the BERT, RoBERTa [12,25], DistilRoBERTa, and DeBERTaV3 models in classifying TD [17,32].

We trained all these model on the train split of the TD datasets [35]. DeBERTaV3 achieves the best overall performance, with the highest accuracy (0.8983),

[2] https://doi.org/10.5281/zenodo.15161451.

precision (0.8635), and F1 score (0.8851). While RoBERTa has the highest recall (0.9236), it lags behind DeBERTaV3 in other metrics. DistilRoBERTa, a distilled version of RoBERTa, shows competitive performance, demonstrating the effectiveness of knowledge distillation in maintaining accuracy while reducing model size. BERT, while still strong, generally exhibits the lowest performance across these metrics. The Matthew's Correlation Coefficient (MCC) further supports these observations, with DeBERTaV3 achieving the highest MCC of 0.7947, indicating superior performance in binary classification . These models trained using TD-Suite perform comparatively better in all classification performance metrics compared to other deep learning models like CNNs, RNNs, and LSTMs [3,23,40] for TD text classification task.

5.4 Resource Usage and Carbon Emissions

Table 2. Comparison of Resource Usage and Carbon Emissions

Parameter	BERT	RoBERTa	DistilRoB.	DeBERTaV3
Inference				
Emissions ($kgCO_2e$)	0.00103	0.00109	0.00059	0.00158
Duration (s)	143.46	151.72	81.99	215.23
Training				
Emissions ($kgCO_2e$)	0.03677	0.03710	0.01904	0.05566
Duration (s)	5140.70	5183.37	2663.26	7674.37

Table 2 provides a comparison of the resource usage and carbon emissions for the four models during both inference and training obtained from TD-Suite framework when Training in the train split and running inference on the test split of the TD Dataset [35]. DistilRoBERTa demonstrates the lowest resource consumption, with the shortest inference duration (81.99 s) and the lowest training emissions (0.01904 $kgCO_2e$). In contrast, DeBERTaV3, while achieving the best performance, exhibits the highest inference duration (215.23 s) and training emissions (0.05566 $kgCO_2e$). BERT and RoBERTa show similar resource usage, with RoBERTa having slightly higher emissions and duration than BERT. These results highlight the trade-off between model performance and computational cost. Distillation, as seen with DistilRoBERTa, offers an effective strategy for reducing resource usage and environmental impact with almost comparable performance as shown in Table 1.

5.5 Identify Different Technical Debt Types

We evaluated the effectiveness of the TD-Suite framework in identifying distinct types of Technical Debt (TD). Specifically, we analyze the performance of DistilRoBERTa binary classification models on a test split unseen during training. We used two stage ensemble approach for classifying specific TD types across four representative categories: Test, Architecture, Code, and Documentation Debt.

Table 3 presents the performance metrics: Recall, Accuracy, and F1 Score alongside the support count for each category.

Table 3. Performance of Binary Classification (DistilRoBERTa) Models on Different Technical Debt Types

Category	Recall	Accuracy	F1	Support
Test	0.825	0.825	0.904	1950
Architecture	0.755	0.755	0.860	49
Code	0.736	0.736	0.848	469
Documentation	0.856	0.856	0.922	528

The type-specific classifiers demonstrate moderate success, with Recall and Accuracy values ranging from 0.736 for Code Debt up to 0.856 for Documentation Debt, and corresponding F1 scores falling between 0.848 and 0.922.

While identifying specific types of technical debt using binary classification is feasible to a reasonable degree, nuanced differences between specific TD types are more challenging for the model to distinguish compared to the broader distinction between the presence and absence of TD.

Given the varying performance of the specific binary classifiers shown in Table 3 and the limitations observed in multi-class classifiers and following the findings from Shivashankar et al. [35] ensemble of two distinct binary classification stages to effectively identify different TD types.

The first stage, **Initial TD Detection**, uses a highly effective general binary classifier. This model acts as a gatekeeper, accurately identifying whether a given software issue or text snippet contains any form of technical debt. Its high recall ensures that the vast majority of TD instances are captured at the outset.

If the first model positively identifies the presence of TD, a second stage is triggered: **Specific TD Type Classification**. This stage employs the specific "Binary types" classifiers, such as those evaluated in Table 3. While these models have lower performance than the general TD detector see Table 1, they are better optimized for pinpointing the specific category—such as Code Debt, Test Debt, or Documentation Debt—than a direct multi-class model would be.

This two-stage ensemble approach offers several distinct advantages. Primarily, it leverages the strengths of both modeling strategies: the high detection accuracy of the general TD model and the type-identification capabilities of the specific models. Furthermore, it circumvents the complexities and poor performance often observed when attempting to make a single model distinguish between many specific TD types simultaneously. By decomposing the problem into two simpler binary classification steps—first determining if it is TD, and then determining which type—the overall classification accuracy and reliability for identifying specific TD types are improved [35].

6 Deployment and Usability Features

Beyond the core classification capabilities and robust implementation, the practical success of a framework like TD-Suite hinges critically on its ease of deployment, accessibility, and overall usability for its intended audience: software engineers and researchers [13,24]. Recognizing this, TD-Suite incorporates several features specifically designed to streamline its integration into development workflows and make its powerful analytical tools readily available to users with potentially varying levels of machine learning expertise. These features span interactive interfaces and easy evaluation and testing of these different TD and its types models on custom datasets.

6.1 Web Interface

TD-Suite includes an interactive web interface built with Gradio, providing a graphical front-end that simplifies model training and evaluation without command-line interaction. It features distinct "Fine-tune Model" and "Evaluate Model" tabs. In the fine-tuning tab, users upload CSV datasets and use controls like sliders to set preprocessing parameters (e.g., train/test split percentage, minimum word length). Processing the CSV handles data loading, cleaning, filtering, splitting, and saving, showing status and a data preview. Users then select a base model and click to fine-tune. The interface displays progress and results, including metrics (accuracy, classification report), a confusion matrix, an annotated data preview, and a download link for the full results.

The "Evaluate Model" tab allows uploading a dataset and selecting one or multiple models via checkboxes. After processing, evaluation begins, potentially using GPU acceleration. The interface displays a preview of the data with predictions from each model and provides a downloadable spreadsheet with the complete evaluation results. This significantly lowers the barrier to entry, enabling rapid experimentation and straightforward model use without coding.

6.2 Containerized Deployment

To simplify setup and handle complex dependencies (like specific library versions and GPU drivers), TD-Suite uses Docker for containerized deployment. The Dockerfile, provided in the Zenodo replication package, defines the configuration. It specifies a base image with CUDA/cuDNN for GPU support, installs system packages, copies the application code, and sets the Gradio web app as the default launch command.

This Docker approach offers key advantages: it ensures a consistent, reproducible runtime environment across different machines, eliminating setup inconsistencies. Dependency management is encapsulated, simplifying setup for end-users who only need Docker installed. This streamlines deployment compared to manual configuration, promoting wider adoption and ensuring reliable operation.

7 Evaluation on Industry Projects

To validate the robustness of our approach, we conducted evaluations on industrial datasets provided by Visma, a multinational software company comprising over 180 entrepreneurial software companies. Visma's unique structure, characterized by high autonomy among its constituent companies and diverse team practices, offers an ideal environment for assessing model performance across a range of project contexts.

We first evaluated our DistilRoBERTa TD fine-tuned model on a dataset consisting of approximately 1,100 Jira issues from six different projects across three countries, with about 400 issues labeled as TD.

Table 4 presents the model's performance before and after fine-tuning with 30% of the Visma dataset. The results show significant improvements across all metrics after fine-tuning. Notably, accuracy increased from 56.8% to 73.7%, and precision from 45.1% to 60.8%. Recall, which is crucial for identifying potential TD issues in environments with inconsistent tagging, remained high at 79.1% and improved slightly to 80.1%.

Table 4. Classification Metrics for Technical Debt Before and After 30% Fine-Tuning with Visma Dataset [35]

Metric	Before Fine-Tuning	After 30% Fine-Tuning
Accuracy	0.568	0.737
Precision	0.451	0.608
Recall	0.791	0.801
F1-Score	0.574	0.691
MCC	0.664	0.707
AUC	0.615	0.750

We further evaluated our fine-tuned Security binary classification model, collaborating with Visma's Chief Software Quality Engineer and a Security Business Analyst [36]. For this evaluation, a dataset comprising of 173 issues from two projects. These issues were initially tagged manually by developers as "NFR" (Non-Functional Requirements). The label of primary interest was "Security". One of the participants, possessing a security background, verified the ground truth by mapping existing labels (including those from automated tools) to the "Security" label.

Table 5 presents the results for this Security test dataset. The Security class exhibits high precision (0.98) but a recall of 0.80. This leads to an F1-score of 0.88. While the model performs reasonably well, the difference between the high precision and the slightly lower recall suggests that the model might be dealing with some ambiguity or overlap between the security and non-security classes within this specific project context.

Table 5. Performance metrics for Security and Non-Security Classes [36]

Class	Precision	Recall	F1-Score	MCC
Non-Security (0)	0.62	0.95	0.75	0.64
Security (1)	0.98	0.80	0.88	

The evaluations presented in this study highlight the individual strengths of our finetuned models in industrial settings. To maximize these capabilities, the comprehensive **TD-Suite** framework incorporates all models used in both the QualiTagger [36] and BEACon-TD [35] . By integrating these approaches, the TD-Suite utilizes datasets trained to identify 13 distinct types of Technical Debt [5], providing a robust, multi-faceted tool for software quality assurance and debt management in diverse development environments.

8 Discussion

8.1 Implications for Agile Practice

The integration of TD-Suite into the Agile lifecycle facilitates a fundamental shift from reactive to proactive debt management, embedding quality assurance directly into the project management workflow. By automatically tagging issues with specific debt categories, the tool provides real-time visibility into the accumulation of debt [7], effectively bridging the communication gap between technical teams and stakeholders. This automated classification reduces the cognitive load on developers, who no longer need to manually categorize every issue, and allows Product Owners to make data-driven decisions during backlog grooming and sprint planning. Furthermore, this continuous monitoring enables longitudinal analysis of project health; for instance, if the tool detects a sudden spike in "Design Debt" tags, the team can statistically justify the allocation of a "refactoring sprint" to address architectural stability before it negatively impacts development velocity [2].

8.2 The Role of Green AI in Software Engineering

Our findings on the carbon footprint of transformer models highlight a critical, yet often overlooked, ethical dimension of deploying AI within Software Engineering workflows. While maximizing predictive accuracy is often the default objective in academic research, the marginal performance gains offered by massive models like DeBERTaV3 may not justify their substantial environmental cost, particularly when deployed in continuous integration environments [13,24]. As these tools are intended to run frequently—potentially on every commit or pull request—the cumulative energy consumption becomes significant. TD-Suite empowers teams to quantify this trade-off between precision and sustainability. We advocate for a "Green AI" approach where computationally efficient models like DistilRoBERTa are the default configuration, and heavier, energy-intensive models are reserved strictly for specific, high-stakes tasks where minor improvements in recall are critical [35].

9 Threats to Validity

Construct Validity: The definition of "Technical Debt" can be subjective. We mitigate this by using datasets labeled by experts, but ambiguity remains in edge cases.
Internal Validity: Hyperparameter tuning was not exhaustive due to computational constraints. It is possible that better configurations exist for specific models. We controlled for randomness using fixed seeds and cross-validation.
External Validity: While we tested on OOD data, the datasets are primarily from Open Source and one industrial partner. Generalization to proprietary, closed-source projects with different domain-specific jargon requires further validation.

10 Conclusion

We introduced TD-Suite, a comprehensive framework that aligns with the themes of sustainability and expanding Agile practices. By leveraging transformer-based language models, TD-Suite automates the classification of technical debt from issue trackers, enabling faster feedback loops. The framework integrates data processing, model training, rigorous evaluation, and sustainable computing practices into a user-friendly, containerized solution. Our results demonstrate that while large models like DeBERTaV3 offer peak accuracy, distilled models like DistilRoBERTa provide a sustainable, high-performance alternative suitable for real-time Agile workflows. This empowers Agile teams to proactively manage debt, shaping a more sustainable and inclusive future for software engineering.

References

1. Aggarwal, C.C., et al.: A survey of text classification algorithms. In: Mining Text Data, pp. 163–222. Springer (2012)
2. Ajibode, A., et al.: Systematic literature review on forecasting and prediction of technical debt evolution. arXiv preprint arXiv:2406.12026 (2024)
3. Alhefdhi, A., et al.: A framework for technical debt identification and description. In: Proceedings of the 17th International Conference on Evaluation of Novel Approaches to Software Engineering (ENASE), pp. 313–320. SciTePress (2022). https://doi.org/10.5220/0011096100003209
4. Allamanis, M., et al.: A survey of machine learning for big code and naturalness. ACM Comput. Surv. (CSUR) **51**(4), 1–37 (2018)
5. Alves, N.S.R., et al.: Towards an ontology of terms on technical debt. In: 2014 Sixth International Workshop on Managing Technical Debt, pp. 1–7. IEEE (2014)

6. Anthony, L.F.W., et al.: Carbontracker: tracking and predicting the carbon footprint of training deep learning models. arXiv preprint arXiv:2007.03051 (2020)
7. Buschmann, F.: To pay or not to pay technical debt. IEEE Softw. **28**(6), 29–31 (2011)
8. Chernyavskiy, A., et al.: Transformers in text classification: a review. In: International Conference on Analysis of Images, Social Networks and Texts, pp. 17–29. Springer (2021)
9. Chicco, D., et al.: The advantages of the Matthews correlation coefficient (MCC) over F1 score and accuracy in binary classification evaluation. BMC Genomics **21**(1), 6 (2020). ISSN: 1471-2164. https://doi.org/10.1186/s12864-019-6413-7. Accessed 21 Feb 2022
10. Codabux, Z., et al.: Technical debt in the peer-review documentation of R packages: a rOpenSci case study. In: Proceedings of the 18th International Conference on Mining Software Repositories (MSR), MSR 2021, pp. 195–206. IEEE (2021). https://doi.org/10.1109/MSR52588.2021.00032
11. Datasets. https://huggingface.co/docs/datasets/en/index. Accessed 24 Aug 2024
12. Devlin, J., et al.: Bert: pre-training of deep bidirectional transformers for language understanding. In: Proceedings of the 2019 Conference of the North American chapter of the Association for Computational Linguistics: Human Language Technologies, vol. 1 (Long and Short Papers), pp. 4171–4186 (2019)
13. Ernst, N., et al.: Technical Debt in Practice: How to Find It and Fix It. MIT Press (2021)
14. Feng, Z., et al.: Codebert: a pre-trained model for programming and natural languages. arXiv preprint arXiv:2002.08155 (2020)
15. Flisar, J., et al.: Detecting self-admitted technical debt using word embeddings. In: Proceedings of the 13th International Conference on Software Technologies (ICSOFT 2018), pp. 591–598. SciTePress (2018). https://doi.org/10.5220/0006899705910598
16. Gu, H., et al.: Self-admitted technical debts identification: how far are we? In: 2024 IEEE International Conference on Software Analysis, Evolution and Reengineering (SANER), pp. 804–815. IEEE (2024)
17. He, P., et al.: DeBERTaV3: improving DeBERTa using ELECTRA-style pre-training with gradient-disentangled embedding sharing. In: The Eleventh International Conference on Learning Representations (2023)
18. Howard, J., et al.: Universal language model fine-tuning for text classification. In: Proceedings of the 56th Annual Meeting of the Association for Computational Linguistics (Volume 1: Long Papers), pp. 328–339 (2018)
19. Huang, Q., et al.: Identifying self-admitted technical debt in open source projects using text mining. Empirical Softw. Eng. **23**(1), 418–451 (2018). https://doi.org/10.1007/s10664-017-9522-1
20. Khan, J.Y., et al.: Automatic Detection and Analysis of Technical Debts in Peer-Review Documentation of R Packages. arXiv preprint arXiv:2201.04241 (2022). arXiv:2201.04241 [cs.SE]
21. Kowsari, K., et al.: Text classification algorithms: a survey. Information **10**(4), 150 (2019)
22. Lenarduzzi, V., et al.: The technical debt dataset. In: Proceedings of the 15th International Conference on Predictive Models and Data Analytics in Software Engineering (PROMISE 2019). PROMISE 2019, pp. 64–73. ACM (2019). https://doi.org/10.1145/3345629.3345630

23. Li, J., et al.: Identifying self-admitted technical debt in issue tracking systems using text classification. In: Proceedings of the 30th IEEE International Conference on Software Analysis, Evolution and Reengineering (SANER), pp. 634–645. IEEE (2023). https://doi.org/10.1109/SANER56736.2023.00066
24. Li, Z., et al.: A systematic mapping study on technical debt and its management. J. Syst. Softw. **101**, 193–220 (2015). https://doi.org/10.1016/j.jss.2014.12.027
25. Liu, Y., et al.: RoBERTa: A Robustly Optimized BERT Pretraining Approach (2020)
26. Maldonado, E.C., et al.: Detecting and characterizing architectural roots from self-admitted technical debt. In: 2017 IEEE International Conference on Software Architecture (ICSA), pp. 161–170 (2017). https://doi.org/10.1109/ICSA.2017.16
27. Maldonado, E., et al.: Detecting and classifying self-admitted technical debt in source code comments. In: 2017 IEEE 24th International Conference on Software Analysis, Evolution and Reengineering (SANER), pp. 174–184. IEEE (2017)
28. Medhat, W., et al.: Sentiment analysis algorithms and applications: a survey. Ain Shams Eng. J. **5**(4), 1093–1113 (2014)
29. Melin, E.L., et al.: Exploring the advances in using machine learning to identify technical debt and self-admitted technical debt. In: Proceedings of the 1st International Workshop on AI Engineering - Software Engineering for AI (WAIN). WAIN 2024, pp. 139–143. ACM (2024). https://doi.org/10.1145/3644673.3644817
30. OBrien, D., et al.: 23 shades of self-admitted technical debt: an empirical study on machine learning software. In: Proceedings of the 30th ACM Joint European Software Engineering Conference and Symposium on the Foundations of Software Engineering (ESEC/FSE 2022). ESEC/FSE 2022, pp. 734–746. ACM (2022). https://doi.org/10.1145/3540250.3549088
31. Ren, X., et al.: Characterizing and identifying self-admitted technical debt in infrastructure as code. In: Proceedings of the 34th IEEE/ACM International Conference on Automated Software Engineering (ASE). ASE 2019, pp. 617–629. IEEE Press (2019). https://doi.org/10.1109/ASE.2019.00062
32. Sanh, V., et al.: DistilBERT, a distilled version of BERT: smaller, faster, cheaper and lighter. arXiv preprint arXiv:1910.01108 (2019)
33. Santos, G., et al.: Identifying requirement and design self-admitted technical debt using recurrent neural networks. In: Proceedings of the 36th International Conference on Software Maintenance and Evolution (ICSME), pp. 669–673. IEEE (2020). https://doi.org/10.1109/ICSME46990.2020.00068
34. Sharma, H., et al.: A comparative analysis of machine learning algorithms for email spam detection. Cybern. Inf. Technol. **23**(1), 151–166 (2023)
35. Shivashankar, K., et al.: BEACon-TD: classifying technical debt and its types across diverse software projects issues using transformers. J. Syst. Softw. 112435 (2025)
36. Shivashankar, K., et al.: QualiTagger: automating software quality detection in issue trackers. arXiv preprint arXiv:2504.11053 (2025)
37. Skryseth, D., et al.: Technical debt classification in issue trackers using natural language processing based on transformers. In: Proceedings of the 2023 ACM/IEEE International Conference on Technical Debt (TechDebt). TechDebt 2023, pp. 92–101. IEEE (2023)
38. Sutoyo, E., et al.: Self-admitted technical debt detection approaches: a decade systematic review. arXiv preprint arXiv:2312.15020 (2023)
39. Transformers. https://huggingface.co/docs/transformers/en/index. Accessed 13 Apr 2025

40. Tsoukalas, D., et al.: Predicting technical debt prone modules using machine learning. In: Proceedings of the 25th International Conference on Evaluation and Assessment in Software Engineering (EASE 2021). EASE 2021, pp. 11–20. ACM (2021). https://doi.org/10.1145/3463274.3463326
41. Tufano, M., et al.: An empirical study on developer-related factors characterizing fix-inducing commits. J. Softw. Evol. Process **29**(1), e1797 (2017)
42. Vaswani, A., et al.: Attention is all you need. In: Advances in Neural Information Processing Systems, vol. 30 (2017)
43. Wattanakriengkrai, S., et al.: Identifying design and requirement self-admitted technical debt using N-gram IDF. In: 2018 IEEE International Conference on Software Maintenance and Evolution (ICSME), pp. 529–533 (2018). https://doi.org/10.1109/ICSME.2018.00063
44. Wolf, T., et al.: Huggingface's transformers: state-of-the-art natural language processing. In: Proceedings of the 2020 Conference on Empirical Methods in Natural Language Processing: System Demonstrations, pp. 38–45 (2019)
45. Zampetti, F., et al.: Recommend me an action! Classifying and recommending SATD removal strategies. In: Proceedings of the 28th International Conference on Program Comprehension (ICPC 2020). ICPC 2020, pp. 35–46. ACM (2020). https://doi.org/10.1145/3387904.3389149

AI Augmented Software Engineering

Evaluating the Quality of User Stories: An Extended Comparative Study of Multiple LLMs and Rule-Based Tools

Izabella Silva(✉), João Paiva, Mirko Perkusich, Danyllo Albuquerque, Emanuel Dantas, Kyller Gorgônio, and Angelo Perkusich

VIRTUS Research, Development and Innovation Center, Federal University of Campina Grande, Campina Grande, PB 58429-900, Brazil
{izabella.silva,joao.paiva,mirko,danyllo.albuquerque, emanuel.dantas,kyller,perkusich}@virtus.ufcg.edu.br

Abstract. Background: Ensuring the quality of user stories is vital to Agile Software Development. Rule-based tools like AQUSA, based on the Quality User Story (QUS) framework, offer reliable structural checks but struggle with context-sensitive or pragmatic issues. Large Language Models (LLMs) have emerged as potential alternatives, yet prior studies often rely on small datasets, older models, or lack direct comparison with rule-based baselines. **Objective:** This study aims to assess the effectiveness of modern LLMs relative to a rule-based tool (AQUSA) for detecting defects in user stories, considering both structural and contextual dimensions. **Method:** We conduct a large-scale comparative evaluation involving AQUSA and three GPT-family LLMs (GPT-5, GPT-5-mini, and GPT-4), using 182 user stories drawn from three industrial datasets. We apply both quantitative metrics (precision, recall, F1-score) and qualitative analysis of feedback clarity and defect relevance. **Results:** GPT-5-mini achieved the highest recall (0.81) and overall F1-score (0.62), while AQUSA attained the highest precision (0.61) with significantly fewer false positives. GPT-5 showed high hallucination rates and instability; GPT-4 was overly conservative, leading to under-detection of defects. **Conclusion:** Neither rule-based nor GPT-family LLM-based approaches suffice in isolation. Rule-based tools enforce structural rigor, while LLMs capture nuanced linguistic and pragmatic flaws. We advocate a hybrid "Dual-gate" strategy—using AQUSA for structural validation followed by lightweight LLMs for contextual refinement—to improve the reliability and scalability of user story quality assessment in agile environments.

Keywords: User Stories · Quality Assessment · Agile Requirements Engineering · Prompt Engineering · Large Language Models · AQUSA Tool · QUS Framework

1 Introduction

In Agile Software Development, user stories are the dominant format for capturing and communicating requirements [5]. Typically written as "As a ⟨role⟩, I

A. Goldman et al. (Eds.): XP 2026, LNBIP 578, pp. 155–174, 2026.
https://doi.org/10.1007/978-3-032-22375-3_10

want ⟨feature⟩ so that ⟨benefit⟩," they facilitate shared understanding between technical teams and business stakeholders [8]. Despite their simplicity, user stories are prone to quality issues. Prior research shows that vague, inconsistent, or incomplete stories introduce ambiguity, misalignment, and rework—factors that jeopardize project outcomes [2].

To address these concerns, Lucassen et al. proposed the Quality User Story (QUS) framework [6], which classifies quality into syntactic, semantic, and pragmatic dimensions. AQUSA (Automatic Quality User Story Artisan), a rule-based tool built on this framework, uses natural language processing to detect structural defects. While AQUSA offers deterministic and reproducible feedback, its reliance on handcrafted rules limits its ability to identify subtle context-dependent, pragmatic, or semantic defects. [4].

Recent progress in Large Language Models (LLMs) has created new opportunities in Requirements Engineering [15] and broader Intelligent Software Engineering [10]. Models in the GPT family exhibit strong capabilities in natural-language understanding, critique, and reformulation [1,19], motivating empirical studies on their use for user story analysis. For example, Ronanki et al. [13] examined ChatGPT's ability to detect QUS violations and found good alignment with human judgment, though concerns about inconsistency and overgeneralization remained.

More recently, Sharma and Tripathi [14] benchmarked GPT-3.5-Turbo, GPT-4-Turbo, and GPT-4o on user story defect detection, reporting strong performance on syntactic and pragmatic criteria but persistent difficulty with semantic aspects. However, most existing studies rely on earlier LLM generations, omit qualitative feedback analysis, or do not include direct comparisons with rule-based baselines such as AQUSA.

This study expands the empirical evidence by benchmarking AQUSA against three recent GPT models—GPT-5, GPT-5-mini, and GPT-4—using 182 user stories from three industrial projects. Unlike our earlier pilot study, which included DeepSeek on a small dataset, the present work focuses on a controlled, large-scale comparison within a single model family to isolate the effects of architectural scale and optimization. Our evaluation uses QUS-aligned prompts and expert validation to establish ground truth. In addition to quantitative metrics, we assess the clarity, contextual relevance, and actionability of the feedback each tool provides. Throughout this paper, empirical claims are therefore restricted to the evaluated GPT-family models; while these models are widely adopted as commercial baselines in Software Engineering research, they represent only a subset of the broader LLM ecosystem, and the findings should not be generalized to all large language models.

Our contributions are:

- A scalable methodology for benchmarking user story quality using recent LLMs and a rule-based baseline.
- A comparative analysis of AQUSA, GPT-5, GPT-5-mini, and GPT-4 on defect coverage and expert agreement across 182 real-world user stories.

- A qualitative assessment of feedback clarity, contextual grounding, and failure modes, highlighting the strengths and limitations of rule-based and generative approaches.
- Empirical support for a hybrid "Dual-gate" strategy: using rule-based tools for structural validation and LLMs for pragmatic refinement under human supervision.

The remainder of this paper is organized as follows: Sect. 2 reviews user story quality assessment. Section 3 details the methodology, datasets, and prompting strategy. Section 4 presents and discusses the results. Section 5 explores implications for practice. Section 6 outlines threats to validity, and Sect. 7 concludes with directions for future work.

2 Background and Related Work

This section introduces the theoretical foundations of user story quality and reviews recent advances in applying LLMs to RE, with a focus on user story quality assessment.

User Story Quality and the QUS Framework. The Quality User Story (QUS) framework, proposed by Lucassen et al. [6], defines thirteen quality criteria for user stories, organized along Lindland's three dimensions of model quality: *syntactic* (textual structure independent of meaning), *semantic* (relations and meaning among components), and *pragmatic* (interpretation by the audience). QUS differentiates criteria that apply to individual stories—such as *well-formed* (includes role and means), *atomic* (one feature only), *minimal* (includes only role/means/ends), *conceptually sound*, *problem-oriented*, *unambiguous*, *full sentence*, and *estimatable*—from those that apply across a set of stories, such as *unique*, *conflict-free*, *uniform*, *independent*, and *complete*. These inter-story criteria are grounded in formal relationships like semantic duplication, superclass/-supertype overlap, and dependency chains, providing a rigorous basis for backlog evaluation.

To operationalize QUS, Lucassen et al. developed AQUSA, a rule-based tool that uses natural language processing heuristics and predefined patterns to detect violations of a subset of these criteria [6]. AQUSA is most effective for well-defined syntactic and formatting-related pragmatic issues. It reliably flags missing roles or actions, non-atomic stories, violations of the "roleâĂŞmeansâĂŞend" structure, inconsistent formats, and duplicate entries within a backlog. However, as Lucassen et al. note, AQUSA's handcrafted rules struggle with context-dependent criteria—such as *unambiguous*, *estimatable*, *independent*, and *complete*—which require domain knowledge or subtle semantic interpretation. This limitation shapes our study design: we focus on the five QUS criteria that AQUSA is reported to support—three syntactic (*well-formed*, *atomic*, *minimal*) and two pragmatic (*uniform*, *unique*).

LLMs and User Story Evaluation. LLMs have recently been applied across a range of RE tasks, including elicitation, analysis, refinement, and formalisation [3,7,11,16]. While this broader literature demonstrates the expanding role of LLMs in processing natural-language requirements, the most relevant subset of work targets user story evaluation and improvement.

Early studies explored LLM support for user story refinement. Zhang et al. [19] used agent-based prompting to generate QUS-aligned feedback. Arora et al. [1] and Vogelsang et al. [15] examined LLM-based rewriting and classification, emphasizing ambiguity reduction and stakeholder clarity. Yamani et al. [18] contributed the UStAI dataset by generating user stories from academic abstracts; the dataset was validated using QUS criteria and has been reused in subsequent studies.

Three studies are especially aligned with our research question on comparing LLM-based and rule-based evaluation under QUS-like standards. Ronanki et al. [13] evaluated ChatGPT (GPT-3.5) and AQUSA on 11 user stories, finding ChatGPT more consistent with human judgment but variable across runs. Sharma and Tripathi [14] benchmarked GPT-3.5-Turbo, GPT-4-Turbo, and GPT-4o on 960 synthetic and human-validated stories. They reported strong performance on syntactic and pragmatic criteria—especially for GPT-4o—but consistent difficulty with semantic aspects like ambiguity. Notably, their study did not compare against AQUSA or any rule-based baseline.

In our prior work [9], we conducted a small-sample comparison between AQUSA and the DeepSeek LLM using the original QUS validation set of 15 user stories. Both approaches achieved similar F1-scores, but differed in their strengths: AQUSA showed higher precision for structural issues, while the LLM provided richer pragmatic feedback. However, the limited dataset size and the use of an earlier-generation model restricted the generalizability of the findings.

The present study is explicitly designed as a replication-and-extension of that work. We substantially increase the empirical basis (from 15 to 182 real industrial user stories), evaluate a new generation of commercial LLMs (GPT-4, GPT-5, and GPT-5-mini), and introduce additional analytical dimensions that were not feasible at small scale. In particular, the larger dataset enables the observation of systematic model-level phenomena—such as the performance trade-off between frontier and optimized models—and supports a qualitative analysis of feedback usefulness and failure modes. Together, these extensions provide new evidence that goes beyond confirming prior results and strengthens their external validity.

Together, these studies suggest that (i) modern LLMs are increasingly competitive with rule-based tools for user story quality assessment; (ii) syntactic criteria remain more accessible to LLMs than semantic ones; and (iii) comparisons between LLMs and tools like AQUSA remain limited, often constrained by small samples or outdated models. This motivates our study: a broader, more systematic comparison using recent GPT-family models and a larger, more diverse dataset of real user stories.

3 Research Design

This study investigates how a traditional rule-based tool (AQUSA) compares with three GPT-family models (GPT-4, GPT-5, and GPT-5-mini) in detecting user story quality defects. The decision to focus exclusively on the GPT family was made to ensure architectural consistency and experimental control, enabling a direct comparison between frontier and optimized variants under identical prompting and execution conditions.

To ensure measurement equivalence, we restrict our analysis to the five high-level QUS criteria that AQUSA is reported to support: three syntactic factors (*well-formed*, *atomic*, *minimal*) and two pragmatic ones (*uniform*, *unique*). This restriction is a deliberate methodological choice to enable a fair, like-for-like comparison with a rule-based baseline. Rather than favoring AQUSA, it creates a conservative evaluation setting in which LLMs are assessed precisely on the criteria where handcrafted rules are expected to perform best.

For operational purposes, two of these criteria (*well-formed* and *minimal*) are decomposed into more fine-grained defect types in the prompt, resulting in seven operational defect types used during LLM evaluation.

We address the following research questions:

RQ1: How do AQUSA and GPT-family LLMs (GPT-4, GPT-5, GPT-5-mini) compare in detecting user story defects under the five supported QUS criteria?
RQ2: How does the clarity and usefulness of the feedback produced by AQUSA compare to that produced by the LLMs?

To answer these questions, we followed the five-step process shown in Fig. 1 and described below.

Step 1: Selection of User Stories. We used the benchmark dataset of Robeer et al. [12], which contains 28 curated groups of real-world user stories drawn from industrial and open-source contexts. Each group represents a coherent product backlog from a distinct system or organizational setting.

We selected Groups 13, 21, and 28, yielding 182 user stories. These were chosen to maximize variation in domain, writing style, structural quality, and historical context—key dimensions for evaluating defect-detection performance. The groups are summarized as follows:

- **Group 13—PlanningPoker (53 stories):** Early-stage backlog for a collaborative estimation tool.
- **Group 21—BADCamp (69 stories):** User stories from a conference website GitHub repository.
- **Group 28—Zooniverse/MICO (60 stories):** Requirements from the EU-funded MICO project, covering research and media platforms.

Each group was treated as an independent product backlog in both AQUSA and LLM evaluations, preserving contextual integrity.

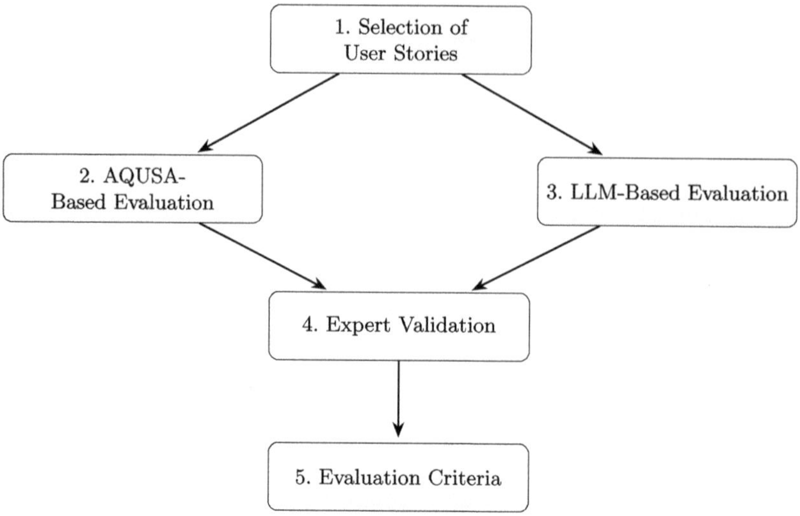

Fig. 1. Research design workflow.

Step 2: AQUSA-Based Evaluation. AQUSA [6] was run separately on each group. It analyzes stories using rule-based QUS patterns and outputs a plain-text list of defects, each labeled with a QUS code and an explanatory message. For example:

```
minimal.indicator_repetition  Message: As a moderator, I want to add
an item to the list of items to be estimated, [* so that *] [* so *] that
we can be flexible and accommodate situations where we think of a new
story while playing.
```

In AQUSA outputs, the notation [* ... *] is used to mark the exact token sequence identified as problematic; in this example, the second occurrence of the benefit indicator ("so that") is highlighted to signal syntactic repetition.

We converted AQUSA's output into a structured spreadsheet, with one row per defect and columns for story ID, defect type, and feedback message. This transformation preserved all defect content and only normalized the format for analysis.

Step 3: LLM-Based Evaluation. The same 182 user stories were processed using GPT-4, GPT-5, and GPT-5-mini via the OpenAI API (November 26âĂŞ27, 2025), with `temperature = 0` to ensure deterministic outputs and reproducibility. This configuration is standard in classification-oriented benchmarking, as it minimizes stochastic variation and ensures that observed differences across models can be attributed to their intrinsic behavior rather than sampling randomness. Each model was run once per group-level backlog, mirroring AQUSA's evaluation scope.

We used a shared instruction prompt that incorporates two key prompting strategies: *few-shot prompting*, through embedded examples for each QUS criterion, and *chain-of-thought prompting*, via explicit stepwise instructions for evaluating individual stories and cross-story comparisons. The prompt required the model to (i) evaluate each story against five QUS criteria, (ii) detect duplicates and format inconsistencies across the backlog, and (iii) return structured JSON output reporting each defect and an aggregate summary.

Due to space constraints, only the prompt's high-level structure is shown below; the full version is available in the Supplementary Material[1]. The supplementary repository also includes a mapping between the seven operational defect types used in the prompt and their corresponding five high-level QUS criteria, ensuring conceptual consistency between the methodology and the evaluation.

LLM Prompt Skeleton

System: You will serve as a quality analyzer for user stories based on the QUS Framework, focusing on five high-level QUS criteria, operationalized through seven specific defect types for evaluation.

- **QUS Framework Definition:** Defines 5 QUS criteria (3 syntactic, 2 pragmatic) and assigns each a defect code
- **Few-Shot Examples:** Each criterion is illustrated with a realistic user story and a corresponding annotated correction. These examples teach the model how to classify and format outputs.
- **Analysis Instructions:**
  - Evaluate each story individually (syntactic/pragmatic criteria).
- **Output Specification:** Requires a strict JSON object with two keys:
  - `"defects"` — list of defect objects, each containing:
  - `"summary"` — totals for `total_stories`, `total_defects`, and a count per defect type.

Step 4: Expert Validation. To construct the ground truth, one expert in Agile Software Development and the QUS framework reviewed all outputs. Each defect reported by AQUSA or the LLMs was validated as a true or false positive. The expert also manually inspected all stories to identify any missed defects (false negatives).

Because the analyzed QUS criteria are deterministic or low-ambiguity, the task involved minimal subjectivity. A single expert was therefore considered adequate.

Step 5: Evaluation Criteria. We compared AQUSA and the LLMs using four evaluation perspectives:

[1] https://github.com/izabellaribeiro/xp-llm-quality.git.

1. **Defect count**—total defects per story, per group, and overall.
2. **Defect type distribution**—coverage across the five QUS criteria.
3. **Overlap and divergence**—shared versus uniquely detected defects.
4. **Feedback quality**—qualitative assessment of clarity, specificity, and actionability, evaluated using a structured feedback evaluation rubric (provided in the Supplementary Material) derived from prior QUS-based studies.

Quantitative accuracy was assessed using precision, recall, and F1-score, computed against the expert-confirmed ground truth. Precision is defined as the proportion of detected defects that were confirmed as valid (TP/(TP + FP)), recall as the proportion of valid defects that were successfully detected (TP/(TP + FN)), and F1-score as the harmonic mean of precision and recall. These metrics are standard in defect detection and classification tasks and were computed for each tool.

All scripts, prompt templates, raw model outputs, and validated defect annotations produced by AQUSA and the LLMs are publicly available in the Supplementary Material, enabling full replication, independent assessment of prompt adequacy, and verification of the evaluation pipeline.

4 Results and Discussion

This section presents the results of our comparative evaluation of AQUSA and three state-of-the-art GPT-family LLMs (GPT-4, GPT-5, and GPT-5-mini), structured around the research questions introduced in Sect. 3. For each question, we report quantitative findings followed by qualitative analysis. Section 4.3 then situates our results within the context of related work.

4.1 RQ1: How Do AQUSA and GPT-Family LLMs (GPT-4, GPT-5, GPT-5-Mini) Compare in Detecting User Story Defects Under the Five Supported QUS Criteria?

To address RQ1, we compared the defect-detection accuracy of all tools across the 182 User Stories using the expert-validated ground truth. This analysis covers Perspective 1 (Defect Count), Perspective 2 (Defect Type Distribution), and Perspective 3 (Overlap and Divergence), as defined in Step 5 of the research design. We report true positives (TP), false positives (FP), false negatives (FN), and the derived precision, recall, and F1-score for each dataset group and in aggregate. All quantitative results are reported at the level of the five high-level QUS criteria supported by AQUSA, with operational defect types internally aggregated to their corresponding criteria. Table 1 summarizes the results and enables inspection of performance trends. The results reveal big and consistent differences among tools, both in aggregate and within dataset groups. Below, we describe these patterns in detail, grounded in the numeric evidence.

To better understand where these differences originate, we further analyzed the per-criterion performance of the best-performing LLM (GPT-5-mini) across

Table 1. Performance of AQUSA and LLMs Across All Dataset Groups (N=182). Green = best values, Yellow = mid-range, Red = poor.

Group	Model	TP	FP	FN	Precision	Recall	F1
Group 13	AQUSA	4	2	1	0.67	0.80	0.73
	GPT-5-mini	3	3	2	0.50	0.60	0.55
	GPT-4	1	0	4	1.00	0.20	0.33
	GPT-5	3	17	2	0.15	0.60	0.24
Group 21	AQUSA	10	6	34	0.63	0.23	0.33
	GPT-5-mini	39	43	5	0.48	0.89	0.62
	GPT-4	1	4	43	0.20	0.02	0.04
	GPT-5	13	7	31	0.65	0.30	0.41
Group 28	AQUSA	10	7	4	0.59	0.71	0.64
	GPT-5-mini	9	4	5	0.69	0.64	0.66
	GPT-4	0	0	14	0.00	0.00	0.00
	GPT-5	14	61	3	0.19	0.82	0.30
Aggregate	AQUSA	24	15	39	0.61	0.38	0.47
	GPT-5-mini	51	50	12	0.50	0.81	0.62
	GPT-4	2	4	61	0.33	0.03	0.05
	GPT-5	30	85	36	0.26	0.45	0.33

the five supported QUS criteria. Table 2 reports precision, recall, and F1-score broken down by defect type, illustrating how GPT-5-mini behaves across different quality criteria.

Table 2. Per-criterion performance of GPT-5-mini.

Criterion	Precision	Recall	F1
Well-formed	0.60	1.00	0.75
Atomic	0.75	0.60	0.67
Minimal	1.00	1.00	1.00
Uniform	0.40	0.90	0.55
Unique	0.00	0.00	0.00

The per-criterion analysis, when interpreted alongside the aggregated results in Table 1, reveals clear specialization patterns. AQUSA consistently achieves higher precision on syntactic criteria such as *well-formed* and *minimal*, reflecting the strengths of its handcrafted rules.

Aggregate Effectiveness. Across all datasets, GPT-5-mini achieved the highest overall F1-score (0.62), driven by the highest recall (0.81) and moderate precision (0.50). It correctly identified 51 valid defects—more than twice AQUSA's 24—and missed only 12, compared to AQUSA's 39. AQUSA attained the highest precision (0.61) but substantially lower recall (0.38), resulting in an F1-score of 0.47. Its false-negative count indicates that many defects, particularly pragmatic ones, lie outside the scope of its rule base. GPT-5 exhibited high recall (0.45) but very low precision (0.26), with an exceptionally large number of false positives (85). GPT-4 performed the worst, with an F1-score of 0.05, detecting only 2 true defects and missing 61.

Group-Level Analysis. A group-wise breakdown provides further insight:

Group 13 (Shorter, Structurally Straightforward Stories). AQUSA obtained the best performance in this subset (F1 = 0.73), with only one false negative. GPT-5-mini performed moderately (F1 = 0.55). GPT-4 detected almost no defects (F1 = 0.33), and GPT-5 generated 17 false positives for only 3 true positives.

Group 21 (Largest and Most Defect-Prone Dataset). GPT-5-mini again performed best (F1 = 0.62), identifying 39 valid defects and missing only 5. AQUSA struggled (F1 = 0.33), missing 34 valid defects. GPT-5 produced 43 false positives, and GPT-4 failed to detect most issues (1 true positive, 43 false negatives).

Group 28 (More Homogeneous Set with Moderate Defect Density). AQUSA and GPT-5-mini achieved similar performance (F1 = 0.64 and 0.66, respectively). GPT-5 had high recall (0.82) but produced 61 false positives. GPT-4 detected no defects in this group.

While the group-level analysis highlights overall performance differences, a finer-grained understanding requires examining how each tool behaves across datasets with varying defect density and linguistic variability. In particular, Group 21 contains the highest concentration of pragmatic and context-dependent issues, which increases both false positives (template-driven critiques) and false negatives (missed subtle defects), making it a harder and more realistic benchmark than small curated sets.

Perspective 2: Defect-Type Distribution. Although the study focuses only on the five QUS-related factors supported by AQUSA, clear patterns emerged across tools and defect types.

First, AQUSA performed best on syntactic defects (for example, missing or malformed roles and actions, repeated indicators, basic atomicity violations) and on formatting-based pragmatic defects (uniformity issues). These are precisely the kinds of patterns encoded in its rule base and explain its strong performance in Group 13 and its competitive results in Group 28.

Second, GPT-5-mini was more effective in detecting pragmatic defects that require semantic and contextual interpretation. A representative case is US#53 in Group 21 (beginning with 'As a Mike, I want to..."), which was confirmed by the expert as a *well_formed.no_role* violation. While the story is syntactically well-formed, the actor is a proper name rather than a stakeholder role. AQUSA did not flag this issue because it treats the sentence as structurally valid, whereas GPT-5-mini was able to recognize that "Mike" is unlikely to denote a generic role in the domain context. This type of semantic anomaly helps to explain why GPT-5-mini achieves much higher recall in Group 21.

Third, the LLMs exhibited characteristic failure modes. GPT-5 in particular tended to over-generalize ambiguity and granularity issues: in several cases it flagged user stories that the expert judged as acceptable, often because they deviated from an "idealized" template, inflating false-positive counts (especially in Groups 21 and 28). GPT-4, in contrast, adopted a highly conservative stance, rarely flagging pragmatic defects unless there was an explicit structural cue, which explains its very low recall.

Perspective 3: Overlap and Divergence. Across the dataset, AQUSA and the GPT-family models exhibited limited overlap in the defects they identified. AQUSA primarily detected syntactic and formatting-related issues, whereas GPT-5-mini uncovered a substantial number of pragmatic defects that were systematically missed by the rule-based approach. This asymmetric overlap indicates that the tools fail in different ways—AQUSA by omission and LLMs by over-classification—highlighting their complementary detection profiles.

Overall, these patterns suggest that AQUSA and GPT-5-mini have complementary strengths and weaknesses.

4.2 RQ2: How Does the Clarity and Usefulness of the Feedback Produced by AQUSA Compare to that Produced by the LLMs?

The second research question addresses Perspective 4 (Feedback Quality), focusing on the nature of the feedback produced by each tool and its usefulness for practitioners who need to refine User Stories. The qualitative findings reported in this section are based on a structured feedback evaluation rubric (see Supplementary Material), which assesses clarity, specificity, and actionability.

Based on the structured rubric evaluation, AQUSA provides deterministic, pattern-based feedback that scores high on clarity but lower on actionability. For each detected violation, it returns the defect type and highlights the offending fragment, sometimes accompanied by short generic suggestions embedded in its rule base. For example, in US#6 from Group 13 ("As a moderator, I want to add an item to the list of items to be estimated, so that so that we can be flexible and accommodate situations where we think of a new story while playing."), AQUSA correctly identified a *minimal.indicator_repetition* defect and returned a literal highlight of the repeated indicator:

As a moderator, I want to add an item..., [* so that *] [* so *] that we can be flexible...

This style is precise and reproducible, but it offers limited guidance beyond pointing to the problematic token. The user still needs to decide how to rewrite the story to resolve the issue.

In contrast, the LLMs—particularly GPT-5-mini—tended to produce more explicit and actionable reformulations. For the same story, GPT-5-mini not only flagged the repetition but also suggested a concrete correction:

> Remove the repeated indicator phrase by changing "so that so that we can be flexible..." to "so that we can be flexible and accommodate situations where we think of a new story while playing."

Across the dataset, GPT-5-mini frequently offered short rewrites, clarified the intended meaning when roles or goals were ambiguous, and proposed alternative role names grounded in typical agile terminology (for example, suggesting "product owner", "admin", or "stakeholder" instead of a person's name). In the case of US#53 ("As a Mike..."), for instance, the model not only flagged the invalid role but also recommended replacing the personal name with a meaningful role, which reduces the cognitive effort required from the practitioner.

Taken together, the rubric-based qualitative analysis indicates that AQUSA consistently scores higher on clarity, due to its deterministic and token-level feedback, while GPT-5-mini scores higher on specificity and actionability by providing concrete reformulation suggestions. AQUSA offers shallow but stable feedback tightly aligned with its rule base, whereas GPT-5-mini provides deeper and more actionable guidance that supports the immediate refinement of User Stories, at the cost of occasional speculative justification and stylistic bias. In a few cases, this manifested as *prompt contamination*, where the model's explanation echoed patterns from the prompt examples rather than the story itself, resulting in off-topic rationale.

4.3 Comparison with Previous Studies

Three prior studies have investigated LLM-based User Story quality evaluation with goals similar to ours: Ronanki et al. [13], Sharma and Tripathi [14], and our earlier work [9]. The findings of the present study both reinforce and extend insights from these investigations.

Ronanki et al. [13]**.** Ronanki et al. evaluated the March 2023 release of ChatGPT (GPT-3.5) on a sample of eleven User Stories, comparing its assessments against AQUSA and human reviewers. They reported that ChatGPT aligned more closely with human judgments than AQUSA, while also noting substantial instability across runs. Our results corroborate two of their conclusions: (i) modern LLMs exhibit broader semantic coverage than AQUSA, and (ii) variability persists, though at a markedly reduced level in GPT-5 and GPT-5-mini. However, using a considerably larger and more diverse dataset (182 real User Stories), we observe that the alignment between LLMs and human expectations is less consistent than originally suggested. State-of-the-art models outperform

AQUSA in recall but sometimes introduce false positives and occasionally hallucinate defects. These issues were only anecdotally mentioned by Ronanki et al., but our fine-grained analysis shows that even modern LLMs require caution when used as automated QA instruments. Here, the term *hallucinated defects* refers to content-level false positives or unjustified explanations, rather than to the introduction of unsupported defect categories, as all models were constrained to the predefined QUS schema.

Sharma and Tripathi [14]. Sharma and Tripathi conducted the largest LLM benchmark to date, evaluating GPT-3.5, GPT-4-Turbo, and GPT-4o on 960 synthetically generated User Stories. They concluded that newer models outperform earlier ones, especially on syntactic and formatting criteria, while semantic criteria remain challenging regardless of prompt richness. Our results are consistent with both observations but provide two refinements. First, although we also observe a performance increase from GPT-4 to GPT-5, we find that GPT-5-mini surpasses GPT-5 in recall and output stability, challenging the assumption—implicit in prior work—that larger models necessarily perform better. Second, whereas Sharma and Tripathi relied on synthetic stories, our evaluation uses real industrial User Stories, revealing substantially greater semantic complexity. As a result, criteria such as *Ambiguous*, *Conceptually Sound*, and *Estimatable* show lower agreement across LLMs, confirming their findings under more ecologically valid conditions. Finally, since their study did not include rule-based baselines, our results provide new evidence that LLMs complement—rather than replace—the structural precision of AQUSA.

Perkusich et al. [9]. Our previous study compared AQUSA and the DeepSeek LLM using the original QUS validation set of fifteen User Stories, serving as a pilot investigation. Although that study reported a higher F1-score than the present benchmark, the two results are not directly comparable: the pilot relied on a small curated dataset, whereas the present study evaluates 182 industrial stories spanning three heterogeneous backlogs. The larger and more diverse dataset introduces substantially higher semantic and pragmatic variability—such as role misuse, stylistic drift, and cross-story effects—yielding a more conservative but more realistic estimate of performance. In contrast, the present study shifts the focus to a larger-scale evaluation using recent GPT-family models, enabling a more robust analysis of defect detection behavior under contemporary commercial LLM architectures. That work indicated potential complementarity: AQUSA provided higher-precision structural checks, whereas the LLM captured a broader range of pragmatic and stylistic issues. The present study validates and extends these insights through (i) a substantially larger dataset, (ii) multiple contemporary GPT-family models, and (iii) detailed quantitative and qualitative analyses. The complementarity pattern persists: LLMs achieve consistently higher recall and detect more subtle linguistic or pragmatic issues, but their precision varies considerably across criteria and models. Finally, our analysis demonstrates that both rule-based and GPT-family LLM-based approaches systematically miss defects requiring rich contextual or domain-specific reasoning, a limitation only briefly noted in our earlier work.

Synthesis. Overall, our findings suggest that LLM support for User Story evaluation is expanding in capability—particularly in contextual coverage and the actionability of feedback—while aggregate accuracy metrics such as F1-score remain highly sensitive to dataset scale and difficulty. As a result, performance figures should be interpreted within comparable benchmarks: higher scores on small curated sets and lower scores on large industrial backlogs do not necessarily indicate regression in model capability. Second, the superior performance of GPT-5-mini over GPT-5 suggests that architectural and alignment choices—not only model scale—play a critical role in requirements-focused tasks. Third, this study provides one of the first large-scale, unified comparisons of AQUSA and multiple state-of-the-art GPT models on real industrial data, showing that neither family of techniques is sufficient on its own; instead, a combined use of rule-based and GPT-family LLM-based approaches is likely to yield the most reliable outcomes for agile teams.

Taken together, these comparisons indicate that the present study goes beyond a scaled replication of earlier work. The larger dataset enables the identification of systematic and repeatable behavioral patterns—such as the superior stability of GPT-5-mini over a frontier model and the divergence between detection accuracy and feedback usefulness—that could not be reliably observed in small-sample evaluations. These insights directly inform the design of hybrid, neuro-symbolic quality-assurance pipelines and refine our understanding of how different classes of LLMs should be positioned within such pipelines.

5 Implications for Research and Practice

The findings of this study yield several implications for both practitioners and researchers in the field of agile requirements engineering.

Importantly, our findings should be interpreted in light of agile practice, where user stories are not complete specifications but intentionally lightweight artifacts that serve as triggers for conversation between stakeholders and development teams. The goal of the proposed approach is therefore not to enforce "perfect" user stories or upfront completeness, but to support teams in ensuring that stories are good enough to enable productive discussion. In this sense, the Dual-gate strategy is best positioned as a continuous, iterative aid during backlog refinement, rather than as a rigid quality gate applied only at planning time. As user stories evolve through negotiation and learning, the feedback provided by AQUSA and LLMs can be reapplied incrementally, aligning with agile principles of adaptability and just-in-time elaboration rather than big upfront planning.

From a Practical Standpoint. The results reinforce that while rule-based tools such as AQUSA provide a necessary baseline for structural improvement, they are insufficient for detecting many pragmatic quality issues in complex industrial scenarios. AQUSA demonstrated high stability in enforcing rigid structural standards and formatting consistency, making it a suitable candidate for "sanitary gates" in continuous integration pipelines where false positives must be minimized. Conversely, GPT-family models—in particular GPT-5-mini—were more effective at capturing context-dependent defects (for example, inappropriate roles or subtle inconsistencies between stories) that systematically evade rule-based detection.

Our analysis also highlights a critical trade-off regarding model selection: bigger is not always better. The optimized GPT-5-mini model achieved the highest overall effectiveness, balancing sensitivity (recall) and precision, whereas the larger GPT-5 model exhibited substantially higher false-positive rates and less stable behavior. For organizations, this suggests that deploying specialized, lower-latency models can be not only more cost-effective but also more reliable than always resorting to the largest available models for this type of classification task.

At the same time, the introduction of generative AI brings new risks that differ fundamentally from traditional tools. While AQUSA failed primarily by omission (false negatives), the LLMs failed primarily by over-reporting defects (false positives), sometimes accompanied by off-topic or prompt-contaminated justifications (i.e., cases where the model's explanation is influenced by examples or assumptions present in the prompt rather than by evidence in the user story itself). This behavior underscores the necessity of a human-in-the-loop approach. Teams cannot blindly trust the output of an LLM, as it may critique a User Story using reasoning that refers to unrelated context or stylistic preferences rather than genuine defects. Consequently, our results support the adoption of a hybrid, layered strategy: using AQUSA to automatically block clear structural violations and employing LLMs as advisory agents or "agile coaches" to suggest pragmatic improvements, with the mandatory requirement that a Product Owner or requirements engineer validates the AI's suggestions. Importantly, even this "Dual-gate" approach does not eliminate the need for expert review: both families of tools systematically missed defects that required rich contextual or domain-specific knowledge.

For researchers and tool developers, this study points toward a concrete agenda for neuro-symbolic quality assurance. First, the evidence suggests that future tools should not rely on a single paradigm. Instead, researchers should explore architectures that integrate deterministic rule engines to constrain the search space of generative models, thereby reducing spurious defect reports and off-topic rationales. For instance, a system could use AQUSA (or similar rule-based components) to validate syntax and basic QUS criteria, and then pass only structurally valid stories to an LLM configured to focus on pragmatic and semantic aspects.

Second, the variance in performance across our three datasets indicates a need for more granular benchmarks. Future work should focus on curating datasets that clearly separate structural defects from context-dependent pragmatic nuances, allowing more precise evaluation of model competencies and failure modes. Third, given the observed hallucinations and stylistic biases in explanations, investigations into prompt and system-design strategies that minimize context leakage and encourage faithful justifications are essential to building trust in AI-assisted requirements engineering tools. Finally, our findings suggest that evaluation protocols should go beyond aggregate metrics, incorporating both defect-type breakdowns and feedback-quality analyses to guide the design of next-generation hybrid tools.

6 Threats to Validity

This section discusses several threats to validity, structured according to the common classifications: internal, construct, external, and conclusion validity [17]. For each category, we outline potential risks and the measures taken to mitigate their impact.

Internal validity concerns whether the observed differences between AQUSA and the LLMs can be attributed to the tools' detection capabilities rather than to uncontrolled factors. A critical threat in LLM-based evaluations is prompt sensitivity, as variations in instructions, examples, or output constraints may substantially influence model behavior. In this study, prompt engineering is treated explicitly as a potential confounding factor and mitigated through a control-by-standardization strategy: all models were evaluated using the same rigorously defined prompt, identical few-shot examples, identical output schema, and identical execution settings. This design prioritizes measurement equivalence over prompt optimization, ensuring that observed differences reflect intrinsic model behavior rather than prompt-tuning effects.

A related phenomenon is context leakage or *prompt contamination*, in which the model's justification is unintentionally shaped by patterns introduced in the prompt (e.g., few-shot examples) rather than by the content of the evaluated user story. To reduce this risk, the few-shot examples used in the prompt were drawn from domains unrelated to the datasets under study. In addition, all LLMs were executed with `temperature = 0`, eliminating sampling randomness and ensuring that differences observed across models (e.g., GPT-5-mini vs. GPT-5) reflect systematic behavioral tendencies rather than stochastic variation. This choice favors stability and precision in defect detection tasks, but may limit generative diversity in feedback formulation, which could be advantageous in less constrained refinement scenarios.

Another internal validity threat concerns the construction of the ground truth, which was derived from expert validation of tool outputs rather than from an independent pre-annotation phase. To mitigate this risk, the expert did not merely review tool-generated defects, but also conducted a full independent manual inspection of all 182 user stories to identify missed defects (false negatives). Moreover, the five QUS criteria analyzed are predominantly syntactic or low-ambiguity pragmatic factors with clear, structurally observable manifestations, which reduces subjective interpretation. Nevertheless, reliance on a single expert remains a limitation, and future studies should employ multiple annotators to assess inter-rater agreement.

A further internal validity threat concerns model and version volatility inherent to commercial LLM APIs. Providers may update models without explicit versioning, potentially affecting reproducibility over time. To mitigate this risk, all experiments were executed within a fixed time window (November 26âĂŞ27, 2025), using deterministic settings, and all raw model outputs were archived and released in the supplementary repository. While this does not eliminate version drift, it enables independent inspection and future re-analysis of the exact outputs used in this study.

Construct validity relates to whether the measurements truly reflect the QUS constructs under investigation. One potential threat arises from interpreting the defects reported by the LLMs, particularly because generative models may introduce stylistic preferences or speculative justifications. However, this risk is reduced in our study because the prompt constrained all models to output defects exclusively within the five QUS categories supported by AQUSA, using a fixed JSON schema that prevented category drift or the introduction of new defect types. Furthermore, every reported defect was manually validated using a structured rubric derived from prior QUS work. While this mitigates misclassification risks, it does not eliminate the possibility that LLMs may produce convincing but off-topic explanations, which we accounted for through supplementary qualitative analysis.

External validity concerns the generalizability of the results. Our evaluation covers 182 real User Stories across three industrial backlogs, offering stronger ecological validity than studies based on small samples or synthetic stories. However, these datasets come from specific domains (estimation tools, event management, and multimedia platforms), and results may not generalize to other agile contexts, particularly safety-critical or highly regulated environments. In addition, this study focuses exclusively on the GPT family (GPT-4, GPT-5, and GPT-5-mini). The exclusion of other LLM architectures, such as DeepSeek, Claude, or Llama, represents a deliberate limitation of scope. While this choice supports controlled intra-family comparison, GPT-family models should be understood as widely used commercial baselines in recent Software Engineering research rather than universal state-of-the-art solutions across all natural language understanding tasks. Consequently, the generalization of results across different model families remains an open question for future benchmarking studies.

Conclusion validity pertains to the robustness of our inferences. One threat lies in the accuracy of the ground truth, as expert validation was used instead of independent dual-annotation. Although subjectivity is limited due to the nature of the five QUS criteria studied, subtle errors remain possible. Another threat concerns the distribution of defects in the dataset: some criteria have relatively few instances, which may amplify small fluctuations in precision or recall. To mitigate these risks, we complement quantitative metrics (precision, recall, F1-score) with qualitative analysis of feedback quality and characteristic failure modes, including hallucinated explanations and template-driven false positives. This triangulation increases confidence that the observed complementarity between AQUSA and the LLMs—particularly the higher recall of GPT-5-mini and the higher precision of AQUSA—is supported by both statistical evidence and detailed behavioral analysis.

7 Final Remarks

This study presented a comparative evaluation of the rule-based AQUSA tool and three state-of-the-art Large Language Models (GPT-4, GPT-5, and GPT-5-mini) applied to User Story quality assessment across 182 real industrial requirements. The findings demonstrate that neither rule-based nor LLM-based techniques are sufficient in isolation. Instead, they exhibit complementary strengths that point toward a hybrid, neuro-symbolic future for requirements quality assurance. AQUSA provides deterministic and reproducible structural checks, whereas LLMs, particularly GPT-5-mini, deliver broader semantic and pragmatic coverage.

Quantitatively, the results challenge the widespread assumption that larger models necessarily perform better. The optimized GPT-5-mini achieved the highest overall effectiveness, with the best Recall (0.81) and F1-score (0.62), while generating substantially fewer false positives than GPT-5. In contrast, the frontier GPT-5 model exhibited strong sensitivity but suffered from systematic over-classification, producing 85 false positives. GPT-4 adopted an overly conservative behavior, resulting in extremely low recall. AQUSA achieved the highest precision (0.61) but missed a large proportion of valid defects due to its limited coverage of pragmatic and semantic QUS criteria.

Qualitatively, the contrast between approaches was equally clear. AQUSA consistently enforced rigid textual and structural standards with no off-topic explanations, making it a reliable gatekeeper for low-level hygiene. By comparison, GPT-5-mini excelled in detecting subtle contextual anomalies—such as improper roles or conceptually ambiguous ends—and provided actionable natural-language rewrites that resemble human review. However, LLM feedback occasionally included off-topic justifications or stylistic biases, underscoring the need for human validation and for mechanisms that constrain generative reasoning.

Overall, the results support a "Dual-gate" quality strategy: (i) rule-based tools for deterministic structural validation, and (ii) LLMs as advisory agents for pragmatic refinement, with explicit human oversight. This layered design leverages the precision of symbolic rules together with the adaptive reasoning of LLMs while mitigating the weaknesses of each paradigm.

Future work will pursue three main directions: (i) developing a neuro-symbolic prototype that integrates AQUSA's rule engine to constrain and ground LLM outputs, thereby reducing false positives and speculative explanations; (ii) benchmarking additional model families (such as Claude, Llama, and DeepSeek); and (iii) conducting longitudinal studies to evaluate whether AI-assisted quality gates measurably reduce rework, improve backlog clarity, or impact team velocity. In this context, future hybrid implementations will also explore different temperature settings, using low temperature for deterministic defect detection and higher temperature values for generating alternative reformulations during contextual refinement.

References

1. Arora, C., Grundy, J., Abdelrazek, M.: Advancing requirements engineering through generative ai: assessing the role of llms. In: Generative AI for Effective Software Development, pp. 129–148. Springer, Heidelberg (2024)
2. Brhel, M., Meth, H., Maedche, A., Werder, K.: Exploring principles of user-centered agile software development: a literature review. Inf. Softw. Technol. **61**, 163–181 (2015)
3. Endres, M., Fakhoury, S., Chakraborty, S., Lahiri, S.K.: Formalizing natural language intent into program specifications via large language models. arXiv preprint arXiv:2310.01831 (2023)
4. Kasauli, R., Knauss, E., Horkoff, J., Liebel, G., de Oliveira Neto, F.G.: Requirements engineering challenges and practices in large-scale agile system development. J. Syst. Softw. **172**, 110851 (2021)
5. Leffingwell, D.: Agile Software Requirements: Lean Requirements Practices for Teams, Programs, and the Enterprise. Addison-Wesley Professional, Boston (2010)
6. Lucassen, G., Dalpiaz, F., van der Werf, J.M.E., Brinkkemper, S.: Improving agile requirements: the quality user story framework and tool. Requir. Eng. **21**, 383–403 (2016)
7. Ma, L., Liu, S., Li, Y., Xie, X., Bu, L.: Specgen: automated generation of formal program specifications via large language models. arXiv preprint arXiv:2401.08807 (2024)
8. Pacheco, C., García, I., Reyes, M.: Requirements elicitation techniques: a systematic literature review based on the maturity of the techniques. IET Softw. **12**(4), 365–378 (2018)
9. Perkusich, M., Silva, I., Albuquerque, D., Gorgônio, K., Perkusich, A.: Evaluating the quality of user stories: a comparative study of large language models and rule-based tool. In: 2025 International Conference on Software, Telecommunications and Computer Networks (SoftCOM), pp. 1–6. IEEE (2025)
10. Perkusich, M., et al.: Intelligent software engineering in the context of agile software development: a systematic literature review. Inf. Softw. Technol. **119**, 106241 (2020)
11. Poudel, A., Lin, J., Cleland-Huang, J.: Leveraging transformer-based language models to automate requirements satisfaction assessment. arXiv preprint arXiv:2312.04463 (2023)
12. Robeer, M., Lucassen, G., van der Werf, J.M.E., Dalpiaz, F., Brinkkemper, S.: Automated extraction of conceptual models from user stories via nlp. In: 2016 IEEE 24th International Requirements Engineering Conference (RE), pp. 196–205. IEEE (2016)
13. Ronanki, K., Cabrero-Daniel, B., Berger, C.: Chatgpt as a tool for user story quality evaluation: trustworthy out of the box? In: International Conference on Agile Software Development, pp. 173–181. Springer, Heidelberg (2022)
14. Sharma, A., Kumar Tripathi, A.: Evaluating user story quality with llms: a comparative study. J. Intell. Inf. Syst. 1–29 (2025)

15. Vogelsang, A., Fischbach, J.: Using large language models for natural language processing tasks in requirements engineering: a systematic guideline. In: Handbook on Natural Language Processing for Requirements Engineering, pp. 435–456. Springer, Heidelberg (2025)
16. White, J., Hays, S., Fu, Q., Spencer-Smith, J., Schmidt, D.C.: Chatgpt prompt patterns for improving code quality, refactoring, requirements elicitation, and software design. In: Generative AI for Effective Software Development, pp. 71–108. Springer, Heidelberg (2024)
17. Wohlin, C., et al.: Experimentation in Software Engineering, vol. 236. Springer, Heidelberg (2012)
18. Yamani, A., Baslyman, M., Ahmed, M.: Leveraging llms for user stories in AI systems: Ustai dataset. arXiv preprint arXiv:2504.00513 (2025)
19. Zhang, Z., Rayhan, M., Herda, T., Goisauf, M., Abrahamsson, P.: Llm-based agents for automating the enhancement of user story quality: an early report. In: International Conference on Agile Software Development, pp. 117–126. Springer, Cham (2024)

An AI Driven Decision System for Value Aware Regression Testing

Suddhasvatta Das(✉) and Kevin Gary

Arizona State University, Tempe, AZ, USA
{sdas76,kgary}@asu.edu

Abstract. In agile software development, regression testing is an ongoing process activity. However, real-world time constraints necessitate selecting a subset of tests to run. Current regression test selection algorithms primarily focus on technical metrics such as requirement coverage while overlooking the business value each test validates. This study reframes regression test selection as a multi-objective optimization problem in which tests are selected to maximize business value within a constrained testing time while maintaining adequate requirement coverage. We apply an artificial intelligence-based search algorithm, and our results show that the proposed method consistently selects tests with higher business value than baseline approaches when time is limited, while maintaining comparable requirement coverage. These findings suggest that a driven value-aware selector can be incorporated into agile teams for decisions on allocating limited regression testing resources.

Keywords: Agile · Continuous Integration · Business Value · Regression Testing · AI-Search Optimization. · Multi Objective Optimization · Genetic Algorithms

1 Introduction

Agile now dominates software development, with over 70% of organizations adopting it for rapid, incremental value delivery [32]. Its success hinges on flexible planning, iterative feedback, and automated testing to maintain high quality. Continuous regression testing is essential to prevent new changes from breaking key functionality or stakeholder value [9,30,33,37], but the main challenge is selecting the right tests, not running them [43]. Most Regression Test Selection (RTS) research remains focused on technical metrics, often overlooking end-to-end business workflows and Business Value (BV), typically validated with User Acceptance Tests (UATs) [13,25]. Neglecting value-driven regression testing exposes agile teams to risks that automation alone cannot prevent, as seen in the 2024 CrowdStrike incident [8]. This work proposes a value-driven regression testing approach that guides UAT selection by business value, the core agile success metric [2].

In agile development, business value encompassing financial and non-financial outcome measures progresses and guides trade-offs [21]. BV links software

A. Goldman et al. (Eds.): XP 2026, LNBIP 578, pp. 175–190, 2026.
https://doi.org/10.1007/978-3-032-22375-3_11

to organizational goals, adapts to shifting priorities, and ensures each increment benefits stakeholders. Consistent with Lean Engineering [31], all activities, including regression testing, must preserve value. While regression testing does not create new value, it is essential for safeguarding delivered value in agile.

While agile's emphasis on business value, most regression testing research relies on technical metrics such as test coverage, fault detection, or testing time, which assume equal business impact for all requirements [9]. While some studies weight requirements by priority [6,38], these weights rarely reflect actual post-delivery value. As Svensson et al. and Trujillo et al. show [39,41], high-priority features do not always equate to high value, and lower-priority ones can be highly beneficial. Thus, integrating business value into regression testing remains a key gap in agile.

Agile's continuous delivery imposes strict time constraints, making regression testing inherently time-limited [9,30,37]. As systems grow, exhaustive testing after each change becomes infeasible [14,30,37]. Thus, regression testing becomes a resource allocation problem: teams must use limited testing time to maximize business value, not just technical metrics. This reframes regression testing as a multi-objective optimization selecting test subsets that maximize business value under time and coverage constraints [19,36]. Each subset is a trade-off among time, coverage, and value. Manual selection is inefficient and biased; agile's shifting priorities require adaptive, evidence-based decision mechanisms.

This is where Artificial Intelligence (AI) based optimization becomes helpful. AI aids decision-making by selecting tests that maximize value and coverage within time limits. Search and learning-based algorithms evaluate test combinations for business value and time [18]. While ML can predict critical tests from historical data [30,37,43], such models often miss agile-specific factors like user stories and business value [30]. The focus is on optimizing test selection for cumulative business value within time constraints, supporting agile goals beyond defect detection.

Thus, this research addresses the lack of value-driven, time-efficient regression test selection in agile, aiming to align testing with stakeholder value. *The goal is to develop and empirically evaluate a value-driven, time-aware framework for regression test selection that operationalizes agile principles of business value preservation and time efficiency through intelligent, optimization-based decisions.* The paper is organized as follows: background, methods, empirical study, future work, and conclusion.

2 Background

This section covers relevant conceptual background that directly motivates this work and positions the gap in current research.

Agile regression testing safeguards validated functionality during rapid iteration and continuous integration [37]. Automated pipelines accelerate verification, but business value is rarely a core metric [9]. Recent advances include clustering for better fault detection [24], code coverage with change-impact analysis [1], dependency-based selection for faster feedback [26], and scalable continuous integration methods [14]. Class-level RTS is more precise but slower than module-level [35], and RTS is especially important for frequent, small code changes [43].

Regression Test Selection selects tests to ensure code changes do not break existing behavior, using static or dynamic analysis to identify those affected [25]. Safe approaches keep all tests that might reveal faults, omitting others for efficiency [33]. Classic RTS used dependency analysis (e.g., DejaVu, RETEST) [20], and has expanded to distributed version control, embedded, aspect-oriented, and GUI-based systems [4,5,12,17]. Increasingly, algorithms leverage requirements, linking them to validating tests [3,6,38]. Chittimalli et al. introduced requirement–test traceability and criticality-based prioritization; Srivastava et al. ranked tests using stakeholder-defined priority and risk, and Khalid et al. applied priority ranking to black-box test cases.

Search-Based Regression Testing (SBRT) applies Search-Based Software Engineering (SBSE) to automate test selection, prioritization, and minimization as search problems evaluated by fitness functions. Traditional SBRT often uses proxies like code coverage or execution cost, which may be unreliable [28]. Greedy algorithms are fast but get stuck in local optima; metaheuristics (Genetic Algorithms, Simulated Annealing, PSO) better explore the space. Li et al. found Genetic Algorithms consistently outperformed other heuristics [28]. De Souza et al. used Binary Constrained PSO for cost-aware test selection, greatly improving requirement coverage per unit cost over random and greedy baselines [16,18,23,36].

In summary, RTS has evolved from static and dependency-based to cost and search-based methods, but most optimize only one criterion i.e. coverage, fault detection, or cost and rarely incorporate business value [25,28,36]. Agile teams must maximize business value, maintain coverage, and meet tight deadlines, yet existing RTS and SBRT rarely address all three. This creates risks of misaligned regression decisions and poor trade-offs between speed and critical functionality. This paper addresses the gap by formalizing regression testing as a value-aware, time-constrained multi-objective optimization and proposing a method that explicitly balances value, coverage, and time.

3 Methods

This section formalizes business value driven RTS as a multi-objective optimization balancing business value and requirement coverage within time constraints.

Problem Formulation and Approach: We formalize regression testing as follows: Fig. 1a from Jorgenson [22] illustrates requirements (S), code (P), and tests (T). In any SDLC, a subset of requirements $S_i \subseteq S$ is implemented as P_i and tested by T_i. Regression testing targets only delivered, tested requirements (region 1 in Fig. 1a). In each new version (P_{i+1}, T_{i+1}), regression tests are those in $T_i \cap T_{i+1}$, ensuring shared requirements remain intact [33]. Due to time constraints [9,30], running all these tests is often impractical. RTS selects the most effective subset of $T_i \cap T_{i+1}$ within the Regression Test Window $(\Delta\tau)$, prioritizing requirements present in both versions. Non-overlapping regions represent new or removed requirements and are excluded. The objective is to select tests that maximize business value and requirement coverage within Regression Test Window (RTW), given each requirement's BV and execution time of tests associated to the requirements. Thus, time-aware BV-driven RTS is formulated as:

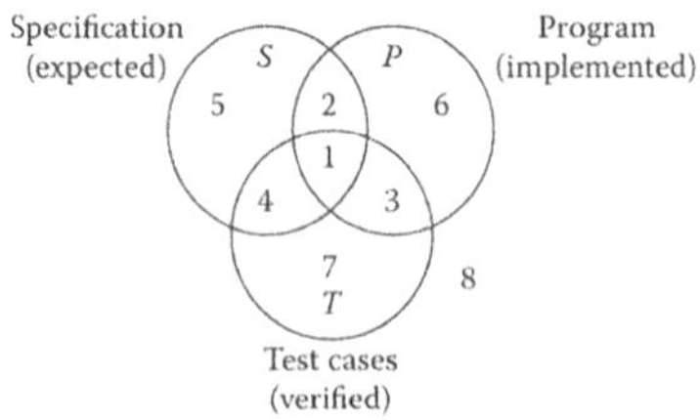

(a) Relationship of P,S,T [22]

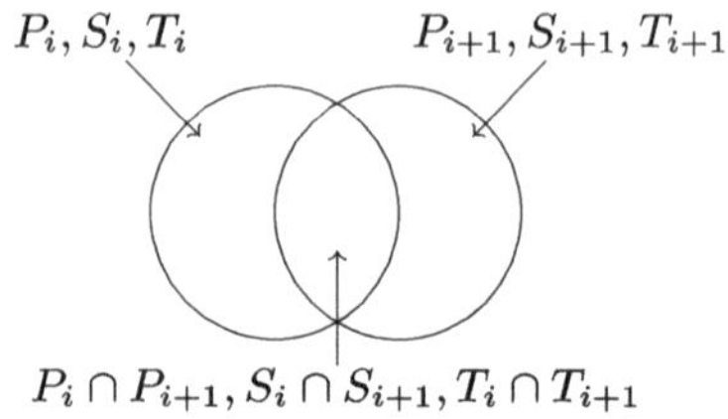

(b) Region 1 of Fig. 1a Zoomed

Fig. 1. Regression Test - Mathematical Definition

Problem Definition: Given the program versions P_i and P_{i+1}, the overlapping test pool $T_i \cap T_{i+1}$, the overlapping requirement set $S_i \cap S_{i+1}$, and the available regression test window $\Delta\tau$, the objective is to select subsets $(T_i \cap T_{i+1})' \subseteq (T_i \cap T_{i+1})$ and $(S_i \cap S_{i+1})' \subseteq (S_i \cap S_{i+1})$ that maximize the two criteria of (i) total BV $\sum_{s \in (S_i \cap S_{i+1})'} BV(s)$ and (ii) requirement coverage $\frac{|(S_i \cap S_{i+1})'|}{|(S_i \cap S_{i+1})|} \times 100$. The selection must satisfy the time constraint $\sum_{t \in (T_i \cap T_{i+1})'} ex(t) \leq \Delta\tau$, and each requirement s included in $(S_i \cap S_{i+1})'$ must have all of its validating tests selected; that is, tests$(s) \subseteq (T_i \cap T_{i+1})'$.

Algorithm: We implement our approach using Non-dominated Sorting Genetic Algorithm II (NSGA-II) [10,11], encoding solutions as binary vectors that indicate test selection. Fitness is assessed by two objectives: 1) total business value of covered requirements and 2)percentage of requirements in the regression test window covered. A population of feasible solutions is initialized within the execution-time budget $\Delta\tau$. Offspring are generated using tournament selection (k), crossover (p_c), and mutation (p_m), with a repair operator ensuring time constraints. NSGA-II then partitions solutions into Pareto fronts, using crowding distance to maintain diversity. This process is repeated for G generations, after which the first Pareto front provides trade-off solutions. Only requirements with all associated tests selected are counted, enforcing a strict 'definition of done' [29]. For evaluation, we select the solution with the highest business value, or, if tied, the one with the highest coverage, to compare with BCPSO and random algorithms. While the full Pareto front remains available for alternative goals, and teams can pick based on their quality goals, we report a single recommended test set per RTW for analysis.

Algorithm 1. NSGA-II for Test↔Requirement Selection

Input: requirements' BV, tests' exec-time, budget Δ_T, population size N, generations G, tournament size k, crossover prob p_c, mutation prob p_m
Sets: P population, O offspring, R combined pool
$P \leftarrow$ INITIALIZE-POPULATION(N, s, Δ_T)
for $g = 1$ to G **do**
  $O \leftarrow \varnothing$
  while $|O| < N$ **do**
    $p_1 \leftarrow$ TOURNAMENT-SELECT(P, k)
    $p_2 \leftarrow$ TOURNAMENT-SELECT(P, k)
    $(c_1, c_2) \leftarrow$ CROSSOVER(p_1, p_2, p_c)
    $c_1 \leftarrow$ MUTATE(c_1, p_m); $c_2 \leftarrow$ MUTATE(c_2, p_m)
    $c_1 \leftarrow$ REPAIR-FEASIBLE(c_1, Δ_T); $c_2 \leftarrow$ REPAIR-FEASIBLE(c_2, Δ_T)
    $O \leftarrow O \cup \{c_1, c_2\}$
  $R \leftarrow P \cup O$
  Evaluate each $r \in R$: $F_1 = \sum_s BV(s)$; $F_2 = \frac{|\text{covered reqs}|}{|S_i \cap S_{i+1}|} \times 100$
  $F \leftarrow$ NON-DOMINATED-SORT(R)
  $P \leftarrow$ SELECT-NEXT-GENERATION(F, N)
$PF \leftarrow$ first front of NON-DOMINATED-SORT(P)
return PF

4 Empirical Study

This section empirically evaluates the business value driven regression test selection. NSGA-II is compared to a baseline and random selection methods for effectiveness in terms of BV and requirement coverage. The research questions addressed are below:

RQ1: How does the proposed multi-objective algorithm balance business value and Requirement coverage under different RTWs?
RQ2: What is the business value/unit time of the proposed algorithm compared to baseline and random selection?

Baseline: We evaluated our BV-driven RTS against a requirement-coverage baseline under similar time constraints. Most requirement-coverage RTS studies use test-centric metrics such as average percentage of fault detected (APFD) or code coverage, but Kazmi et al. [25] found that requirement coverage is better for verifying satisfaction. De Souza et al. [36] provide a relevant baseline, using Binary Constrained Particle Swamp Optimization (BCPSO) to maximize requirement coverage within a time budget, treating coverage as the objective and cost as a constraint. For agile relevance, we require all tests for a requirement to pass for it to count as covered; partial coverage is insufficient, aligning with the definition of done. Our evaluation aggregates covered requirements and their cumulative BV as the metric.

Data: De Souza et al. [36] report aggregate execution-time budgets and measure solution quality by requirement coverage. Without a replication package, we reverse-engineered synthetic test sets, preserving the aggregate budget and mean pairwise Jaccard similarity (14.09%). For BV-driven RTS, 248 requirements were assigned Fibonacci business values (2–89) to reflect agile scaling [27,34], resulting in a right-skewed value distribution [7,40]. Test execution times were drawn from

Table 1. Datasets

Parameter	Dataset 1	Dataset 2
# of Test Cases	80	40
Total Exec Time	699.31	349.65
Skewness (Exec Time)	3.26	2.84
Range (Exec Time, min–max)	1.16–101.14	1.27–79.41
# of Requirements	248	124
Total Business Value	3786	2480
Skewness (BV)	2.30	1.70
Range (BV)	2–89	2–89
Redundancy (%)	14.09	14.09

an exponential distribution with the observed mean, matching the baseline's total budget and realistic profiles [15]. To study input size, we halved the number of test cases and requirements, holding other factors constant. This one-factor experiment isolates test set size as the independent variable [42]. *Note: Both datasets represent requirements and tests in* $S_i \cap S_{i+1}, T_i \cap T_{i+1}$ *of Figure* 1*b the unchanged behaviors across versions.*

Experiment Execution: Each algorithm was executed on the two datasets [Table 1] under varying RTW. Each configuration was repeated 30 times to account for the stochastic nature of the algorithms. The experimental setup is summarized below:

- Datasets: one re-created from the baseline and another created which has half number of requirements and tests, we call them 80–248 and 40–124 respectively.
- Algorithms: NSGA-II, BCPSO (baseline), and Random selection.
- RTWs: 5%–95% of total execution time in 5% increments (19 levels).
- Replications: 30 independent runs per configuration.
- Total executions: 3 algorithms × 19 levels × 30 replications = 1710 runs.
- NSGA-II Configuration: generations = 150, crossover probability = 0.9, mutation probability = $1/L$ where L is the chromosome length (i.e., the number of test cases)

Results: This section presents the results of our experiments. First plots and tables are presented followed by explanation of results.

Business Value: In Fig. 2a, b we see BV followed similar monotonic growth. NSGA-II consistently produced the highest BV throughout most RTWs and especially led between 10% and 40%. Baseline also increased steadily in BV, generally tracking just below NSGA-II, while Random produced substantially lower BV in early and mid RTWs. However, as RTW increased, Random's BV improved and the performance gap narrowed. In the final RTW intervals, all

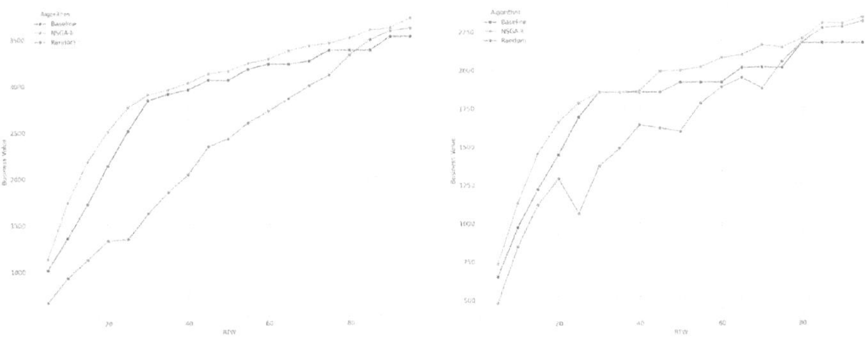

(a) Dataset 1 (b) Dataset 2

Fig. 2. Business Value achieved by NSGA-II, Baseline, and Random across RTWs

three methods approached similar upper BV levels, with NSGA-II maintaining a small lead, Baseline just behind, and Random closing in but not exceeding the others.

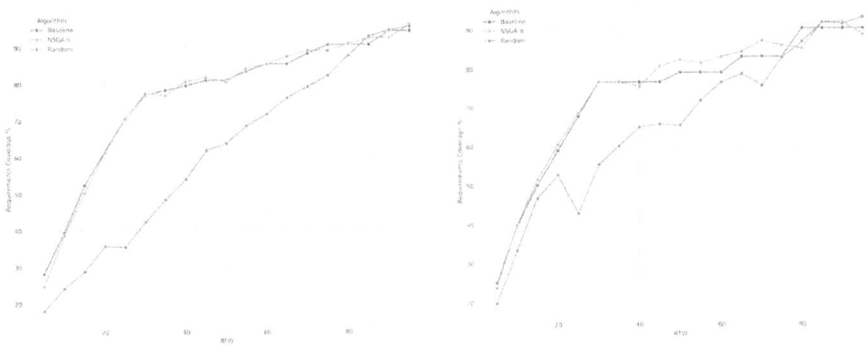

(a) Dataset 1 (b) Dataset 2

Fig. 3. Requirement Coverage achieved by NSGA-II, Baseline, and Random across RTWs

Requirement Coverage: Across both datasets in Fig. 3a, b we see requirement coverage increased steadily for all methods as the RTW grew. NSGA-II and Baseline showed the fastest coverage gains early, both surpassing 50% by about 20% RTW, and tracked closely through the mid-range (approximately 30–60% RTW), with NSGA-II holding slight advantages at several points. Random selection had slower early gains and lagged behind NSGA-II and Baseline through the first third of the RTW range, but its coverage improved steadily as RTW expanded. In the higher RTW intervals (above 75%), all methods converged, each exceeding 85–90% coverage, and differences became minimal.

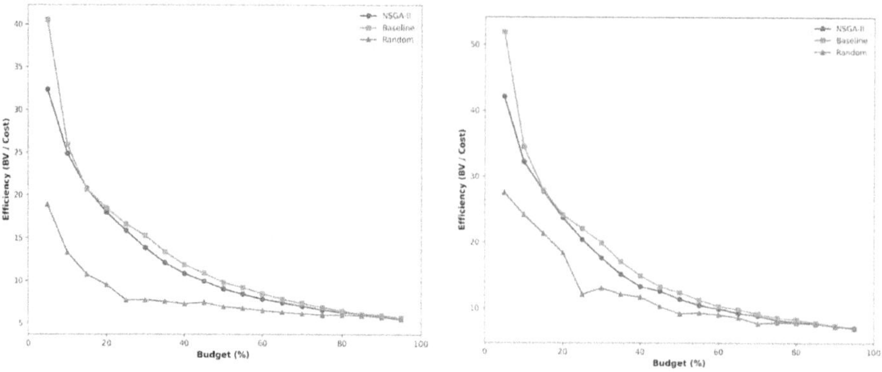

(a) Dataset 1

(b) Dataset 2

Fig. 4. BV/Unit Time by NSGA-II, Baseline, and Random across RTWs

Efficiency: Figure 4a, b shows that efficiency (BV per unit cost) steadily decreased as RTW increased across both datasets. At 10–15% RTW, Baseline and NSGA-II had the highest efficiency, with Baseline slightly behind; Random was much lower. The largest method separation occurred in this interval. From 20–65% RTW, all methods' efficiency declined, with Baseline and NSGA-II tracking closely and staying above Random, which dropped more sharply and plateaued well below the others. Above 70% RTW, efficiency values for all methods converged, and by 85–95% RTW, the three were nearly equal, with only minor differences across datasets.

Table 2. ANOVA results for Dataset 1 (D1) and Dataset 2 (D2).

RTW	Business Value		Requirement Coverage	
	D1	D2	D1	D2
5%	<0.001	<0.001	<0.001	<0.001
10%	<0.001	<0.001	<0.001	<0.001
15%	<0.001	<0.001	<0.001	<0.001
20%	<0.001	<0.001	<0.001	0.004
25%	<0.001	<0.001	<0.001	<0.001
30%	<0.001	<0.001	<0.001	<0.001
35%	<0.001	<0.001	<0.001	<0.001
40%	<0.001	<0.001	<0.001	<0.001
45%	<0.001	<0.001	<0.001	<0.001
50%	<0.001	<0.001	<0.001	<0.001
55%	<0.001	<0.001	<0.001	<0.001
60%	<0.001	<0.001	<0.001	0.009
65%	<0.001	0.024	<0.001	0.033
70%	<0.001	<0.001	<0.001	<0.001
75%	<0.001	<0.001	<0.001	0.031
80%	<0.001	0.541	0.012	<0.001
85%	<0.001	0.008	0.107	0.585
90%	<0.001	<0.001	<0.001	0.465
95%	<0.001	<0.001	0.044	<0.001

Table 3. Tukey HSD Comparisons for Business Value and Requirement Coverage for Dataset1 (D1) and Dataset2 (D2)

Business Value					
RTW	Pair	Mean Diff (D1)	95% CI (D1)	Mean Diff (D2)	95% CI (D2)
10%	Baseline vs Random	−427.33	[−564.74, −289.92]	−133.60	[−207.37, −59.83]
	NSGA-II vs Random	−810.10	[−947.51, −672.69]	−257.80	[−331.57, −184.03]
	Baseline vs NSGA-II	382.77	[245.36, 520.18]	124.20	[50.43, 197.97]
50%	Baseline vs Random	−688.50	[−852.30, −524.70]	−554.10	[−700.00, −208.20]
	NSGA-II vs Random	−689.70	[−854.40, −525.00]	−358.80	[−507.40, −210.20]
	Baseline vs NSGA-II	1.10	[−163.60, 165.80]	−195.30	[−342.60, −48.00]
90%	Baseline vs Random	60.90	[21.80, 100.00]	106.47	[36.78, 176.16]
	NSGA-II vs Random	−36.83	[−75.94, 2.27]	−24.53	[−94.22, 45.16]
	Baseline vs NSGA-II	97.73	[58.63, 136.84]	131.00	[61.31, 200.69]
Requirement Coverage					
RTW	Pair	Mean Diff (D1)	95% CI (D1)	Mean Diff (D2)	95% CI (D2)
10%	Baseline vs Random	−15.3360	[−18.8848, −11.7872]	−6.2634	[−7.5147, −5.0121]
	NSGA-II vs Random	−14.4758	[−18.0246, −10.9270]	−6.5860	[−7.8373, −5.3347]
	Baseline vs NSGA-II	−0.8602	[−4.4090, 2.6886]	0.3226	[−0.9287, 1.5739]
50%	Baseline vs Random	−17.3790	[−21.9691, −12.7890]	−13.6559	[−19.8842, −7.4277]
	NSGA-II vs Random	−16.9624	[−21.5524, −12.3723]	−16.8817	[−23.1100, −10.6535]
	Baseline vs NSGA-II	−0.4167	[−5.0067, 4.1734]	3.2258	[−3.0024, 9.4541]
90%	Baseline vs Random	0.2285	[−0.9178, 1.3748]	1.1559	[−2.0332, 4.3451]
	NSGA-II vs Random	2.0565	[0.9102, 3.2027]	−0.4570	[−3.6461, 2.7322]
	Baseline vs NSGA-II	−1.8280	[−2.9742, −0.6817]	1.6129	[−1.5763, 4.8021]

One-way ANOVA revealed significant performance differences among NSGA-II, Baseline, and Random ($p < 0.001$), especially at low and mid RTWs. Tukey's HSD tests at 10%, 50%, and 90% RTW (shown due to space) indicate NSGA-II and Baseline were closely matched on coverage, but NSGA-II consistently achieved higher business value. Full results are in the replication package[1].

Random lagged behind in both metrics at lower and mid RTWs, narrowing the gap as budgets increased. Efficiency declined for all methods as RTW rose, with NSGA-II and Baseline most efficient at low RTWs and converging with Random at the highest budgets. These results confirm NSGA-II's advantage in balancing business value and coverage (see Tables 2 and 3).

5 Discussion

In this section, we present our interpretation of the results and answer the research questions.

RQ1. How does the proposed multi-objective algorithm balance business value and requirement coverage under different RTWs?: The behavior of NSGA-II across RTWs suggests that regression testing in agile can indeed be treated as a value-preserving allocation problem, rather than a purely technical coverage

[1] https://github.com/Suddhasvatta007/An-AI-Driven-Decision-System-for-Value-Aware-Regression-Testing.

exercise. When the RTW is tight, the algorithm is forced to expose its "preferences": it consistently converges on configurations that protect fewer, but more valuable requirements, while still respecting the requirement-level definition of done. This pattern indicates that the multi-objective formulation successfully internalizes Agile's central principle of maximizing stakeholder value under constraints: instead of distributing time thinly across many low-impact behaviors, NSGA-II concentrates the available budget on high-value slices of functionality whose failure would be most damaging.

At the same time, the results show that this emphasis on value does not come at the expense of requirement coverage. Because the algorithm operates at the requirement level and counts a requirement as covered only when all of its validating tests are selected, the search is implicitly encouraged to form cohesive "bundles" of tests that complete requirements, rather than scattered partial selections. This creates a natural coupling between value and coverage, i.e., high-value requirements are protected end-to-end, while the algorithm continues to explore solutions that expand coverage as more time becomes available. The fact that NSGA-II tracks the requirement coverage driven baseline closely, while often achieving higher cumulative business value, indicates that value and coverage can be jointly optimized rather than treated as competing objectives.

The way NSGA-II behaves across the RTW range also reveals something about different operating regimes for agile teams. In very small RTWs, the algorithm's selections embody a "core value shield". The pipeline has just enough time to guard the most valuable behaviors, while accepting that some peripheral functionality will remain temporarily untested. As the RTW grows into a midrange, NSGA-II's solutions become more balanced, progressively incorporating medium-value requirements and thereby expanding coverage without losing sight of value. Once the RTW is large enough to admit most tests, the optimization problem becomes almost degenerate, and all approaches converge to similar BV and coverage, with the specific balancing strategy mattering far less. This reinforces that intelligent selection is most needed exactly where agile teams feel the most pressure when feedback must be fast, and budgets are tight.

From a conceptual standpoint, the observed balance between BV and requirement coverage suggests that RTS should be explicitly framed as a multi-objective decision rather than a single-metric optimization. NSGA-II's search does not commit to a single "best" trade-off; it generates a frontier of alternatives that differ in how they balance value concentration versus breadth of coverage. In practice, this gives product owners and quality assurance teams a spectrum of defensible choices, for example, preferring a solution that best suites their quality goals. In this way, the algorithm does not replace human judgment; it structures it, making explicit the trade-offs that are often handled informally or heuristically in current agile regression practice. Moreover, this philosophy also aligns with the concept of using value as metric for regression testing along with the current technical metrics we have as mentioned by Das and Gary [9].

Finally, the fact that the same qualitative balancing behavior emerges on two datasets of different sizes indicates that the approach is not overly sensitive to the scale of the regression test set. Whether the team faces a smaller or larger pool of UATs, NSGA-II consistently allocates limited test time to protect high-value requirements while maintaining competitive coverage. This supports the broader claim that value-aware, time-constrained multi-objective optimization is a viable foundation for RTS in agile, rather than merely an artifact of a particular dataset or configuration.

RQ2. What is the BV/unit time of the proposed algorithm compared to BCPSO and Random?: Interpreting *BV per unit time as efficiency = (total BV of requirements whose all tests are selected/execution time of selected tests).* The results show that NSGA-II and the BCPSO baseline are broadly similar in efficiency, and both clearly outperform Random, especially at low and mid RTWs. As RTW grows, all three methods exhibit steadily declining BV/unit time and eventually converge, reflecting the expected diminishing returns: once most requirements are covered, each extra minute of testing buys proportionally less additional value. From an agile perspective, this reinforces the idea that early minutes are much more valuable than late ones.

The more interesting behavior appears in the small and mid RTWs, where we sometimes observe that the baseline achieves slightly higher BV/unit time than NSGA-II, even though NSGA-II delivers more total BV over the same RTW grid. This is not a contradiction; it is a direct consequence of what each algorithm is optimizing. NSGA-II is explicitly tuned to maximize (i) total business value and (ii) requirement coverage, under the hard time constraint, with a strict "definition of done" that only counts a requirement if all its tests are executed. In practice, this means NSGA-II is willing to "pay" for some high-value but relatively expensive requirements if they help the solution move up on the BV axis, even when their test bundles consume a substantial portion of the budget. BCPSO, in contrast, is designed to maximize requirement coverage within a given cost; it naturally favors cheaper requirements and test clusters, because they let it cover more distinct requirements within the same time budget. When we then compute BV/unit time using the actual execution time of the selected tests, this coverage-centric behavior can yield slightly higher value density per second for BCPSO, even though the absolute value protected is lower.

The characteristics of the datasets accentuate this effect. Business value assignments follow a right-skewed distribution, and execution times are sampled from a right-tailed exponential distribution, with no enforced correlation between the two, following the baseline's idea. As a result, there exist clusters of cheap, medium-BV requirements and expensive, high-BV requirements. NSGA-II's BV objective pulls it toward including some of the expensive, high-BV requirements once the "cheap head" is mostly exploited, whereas BCPSO continues to accumulate many low-to-medium value requirements with short tests. In pure efficiency terms, the baseline is effectively skimming "cheap value" first, so its BV/unit-time curve can sit slightly above NSGA-II's in some bands, even as NSGA-II secures a larger share of the total BV available in the system.

Seen through an agile lens, this trade-off is meaningful rather than problematic. A team that optimized solely for BV per minute could end up with a portfolio dominated by small, inexpensive stories that collectively look very efficient but leave some high-stakes workflows under-tested. NSGA-II, on the other hand, behaves more like a product owner under time pressure. It uses the available window to ensure that a larger portion of the release's high-value requirements are fully exercised, accepting that the resulting test set may not maximize BV/unit time at every RTW. The efficiency results, therefore, suggest that our multi-objective approach is making a deliberate trade: it sacrifices a small amount of value density per second to protect more of what matters most, while remaining within the same efficiency range as a cost-sharpened coverage baseline and well ahead of uninformed selection. For agile teams, that trade-off aligns with the core goal of regression testing: not to win an efficiency metric in isolation, but to spend limited regression time in a way that most robustly preserves delivered business value.

6 Threats to Validity

In this section, we discuss potential threats to the validity of our study along the four common dimensions of internal, construct, external, and conclusion validity.

Internal validity may be affected by using synthetic datasets and assumptions about BV and execution-time distributions, as well as dataset scaling and NSGA-II parameter choices, although replication and literature-backed settings help mitigate some of this risk.

Construct validity is limited by the strict requirement-level "definition of done" and the Fibonacci-based BV distribution, which may differ from real-world practices.

External validity is constrained by the use of synthetic datasets and a narrow set of baselines, which may reduce generalizability to industrial UAT suites and diverse agile teams.

Conclusion validity is supported by statistical significance testing (ANOVA, Tukey HSD), but is weakened by the absence of effect sizes and adjustments for multiple comparisons; replication and trend consistency support our conclusions, though additional statistical detail would further increase confidence.

Overall, these threats indicate that our results should be interpreted as an initial, controlled evaluation of value-aware, time-constrained regression test selection rather than definitive evidence of performance in all industrial settings. Nonetheless, the consistency of trends across replications and the use of literature-informed parameters suggest that the observed advantages of the proposed approach are meaningful and warrant further investigation with real-world datasets and broader baselines.

7 Conclusion and Future Work

In conclusion, this work re-frames agile regression testing as a business value preservation problem, formalizes it as a multi-objective optimization maximizing BV and requirement coverage within a finite RTW, and demonstrates it with an NSGA-II–based approach. Empirical results show that, especially under tight and mid-range budgets, the method consistently protects more business value while maintaining competitive coverage, converging with other methods only when time is abundant. The core contribution is conceptual: for the first time, AI and business metrics are combined for test and resource management, positioning regression selection as an AI-supported, value-focused decision. AI makes trade-offs explicit, supporting agile's goal of continuously safeguarding delivered stakeholder value.

Moreover, future work will enhance AI-based decision-making and data quality. NSGA-II can evolve into value-aware optimization services integrated into CI/CD pipelines, continuously providing Pareto-optimal test sets as decision-support tools. Here, the RTS engine acts as a service, recommending test subsets per change based on business value, coverage, and time, and making trade-offs transparent for stakeholders. A key challenge is the "starvation effect": optimizing cycles in isolation can cause some requirements to be repeatedly skipped. Addressing this requires richer data tracking cross-cycle history and recency, adding anti-starvation constraints, and collaborating with industry for longitudinal agile datasets with requirements, tests, BV, and pipeline telemetry. Ultimately, AI needs only business value as a semantic signal, quantified however an organization chooses, as measurement itself shapes what is observed [21].

Acknowledgment. This work acknowledges the assistance of a Large Language Model (LLM) used explicitly for grammar and spelling-checking purposes. The author has reviewed all content to ensure accuracy, integrity, and correctness.

References

1. Ali, S., Hafeez, Y., Hussain, S., Yang, S.: Enhanced regression testing technique for agile software development and continuous integration strategies. Software Qual. J. **28**, 397–423 (2020). https://doi.org/10.1007/s11219-019-09492-2
2. Alliance, A.: Manifesto for agile software development (2001). https://agilemanifesto.org. Accessed 12 Sept 2024
3. Arafeen, M.J., Do, H.: Test case prioritization using requirements-based clustering. In: Proceedings of the 2013 IEEE 6th International Conference on Software Testing, Verification and Validation, pp. 312–321. IEEE (2013)
4. Biswas, S., Mall, R., Satpathy, M.: A regression test selection technique for embedded software. ACM Trans. Embed. Comput. Syst. **13**, 47:1–47:39 (2013). https://doi.org/10.1145/2539036.2539043. https://consensus.app/papers/a-regression-test-selection-technique-for-embedded-biswas-mall/bc0778b835c25d9ebf6a741de1978a15/?utm_source=chatgpt
5. Chesser, C.: A Regression Test Selection Technique for Graphical User Interfaces (Doctoral dissertation, University of Kansas) (2012)
6. Chittimalli, P.K., Harrold, M.J.: Regression test selection on system requirements. In: Proceedings of the 1st India Software Engineering Conference, pp. 87–96. ACM (2008)

7. Cottmeyer, M.: Small agile user stories reduce variability and improve predictability (2014). https://www.leadingagile.com/2014/01/small-stories-reduce-variability-velocity-improve-predictability. Accessed 23 Oct 2025
8. CrowdStrike: Channel file 291 incident root cause analysis. Technical report, CrowdStrike, Inc., Austin, TX (2024). https://www.crowdstrike.com/wp-content/uploads/2024/08/Channel-File-291-Incident-Root-Cause-Analysis-08.06.2024.pdf, retrieved from CrowdStrike website
9. Das, S., Gary, K.: Regression testing in agile–a systematic mapping study. Software **4**(2), 9 (2025)
10. Deb, K.: An efficient constraint handling method for genetic algorithms. Comput. Methods Appl. Mech. Eng. **186**(2–4), 311–338 (2000)
11. Deb, K.: Multi-objective optimisation using evolutionary algorithms: an introduction. In: Multi-objective Evolutionary Optimisation for Product Design and Manufacturing, pp. 3–34. Springer, London (2011)
12. Delamare, R., Baudry, B., Le Traon, Y.: Regression test selection when evolving software with aspects. In: ACM SIGSOFT International Symposium on Software Testing and Analysis, p. 7 (2008). https://doi.org/10.1145/1404953.1404960. https://consensus.app/papers/regression-test-selection-when-evolving-software-with-delamare-baudry/67d5b2447c425a51b2ed22ecc9456bbf/?utm_source=chatgpt
13. Edin, A., Qorbanzada, M.: An ambidextrous approach to user acceptance testing management and automation: how software customers can optimize their processes to explore new technology as well as current performance to improve the effectiveness of user acceptance testing (2022)
14. Elbaum, S., Rothermel, G., Penix, J.: Techniques for improving regression testing in continuous integration development environments. In: Proceedings of the 22nd ACM SIGSOFT International Symposium on Foundations of Software Engineering, pp. 235–245. ACM, New York (2014)
15. Elbaum, S., Malishevsky, A.G., Rothermel, G.: Test case prioritization: a family of empirical studies. IEEE Trans. Software Eng. **28**(2), 159–182 (2004)
16. Elbeltagi, E., Hegazy, T., Grierson, D.: Comparison among five evolutionary-based optimization algorithms. Adv. Eng. Inform. **19**(1), 43–53 (2005)
17. Gligorić, M., Majumdar, R., Sharma, R., Eloussi, L., Marinov, D.: Regression test selection for distributed software histories. In: International Conference on Fundamental Approaches to Software Engineering, pp. 293–309 (2014). https://doi.org/10.1007/978-3-319-08867-9_19. https://consensus.app/papers/regression-test-selection-for-distributed-software-gligoric-majumdar/f5cf99835d7d5a42b456a21daa8f4304/?utm_source=chatgpt
18. Harman, M., Jones, B.F.: Search-based software engineering. Inf. Softw. Technol. **43**(14), 833–839 (2001)
19. Harman, M., McMinn, P.: A theoretical and empirical study of search-based testing: local, global, and hybrid search. IEEE Trans. Software Eng. **36**(2), 226–247 (2009)
20. Harrold, M.J., et al.: Regression test selection for java software. In: Proceedings of the 16th ACM SIGPLAN Conference on Object-Oriented Programming, Systems, Languages, and Applications, pp. 312–326 (2001). https://doi.org/10.1145/504282.504305. https://consensus.app/papers/regression-test-selection-for-java-software-harrold-jones/71258751df6e54df983339c8c182f60e/?utm_source=chatgpt
21. Heidenberg, J., Weijola, M., Mikkonen, K., Porres, I.: A model for business value in large-scale agile and lean software development. In: Systems, Software and Services

Process Improvement: 19th European Conference, EuroSPI 2012, Vienna, Austria, 25–27 June 2012. Proceedings, vol. 19, pp. 49–60. Springer, Heidelberg (2012). https://doi.org/10.1007/978-3-642-31199-4_5
22. Jorgensen, P.C.: Software testing: a Craftsman's approach. Auerbach Publications, Boca Raton (2013)
23. Kachitvichyanukul, V.: Comparison of three evolutionary algorithms: GA, PSO, and DE. Ind. Eng. Manage. Syst. **11**(3), 215–223 (2012)
24. Kandil, P., Moussa, S., Badr, N.: Cluster-based test cases prioritization and selection technique for agile regression testing. J. Softw. Evol. Process **29**(6), e1794 (2017). https://doi.org/10.1002/smr.1794
25. Kazmi, R., Jawawi, D.N., Mohamad, R., Ghani, I.: Effective regression test case selection: a systematic literature review. ACM Comput. Surv. (CSUR) **50**(2), 1–32 (2017)
26. Koivuniemi, J.: Shortening feedback time in continuous integration environment in large-scale embedded software development with test selection. Master's thesis, J. Koivuniemi (2017)
27. Leffingwell, D.: Agile Software Requirements: Lean Requirements Practices for Teams, Programs, and the Enterprise. Addison-Wesley Professional (2010)
28. Li, Z., Harman, M., Hierons, R.M.: Search algorithms for regression test case prioritization. IEEE Trans. Software Eng. **33**(4), 225–237 (2007)
29. Nidhra, S., Dondeti, J.: Black box and white box testing techniques: a literature review. Int. J. Embed. Syst. Appl. (IJESA) **2**(2), 29–50 (2012)
30. Pan, R., Bagherzadeh, M., Ghaleb, T.A., Briand, L.: Test case selection and prioritization using machine learning: a systematic literature review. Empir. Softw. Eng. **27**(2), 29 (2022). https://doi.org/10.1007/s10664-021-10046-1
31. Poppendieck, M.: Principles of lean thinking. IT Manage. Select **18**, 1–7 (2011)
32. Institute of Project Management: 16th annual state of agile report (2022). https://instituteprojectmanagement.com/wp-content/uploads/2023/01/AR-SA-2022-16th-Annual-State-Of-Agile-Report.pdf. Accessed 12 Sept 2024
33. Rothermel, G., Harrold, M.J.: A safe, efficient regression test selection technique. ACM Trans. Softw. Eng. Methodol. (TOSEM) **6**(2), 173–210 (1997)
34. Salem, A.B.: What is WSJF – weighted shortest job first safe? (2022). https://scrum-master.org/en/what-is-wsjf-weighted-shortest-job-first-safe/?utm_source=chatgpt.com. Accessed 23 Oct 2025
35. Shi, A., Zhao, P., Marinov, D.: Understanding and improving regression test selection in continuous integration. In: Proceedings of the 2019 IEEE 30th International Symposium on Software Reliability Engineering (ISSRE), pp. 228–238. IEEE, New York (2019)
36. de Souza, L.S., et al.: Search based constrained test case selection using execution effort. Expert Syst. Appl. **40**(12), 4887–4896 (2013)
37. Spieker, H., Gotlieb, A., Marijan, D., Mossige, M.: Reinforcement learning for automatic test case prioritization and selection in continuous integration. In: Proceedings of the 26th ACM SIGSOFT International Symposium on Software Testing and Analysis, pp. 12–22. ACM, New York (2017)
38. Srivastva, P.R., Kumar, K., Raghurama, G.: Test case prioritization based on requirements and risk factors. ACM SIGSOFT Softw. Eng. Notes **33**(4), 1–5 (2008)
39. Svensson, R.B., Torkar, R.: Not all requirements prioritization criteria are equal at all times: a quantitative analysis. J. Syst. Softw. **209**, 111909 (2024)
40. Team, I.A.J.E.: Estimating the business value of stories (2020). https://integralagile.com/journal/estimating-business-value-stories. Accessed 23 Oct 2025

41. Trujillo, T.: Business value and prioritization: what work should you do first? (2023). https://www.catalyte.io/insights/business-value-and-prioritization-what-work-should-be-done-first/. Accessed 07 Aug 2025
42. Wohlin, C., Runeson, P., Höst, M., Ohlsson, M.C., Regnell, B., Wesslén, A.: Experimentation in Software Engineering, vol. 236. Springer, Berlin (2012)
43. Yu, T., Wang, T.: A study of regression test selection in continuous integration environments. In: Proceedings of the 2018 IEEE 29th International Symposium on Software Reliability Engineering (ISSRE), pp. 135–143. IEEE (2018)

ArchHypo.AI: An LLM-Based Tool for Managing Software Architecture Uncertainty with Hypothesis Engineering in Agile Boards

Jonathan Carvalho[1], Vinicius da Silva Dias[1], Fábio Fagundes Silveira[1](✉), Eduardo Guerra[4], Paulo Gabriel Gadelha Queiroz[2], and Joelma Choma[2,3]

[1] Federal University of São Paulo, São José dos Campos, Brazil
{jonathan.carvalho,dias.vinicius,fsilveira}@unifesp.br
[2] Free University of Bozen-Bolzano, Bolzano, Italy
pgabriel@ufersa.edu.br, jchoma@ufscar.br
[3] Federal Rural University of the Semi-Arid Region, Mossoró, Brazil
[4] Federal University of São Carlos, São Carlos, Brazil
eduardo.guerra@unibz.it

Abstract. Agile software development often faces challenges related to architectural uncertainty. ArchHypo addresses this by providing a hypothesis-driven architecture technique that helps teams formulate, test, and learn from architectural assumptions iteratively. However, studies have shown that the lack of tooling integrated into everyday development workflows is a significant barrier to its adoption. In this paper, we present `ArchHypo.AI`, a Trello plugin that integrates hypothesis-driven architectural reasoning directly into agile boards and validates the ArchHypo technique in real projects. The plugin uses an LLM and a RAG mechanism to help teams generate and classify architectural hypotheses, develop technical plans, and link actions to architecture decision patterns. By operating on top of an existing project management tool, `ArchHypo.AI` aims to lower the adoption cost of hypothesis engineering and to make architectural decision processes more observable. We evaluated `ArchHypo.AI` in a controlled study with software professionals working on a realistic architecture scenario. The results indicate that the plugin helps structure architectural discussions, reduces manual effort in documenting hypotheses and plans, clarifies procedural steps, and surfaces differences in risk perception within teams. Qualitative feedback suggests that AI-assisted support facilitates collaborative reasoning about architecture. Our findings show that LLM-based tools can effectively support hypothesis-driven architecture in agile settings and highlight design considerations for integrating such tools into existing workflows.

Keywords: Hypothesis-Driven Architecture · GenAI SE Tools · Agile Software Development

A. Goldman et al. (Eds.): XP 2026, LNBIP 578, pp. 191–207, 2026.
https://doi.org/10.1007/978-3-032-22375-3_12

1 Introduction

Agile software development is a mainstream approach to software development that supports incremental deliveries, continuous collaboration, and adaptation to change [23]. However, as systems evolve and become more complex, challenges and uncertainties arise related to architectural decision-making [20,21]. These uncertainties, if not managed effectively, can result in rework, technical debt, and system vulnerability [15].

Based on patterns identified in agile architecture approaches, the ArchHypo technique [15] proposes hypothesis engineering as a way to address uncertainties in software architecture. This technique allows teams to establish, evaluate, and confirm assumptions about architectural choices, promoting traceability and continuous learning [16]. ArchHypo was created within an adaptable format that can be used in various agile development methodologies. Although some benefits of ArchHypo have been recognized, professionals have reported practical challenges in its adoption, particularly the lack of tools for recording and tracking architectural hypotheses within the team's daily workflow, which has been identified as a barrier to effective use [16].

To overcome these limitations, we developed a Trello[1] plugin that connects ArchHypo directly to the development workflow. Trello is a project management tool where tasks, represented as cards, are organized into columns that reflect workflow stages. We chose Trello for its widespread popularity, adaptability, and support for agile processes. By integrating Large Language Models (LLMs) into the plugin, we provide intelligent support for decision-making, justification, and hypothesis refinement based on historical data and recurring patterns [24]. To our knowledge, no existing tools provide this level of LLM-supported hypothesis engineering integration.

The main objective is to present and evaluate the adoption of the ArchHypo technique through an empirical study with specialists, and to propose an LLM-based tool to support this adoption. Furthermore, it seeks to encourage continuous experimentation and data-driven decision-making, in line with recent initiatives such as Evidence-Based Agile [17] and Lean Experimentation [21].

The paper is organized as follows: Sect. 2 reviews the foundations of hypothesis-driven architecture and AI in software engineering. Section 3 details the `ArchHypo.AI` plugin and its implementation. Section 4 describes the research design and participants. Section 5 reports artifact analysis and feedback. Finally, Sects. 6 and 7 discuss implications, limitations, and future directions.

2 Background

Agile software development prioritizes cyclical delivery, collaborative work with the client, and rapid response to changes. Its principles are widely used in many fields, empowering teams to deliver value in constantly changing environments [23]. However, choosing architectural solutions in agile environments

[1] https://trello.com.

remains a complex task, often affected by changing requirements and stakeholder uncertainty [20].

To address architectural uncertainty, the *ArchHypo technique* was developed, which applies hypothesis engineering to architecture [15]. This technique motivates teams to consider architectural decisions as hypotheses that should be tested through experimentation, in alignment with the agile values of flexibility and learning. The approach is grounded around a set of patterns that define its principles and guide its application in agile environments [12,14].

Patterns are essential in agile architecture, offering reusable solutions to recurring design problems. Research has documented patterns for the evolution of architecture in agile projects [22], for initial architectural design [6], and for the maintenance of architectural health through continuous inspections [11]. These patterns provide a foundation for integrating hypothesis-driven practices into agile workflows.

Experimentation is fundamental for agile decision-making, and prior work has proposed software analytics patterns to supports experimentation and learning in development teams [2,3]. Such patterns help establish quality criteria, learn from experiments, and manage measurement processes.

Current developments in artificial intelligence have provided new opportunities to support agility. Implementing the LLM model in development workflows provides intelligent assistance in formulating, prioritizing, and refining hypotheses [24]. This aligns with the *Evidence-Based Agile* initiative, which advocates for data-driven decisions and continuous validation [17].

Lean experimentation complements these strategies by promoting agile testing of ideas with limited resources, reducing risks, and accelerating learning [21]. Together, these concepts establish a solid foundation for improving the architectural decision-making process in agile environments.

3 ArchHypo.AI: Intelligent Hypothesis Management in Agile Tools

In agile development environments, architectural decisions are often made under conditions of uncertainty, directly affecting Non-Functional Requirements (NFRs). To address this situation, Silva et al. [15] proposed the *ArchHypo technique*, which is based on an iterative cycle designed to progressively reduce architectural uncertainty. The process begins with *Uncertainty Identification*, followed by *Hypothesis Formulation*, where the NFRs in question are categorized and their impact and degree of uncertainty are analyzed. Then a *Technical Plan* is developed, describing the experiments, examining the trade-offs, and employing ArchHypo patterns such as *Architectural Spike* or *Proof of Concept*, supported by *Retrieval Augmented Generation (RAG)* [25]. After the experiments are executed and verified, the *Analysis and Learning* phase takes place, generating insights that will inform future decisions and backlog improvement.

To support this iterative process, we created `ArchHypo.AI`[2], a Trello add-on that leverages the capabilities of Large Language Models (LLMs) [18] to aid in architectural reasoning activities. The current version uses Google Gemini Pro[3]; however, its versatile structure enables compatibility with other LLMs.

To provide highly accurate, low-latency responses, the add-on uses prompts engineering techniques alongside a vector database. This strategy allows `ArchHypo.AI` to quickly store and retrieve contextual project information, including previous architectural decisions and relevant discussions. The retrieved information is then integrated into prompts, providing the LLM with the essential context to produce more detailed and informed analyses.

This structure not only enhances the quality of the generated justifications and classifications but also ensures fast and effective interaction directly within the Trello workflow, promoting informed decision-making and encouraging a continuous learning cycle.

3.1 Core Features and Functionalities

The plugin was developed to integrate with the existing Trello workflow, offering a set of AI-powered features that convert uncertainties into tangible actions, such as: **Hypothesis Generation from Uncertainties:** The user presents a technical uncertainty in natural language. The LLM examines the description and automatically generates a well-structured technical hypothesis; **LLM-Assisted Classification:** During the hypothesis creation process, the LLM proposes classifications for essential attributes, such as the related Non-Functional Requirement (NFR) (e.g., Performance, Safety), the intensity of the uncertainty, and the possible impact on the project. Each suggestion is accompanied by an explanation, promoting clarity in decision-making; **Technical Plan Generation:** Based on a hypothesis, the user can request the development of a technical plan. The LLM develops a set of actions (e.g., Architectural Prototypes, Proofs of Concept, etc.) with the goal of validating the hypothesis and reducing uncertainty; **Classification with Architectural Patterns:** Each action in the technical plan is automatically categorized with an architectural decision pattern, such as *Architectural Spike*, *Tracer Bullets*, or *Postpone Uncertain Decisions*. This categorization is performed by LLM, using a predefined pattern catalog accessed via RAG, which helps standardize risk mitigation strategies; **Visualization of Metrics:** The plugin provides a visual dashboard that compiles information from the cards, allowing the team to observe the distribution of hypotheses based on their level of impact, uncertainty, Non-Functional Requirements (NFRs), and Architectural Patterns, thus facilitating prioritization and strategic monitoring.

3.2 LLM-Driven Architectural Support

The `ArchHypo.AI` offers two main functionalities to support architectural decisions in agile environments: (i) the *(RAG* technique for classifying architectural

[2] https://github.com/jonathancs-tester/ArchHypo-Trello-Plugin.
[3] https://gemini.google.com.

patterns, and (ii) an *Interactive User Feedback* mechanism, which ensures continuous adaptation of the model. Figure 1 shows the operational flow of these functionalities.

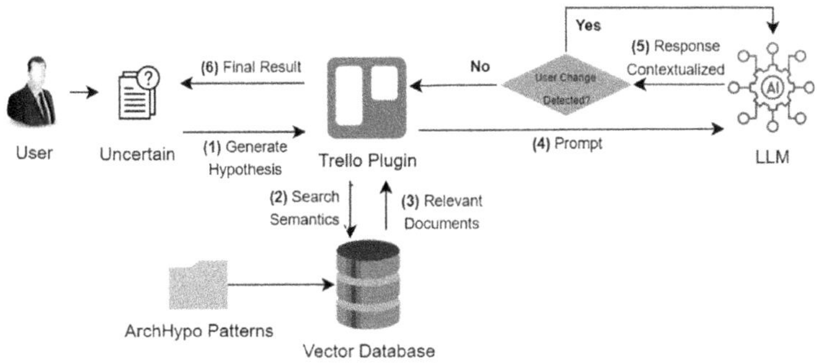

Fig. 1. Operational flow of LLM-based architectural support in `ArchHypo.AI`, integrating RAG and user feedback mechanisms for hypothesis management.

The **RAG** approach enables the LLM to access a dynamic, up-to-date knowledge base of *ArchHypo Patterns*, overcoming the limitations of pre-trained knowledge. The process occurs in four stages: (1) the architectural hypothesis is received as input; (2) it is encoded into a *embedding* vector and used to query a vector database in *Pinecone*[4] with 0.0 temperature and 2k chunk size; (3) the most relevant documents are retrieved and concatenated with the original hypothesis, forming a *prompt optimization* with 2k–20k max tokens; (4) the LLM generates a response in JSON format with the most appropriate pattern and the justification for the choice.

However, the **Interactive User Feedback** ensures that the system evolves based on user corrections. During the creation of hypothesis and technical plans, the user can adjust LLM suggestions, such as hypotheses, NFRs, uncertainty levels, and architectural patterns. Each adjustment is recorded and structured in the LLM context using Trello APIs that can be used to align the model with the team's preferences. This continuous cycle makes LLMs more accurate, adaptive, and integrated into agile workflows.

4 Methodology

This study aimed to evaluate the use of the `ArchHypo.AI` plugin in assisting architects and software developers in identifying, documenting, and planning the resolution of architectural uncertainties. To guide the study, three research questions were formulated:

[4] https://www.pinecone.io.

- **RQ1 (Effectiveness):** Can professionals effectively use the `ArchHypo.AI` plugin to transform unstructured architectural concerns into structured hypotheses and actionable technical plans?
- **RQ2 (Usefulness):** Does the `ArchHypo.AI` plugin generate relevant suggestions, such as hypotheses, technical plans, and classifications, that are aligned with the initial architectural uncertainties?
- **RQ3 (Usability):** What usability benefits and challenges do participants face when using the `ArchHypo.AI` plugin to support architectural decision-making?

4.1 Participant Profile

The study participants were 10 professionals enrolled in the joint Master's Program in Computer Science at the State University of Rio Grande do Norte and the Federal Rural University of the Semi-Arid Region (Mossoró, Brazil), most of whom had over 5 years of professional experience in software engineering. Table 1 provides a summary of the participants' professional profiles. As shown in the table, participants were divided into four balanced groups. Each group was expected to collaboratively discuss architectural uncertainties and assess whether the AI-generated classifications aligned with their assumptions and the technical planning aspects considered in the study.

Table 1. Participant demographics and roles in the `ArchHypo.AI` evaluation study.

Board	Participant	Current Position	Experience	Arch. Level	Team Size	Company Type
Board 1	P1	Solutions Architect	>10 years	Senior	6–10 people	IT Consulting
	P2	Software Engineer Senior	5–10 years	Medium	6–10 people	Large Company
	P3	Mid-Level Developer	2–5 years	Low	3–5 people	Startup
Board 2	P4	Tech Lead	>10 years	High	11–15 people	Digital Product
	P5	Senior Software Engineer	5–10 years	Medium	6–10 people	Large Company
	P6	Junior Developer	1–2 years	Low	11–15 people	IT Consulting
Board 3	P7	Specialist Software Engineer	>10 years	High	3–5 people	Startup
	P8	Mid-Level Developer	5–10 years	Medium	6–10 people	Product Digital
Board 4	P9	Software Architect	>10 years	Senior	>15 people	Large Enterprise
	P10	Senior DevOps Engineer	5–10 years	Medium	6–10 people	IT Consulting

* *Arch. Level: Self-assessed Architecture Knowledge Level.*

4.2 Data Collection and Study Procedure

The study was conducted within the context of the "Special Topics in Software Engineering and Computational Systems" course. Although the activity was carried out with all enrolled participants, they were explicitly informed that participation in the research component was entirely voluntary, and formal consent was obtained. No academic assessment was based on individual performance in the activity or on the answers provided in the questionnaire. Despite being embedded in an academic setting, the course was specifically designed for and attended by experienced software professionals. The study followed an organized workflow consisting of three main stages: onboarding and training, activity execution, and data validation.

In the initial stage, participants underwent an onboarding process to ensure they understood the study's objectives and the tools used. First, they reviewed and signed a free and informed consent form that detailed the purpose of the investigation, the measures taken to protect data privacy, and the voluntary nature of their participation. To promote understanding of the `ArchHypo.AI` plugin, participants received two essential documents: a *User Guide* containing detailed instructions for using the tool, and a *Pattern Catalog* describing the ArchHypo Patterns [12,14,15] used by the plugin. Following this, a practical training session took place, during which participants practiced formulating an example of uncertainty, developing a hypothesis, and creating a technical plan using the plugin.

In the second stage, participants were presented with an authentic scenario that illustrated the architectural uncertainties described in a text. Based on this scenario, participants were instructed to identify three different architectural uncertainties, create corresponding hypotheses in `ArchHypo.AI` and develop technical plans for each hypothesis.

The text describing the uncertainties was created based on three hypotheses derived from a case study [15]. These hypotheses correspond to the H1, H2, and H5 labels in the original work. These hypotheses were chosen because they relate to important quality attributes, specifically performance, security, and flexibility. Moreover, since they were derived from a real project, they represent a realistic scenario, and the original project's data can serve as a reference to evaluate the study's outcomes. In addition to identifying and classifying the hypotheses, the groups should also propose concrete actions for the technical plan, based on documented patterns for handling architectural uncertainty.

The third stage involved exporting and validating the data from the Trello boards developed by each team, encompassing all assumptions, technical strategies, and content generated by `ArchHypo.AI`. Following this activity, participants were asked to complete a questionnaire[5] containing both closed and open-ended questions to indicate (i) the most useful aspects of `ArchHypo.AI` (ii) report any difficulties or limitations encountered, and (iii) suggest improvements or new features. In this form, they also provided informed consent to participate in the study.

4.3 Data Analysis

To address RQ1 (effectiveness) and RQ2 (usefulness), we conducted a comparative analysis between the data extracted from the Trello artifacts produced by

[5] https://forms.gle/BBAPnbKuR67tChGm6.

the teams throughout the study and the proposals based on input from software architecture specialists who had previously created and validated patterns and processes for this architecture. These discussions occurred during video calls and were documented to inform the design and refinement of the approach. This analysis evaluated the coherence and relevance of the proposals discussed, considering different perspectives and the context of the original project.

In addition, we systematically reviewed hypotheses and technical plans developed by the participants, evaluating their relevance, coherence, and congruence with the architectural scenario presented at the beginning. Since there are several valid approaches to handling the same software uncertainty, the original project's actions were considered for comparison, but not as the only correct direction. The aim is to verify whether the plugin actually assisted in developing meaningful, contextually grounded architectural reasoning.

Regarding RQ3 (usability), we analyzed responses to the post-activity questionnaire using thematic analysis [1] to identify recurring patterns related to positive aspects, limitations, and suggestions for usability improvements. This allowed us to evaluate the tool's usability and identify areas for improvement in the plugin. A combined analysis enabled a comprehensive understanding of how the `ArchHypo.AI` contributes to architectural decision-making in agile environments.

5 Results

This section presents the results of the hypothesis evaluation performed by the participants and alignment with architectural patterns compared to the reference data established by the specialists (Sect. 5.1) and the participants' feedback on the usability of the `ArchHypo.AI` plugin (Sect. 5.2).

5.1 Effectiveness and Usefulness of the ArchHypo.AI

In Tables 2 and 3, the colors indicate the degree of alignment between the groups' results and the specialists. **Green** represents total convergence, meaning the result and the justification coincide with those of the specialists. **Yellow** indicates partial divergence: the result differs, but the justification presented is coherent and makes sense. **Red** indicates complete divergence, when neither the result nor the justification is aligned with the specialists view.

The hypothesis comparison focused on the categorical fields associated with each hypothesis, such as Non-Functional Requirements (NFR), Level of Uncertainty, and Level of Impact, for each group. Table 2 illustrates a comparison of these categorical fields for each group that corresponded to the specialists' evaluation.

Overall, this assessment reveals that, although the groups had risk topics similar to those of the specialists, their perceptions of the importance of each risk differed. The `ArchHypo.AI` plugin effectively exposes these perception disparities, promoting a structured dialogue about architectural decisions and allowing

Table 2. Comparison of hypothesis classifications (NFR, Uncertainty, Impact) between specialists and participant groups.

Group	Hypothesis	NFR	Uncertainty Level	Impact Level
Original Data (Specialist)	H1	Performance	High	High
	H2	Security	High	Very High
	H5	Flexibility	High	High
Group 1	H1	Performance	Low	Medium
	H2	Security	Medium	High
	H5	Flexibility	Medium	Medium
Group 2	H1	Performance	Medium	High
	H2	Security	Low	Medium
	H5	Flexibility	Medium	High
Group 3	H1	Reliability	Low	High
	H2	Security	High	Very High
	H5	Performance	Low	Medium
Group 4	H1	Performance	High	Very High
	H2	Security	Medium	High
	H5	Flexibility	Medium	High

teams to come together not only to identify risks but also to prioritize them and assess their potential impact. Regarding the *Performance hypothesis*, all groups recognized the risk associated with using a single server, showing only variations in uncertainty (from low to high). Under the *Security hypothesis*, there was unanimity on the importance of integration with the government's SSO, with impact levels that proved to be consistently high, reflecting the specialists' view. Finally, within the *Flexibility hypothesis*, the groups discussed the coexistence of legacy (XML) and new (JSON) data in a similar manner, further strengthening the specialists' perception of the architectural consequences of this choice.

After that, the architectural patterns used by the participating groups and the specialists were compared across the hypotheses. For each item determined by the group, it was verified whether the selected architectural pattern was consistent with the specialists' choice. Table 3 provides the convergence and divergence results between the groups' and the specialists' views.

A comparison between the patterns selected by the specialists and those of four distinct groups revealed differences in theoretical alignment in their approach to solving software architecture-related problems.

To address performance and scalability challenges, the specialists adopted the *Software Analytics* methodology [2]. The groups took varied paths: Group 4 most closely resembled the specialist's approach, combining *Architectural Spike* and *Software Analytics*. In contrast, the other groups chose tactics such as practical infrastructure testing (Group 1), emphasis on resilience and early monitoring (Group 2), and a focus on redundancy (Group 3).

Table 3. Comparison of architectural patterns used by participant groups and the specialists across hypotheses, highlighting convergence and divergence in decision strategies.

Hypothesis	Original Data (Specialist)	Group 1	Group 2	Group 3	Group 4
H1	Software Analytics	Software Analytics	Software Analytics	Software Analytics	Software Analytics
		Architectural Spike	Architectural Trigger	Architectural Trigger	Architectural Spike
		Architectural Trigger	Protective Guideline		
H2	Architectural Spike	Architectural Spike	Architectural Spike	Architectural Spike	Architectural Spike
	Tracer Bullets		Tracer Bullets	Software Analytics	Tracer Bullets
			Plan for Preparation	Bring the Specialist	Bring the Specialist
H3	Architectural Spike	Architectural Spike	Architectural Spike	Software Analytics	Architectural Spike
		Software Analytics	Software Analytics		Software Analytics
		Tracer Bullets	Tracer Bullets		Postpone Decision

Regarding security and authentication (SSO), the specialists' approach integrated *Architectural Spike* and *Tracer Bullets*. Groups 1 and 2 demonstrated strong alignment by applying *Architectural Spike* to their proofs of concept. Group 3 opted to consult an external specialist while Group 4, again following the specialists' example, effectively combined various techniques.

Regarding data integration and interoperability, the specialists focused their analysis on the use of *Architectural Spike*. The groups presented different solutions: Groups 1 and 2 expanded the approach with cyclical validation and abstraction; Group 3 employed an analysis strictly focused on *Software Analytics*; and Group 4 demonstrated strategic planning and flexibility by combining the late adoption of uncertain decisions with experimentation.

In summary, the analysis concluded that Groups 2 and 4 showed the highest alignment with the specialists' reasoning across all contexts. On the other hand, Group 3 showed the most significant disparity in the strategies selected. This investigation provides insight into how teams converge or diverge in identifying risks and selecting solutions to minimize them, emphasizing theoretical and practical consistency in architectural decisions.

5.2 Usability of the ArchHypo.AI

The feedback analysis was based on participants' responses to three open-ended questions. Figure 2 illustrates the distribution and recurrence of ideas between participants, where the size of each node reflects the number of participants who reported that specific insight. As a result, we identified 15 themes, which were grouped into four categories: positive aspects, challenges, tool perception, and improvement suggestions. To ensure traceability and enrich the thematic interpretation, direct quotes are included in the following paragraphs, each attributed to participants labeled P1–P10.

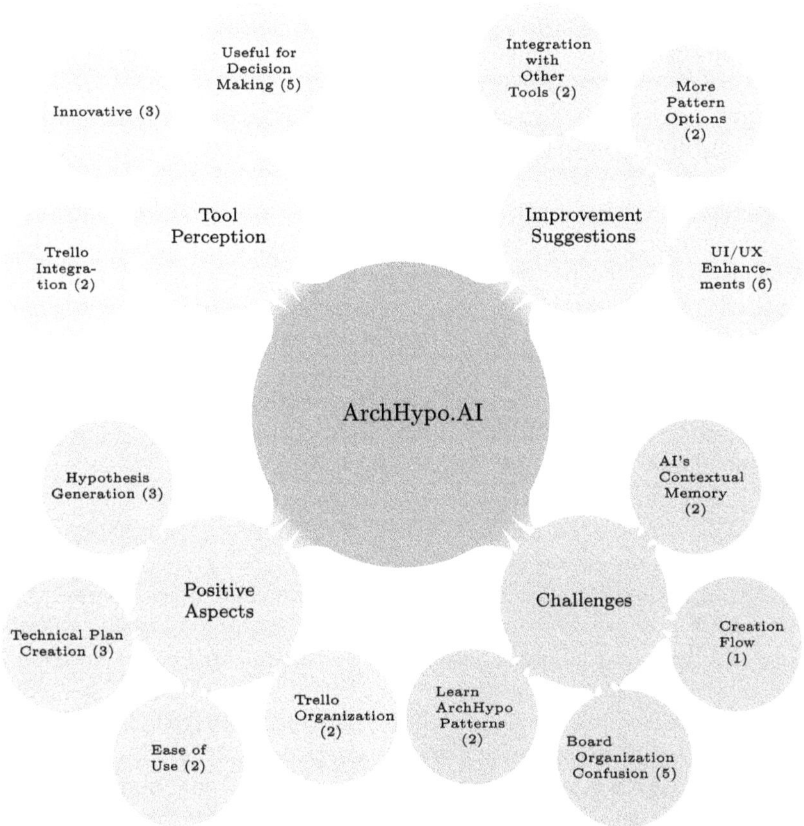

Fig. 2. Thematic map showing the distribution and recurrence of participant-reported insights about ArchHypo.AI. Node size indicates the number of participants who mentioned each insight.

Regarding the **Positive Aspects**, the most praised feature was the *"automatic generation of hypotheses and technical plans"*, mentioned by eight out of ten interviewees. This feature was recognized for its efficiency in saving time and providing a structured starting point for architectural reflection. For example, participant P3 commented that *"the fact that it generates based on my uncertainty and I just need to verify if it makes sense, helps a lot"*, while P7 highlighted that *"it saves time to elaborate both and gives more time to analyze"*. Furthermore, two participants (P2 and P9) emphasized the *"ease and practicality of use"*, characterizing the tool as *"very easy to use"* and *"practical"*, indicating low adoption barriers and an intuitive interaction.

As for the **Challenges**, the most frequently cited problem, reported by four participants (P1, P4, P6, and P10), was the *"confusion in board organization"* in Trello. The arrangement of generated uncertainties and hypotheses was considered complicated, with P4 suggesting: *"There should be a column for hypotheses* *and uncertainties because our team got confused about what each thing was in Trello"*. Other challenges included the tendency of AI to *"repeat the context of previous cards"* formulating new responses (P2 and P8) and minor errors related to *"classification or metric visualization"* (P5 and P9). In particular, two participants (P3 and P7) reported not encountering *"difficulties"*, indicating a variation in user experience.

With respect to the **Improvement Suggestions**, participants offered several recommendations to enhance the tool's usability and effectiveness. The most common suggestion was to *"improve the board structure"* in Trello, with four participants (P1, P4, P6, and P10) proposing the creation of separate columns for uncertainties and hypotheses to improve clarity and workflow. The participant P6 observed: *"I suggest creating a hypothesis column, so that when [...] a hypothesis is generated, the card is moved to the hypothesis column. Because having a hypothesis card in the uncertainty column causes some confusion."* Other suggestions included *"integration with other tools"* such as Jira (P2 and P8), as well as the addition of functionalities such as *"automatic inclusion of metrics (labels)"* and the ability to *"suggest technical trade offs"* (P5 and P9), reflecting a desire for more in-depth analytical support.

Finally, regarding the **Tool Perception**, where participants demonstrated a predominantly positive view of `ArchHypo.AI`, recognizing its ability to enhance architectural decision-making. The tool was considered *"useful for decision making"* (P1 and P3) and *"innovative"* (P6 and P10), indicating its alignment with modern software architecture practices. Integration with Trello was also seen as advantageous, and P2 emphasized *"Trello integration"* as an important feature. These perceptions suggest that `ArchHypo.AI` is not only functional but also resonates with users as an innovative solution that supports strategic alignment and collaborative reflection in architectural processes.

6 Discussion

Our findings offered valuable insights into the effectiveness, usefulness, and usability of the `ArchHypo.AI` plugin.

The review of the elements in Trello, summarized in Tables 2 and 3, revealed an intriguing phenomenon: although the groups and the specialists recognized the same NFRs (performance, safety, and flexibility), their analyses of the levels of uncertainty and impact, as well as the mitigation tactics (architectural patterns), differed. This divergence does not represent a failure but rather highlights the tool's main functionality: acting as a mediator that makes visible and organizes various perceptions of risk. By highlighting these differences, `ArchHypo.AI` encourages a more in-depth architectural debate, forcing teams not only to identify risks but also to negotiate and synchronize their strategic priorities [10,15]. This mediating function aligns with the idea that AI tools should enhance human collaboration rather than simply automating tasks [24].

As shown in the feedback mind map (Fig. 2), the automated generation of hypotheses and technical plans was the most appreciated feature. Comments such as *"saves time developing both and gives more time for analysis"* indicate that the tool addresses a crucial aspect of software engineering: the high cognitive load and time spent documenting architectural decisions. By automating the most bureaucratic step in the process, `ArchHypo.AI` lowers the barrier to adopting hypothesis-driven development practices, a recognized difficulty in agile environments [3].

The difficulties pointed out in Sect. 5, especially the *"confusion in the organization of the board"*, demonstrate a disconnect between the tools workflow and the user's understanding of Trello. The proposal to *"automatically move cards to a Hypotheses column after creation"* is a valuable insight into the need for seamless integration with the team's already established practices [5]. Furthermore, the observation that *"the AI repeats the context of previous cards"* reveals a known limitation of LLMs: managing context in sequential interactions. Improving contextual memory and workflow design are essential steps in evolving the tool from a functional assistant to a true team collaborator [25].

The findings suggest that the value of AI tools in software engineering extends beyond automation to their ability to organize knowledge and facilitate evidence-based decision-making. The use of RAG to classify architectural patterns, as discussed in Sect. 3, is an example of how AI can offer specialized knowledge as needed, aligning with the demand for maintaining the health of the architecture in agile projects [11]. However, the participant's request for more advanced functionalities, such as *"the suggestion of technical trade-offs"*, indicates a desire for AI to go beyond creating plans and begin assisting in the analysis of complex decisions, an open challenge in AI research focused on software engineering [8].

6.1 Threats to Validity

Although there are alternative approaches to structuring validity threats in qualitative research [9,19], we adopted the framework proposed by Runeson and Höst [13], which is widely used in empirical software engineering [7]. This framework distinguishes four dimensions of validity: *construct*, *internal*, *external*, and *reliability*.

Construct Validity: we asked participants to create between three and five technical plan items per hypothesis when using the RAG-based support in `ArchHypo.AI` (Table 3). This design choice may have inflated the number of proposed actions compared to what teams would typically define in real projects, possibly affecting how the tool's output was perceived. Although we provided a catalog of patterns and a user guide, participants' familiarity with and interpretation of these patterns varied, which may have introduced bias in how hypotheses and plans were constructed and, consequently, in how the tool was evaluated.

Internal Validity: participants had access only to a summarized view of the original project scenario, with limited information about the development team and the technologies employed. This partial context may have influenced how they interpreted architectural uncertainties, classified hypotheses, and selected patterns (Table 2), making it difficult to distinguish the tool's impact from that of individual assumptions or prior experience. Furthermore, the study was conducted in a classroom setting and in group discussions, which may have introduced social and collaborative dynamics that influenced decisions independently of the plugin. Additionally, the use of LLMs introduces well-known risks such as over-reliance on generated outputs, and excessive resource consumption, which may have further affected participants' reasoning and decision-making processes.

External Validity: the evaluation was conducted with a small convenience sample of 10 professionals across 4 groups, using a single scenario (a document management system) and a specific tool configuration. As a result, the outcomes may not transfer directly to larger or more heterogeneous teams, to projects with different architectural characteristics, or to organizations that use other project management platforms or other LLMs. The controlled, time-bounded setting of the experiment may also differ from the pressures and constraints of day-to-day industrial practice.

Reliability: our procedures were based on a predefined study protocol (scenario description, onboarding and training activities, task instructions, and post-activity questionnaire), which supports the repeatability of data collection. However, the qualitative analysis of Trello artifacts and open-ended questionnaire responses involves researcher interpretation, and another team might code and cluster themes differently. This limitation reduces the richness of the evidence on which recommendations are based and may affect the reproducibility of the model's exact outputs, a challenge already highlighted in studies on architectural refactoring that emphasize the importance of architectural visibility for service reuse and decision-making in microservice contexts [4].

7 Conclusion

This paper presented `ArchHypo.AI` a Trello plugin that uses LLM to support and validate the ArchHypo technique for decision-making in real projects. Our evaluation confirms its feasibility, usefulness, and positive impact on user experience within agile workflows. Research has shown that artificial intelligence functionalities significantly facilitate the formulation and management of architectural hypotheses, which was deeply appreciated by the participants.

The main contribution of this study is the demonstration that AI-based tools can facilitate the adoption of formal methods for hypothesis management. However, our conclusions also highlight the relevance of usability, as opinions suggested the need for a more intuitive workflow in Trello and more contextually relevant AI recommendations.

Furthermore, we noted that the LLM generated a greater number of Technical Plans Items compared to the project itself. However, it is worth noting that one of the project tasks modified by LLM exhibited a repetitive pattern and received the same rating in multiple evaluations. This observation indicates a promising ability of AI to replicate and identify patterns, even without a complete context provided.

Additionally, the research's limitations, such as the lack of a complete project context, the absence of detailed knowledge about the team and the source code used by the participants, as well as the variability in the criteria considered among the different evaluation groups, may have impacted some ratings and perceptions. It is essential to consider these limitations for a more accurate interpretation of the results.

Future work will focus on improving the user interface, adapting the AI model in light of the feedback received, and investigating integration with other project management platforms, such as Jira, and version control tools as requested in participant feedback. We also intend to conduct a quantitative study to assess the long-term impact of `ArchHypo.AI` on team productivity and software quality.

Acknowledgments. The authors would like to thank the São Paulo Research Foundation (FAPESP) – grant 2023/14646-1 – for financial support.

References

1. Braun, V., Clarke, V.: Using thematic analysis in psychology. Qual. Res. Psychol. **3**(2), 77–101 (2006)
2. Choma, J., Guerra, E.M., Silva, T.S.: Patterns for implementing software analytics in development teams. In: 24th Conference on Pattern Languages of Programs, p. 12. ACM (2017)
3. Choma, J., Guerra, E.M., Silva, T.S.: Learning from experiments, define quality standards, suspend measurement: three patterns in a software analytics pattern language. In: 12th Latin American Conference on Pattern Languages of Programs (SLPLoP), p. 10. ACM (2018)
4. Daniel, J., Mota, G., Wang, X., Guerra, E.: Architecture refactoring towards service reusability in the context of microservices. In: 26th International Conference on Agile Software Development (XP 2025), pp. 129–144. Agile Alliance (2025)
5. Guerra, E., Melegati, J.: Hypotheses engineering in software startups: from business to architecture. In: Advances in Software Startups - Generative AI, Product Engineering and Business Development. Springer (2025)
6. Guerra, E., Wirfs-Brock, R., Yoder, J.: Patterns for initial architectural design on agile projects. In: 4th Asian Conference on Pattern Languages of Programs (AsianPLoP) (2015)
7. Härtel, J., Lämmel, R.: Operationalizing validity of empirical software engineering studies. Empir. Softw. Eng. **28**, 153 (2023)
8. Jin, H., Huang, L., Cai, H., Yan, J., Li, B., Chen, H.: From LLMs to LLM-based agents for software engineering: a survey. In: Journal preprint (2024)
9. Lago, P., Runeson, P., Song, Q., Verdecchia, R.: Threats to validity in software engineering – hypocritical paper section or essential analysis? In: 18th IEEE International Symposium on Empirical Software Engineering and Measurement (ESEM 2024), pp. 314–324. ACM (2024)
10. Lupafya, C.: A framework for managing uncertainty in software architecture. In: 13th European Conference on Software Architecture - Volume 2, pp. 71–74. Association for Computing Machinery, New York (2019)

11. Merson, P., Yoder, J.W., Guerra, E.M., Aguiar, A.: Continuous inspection: a pattern for keeping your code healthy and aligned to the architecture. In: AsianPLoP 2014-Asian Conference on Pattern Languages of Programs, 3 (2014)
12. Paris, A., Guerra, E., Silveira, F., Silva, K.: Patterns for small adjustments in the development process to deal with architectural uncertainties. In: 29th European Conference on Pattern Languages of Programs, People, and Practices, pp. 1–8 (2024)
13. Runeson, P., Höst, M.: Guidelines for conducting and reporting case study research in software engineering. Empirical Softw. Eng. **14**(2), 131–164 (2009). ISSN 1382-3256
14. Silva, K., Adolfo, L.B., Coppe, A., Silveira, F.F., Ferreira, M., Guerra, E.: Patterns for using hypothesis engineering to manage architectural uncertainties. In: Proceedings of the 29th European Conference on Pattern Languages of Programs, People, and Practices, pp. 1–8 (2024)
15. Silva, K., Melegati, J., Silveira, F., Wang, X., Ferreira, M., Guerra, E.: ArchHypo: managing software architecture uncertainty using hypotheses engineering. IEEE Trans. Softw. Eng. (2025)
16. Silva, K., Melegati, J., Wang, X., Ferreira, M., Guerra, E.: Using hypotheses to manage technical uncertainty and architecture evolution in a software start-up. IEEE Software **41**(4), 7–13 (2024)
17. Stotz, N., Drews, P.: Metrics for experimentation programs: categories, benefits and challenges. In: 26th International Conference on Agile Software Development (XP 2025), pp. 1–10. Agile Alliance (2025)
18. Vaswani, A., Shazeer, N., Parmar, N., Uszkoreit, J., Jones, L., Gomez, A.N., et al.: Attention is all you need. Adv. Neural. Inf. Process. Syst. **30**(1), 261–272 (2017)
19. Verdecchia, R., Engström, E., Lago, P., Runeson, P., Song, Q.: Threats to validity in software engineering research: a critical reflection. Inf. Softw. Technol. **164**, 107329 (2023)
20. Vidgen, R., Wang, X.: Coevolving systems and the organization of agile software development. Inf. Syst. Res. **20**(3), 355–376 (2009)
21. Wahid, M.K.A., Dawood, L.M.: Lean, agile, leagile manufacturing systems pros and cons: a literature survey. In: AIP Conference Proceedings, vol. 3079 (2024)
22. Wirfs-Brock, R., Yoder, J., Guerra, E.: Patterns to develop and evolve architecture during an agile software project. In: Proceedings of the 22nd Conference on Pattern Languages of Programs, pp. 1–18 (2015)
23. Yang, N., Wang, X., Siemon, D., Hyrynsalmi, S., Zhang, Z.: Core theories in agile software development. In: 26th International Conference on Agile Software Development (XP 2025), pp. 3–18. Agile Alliance (2025)
24. Zhang, Z.: AI and agile software development: a research roadmap from the XP2025 workshop. In: XP2025 Workshop on AI and Agile. Agile Alliance (2025)
25. Zhao, S., Yang, Y., Wang, Z., He, Z., Qiu, L.K., Qiu, L.: Retrieval augmented generation (RAG) and beyond: a comprehensive survey. In: arXiv preprint arXiv:2409.14924 (2024)

Product and Design

Integration of UX Research Practices Into Agile Requirements Engineering: A Study in Software Industry

Leonardo Ciscon[1(✉)], Marcelo de Oliveira[2], Adler Diniz[2], Joelma Choma[1], and Luciana Zaina[1]

[1] Federal University of São Carlos, Sorocaba, Brazil
leonardo.ciscon@estudante.ufscar.br, jh.choma@hotmail.com, lzaina@ufscar.br

[2] Federal University of Itajubá, Itajubá, Brazil
{marcelo_sinf,adlerdiniz}@unifei.edu.br

Abstract. Agile Requirements Engineering (Agile RE) has been widely studied, but gaps remain regarding how user-centered research practices, specifically UX Research, are integrated into Agile RE. This paper investigates how UX Research is applied within Agile RE activities and identifies the positive and negative aspects of this integration. We conducted a multiple-case study with four distinct organizations, collecting data through interviews with 12 agile and UX professionals. Our results revealed that UX Research practices and tools are most frequently employed to discover requirements, both in organizations with and without UX professionals. However, the findings also indicate that although UX Research practices provide valuable input for requirements specification, there remains a need to better structure and communicate UX-related aspects so they become more visible to the agile team in all Agile RE activities. Our study contributes by discussing how UX Research practices and tools are employed across the stages of the Agile RE cycle, as well as the roles of the different stakeholders involved in these stages in different companies.

Keywords: agile requirements engineering · user experience · UX Research · UX · case study

1 Introduction

The integration of User Experience Design (UXD) and Agile Software Development is not new. The literature have explored this topic [1,3,4,12,14] in different perspectives. Organizations have increasingly recognized the importance of applying UXD methods and techniques in software development to produce high-quality software, which consequently affects user visibility and acceptance [12]. In agile context, teams have worked to incorporate user experience (UX)

A. Goldman et al. (Eds.): XP 2026, LNBIP 578, pp. 211–227, 2026.
https://doi.org/10.1007/978-3-032-22375-3_13

into agile projects for many years [5,24,26]. However, companies still face difficulties in synchronizing development and UX tasks [6].

The focus on user-centered requirements has shifted from usability to UX, maintaining a concentrated focus on efficiency and ease of use while also reflecting users' emotions and beliefs (e.g., product value and engagement with the product) [6,12]. According to ISO 9241-210:2019 [9] usability refers to how well a system, product, or service helps specific users accomplish their goals effectively, efficiently, and with satisfaction in a given context of use. This ISO standard further defines UX as "a person's perceptions and responses that result from the use and/or anticipated use of a system, product, or service". The UX definition encompasses emotions, beliefs, preferences, behaviors, and task accomplishments before, during, and after interaction, which is influenced by the system, user, and context.

In particular, Agile Requirements Engineering (Agile RE) activities play an important role in building a good UX [12,21]. Agile RE typically uses a just-in-time model to refine high level requirements into low level tasks that can be implemented by developers, fostering collaboration among stakeholders, users, and developers [21]. The literature indicates that Agile RE does not follow a fixed set of stages and the activities are often overlapping rather than clearly defined [2,27]. Schön et al. [21] outline the core activities of Requirements Engineering as elicitation, documentation, validation, negotiation, and management, noting that in Agile RE these activities are often intertwined rather than clearly delineated.

To effectively incorporate UXD into Agile RE, practitioners have to elicit and understand users' needs by conducting UX Research activities. Kieffer et al. [11] and Krout et al. [13] define UX Research as the systematic investigation and evaluation of end-user experience to generate insights for product development. UX Research helps designers understand user needs and develop solutions that better meet them, and it can be applied at any stage of the design process using methods such as interviews, user testing, and user observation [7].

In light of the importance of incorporating UXD into Agile RE, prior work has proposed approaches to connect UX Research with Agile RE and has documented the challenges of this convergence [1,3,12]. This alignment is widely seen as beneficial for improving product quality by strengthening collaboration and supporting iterative development cycles [22,23]. Nevertheless, the literature indicates that making this integration work in practice remains difficult. The time-boxed nature of agile, workload balance between agile and UX teams, and the prioritization of functionality over usability/UX are seen as challenges [1]. Some recurring issues, such as limited user participation, weak shared understanding of requirements between designers and developers, insufficient specification of usability requirements, and poor requirements documentation, are also frequently problems found [3]. Difficulties in prioritizing UXD tasks in the backlog and confusion between client and end-user roles [18].

Although the literature has extensively examined the integration of UX into agile practices, little has been investigated on UX Research practices employed across the different stages of Agile RE (i.e., requirements discovery, specification, validation, and management). Understanding this integration provides clearer insight into the extent to which UX Research outcomes are effectively incorporated into Agile RE. To explore the topic above, we defined the following research questions (RQs): *RQ1) How are UX Research practices and approaches integrated in Agile RE?* and *RQ2) What are the positive and negative impacts of UX Research on Agile RE?*

To answer the RQs, we conducted a multiple-case study in four agile-focused software companies involving twelve professionals holding different roles (e.g., UX designer, UX researcher, developers, among others). Our results show that UX Research practices (e.g., tools, techniques, and methods) are used mainly during requirements discovery and, while they inform specification, their outcomes are often not structured or communicated in ways that are clearly visible to agile teams. We contribute by mapping how UX Research is distributed across Agile RE stages and who is involved, and by discussing benefits and drawbacks that can guide practitioners in organizing this integration to better support requirements work.

2 Related Work

The integration of UXD and RE in agile contexts (Agile RE) has been widely studied [1,3,14,22], yet aligning UX Research practices with Agile RE remains challenging [12,18].

Schon et al. [22] found that integrating Human-Centered Design (HCD) with Kanban improves UX and makes development more human-centric. Sfetsos et al. [23] proposed a hybrid process that adds lightweight User-Centered Design (UCD) practices, including upfront user research, iterative UI design by a UX designer, and usability testing, thereby improving product quality and reducing defects across sprints. Pillay et al. [18] observed that short sprint cycles hinder user research and usability testing, leading teams to perform UX activities one or two iterations before development. They also reported challenges such as prioritizing UX tasks in the backlog and confusion between client and end-user roles. Good practices identified include creating UX-specific backlogs, conducting quick tests, and using simplified usability methods like heuristic evaluations and low-fidelity prototypes.

Considering the integration of UX and Agile RE from user stories, Ananjeva et al. [4] found that concise user stories and deliberation help integrate UX into agile development without compromising agility. Conversely, Marques et al. [15] utilized the USARP (Usability Requirements with Personas and User Stories) method to define UI/UX requirements in a case study. According to the authors, this method potentially enabled the identification of UI/UX aspects and their relation with functional requirements. Keshk et al. [10] proposed a roadmap to enhance Agile RE through a hybrid process that combines UI prototyping and enriched user stories through a template that includes: user story statement, actors, priority, precondition, post-condition, scenarios, the prototype and other elements. This approach is complemented by additional requirements validation steps.

Several SLRs have examined how to integrate UX Research with Agile RE and the challenges involved. Almeyda et al. [3] summarized common practices and strategies for integrating UX and agile requirements analysis, highlighting recurring problems such as limited user participation, weak shared understanding between designers and developers, insufficient usability-requirements specification, and poor requirements documentation. Al-Razgan et al. [1] cataloged frequently cited UCD practices in Agile development—prototyping, little UI design up front, usability testing, personas, and workshops; they also reported key challenges including agile time-boxing, balancing work between UX and agile teams, prioritization of functionality over usability/UX, user feedback, requirements documentation, and testing (acceptance and usability). Kusuma et al. [14] mapped UX Research techniques to Agile RE stages, citing contextual investigation, contextual interviews, ethnographic observation, and card sorting for elicitation, and personas, questionnaires, surveys, and interviews for user analysis. More recently, Kollmorgen et al. [12] identified 28 challenges and 103 solution approaches to Agile and UX integration, noting challenges such as team collaboration and activity synchronization, organizational structure and unfit processes, resource-capacity constraints, temporal constraints, and unclear responsibilities/roles, alongside approaches such as integrating UX and development specialists, using lightweight artifacts and practices, holding weekly user meetings, and adopting processes like sprint zero and upfront UI design.

The works above address Agile RE and UXD integration mainly at a general level. Recurring challenges include time-boxing and temporal constraints [1,12,18], prioritizing UX tasks in the backlog [1,18], unclear responsibilities and roles [1,18], limited user participation and feedback [12,18], deficient requirements documentation [1,3], and team collaboration/synchronization [12] are the most mentioned challenges. However, little research has examined the role of UX Research in the Agile RE cycles during the day-to-day operations of companies. Our work investigated how UX Research is handled across the stages of Agile RE, considering the dynamics of approach and tool utilization, as well as the individuals involved in this process.

3 Method

We adopted a multiple-case study to conduct our investigation following the guidelines of Runeson and Höst [19]. The five authors (labeled hereinafter as R1 to R5) participated in the study at different steps. R1, R4, and R5 have backgrounds in agile software development and UX Research, with 15+ years of combined experience in academia and industry. R2 and R3 have 5+ and 15+ years of experience, respectively, in agile software development.

Case Selection and Description. Our study examined how Brazilian organizations (i.e., our unit of analysis) integrate UX Research into Agile RE from four

Table 1. Overview of organizations' characteristics and interviewees' roles

Company ID	A	B	C	D
Segment	Education	Software factory	Web/App	Financial
Business Model	B2B	B2B2C	B2C	B2B2C
Foundation	2008	2020	2015	1962
Agile Method	Scrum	Scrum	Scrum/Kanban	Scrum
Total number of employees	~1700	23	66	~700
# employees in SW area	13	14	15	120
# interviewees	3	3	3	3
Roles	P1 to P3	P4 to P6	P7 to P9	P10 to P12

Company A: (P1) Fullstack Developer (5 / 7); (P2) Fullstack Developer (3 / 20); (P3) Product Owner (3 / 16). **Company B:** (P4) Project Manager (3 / 6); (P5) Software Engineer (1 / 7); (P6) UX Designer (1 / 4). **Company C:** (P7) Software Engineer (6 / 6); (P8) UX Designer (2 / 20); (P9) Quality Analyst (3 / 6). **Company D:** (P10) UX Designer (2 / 8); (P11) UX Designer (1 / 6); (P12) Product Owner (5 / 6). * The numbers in parentheses indicate, respectively, the years with the organization and the total years of professional experience.

companies (anonymized as A, B, C, and D) selected from our research group's collaboration network. The study was approved by the Ethics Committee in Brazil (CAAE: 90622025.1.0000.5504) at the Federal University of São Carlos. Twelve software professionals (three from each organization) who held different roles participated in the study, with experience ranging from 4 to 20 years, all working in organizations adopting agile practices. The conduction of UX Research activities was not an inclusion criterion for company selection, since it may be conducted by individuals without dedicated UX roles [16]. Table 1 presents the organizations and participants' information.

Data Collection. Semi-structured interviews were conducted in Portuguese by R1 and R2 between August and September 2025, each lasting 30–60 min (totaling 9 h). The script comprised 12 questions across four sections (see all the questions in the online Appendix[1]), covering participant profiles, UX Research practices in Agile RE, related challenges, and mitigation strategies. The protocol was reviewed by three experts in Agile RE and UX Research with 5+ years of experience. A pilot test with two industry specialists resulted in minor revisions. All sessions were recorded via Google Meet[2], transcribed with Read.ai[3], and reviewed by R1; subsequently, R2 conducted a double-check.

Data Analysis. The interview data were analyzed qualitatively using a closed coding technique [20]. A predefined set of 27 codes derived from a systematic

[1] https://figshare.com/s/da675b6395b055d710d0.
[2] https://meet.google.com.
[3] https://www.read.ai.

literature review (SLR)[4] was mapped to the interview questions and applied to participants' speech segments (see Fig. 1 in the online *Appendix* codebook). The analysis was conducted by R1, R2, and R3, with a final review by R4 and R5. Initially, R1 presented the study goals and predefined codes to R2 and R3, and the researchers maintained asynchronous communication for clarification, if needed. Each researcher independently coded interviews supported by the Taguette tool[5]. The interviews were randomly assigned across organizations to the researchers (R1 analyzed six interviews; R2 and R3, three each). After the first coding round, the researchers collaboratively cross-reviewed, merged, and refined the codes. In a final step, the UX Research findings were categorized into Agile RE into four stages (i.e., requirements discovery, specification, validation/acceptance, and management/monitoring stages) by R1 and revised by R5 [21,27]. Figure 1 illustrates examples of the coding process.

Excerpts	Codes
"We don't have any specific UX methodology, nor any specific scientific methodology or techniques. So, what we do here ends up being very empirical, very intuitive, because we don't have that formal structure". [P3]	Lack of UX Research Knowledge and expertise gaps
"But there are other demands, which the developers themselves discuss and post on Slack during development, and the team, together, gives their opinions, if they want to". [P7	Collaborative Environment Deliberation

Fig. 1. Example of excerpts and codes assigned.

Threat to Validity. To ensure rigor, we consider the recommendations of Runeson and Höst [19] to validity threats. For construct validity, an interview protocol was developed and refined by independent researchers after two pilot interviews to eliminate ambiguities. During data collection, at least two researchers attended each session to clarify any misunderstandings, and recordings were automatically transcribed and manually reviewed for accuracy. To ensure internal validity, we included professionals from different organizations with diverse backgrounds and expertise and examined a broad set of issues, thereby mitigating potential biases. Regarding external validity, participants came from four software companies differing in size and domain, which supports some degree of abstraction while acknowledging that organizational context may limit generalization and that replications in other settings are welcome. Finally, for reliability, analysis had multi-researcher participation at each stage, and cross-checking of transcriptions and codes reduced interpretive discrepancies.

[4] The paper has not yet been published.
[5] https://taguette.org.

4 Findings

This section presents the key findings underlined and split by RQ. Table 1 presents the organizations and participants' information.

4.1 UX Research Practices and Approaches in Agile RE - RQ1

Company A. The participants described a reengineering project involving migrating to new technologies and incorporating new requirements. In this company, UX Research is performed by the undergraduate admissions office[6] due to the absence of dedicated UX professionals. During **requirements discovery**, the agile team uses personas, user journey analysis, and prototyping [P1, P3]. As the agile team does not have contact with end-users, requirements are elicited through meetings and interviews with the undergraduate admissions office. Based on these requirements, the team creates UI prototypes in Figma[7], considered essential artifacts for understanding requirements, as [P1] stated: "*there were the prototypes and throughout the development of the new system (...) it was very necessary*". These prototypes are evaluated by other teams and the undergraduate admissions office: "*The admissions team had to do a lot of testing and validate the flow for us, if it was what they expected, if the new system delivered everything that was needed for this first version*" [P1]. User stories complemented by acceptance criteria (AC) are the main artifacts for **requirements specification**, and GitLab[8] acts as the central requirements repository for different documents managed jointly by the agile team and the undergraduate admissions office; it includes a specification of UI aspects (e.g., components, text, colors, report format). **Requirements validation and acceptance** are conducted in a dedicated environment with support of mockups for rapid visualization of the requirements. Initial validation is carried out by the agile team and subsequently reviewed by the undergraduate admissions office [P3]. Feedback from the undergraduate admissions office is analyzed, and only after approval and the resolution of identified issues are the requirements released to production. Finally, **requirements management and monitoring** are jointly carried out by the agile and business teams. GitLab is also used to track requirement status (e.g., in development, in validation), and to register and reprioritize identified improvements. Team communication with the undergraduate admissions office occurs via Mattermost[9], which supports asynchronous discussions on questions, changes, and deliverable validation. The agile team also receives new demands and change requests via email and the institution's internal ticketing system [P2, P3].

6 The department responsible for the business roles for university entrance exam.
7 https://www.figma.com/.
8 https://about.gitlab.com/.
9 https://mattermost.com/.

Company B. The company focuses primarily on clients rather than on end-users. A support department handles communication with both clients and users to gather feedback and perform other functions. We found that **requirements discovery** begins with meetings and interviews with clients via Google Meet[10] involving the whole agile team. The doubts and clarifications of user needs are gathered from WhatsApp[11] conversation: "*We always created a WhatsApp group with these clients*" [P5]. In the **requirements specification**, the UX professional initially created chatbot prototypes [P4] in Figma: "*We have a complete design that our UX professional creates, which the client reviews and approves point by point*" [P5]. After client approval, requirements are converted into tasks and stored in ClickUp[12]. As the company aims to further mature its UX practices, clients hold the responsibility of **requirements validation and acceptance**: "*it [a requirement] doesn't enter in the development pipeline until the client is 100% satisfied with the proposed chatbot flow*" [P5]. Mockups and prototypes are created from sprint zero [P6] and presented for client validation, with initial approval by the internal testing team [P4]. UX Research activities also include collecting clients and end-users feedback via the chatbot flow and satisfaction surveys. Weekly team meetings discuss survey results and their impact on requirements and product development [P6], carried out by a cross-functional team in a collaborative environment. Finally, ClickUp supports **requirements management and monitoring**, which rely on ongoing communication with users to confirm delivery and identify needed changes [P5]. [P6] added: "*After project delivery, we usually provide a 15-day warranty period, during which the client can request changes*".

Company C. The company also has a customer service department (operations team[13]) that conducts user research, handles user questions, and forwards system issues to other team. **Requirements discovery** is usually led by the operations team, which identifies needs from user feedback collection, i.e., opinion research, user surveys, client campaigns. The operations team works with Marketing and is mainly responsible for user research: "*So, when we want to discover something that really requires getting closer to the users and asking, they are the ones who execute it, it's the operations team*" [P7]. After prioritizing the users' demands, the requirements are described in Slack[14] to encourage participation and deliberation by the company's cross-functional team. As the requirements mature and questions are clarified, the Product Owner (PO) becomes responsible for **specifying requirements** through tickets in Jira[15] and for creating supporting documentation in Confluence[16] [P8, P9]. Most

[10] https://meet.google.com.
[11] https://web.whatsapp.com.
[12] https://clickup.com.
[13] Team responsible for user support and resolving or forwarding system usage problems.
[14] https://slack.com.
[15] https://www.atlassian.com/software/jira.
[16] https://www.atlassian.com/software/confluence.

of the time, this involves creating user stories and personas [P8, P9]. The only UX professional in the company [P8] works on creating designs, mock-ups, and prototypes using Zeplin[17] and Figma, in addition to ChatGPT for heuristic evaluation. Although there is an effort on UX Research activities, the insufficient documentation is noted by [P7]: "*We do not have very effective, up-to-date documentation (...) most conversations about the requirements happen in a public way on Slack*". **Requirements validation and acceptance** is carried out by analyzing user behavior using Datadog[18] and Grafana[19] [P7], and A/B testing to test hypotheses and guide development. Finally, **requirements management and monitoring** are handled by the PO in Jira, with support from the operations team. The results revealed that user research is continuous at company C, enabling ongoing monitoring of required changes: "*If users respond every two months, every two months you have to adjust something—what was good one month may not be the next*" [P8].

Company D. The UX team has four members—three focused on UX design, user research, and prototyping, and one dedicated exclusively to design system development. The **requirements discovery** is highly collaborative with agile and UX teams working together: "*We [UX team] begin working with the agile team on their development discoveries, while we explore user experience, UI requirements, and prototypes—sketching and creating low-, medium-, and high-fidelity prototypes*". The UX team conducts primarily through internal interviews, semi-structured conversations, and observations with the aim of understanding internal users' expectations [P10]. Data collected is organized at Miro[20], which works as a sharing of knowledge environment [P12]. On the other hand, external users' needs are gathered from surveys and benchmarking tests by the UX team [P11]. For the **requirements specification**, the UX team produces UI prototypes in Figma and uses user stories with AC, personas, and use cases [P10, P11, P12] and requirements are documented in Azure DevOps[21] [P11, P12]. The UX-related requirements specification impacts on the production of coding: "*my work directly impacts the development requirements (...) what I define together with the rest of the team will eventually be transformed into code (...) I write a good part of [UX] requirements*" [P11]. The navigation on interactive prototypes during meetings is the main technique used for **requirements validation and acceptance** with internal users using FigJam[22] as a collaborative space for mapping and discussion [P11]. In addition, usability tests are conducted with external users: "*We did a usability test of this new flow, with clients (...) And then we identified that there was a 97.92% success rate in the execution of 48 requested tasks*" [P10]. Requirements must also be approved by internal users before production release [P12].

[17] https://zeplin.io/.
[18] https://www.datadoghq.com/product/session-replay/.
[19] https://grafana.com/.
[20] https://miro.com/.
[21] https://azure.microsoft.com/en-us/products/devops.
[22] https://www.figma.com/figjam/.

Requirements monitoring is mainly handled by the undergraduate admissions office without direct involvement of the UX team [P10]. Finally, the agile team performs the **requirements management** using Azure DevOps [P11].

4.2 Impacts of UX Research Integration in Agile Requirements Engineering - RQ2

To address RQ2, we identified positive aspects related to best practices, useful approaches, and promising results as well as negative aspects associated with difficulties, conflicts, and challenges in integrating UX Research and Agile RE. Our findings are organized by the four stages of requirements engineering (i.e., requirements discovery, requirements specification, requirements validation and acceptance, and requirements management and monitoring), reporting the positive aspects first, followed by the negative aspects.

Requirements Discovery. *Positive Aspects:* Non-technical stakeholders active participation (e.g., undergraduate admissions office (Company A), clients (Company B), operations team (Company C), internal clients (Company D)) in requirements discovery improves understanding of needs; use of user-centered approaches (e.g., design thinking, design sprint) enhances efficiency, reduces rework, and improves UX; and adoption of the discovery meeting ceremony supports clearer requirements definition [P4]. *Negative Aspects:* Non-technical stakeholders (i.e., not involved in software development) often lack UX Research knowledge, leading to ad-hoc, unstructured discovery [P3]; the absence of dedica-ted UX specialists hinders integration and effective requirements discovery [P2, P3, P7, P9]; and requirements discovery sometimes involves only clients, not end-users, limiting understanding of user needs [P4].

Requirements Specification. *Positive Aspects:* the importance of UX professional role shows that inputs originating from the UX team typically arrive pre-validated and mature, which significantly facilitates the work of the PO and the agile team [P5, P9, P10, P11, P12]; requirements templates structured and UX documentation, with user story, personas, prototypes and AC with examples of UI aspects (e.g., suggested components, text, colors, report format) encourage the agile team to think about UX during feature development [P1, P4, P5, P6, P11, P12]. *Negative aspects:* communication challenges, such as a lack of a shared language between clients, users, and the agile team (e.g., use of technical terminology [P5] and when requirements lack clear definition [P6]); and lack of documentation standards impact the requirements specification stage [P7, P10].

Requirements Validation and Acceptance. *Positive Aspects:* performing UX activities in advance enables requirements to be validated by users before they are prioritized for development [P5, P6, P9]; and conducting review and retrospectives meetings enables requirements to be presented and validated by the operations team prior to their release to end-users [P7, P9].

Negative aspects: infrequent involvement with the end-user impedes the collection of feedback and the resolution of doubts during requirements validation [P10, P11].

Requirements Management and Monitoring. *Positive Aspects:* The involvement of the internal areas and clients, facilitated through chat tools (e.g., Mattermost, WhatsApp Groups, and Slack) or dedicated meetings and interviews, enables the active and constant participation of these stakeholders [P1, P4, P7, P9]; and centralized, agile, and frequent communication with non-technical stakeholders streamlines the management and monitoring of requirements subsequent to their release for use [P2, P8, P10, P11]. *Negative aspects:* user unavailability which makes it difficult to understand the needs and resolve doubts [P2, P8, P10, P11].

Integration Across All Stages of Agile RE. *Positive Aspects:* the collaboration between agile teams and UX professionals [P5, P6, P7, P8, P10], the participation of UX specialists in cross-functional teams [P4, P5, P7, P8, P10, P12], and strategic activities performed by UX specialists are instrumental in achieving integration between UX Research and Agile RE, simultaneously promoting the incorporation of UX principles into solution development. Frequent meetings [P4, P6], proactive team performance [P5], continuous deliveries [P5], tests conducted jointly by the team and the users [P6], and close contact with the client [P10] promote continuous involvement from both teams and users. Conducting continuous UX Research to ensure the agile team remains updated on evolving user needs [P8, P9]. *Negative aspects:* lack of knowledge in UX design practices as a factor that can hinder the progress of activities [P1, P3, P4, P5]; lack of professionals with formal UX background who execute their activities without adequate knowledge of UX Research approaches [P11]; conflict between agility and the time consumed by UX work [P3, P7, P8, P9, P10], UX issues have low priority [P1, P2, P3, P7, P11] and insufficiency of resources for UX Research which generates another negative aspect in the integration: conflicting objectives, when the development of functionalities is often prioritized over usability requirements [P3]; and lack of UX Research which is particularly evident in smaller companies with limited team sizes [P1, P2, P3].

5 Discussion

This study examines the integration of UX Research approaches with Agile RE and investigates the resultant positive and negative impacts emerging from this convergence. As previously detailed, the UX Research and Agile RE activities were organized into four stages: requirements discovery, requirements specification, requirements validation and acceptance, and requirements management and monitoring (see Sect. 4).

By answering *RQ1 - How are UX Research practices and approaches integrated into Agile RE?*, we could see that integration efforts range from the use of Agile RE artefacts to describe UX aspects/requirements to more substantive collaborative work between UX and agile teams (as in Company D).

Considering the characteristics of the companies, the results also revealed some similarities among them. Companies B and D share similar business models and adopt the same agile method (Scrum). However, the former conducts UX Research exclusively with clients, whereas the latter involves end-users more directly in the UX Research. The key distinction lies in how work is integrated during requirements discovery, which, in some cases, is conducted collaboratively by agile and UX teams. Integration in Company D appears to occur more organically, whereas in Company B, weekly meetings are the main mechanism sustaining integration. By contrast, in Companies A and C, requirements discovery is conducted by the undergraduate admissions office and operations team, respectively, with other departments involved in executing requirements specification activities in conjunction with the agile team. In general, we also observed that collaborative work between UX and agile teams during requirements discovery yields more structured specification of those requirements.

Only a limited set of UX Research methods is used in these two companies, with interviews and the analysis of user support tickets serving as the main basis for UX Research. The UX expert's work (in Company C) is largely focused on UI design. The combination of user stories and prototypes remains the most widely used approach for specifying and communicating requirements in the studied companies. The combined use of user stories and prototypes, or the incorporation of UX aspects into user stories, has already been discussed in [10,15], respectively. However, our results showed that teams still face challenges in consistently sharing the requirement-related documentation with the agile team and UX experts.

Taking into account the practices and tools that support the Agile RE and UX Research integration, we observed a diverse ecosystem of technologies used across the different stages of Agile RE. Tools such as GitLab, ClickUp, and Azure DevOps are widely adopted as central repositories for requirements and related documentation. Figma is the most commonly used tool for creating UI prototypes and mockups, serving as the primary environment for UI design, as already reported in [17]. Although Almeyda et al. [3] and Alrazgan et al. [1] have identified common practices and strategies for integrating requirements engineering and UX Research (e.g., user stories, low-fidelity prototypes, personas, use cases, and scenarios), they do not detail how these tools and practices are employed in the activities of teams. Despite Kusuma et al. [14] only mentioning stages of Agile RE, our research provided a detailed description of how UX Research practices and tools are embedded in the procedures used at each stage of Agile RE.

Regarding *RQ2 - What are the positive and negative impacts of UX Research on Agile RE?*, among the best practices identified in requirements discovery are the active participation of non-technical stakeholders and the requirements discovery ceremony, both of which facilitate clearer requirements definition. However, it is important to note that this situation also indicates limited end-user involvement, an issue primarily reported by Company B. In requirements specification, the primary positive aspects relate to the use of structured templates in defining requirements, as well as the use of user stories with AC that describe UI/UX aspects, personas, and prototypes within UX documentation. In requirements validation and acceptance, notable practices include the advanced execution of UX activities and review/retrospective meetings involving internal clients. Finally, agile, centralized, and frequent communication with non-technical stakeholders is a practice highlighted for its positive results in requirements management and monitoring. The use of common tools in organizational daily life, such as asynchronous chats, facilitates rapid communication among the teams. Other identified best practices spanning multiple stages of Agile RE are: collaboration between agile teams and the UX professional, cross-functional teams, and the strategic activities performed by UX experts.

We also identified aspects that hinder the integration between UX Research and Agile RE. The lack of knowledge in UX Research, the absence of UX specialists in the company, and low end-user involvement in a client-centered requirements discovery process can introduce several challenges. In the requirements specification, communication challenges and a lack of documentation standards generate conflicts between UX and Agile teams. On one hand, some participants from Companies A, B, and D recognized the UX documentation as a positive aspect. On the other hand, two participants, one from Company C and another from Company D, reported the lack of standardization in documentation as negative for their work. One potential reason for the different opinion may lie in the intensive use of chat tools by teams, which tends to generate informal documentation. Despite the benefits that communication from chat brings to collaborative work, its utilization may discourage the creation of formal and standardized documentation. The non-presence of user and client participation was also pointed out as a challenge in both the requirements validation and acceptance and in requirements management and monitoring. Furthermore, we also observed some problems that occur in more than one stage: lack of professionals with a formal UX background, conflict between agility and the time consumed by UX work, low priority of UX issues, insufficiency of resources for UX Research and conflicting objectives. These factors collectively highlight that some organizations still fail to adequately prioritize UX and user research within their RE activities.

The work of Pillay et al. [18] compiles good practices generally applied to mitigate the difficulties encountered in integration: advancing UX work, having separate backlogs and teams for UX activities, including users in UX testing, among others. Ananjeva et al. [4] cite the use of concise user stories and deliberation as ways to improve the integration of UX work with agile software development. In our work, we also perceived the importance of deliberation between teams and non-technical stakeholders, facilitating the understanding of the needs to be met by the solution.

The SLR by Kollmorgen et al. [12] identified 28 challenges and 103 solution approaches to the integration of Agile and UX. Some of the challenges identified in their work—such as resource constraints, documentation issues, and user and customer engagement—align with our own findings. Conversely, certain differences emerged: we did not identify the lack of collaboration between teams as a challenge, but rather as an existing best practice within the organizations studied. Furthermore, we noted a high level of involvement from internal users, contrasting with limited involvement from external users. Overall, our work differs by detailing both the challenges and the applied best practices based on a case study in four companies of varying sizes and sectors, which, despite its smaller scope, highlights its greater relevance to industrial practice.

Finally, it was observed that most companies still do not conduct UX Research continuously. Only Company C explicitly reported performing continuous UX Research, yet this was limited to critical functionalities, such as the system usage payment plan. According to Humble J. [8], the goal of continuous UX Research is to provide a constant flow of user data to the team, thereby reducing the risks associated with product decisions. This issue therefore emerges as a significant opportunity for future research in the field.

We understand that case studies bring generalization challenges because findings are context-dependent. Following Wieringa [25], case study generalization can be supported through analogical generalization and abductive inference: explanations of observed phenomena enable analogical transfer to similar situations, which are then assessed for applicability. In our case, the relevant analogous situations are software organizations that employ agile RE and UXD practices. Our study included organizations of different sizes and settings, all conducting UX Research to varying degrees (less in company A and more in companies B, C, and D), which allows researchers and practitioners to judge whether the findings can be applied to other organizations with similar characteristics.

6 Conclusion

This study conducted a multiple-case study with four organizations to examine how UX Research is integrated into Agile RE work. We identified practices, techniques, tools, ceremonies, and artifacts (e.g., user research and outcome documents) and mapped them to Agile RE stages (i.e., requirements discovery, specification, validation and acceptance, and management and monitoring). Our results show that UX Research practices and tools are primarily focused on requirements discovery. Although most practices and tools have already reported in the literature, we extend prior work by situating them within the concrete dynamics of Agile RE. The results revealed that although UX Research provides valuable input to requirements specification, its outcomes are often not structured or communicated in ways that make them easily accessible to agile teams.

In addition, our results highlighted both the positive and negative aspects of integrating UX Research and Agile RE, confirming challenges previously reported in the literature. Additionally, our findings showed that collaborative work among teams during Agile RE activities, whether through ceremonies or through artifacts that share UX-related knowledge, is perceived as beneficial for the integration. Conversely, participants indicated the need to make UX Research a continuous activity in the Agile RE process, a new finding that differs from prior studies.

This study contributes to practice by clarifying how UX Research activities are distributed across Agile RE stages and which individuals are involved in each. By unpacking both the benefits and drawbacks of this relationship, our findings also provide concrete guidance on how to structure the integration between UX Research and Agile RE to better support requirements work. As future work, we intend to investigate how positioning UX Research as a continuous activity in Agile RE can affect practitioners' activities and requirements quality. Additionally, we intend to conduct a new data analysis to examine the adoption of high-abstraction approaches as dual-track development in the organizations.

Acknowledgments. We thank all study participants and the financial support of the São Paulo Research Foundation (FAPESP) - grants 2020/00615-9 and 2020/10429-8; CNPq - Brazil - grants 309497/2022-1; Coordenação de Aperfeiçoamento de Pessoal de Nível Superior (CAPES - Brazil) - Finance Code 001, and Federal Institute of Education, Science and Technology of South of Minas Gerais - IFSULDEMINAS.

Data Availability. Due to confidentiality requirements by the organizations, the raw data cannot be provided openly.

References

1. Al-Razgan, M., et al.: Challenges of integrating agile and UX/UCD: aystematic literature review. Int. J. Comput. Appl. **184**(33) (2022)
2. Aleryani, A.Y.: The impact of the user experience (UX) on the quality of the requirements elicitation. Int. J. Digit. Inf. Wirel. Commun. (IJDIWC) **10**(1), 1–9 (2020)
3. Almeyda, S., Zapata Del Río, C., Cohn, D.: Integration of user experience and agile techniques for requirements analysis: a systematic review. In: Soares, M.M., Rosenzweig, E., Marcus, A. (eds.) Design, User Experience, and Usability: UX Research and Design. HCII 2021. LNCS, vol. 12779, pp. 187–203. Springer, Cham (2021). https://doi.org/10.1007/978-3-030-78221-4_13
4. Ananjeva, A., Persson, J., Bruun, A.: Integrating UX work with agile development through user stories: an action research study in a small software company. J. Syst. Softw. **170** (2020). https://doi.org/10.1016/j.jss.2020.110785
5. Brhel, M., Meth, H., Maedche, A., Werder, K.: Exploring principles of user-centered agile software development: a literature review. Inf. Softw. Technol. **61**, 163–181 (2015)
6. Choma, J., Guerra, E.M., Alvaro, A., Pereira, R., Zaina, L.: Influences of UX factors in the agile UX context of software startups. Inf. Softw. Technol. **152** (2022)
7. Interaction Design Foundation: UX research. Interaction Design Foundation (2021). https://www.interaction-design.org/literature/topics/ux-research. Acessado em 27 de Outubro de 2025
8. Humble, J.: What is continuous UX research?. The Fountain Institute (2024). https://www.thefountaininstitute.com/blog/what-is-continuous-ux-research. Accessed 30 Oct 2025

9. International Organization for Standardization: ISO 9241-210:2019 – Ergonomics of human-system interaction – Part 210: Human-centred design for interactive systems (2019). https://www.iso.org/standard/77520.html, standard
10. Keshk, N., El-Ramly, M., Salah, A.: A proposal for enhancing agile requirements engineering with prototyping and enriched user stories. In: Proceedings of the Federated Africa and Middle East Conf on SE, FAMECSE 2022, pp. 59–63. ACM, New York (2022). https://doi.org/10.1145/3531056.3542773
11. Kieffer, S., Rukonic, L., de Meerendré, V.K., Vanderdonckt, J.: Specification of a UX process reference model towards the strategic planning of UX activities. In: Proceedings of the 14th International Joint Conference on Computer Vision, Imaging and Computer Graphics Theory and Applications - Volume 2: HUCAPP, pp. 74–85. INSTICC, SciTePress (2019). https://doi.org/10.5220/0007693600740085
12. Kollmorgen, J., Pilz, J., da Silva, T.S., Thomaschewski, J., Schön, E.M.: State of the art of agile user experience: challenges and solution approaches. Comput. Stand. Interfaces **96**, 104083 (2025). https://doi.org/10.1016/j.csi.2025.104083
13. Krout, K., Carrascal, J.P., Lowdermilk, T.: Lean UX research at scale: a case study. In: Proceedings of Mensch Und Computer 2020, MuC 2020, pp. 53–59. ACM, New York (2020). https://doi.org/10.1145/3404983.3405587
14. Kusuma, W., Jantan, A., Admodisastro, N., Norowi, N.: User experience of customer-centric software process through requirement process: systematic review. JOIV Int. J. Inform. Vis. (2023)
15. Marques, A.B., Costa, A.F., Santos, I., Andrade, R.: Enriching user stories with usability features in a remote agile project: a case study. In: Proceedings of the XXI Brazilian Symposium on Software Quality, SBQS 2022. ACM, New York (2023). https://doi.org/10.1145/3571473.3571496
16. Martinelli, S., Lopes, L.A., Zaina, L.A.M.: UX research practices related to long-term UX: a systematic literature review. Inf. Softw. Technol. **170**, 107431 (2024). https://doi.org/10.1016/J.INFSOF.2024.107431
17. Parizi, R., Moreira, M., Couto, I., Marczak, S., Conte, T.: A tool proposal for recommending design thinking techniques in software development. J. Softw. Eng. Res. Dev. **10**, 3:1–3:15 (2022). https://doi.org/10.5753/jserd.2021.1931
18. Pillay, N., Wing, J.W.: Agile UX: integrating good UX development practices in agile. In: 2019 Conference on Information Communications Technology and Society (ICTAS), pp. 1–6 (2019)
19. Runeson, P., Höst, M.: Guidelines for conducting and reporting case study research in software engineering. Empir. Softw. Eng. **14**(2), 131–164 (2009)
20. Saldana, J.: The Coding Manual for Qualitative Researchers. SAGE Publications (2021). https://books.google.com.br/books?id=RwcVEAAAQBAJ
21. Schön, E., Thomaschewski, J., Escalona, M.J.: Agile requirements engineering: a systematic literature review. Comput. Stand. Interfaces **49**, 79–91 (2017)
22. Schön, E.M., Winter, D., Uhlenbrok, J., Escalona, M., Thomaschewski, J.: Enterprise experience into the integration of human-centered design and Kanban (2016). https://doi.org/10.5220/0005942601330140
23. Sfetsos, P., Angelis, L., Stamelos, I., Raptis, P.: Integrating user-centered design practices into agile web development: a case study. In: 2016 7th International Conference on Information, Intelligence, Systems & Applications (IISA), pp. 1–6 (2016). https://doi.org/10.1109/IISA.2016.7785424
24. da Silva, T.S., Silveira, M.S., Maurer, F., Silveira, F.F.: The evolution of agile UXD. Inf. Softw. Technol. **102**, 1–5 (2018)

25. Wieringa, R.: Empirical research methods for technology validation: scaling up to practice. J. Syst. Softw. **95**, 19–31 (2014). https://doi.org/10.1016/j.jss.2013.11.1097
26. Zaina, L.A., Sharp, H., Barroca, L.: UX information in the daily work of an agile team: a distributed cognition analysis. Int. J. Hum Comput Stud. **147**, 102574 (2021). https://doi.org/10.1016/j.ijhcs.2020.102574
27. Zaveri, A.A., Jaafar, J., Yafi, E., Shehmir, S.: Evolution of requirements engineering in agile methodology – literature review. J. Eng. Technol. Appl. Phys. **6**(2), 57–65 (2024). https://doi.org/10.33093/jetap.2024.6.2.57

Iterative Pilot Testing as a Scalable User Involvement Practice in Large-Scale Agile Software Development

Morteza Moalagh(✉)

Department of Computer Science, Norwegian University of Science and Technology (NTNU), Trondheim, Norway
morteza.moalagh@ntnu.no

Abstract. User involvement is essential for aligning software systems with organizational needs in agile development; however, achieving meaningful engagement becomes challenging in large-scale settings. Large organizations may contain distributed teams and diverse user groups whose limited availability and unfamiliarity with agile practices hinder sustained involvement. Although participatory and user-centered approaches work in smaller contexts, they are challenging to scale, leaving a gap in how to organize user involvement across dispersed organizations and multiple development teams. To address this gap, the present study examines pilot testing in a large-scale agile environment. Drawing on a qualitative case study of a Norwegian public organization, based on interviews with 35 participants from development and user groups, the study defines iterative pilot testing as a scalable practice in which unfinished yet operational solutions are refined gradually through user involvement when functionality is novel or complex. The study demonstrates how this practice can make development work more visible, enable development teams to be closer to their users and their work practices, and facilitate teams in navigating cultural and functional differences, thereby strengthening user involvement in large-scale agile software development.

Keywords: Agile Software Development · Large-scale Agile Software Development · User Involvement · Pilot Testing · Iterative Pilot Testing

1 Introduction

User involvement is a foundational value in agile software development (ASD), helping facilitate ongoing feedback and collaboration, and alignment between evolving user needs and system outcomes [1–3]. However, in large-scale, geographically distributed organizations, engaging users becomes challenging due to hierarchical structures, distributed teams, and conflicting stakeholder interests. Limited access to users, together with delivery pressures, insufficient agile experience, coordination difficulties, and cultural and communication differences, further undermine consistent participation and reduce the effectiveness of user involvement in ASD [4–6]. Research studies in large-scale ASD further show that distributed settings might weaken user accessibility and the

A. Goldman et al. (Eds.): XP 2026, LNBIP 578, pp. 228–243, 2026.
https://doi.org/10.1007/978-3-032-22375-3_14

clarity of user needs, underscoring the necessity for scalable mechanisms that sustain meaningful engagement effectively [7–9].

Pilot testing practices, which are defined as the real-world assessment of a reliable but unfinished system, might offer strong potential to enhance user involvement within large software development projects [10, 11]. In this study, we investigate iterative pilot testing (IPT)-i.e., pilot testing performed in iterative development such as ASD, as a structured user involvement practice within large-scale ASD. By enabling users to work with the system in authentic environments using real data, IPT might generate deeper learning and context-rich feedback compared to prototypes or controlled testing processes [12, 13]. Research also suggests that exposure and proximity to real usage conditions might help development teams uncover latent requirements, socio-technical constraints, and organizational integration issues that might be missed in laboratory-based evaluation [14, 15]. Such characteristics make IPT particularly relevant for large-scale ASD, which may struggle to involve distributed user groups in rapid, iterative cycles and maintain alignment between system evolution, waste reduction, and value delivery [16].

Although IPT practices are advocated as useful in industry and practice [10], they remain less explored within academic research, especially within large-scale ASD. Most studies focus on related activities such as usability testing, prototyping, or user acceptance testing, which typically involve limited user participation in controlled settings rather than real operational environments with real data [17–19]. Research on beta testing highlights benefits like improved user satisfaction and reduced stress [20], yet it rarely examines the complexity of large-scale agile contexts. Challenges such as multi-team coordination and distributed user groups are often overlooked [7, 21]. Reviews of large-scale ASD consistently note difficulties in sustaining user involvement but offer little insight into scalable practices [22]. Consequently, a clear gap remains in understanding how IPT practices effectively help teams navigate uncertainty and minimize unnecessary rework by involving users in the software development process in large-scale and distributed organizations that use ASD.

In this study, we ask: ***How does iterative pilot testing support user involvement in large-scale agile software development?*** This study examines how pilot testing supports user involvement in the Norwegian Labour and Welfare Administration, a 22,000-employee public organization providing welfare, unemployment support, and employment services. Drawing on 35 interviews, this study explores how Oslo-based (Central office) product teams collaborate with internal users (NAV employees) across 264 local offices, utilizing iterative development practices to integrate pilot feedback into ASD.

This study contributes new insight into how IPT supports user involvement in large-scale ASD. It conceptualizes IPT as a practice in which unfinished yet operational solutions are introduced when functionality is novel or complex. Solutions are incrementally refined through direct engagement with users in their everyday work environments, including opportunities to sit with distant users and observe actual practices. The study also shows that the scale of iterative pilots is determined by assessing potential impact, required solution completeness, duration, and involved user groups. Moreover, this approach might strengthen user involvement in the distributed and large-scale organizations by enabling consistent access to dispersed users, revealing context-specific needs, and supporting more grounded and timely feedback.

2 Background

2.1 User Involvement in Large-Scale Agile Software Development

As agile methods became standard in the software industry, large-scale ASD emerged to extend agile principles across multiple teams and organizational units [23, 24]. To support agility at scale, organizations introduced frameworks such as SAFe and LeSS, which seek to balance team autonomy with centralized synchronization and governance [25]. In these complex environments, user involvement becomes essential for maintaining coherence across teams, reducing dependency risks, and ensuring alignment with user needs. It helps anchor development decisions in real usage contexts and supports learning across iterative cycles [26].

Despite its importance, achieving sustained user involvement in large-scale and geographically distributed ASD remains challenging [27]. Users are often spread across departments and remote locations, limiting their ability to participate regularly in iterative feedback and design activities [4, 8]. Development teams and end users may also hold different priorities or expectations, creating tensions that weaken the influence of user input on decisions [5]. Fast delivery pressures in ASD leave even less room for meaningful collaboration [7]. Users unfamiliar with software or agile practices can be harder to engage, resulting in uneven involvement [6]. Securing commitment across functions and navigating cultural and communication differences adds complexity [4, 28], making user involvement challenging.

2.2 Pilot Testing in Large-Scale Agile Software Development

Pilot testing, also called pilot implementation, field testing, pilot studies, or pilot systems, is defined as a systematic field test of a properly engineered but unfinished system in its intended environment using real data to evaluate value, improve design, and reduce implementation risks [10, 11]. In software engineering, several practices involve users in testing, including usability testing, acceptance testing, and prototype trials, each with different scopes and levels of maturity [17]. Prototyping is an early, incomplete model explored in controlled settings, whereas pilot testing involves a reliable but unfinished system used in real conditions to validate performance and value [13].

In software development, pilot testing functions as a transitional stage between design and full implementation, enabling developers and users to identify technical issues, adjust organizational routines, and refine both the system and its integration into everyday work before broader deployment [10, 11]. It operates as a learning process grounded in real use, revealing design shortcomings, technical problems, and organizational barriers while helping reduce risk prior to large-scale rollout [13, 29]. Typical activities involve planning, technical setup, organizational preparation, real-world usage, and structured learning phases [10]. User involvement is central, as users perform actual tasks and provide feedback that informs design and workflow adjustments [10, 13]. Although involvement can be challenging to sustain amid competing demands [30], continuous communication and alignment can facilitate turning user experiences into opportunities for enhancement [12]. In ASD, pilot testing remains a relatively under-examined aspect within academic research. Although some studies have addressed user acceptance testing in agile contexts, such as the work by Pandit and Tahiliani [18] and Otaduy and Díaz [19], who worked on user acceptance test (UAT). However, UAT differs from pilot testing because it confirms business requirements in controlled environments. Obermueller and Eckhardt demonstrate that beta testing can lessen user stress and increase satisfaction, offering valuable insight relevant to this research area [20]. This study, therefore, turns to iterative pilot testing (IPT) within large-scale ASD contexts, showing how the practice operates in such environments and how it enhances user involvement.

3 Research Method

This study examines an emerging phenomenon and seeks to build new conceptual understanding, thus making an exploratory case study an appropriate research method [31, 32]. This method enables a thorough investigation of a complex sociotechnical setting through multiple data sources and repeated interpretive cycles. It supports in-depth exploration of the environment, helping identify recurring patterns and develop meaningful insights [33]. This section outlines the core components of the exploratory case study, including the case context, data collection, and data analysis methods.

3.1 Case Description

The Norwegian Labour and Welfare Administration (NAV) is a major public institution with over 22,000 employees, providing unemployment and welfare benefits, support for children, pregnant, disabled and retired individuals, job-search assistance, and training programs for unemployed workers [34]. Since 2016, NAV has restructured its IT department, adopting in-sourced agile software development (ASD) [35, 36]. Development teams at NAV are based in Oslo and follow a product structure organized into product areas, each comprising multiple teams led by a product area leader. The cross-functional teams include a product leader, technical lead, designer, domain expert, and developers, supported by shared roles such as agile coaches and legal experts (Jurist). Teams have significant autonomy in shaping their work practices [37] and commonly use agile methods like Scrum with local adaptations. A common practice includes sprint planning on Mondays ("Monday Commit") and review or demonstration sessions on Fridays ("Friday Wins") [36, 38].

NAV develops digital solutions for both Norwegian citizens and internal users, such as case workers. Internal users are located at the central headquarters called Direktoratet, in twelve county offices, and in 264 local offices [34]. Local offices support local citizens, and case workers guide users, process applications, and ensure that individuals receive needed services. To maintain user access in a large and distributed organization, development teams work with user representatives in both county and local offices. Counties have implementation coordinators who manage digitalization work, and local offices also appoint change agents or super users, who are often experienced case workers, to gather requirements, test systems, train colleagues, and provide support [26, 27].

3.2 Data Collection and Analysis

Data Collection. Data collection involved individual and group interviews with 17 NAV development employees and 18 internal-user staff. Twenty-three participants took part in semi-structured interviews, while 12 joined four group sessions. Recruitment continued until thematic saturation was reached, meaning further interviews no longer produced new relevant insights [39]. The interview guides were adapted to reflect the participants' diverse professional backgrounds and their involvement in the pilot testing. For example, members of development teams were asked questions such as *"How do development teams organize an iterative pilot test?"* and *"How do development teams communicate with users during an iterative pilot test?"*. On the other side, users were asked questions such as *"How do you experience the iterative pilot test?"* and *"What is your role in the iterative pilot tests?"*. Each interview lasted between 1.5 and 2 h. Table 1 summarizes the data sources, assigning codes to individuals (P1–P23) and group interviews (G1–G4). The number of participants in each group interview is indicated with N values. To maintain confidentiality, information such as department, age, experience, and office location was removed from the dataset reported.

Table 1. Data Sources

Data Collection Technique	Detail	Side	#
Semi-Structured Interview	Implementation Coordinators (P1–P3)	User	23
	Change Agents (P4–P6)	User	
	IT Manager (P7–P9)	Development	
	Jurist (P10)	Development	
	Product Area Leader (P11)	Development	
	Product Leaders (P12–P16)	Development	
	Domain Experts (P17–P18)	Development	
	Designer (P19)	Development	
	Agile Coach (P20)	Development	
	Technical Leads (P21–P22)	Development	
	Nav Contact Centre Specialist (P23)	Development	
Group Interview	Case Workers (G1)(N = 4)	User	12
	Implementation Coordinators (G2)(N = 2)	User	
	Case Workers (G3)(N = 4)	User	
	Implementation Coordinators (G4)(N = 2)	User	

Data Analysis. Following data collection, an abductive thematic analysis has been applied, linking empirical data with theory through both inductive and deductive reasoning [39]. All interviews were translated from Norwegian to English, transcribed, reviewed for relevance, and analyzed through inductive open coding to categorize information and identify patterns, similarities, and differences [40]. The data analysis was conducted by the sole author in Microsoft Excel, using codes extracted from the interview transcripts. As iterative pilot testing (IPT) constituted the unit of analysis, the coding process focused on concepts directly related to this activity. The analysis was carried out in three main stages. First, initial open codes were identified, compared, and refined, enabling meaningful relationships between categories to emerge. Second, these relationships informed the development of axial codes, which grouped related concepts into broader categories associated with IPT practices. Finally, the axial codes were synthesized into overarching themes and documented in a codebook. For example, codes like "Using Microsoft Teams for communication" or "Getting user feedback through iterative pilot testing by sending forms and questionnaires to users" formed the "Communication during pilots" axial codes, and with other axial codes like "Post-pilot feedback and follow-up communication", they formed the theme "Communication and getting feedback through iterative pilot testing". During theme development, relevant theories and prior studies were reviewed to strengthen alignment with existing literature and improve analytical coherence.

4 Findings

This section presents the findings on how iterative pilot testing (IPT) is conducted in NAV, supporting user involvement in large-scale agile software development. For each topic, selected quotations from the interviews are provided to illustrate and substantiate the findings, with references to individual and group interviews indicated in brackets.

4.1 How Iterative Pilot Testing is Conducted in NAV

In NAV, software development has been organized around large-scale agile software development (ASD) practices that facilitate frequent and incremental releases: *"We generally do an average of 2000 changes in production each week... In the old times, we used to have quarterly releases... You might package 100,000 development hours into one release. So we have been moving from 4 a year to 2000 times a week"* [P9, IT manager]. While ASD emphasizes early delivery and frequent user feedback, NAV's development teams apply this principle selectively. For functionalities involving *novelty or complexity,* teams adopt more cautious release strategies, such as utilizing IPT. For example, one of the participants talked about how IPT gave them valuable user insight before releasing the digital assistant as an intelligent and complex software: *"That's a big advantage when testing something as huge as a digital assistant that can hallucinate and give wrong answers. We got very positive feedback, [...] We had meetings with leaders and subject matter experts so everyone could give feedback"* [P17, Domain Expert]. IPT may also highlight real-world features or software performance and uncover challenges prior to broader release in a large and distributed organization: *"Yes, so we often do pilot.*

Sometimes, we conduct pilot tests to gather input on whether a new feature is effective, especially if it's not yet clear if it makes sense" [P15, Product Leader]. As illustrated in Fig. 1, IPT in NAV begins by defining the scale of the pilot test and choosing pilot offices. The process then proceeds with a formal kickoff, user training, and ongoing communication and feedback activities, which are carried out iteratively throughout the pilot period. Throughout the IPT, the system is iteratively refined based on feedback gathered from participating users.

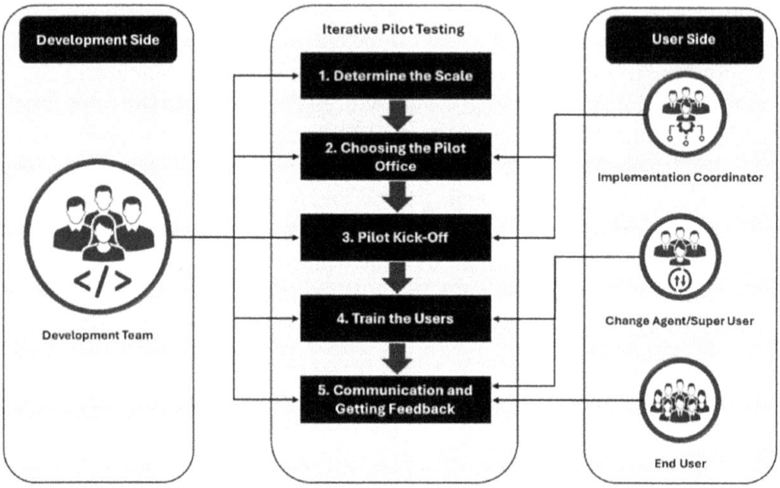

Fig. 1. Iterative pilot testing (IPT) steps and roles in NAV

Determine the Scale: In NAV, the first step in IPT is determining the scale. Determining the pilot scale is based on factors such as *potential impact, solution completeness, duration, and involved user groups*. Pilots in NAV might involve a few offices, enabling closer user engagement, controlled feedback, and reduced risk from immature features: *"With a smaller user group, you can take much more time to explain what the function does, how they should use it, and if there are any consequences, how they should give feedback. Then you have much more control over them. And when you feel confident, you can slowly but surely roll it out further. I think that's a very, very good way to introduce bigger changes"* [P17, domain expert]. On the other hand, IPT might be conducted on a larger scale, like an entire county or multiple offices in different counties: *"Well, the difference is really about scale—whether you run a pilot with just a few people, or roll it out to everyone at once. When it's rolled out to everyone, you naturally get more feedback because it's tested on a much larger scale"* [P23, Call Center Expert].

A second factor in scaling IPT is solution completeness. Instead of awaiting a fully developed system, some teams may release early, limited versions to test key assumptions in real settings, enabling iterative refinement based on actual data rather than speculation and user feedback: *"And now this [...] solution, which is going to be rolled out after the summer, they are piloting this in our county. And so they will be working with first the thin solution and then trying to develop it after the summer"* [G2, Implementation

Coordinators]. In some cases, development teams choose to finalize the initial solution before conducting IPT. During the pilot phase, they collaborate iteratively with users in selected offices to refine and enhance the system, ensuring stability and effectiveness prior to a full-scale release: *"We entered a pilot, which is now likely wrapping up this month, and it has also undergone adjustments throughout the pilot period. So we work a bit differently depending on the situation. […] So when it was good enough to launch, we launched it"* [P11, Product Area Leader].

The third factor influencing the scale of IPT is its duration, determined by whether development teams require intensive user feedback or extended experimentation. For instance, some pilots may span only two weeks, emphasizing high user engagement and rapid iterative adaptation: *"It was also a pilot that was only going to last for 14 days. We had never experienced such a short pilot period before, so it had to be an office that could quickly connect and adapt"* [G4, Implementation Coordinators]. It could also take nearly six months to support deeper experimentation and richer insights into evolving work practices: *"It was half a year. But not that long—maybe a little less. It wasn't over the summer; it started in the spring or something like that, so it wouldn't be so vulnerable. It was just under half a year. […] It was a kind of experiment, where we filled out our time usage"* [G3, Case Workers].

The fourth factor shaping the IPT scale is the involved user groups. Development teams may need users with different skills and work practices to gain diverse perspectives, uncover challenges, and identify support needs or adjustments for improving the digital solution: *"What we did with the first pilot of 24 people was that I sent out a request to everyone: I want one person who is very technically skilled, who can almost figure this out on their own. […] And then I want one person who is a bit old-fashioned, uses old systems, and doesn't have good work methods. We have already chosen two different user groups to accommodate both target groups. Yes, we also included people with less effective work methods. And then we had separate user tests with them so we could find out what their challenges were"* [P17, Domain Expert]. Alternatively, development teams may disregard user group differences and recruit volunteers, focusing on general feedback rather than targeted user insights: "*There was a phase where we transitioned from 'Citrix' to the application portal. That was announced […], and I signed up to participate, partly because I was a change agent, but mostly because I was curious. […] So when it was eventually rolled out to the whole office after many months, I was already familiar with it*" [P4, Change Agent].

Choosing the Pilot Office. After defining the pilot scope, development teams collaborate with implementation coordinators to select suitable local offices, a process influenced by managerial commitment and requiring considerable time and ongoing dialogue between development teams and offices: *"The Directorate needed someone who could quickly step in to test, join a workshop, or act as a pilot. One of the large offices in our county is one of the offices I've found to be development-oriented, along with many others. For a while, we had a list of offices it made sense to contact first"* [G4, Implementation Coordinators]. In this process, implementation coordinators often play a key role, helping development teams negotiate with local offices and identify suitable pilot sites by drawing on their knowledge of both sides and their piloting experience: *"In that process, I'm more of a sparring partner in finding the pilots and maybe not always* *closely involved, but I make sure I'm connected enough to know what's happening on our side"* [P3, Implementation Coordinator].

Pilot Kick-Off. After offices are selected, the pilot kick-off serves as an initial meeting in NAV where users are introduced to the new system or functionality. They will inform about tentative expectations, and given opportunities to share early reflections during the session: *"Before we go out with the pilot, we have a meeting with them and inform them of what we are trying to solve and then that we want them to use it, and give feedback on what I think."* [P6, Jurist]. In addition, development teams prepare documents on the system and functionalities, and present these materials during the meeting to support users' understanding: *"We always write news articles in the meantime, and when we pilot something, everyone else knows what's going on. They also recognize a guide on the list of pilots, so they can go and ask if they have questions. That way, we create a soft introduction even before everyone else gets access"* [P17, domain expert].

Train the Users. IPT also involves gradually training users, beginning with a limited set of offices to build early competence, resolve initial issues, and prepare for broader organizational rollout: *"Now I know, for example, with this system that's coming and supposed to launch. There are two counties in the country, with selected offices in each, that will be the first to start using it. And then one or maybe several other case processing units, as they're called, central ones. However, that's how they've been doing it, to maintain some control and prevent everyone from starting at the same time. They want to start slowly and then gradually train people"* [P18, Domain Expert]. As implementation coordinators support development teams in selecting pilot offices and preparing training materials for an effective pilot, change agents (local super users) receive training directly from the development teams and subsequently train their colleagues during the IPT. By applying a train-the-trainer approach during the IPT, development teams can build trust with change agents, deliver training more efficiently, and better prepare users for the testing period: *"We've also been clear that we're not responsible for training all the caseworkers—that's something they [Change agents] need to do themselves. They become better at the solution if they take ownership of the training. Ideally, we want as few people as possible involved in the initial training, and that they handle it internally within their units"* [P13, Product Leader].

Communication and Getting Feedback Through Iterative Pilot Testing. During the pilot period, development teams and users in the pilot offices work closely together to iteratively change and refine the system: *"This is the system you've built, and often in a pilot, it's a kind of minimum version they've created, which will then be developed further during the pilot. So that's also why we need to be involved early, to be able to say something about it"* [P6, Change Agent]. The teams actively seek feedback and change the system. A primary mechanism is the shared communication channel in Microsoft Teams or Viva Engage, which both groups use to exchange observations, questions, and feedback: *"When you're part of a pilot, the people who produce or develop the system are usually very focused on getting feedback so they can scale it up. [...] there's just a Teams channel opened where you can ask questions, dig into things, or give feedback if something comes up"* [P18, Domain Expert]. Aligned with agile principles of ongoing feedback, NAV's development teams use questionnaires and digital tools like Hotjar to capture user experiences, applying these insights across testing cycles to refine solutions: *"We created a solution just before summer, and it's been in pilot until now. [...] We made sure that all offices in that county got the option in the application, and all caseworkers in that county could sort their task lists. We've also had conversations, and we've placed a Hotjar in the application so that applicants can share their thoughts on the solution"* [P16, Product Leader].

4.2 Iterative Pilot Testing as a Practice for User Involvement in Large-Scale Agile Software Development

Using Iterative Pilot Tests to Make Agile Work Tangible for Users. IPT may make development work more visible in a distributed organization like NAV, especially for users who previously had little contact with development teams. Such involvement could give them a sense that developers remain attentive to evolving needs and open to dialogue and change. As users see their input gradually shaped into design choices, they may begin to sense the rhythms of ASD: *"Yes, the pilots. It's been going on for a while now, and I think it's been really rewarding and fun. It's engaging to be a part of something like this for developing something new. And not least, through this, I've realized how important the competence we have actually is and that the developers also recognize that. They often ask, "Where do you need this?" "How often do you use this?" "Do you ever need that?" And you realize that this process brings clarity, not only for us, but also for those who are going to use the system. In a way, it's also about involving the users, the employees, and employers in shaping the system"* [G1, Implementation Coordinators].

Iterative Pilot Testing as a Way Toward Proximity to Work. IPT in NAV may enable development teams to focus on what users actually do rather than what they say, bringing development work closer to everyday practice: *"So it's in the long run it's more important to look at what people do instead of only what they say because as with our caseworkers, they're quite experienced people. So after we have put things out there, they're able to look at the screen, they're just looking at that data point"* [P21, Technical Lead]. By gaining proximity to users through visits to at least one local office, teams may observe situated work that is difficult to capture through distant requirement discussions. These observable moments could help teams refine the solution in shorter cycles and adapt it more closely to emerging needs: *"When it comes to pilots, we've had proper meetings to give feedback, and in those cases, I've experienced that our input is taken seriously and that changes are actually made based on it"* [P1, Implementations Coordinator].

Iterative Pilot Tests Revealing User Support Needs. IPT in NAV may act as learning cycles, offering insight beyond conventional testing and revealing user demands, enabling teams to identify needed support and observe context-specific challenges that inform subsequent implementation efforts: *"So, it might be that we produce something new, but only within the production environment—meaning only those with that function get access. They can then test the new feature in production and give us feedback. Before we roll it out to the rest of the users, [...] we can gather feedback and make adjustments, either to the solution itself or to the training process we plan to run"* [P22, Technical Lead].

Iterative Pilot Tests Helping Navigate Cultural Differences. IPT in NAV may help address cultural differences across dispersed offices by capturing varied communication styles. For instance, users in northern regions might voice concerns more directly, while those in central areas may be more reserved. Involving multiple locations can widen perspectives, surface otherwise unspoken issues, and support a more balanced understanding that strengthens the value of implemented digital solutions overall: *"The northern one is definitely the one who is quickest to tell when they are displeased. While those here in the closed doors are very much more polite and reserved. While the further north you go, the more direct people are, which is, you know, that's just a culture in Norway, actually. And sometimes the people who are further north are more north than the one in the mid country and the one in the north. [...] They're also direct, so they're a lot easier to tell if they're displaced with something. So it's actually easier to get good results when working with them"* [P14, Product Leader].

5 Discussion

This discussion examines how iterative pilot testing (IPT) supports user involvement in large-scale agile software development (ASD) by first outlining how traditional pilot testing operates in agile contexts and introducing a new concept called IPT. It then considers the scalability of IPT and how different scaling choices allow the practice to adapt to large-scale organizational conditions. The discussion also explores how IPT enables user involvement across geographically dispersed settings, followed by reflections on practical implications.

5.1 Implications for Theory

Iterative Pilot Testing (IPT). The findings contribute to defining IPT as a practice in which an unfinished but reliable system is used by real users in their operational environment to produce early, context-rich feedback. A key distinction emerging from this research, compared with earlier studies on pilot testing [10, 11, 13], is its selective use within an ASD approach. In the studied company, IPT is not employed routinely but is introduced when features are *novel or complex,* enabling development teams to observe how new functionality behaves in realistic settings with authentic data. IPT also serves as a site for collaboration, as communication channels and feedback methods enable development teams to iteratively adjust and enhance the solution based on situated feedback. This continuous improvement process differs from more traditional pilot tests in that it supports ongoing refinement rather than a one-time evaluation. Used in this targeted way, IPT may help teams navigate uncertainty and minimize unnecessary rework, thereby aligning with the core aims of ASD [16].

Scalable Iterative Pilot Testing (IPT). IPT can be understood as a scalable practice, meaning that it can be configured for a small group of users to a large group of users in different locations to address the uncertainties and coordination challenges between the development and user sides of the organization present in large-scale ASD. As shown in Table 2, this study identified key decision areas such as *potential impact*, *solution* *completeness*, *duration*, and *involved user groups* that can be combined in various ways to define and configure the scope of an IPT. This combinational approach illustrates how IPT can be scaled from small to large configurations to address organizational constraints such as distributed users, limited access to participants, and competing priorities in large-scale ASD [4, 5, 8]. In this manner, the scaling approach highlights how IPT can be configured as a flexible practice that supports learning and coordination in large-scale agile environments, thereby complementing prior research [8, 10, 12] that emphasizes the importance of structured user involvement in real operational settings.

Table 2. Decision table for determining the scale of iterative pilot testing

Decision Area	Guiding Question	If Yes	If No
Potential Impact	Is the potential impact high if the solution fails?	Run a pilot with a few offices for close control	Run a pilot, County-wide or multi-office
Solution Completeness	Do we need early-stage feedback before finishing the solution?	Thin solution pilot (minimal viable product)	Near-complete solution pilot
Duration	Is short, intensive feedback enough?	Short pilot (2–4 weeks)	Long pilot (3–6 months)
Involved User Groups	Do you need diverse or contrasting user types to uncover issues?	Multi-group pilot (e.g., tech-savvy + old-fashioned users)	Run a pilot with volunteer users

User Involvement in Iterative Pilot Testing (IPT). IPT may help mitigate challenges arising from hierarchical organizational arrangements, geographically distributed teams, and competing stakeholder interests, which commonly constrain effective user involvement in large-scale settings [28]. In such settings, users are often difficult to reach, spread across departments, and unable to participate regularly in iterative feedback cycles [4, 8]. IPT may make development work more visible and concrete for individuals with limited prior experience with development teams. As users experience their input being translated into design adjustments, tensions stemming from differing priorities and a lack of clarity between developers and frontline staff [5, 7] may be reduced. This hands-on involvement may also help address uneven participation among users unfamiliar with agile practices [5], allowing them to understand agile rhythms through direct engagement rather than abstract discussions of requirements.

In large distributed organizations, development teams may also struggle to interpret user needs consistently because communication styles vary across regions, and high-level requirement discussions fail to reveal context-specific challenges [4, 7]. By observing real workflows during IPT, teams can gain insight into everyday practice across different regions and focus on what users actually do, rather than solely on what they articulate. These insights may also support more accurate refinements and prevent misunderstandings that might otherwise persist through distant communication. IPT additionally reveals user support needs early, allowing adjustments to the solution or implementation approach before full rollout. In this way, IPT becomes a practice for navigating organizational complexity and sustaining meaningful user participation.

5.2 Implications for Practice

The findings have implications for practice in organizations working with large-scale ASD. Iterative pilot testing (IPT) provides a practical and scalable approach to enhancing user involvement when development spans multiple teams and involves dispersed user groups. The recommendations below outline how development teams and Information Technology (IT) managers can effectively utilize the findings of this research.

Implications for Development Teams. Development teams that use an agile approach could use IPT when functionality is novel or complex. Teams might deploy unfinished yet operational solutions to real users to obtain early, context-rich insights and refine solutions continuously. The IPT scope could be shaped by potential impact, solution completeness, duration, and the user groups involved. Conducting pilots in real operational environments allows teams to observe actual work practices and address cultural or communication differences.

Implications for IT managers. IPT could be supported as a coordination mechanism. Managers can encourage development teams, remove participation barriers, and help teams select appropriate pilot scales. IPT reduces implementation risk, builds user trust, enables user participation in software development despite geographic distance, and improves alignment between system design and actual work practices.

6 Conclusion, Limitations, and Future Work

This study examined how iterative pilot testing (IPT) serves as a scalable approach for enhancing user involvement in large-scale agile software development. Drawing on interviews with development teams and user groups in a Norwegian public organization, the findings reveal that IPT is employed selectively when functionality is novel or complex, allowing teams to refine unfinished yet operational solutions through direct user involvement in real-world work environments. The study demonstrates that this proximity helps reveal context-specific needs, surface cultural and communication differences, and make development work more visible to dispersed user groups. By identifying decision areas that guide the scale of IPT, including potential impact, solution completeness, duration, and involved user groups, the research demonstrates how IPT can be scaled and support learning, ultimately reducing rework across large and distributed organizations.

This study has some limitations that should be considered when interpreting the findings. Data analysis was conducted by a single author, which may have influenced interpretations despite the use of systematic procedures. In addition, the study is situated within NAV's specific organizational context, which may limit the generalizability of the findings to other companies. As a qualitative study, the results provide in-depth, context-sensitive insights rather than statistically generalizable conclusions. Future research could examine how IPT and user involvement can be sustained in large-scale agile settings, including challenges related to long-term user involvement, participation fatigue, and the coordination mechanisms required to embed IPT effectively at scale.

Acknowledgments. This research was supported by funding from the Norwegian Labour and Welfare Administration (NAV). I sincerely acknowledge Associate Professor Babak A. Farshchian, Professor Torgeir Dingsøyr, Associate Professor Marius Mikalsen, and Tor Thorsrud Sporsem at Norwegian University of Science and Technology (NTNU) for their valuable feedback on earlier drafts. I also thank the anonymous reviewers for their constructive comments, as well as the NAV employees who generously contributed through interviews, enhancing the quality and rigor of this study.

References

1. Hoda, R., Noble, J., Marshall, S.: The impact of inadequate customer collaboration on self-organizing Agile teams. Inf. Softw. Technol. **53**(5), 521–534 (2011). https://doi.org/10.1016/j.infsof.2010.10.009
2. Schon, E.M., Winter, D., Escalona, M.J., Thomaschewski, J. (eds.): Key challenges in agile requirements engineering. Presented at the Agile Processes in Software Engineering and Extreme Programming (XP 2017), Cologne, Germany. Springer (2017). https://doi.org/10.1007/978-3-319-57633-6
3. Hansson, C., Dittrich, Y., Randall, D.: Agile processes enhancing user participation for small providers of off-the-shelf software. In: Eckstein, J., Baumeister, H., LINK (Online service) (eds.) Extreme programming and agile processes in software engineering: 5th international conference, XP 2004, Garmisch-Partenkirchen, Germany. LNCS, vol. 3092. Springer (2004)
4. Mikalsen, M., Moe, N.B., Wong, S.I., Stray, V.: Agile information system development organizations transforming to large-scale collaboration. In: Proceedings of the Forty-Second International Conference on Information Systems (ICIS 2021), Austin, USA (2021)
5. Barros, L., Tam, C., Varajão, J.: Agile software development projects–Unveiling the human-related critical success factors. Inf. Softw. Technol. **170**, 107432 (2024). https://doi.org/10.1016/j.infsof.2024.107432
6. Zorzetti, M., Signoretti, I., Salerno, L., Marczak, S., Bastos, R.: Improving agile software development using user-centered design and lean startup. Inf. Softw. Technol. **141**, 106718 (2022). https://doi.org/10.1016/j.infsof.2021.106718
7. Dikert, K., Paasivaara, M., Lassenius, C.: Challenges and success factors for large-scale agile transformations: a systematic literature review. J. Syst. Softw. **119**, 87–108 (2016). https://doi.org/10.1016/j.jss.2016.06.013
8. Tam, C., Moura, E.J.D.C., Oliveira, T., Varajão, J.: The factors influencing the success of on-going agile software development projects. Int. J. Project Manage. **38**(3), 165–176 (2020). https://doi.org/10.1016/j.ijproman.2020.02.001
9. Moalagh, M., Svesengen, V., Farshchian, B.A., Mikalsen, M.: user involvement in relational digital transformation: a case study of agile software development practices in a large organization. Presented at the 33rd International Conference on Information Systems Development (ISD 2025), Belgrade, Serbia. AIS (2025). https://doi.org/10.62036/ISD.2025.30
10. Hertzum, M., Bansler, J.P., Havn, E.C., Simonsen, J.: Pilot implementation: learning from field tests in is development. In: CAIS, vol. 30 (2012). https://doi.org/10.17705/1CAIS.03020
11. Mønsted, T., Hertzum, M., Søndergaard, J.: A socio-temporal perspective on pilot implementation: bootstrapping preventive care. Comput. Support. Coop. Work (CSCW) **29**(4), 419–449 (2020). https://doi.org/10.1007/s10606-019-09369-6

12. Wagner, E.L., Piccoli, G.: Moving beyond user participation to achieve successful IS design. Commun. ACM **50**(12), 51–55 (2007). https://doi.org/10.1145/1323688.1323694
13. Hertzum, M., Manikas, M.I., Torkilsheyggi, A.Á.: Grappling with the future: the messiness of pilot implementation in information systems design. Health Informatics J. **25**(2), 372–388 (2019). https://doi.org/10.1177/1460458217712058
14. Bakke, S., Bratteteig, T.: The closer the better: effects of developer-user proximity for mutual learning. In: 17th International Conference, HCI International 2015, Los Angeles, CA, USA. Springer (2015)
15. Chakraborty, S., Sarker, S., Sarker, S.: An exploration into the process of requirements elicitation: a grounded approach. JAIS **11**(4), 212–249 (2010). https://doi.org/10.17705/1jais.00225
16. Alahyari, H., Berntsson Svensson, R., Gorschek, T.: A study of value in agile software development organizations. J. Syst. Soft. **125**, 271–288 (2017). https://doi.org/10.1016/j.jss.2016.12.007
17. Kim, E., et al.: User-centered design roadmapping: anchoring roadmapping in customer value before technology selection. IEEE Trans. Eng. Manage. **69**(1), 109–126 (2022). https://doi.org/10.1109/TEM.2020.3030172
18. Pandit, P., Tahiliani, S.: AgileUAT: a framework for user acceptance testing based on user stories and acceptance criteria. IJCA **120**(10), 16–21 (2015). https://doi.org/10.5120/21262-3533
19. Otaduy, I., Diaz, O.: User acceptance testing for Agile-developed web-based applications: empowering customers through wikis and mind maps. J. Syst. Softw. **133**, 212–229 (2017). https://doi.org/10.1016/j.jss.2017.01.002
20. Obermueller, M., Eckhardt, A., Reibenspiess, V., Blossey, G., Kollmer, T.: How the perception of agile software development affects beta users' stress and satisfaction. Presented at the Hawaii International Conference on System Sciences (2023). https://doi.org/10.24251/HICSS.2023.787
21. Berntzen, M., Alette Engdal, S., Gellein, M., Brede Moe, N. (eds.): Coordination in agile product areas: a case study from a large FinTech organization. In: Proceedings of the 25th International Conference on Agile Software Development XP 2024. LNBI, Bolzano, Italy, vol. 512. Springer, Cham (2024). https://doi.org/10.1007/978-3-031-61154-4_3
22. Tkalich, A., Klotins, E., Sporsem, T., Stray, V., Moe, N.B., Barbala, A.: User feedback in continuous software engineering: revealing the state-of-practice. Empir. Software Eng. **30**(3), 79 (2025). https://doi.org/10.1007/s10664-024-10557-2
23. Dingsoeyr, T., Falessi, D., Power, K.: Agile development at scale: the next frontier. IEEE Softw. **36**(2), 30–38 (2019). https://doi.org/10.1109/MS.2018.2884884
24. Paasivaara, M., Behm, B., Lassenius, C., Hallikainen, M.: Large-scale agile transformation at Ericsson: a case study. Empir. Software Eng. **23**(5), 2550–2596 (2018). https://doi.org/10.1007/s10664-017-9555-8
25. Edison, H., Wang, X., Conboy, K.: Comparing methods for large-scale agile software development: a systematic literature review. IEEE Trans. Softw. Eng. **1** (2021). https://doi.org/10.1109/TSE.2021.3069039
26. Moalagh, M., Svesengen, V., Farshchian, B.A.: Investigating user-side representatives in large-scale agile software development. In: Agile Processes in Software Engineering and Extreme Programming: 26th International Conference on Agile Software Development, XP 2025, Brugg-Windisch, Switzerland, June 2–5, 2025, Proceedings. LNBIP, vol. 545. Springer, Cham (2025). https://doi.org/10.1007/978-3-031-94544-1
27. Moalagh, M., Dahl-Jørgensen, T.C., Svesengen, V., Farshchian, B.A.: User representatives as boundary spanners: case study of large-scale agile software development. In: Proceedings of the 23rd EUSSET Conference on Computer Supported Cooperative Work, Newcastle upon

Tyne, United Kingdom, June 30th – July 4th, 2025. European Society for Socially Embedded Technologies (EUSSET) (2025). https://doi.org/10.48340/ecscw2025_cp06
28. Almeida, F., Espinheira, E.: Large-scale agile frameworks: a comparative review. JASMET **2**(1), 16–29 (2021). https://doi.org/10.31284/j.jasmet.2021.v2i1.1832
29. Savola, R.M., Frühwirth, C., Pietikäinen, A.: Risk-Driven Security Metrics in Agile Software Development – An Industrial Pilot Study
30. Winthereik, B.R.: Enactments of systems development. Scand. J. Inf. Syst. **22**, 49–64 (2010)
31. Yin, R.K.: Designing case studies. In: Qualitative Research Methods, vol. 14 (2003)
32. Oates, B.J., Marie, G., Rachel, M.: Researching Information Systems and Computing. SAGE Publications, London (2022)
33. Baškarada, S.: Qualitative case study guidelines. TQR (2014). https://doi.org/10.46743/2160-3715/2014.1008
34. NAV: What is NAV? (2025). https://www.nav.no/hva-er-nav/en
35. NAV IT: NAV IT. https://www.detsombetyrnoe.no/
36. Bernhardt, H.B.: Digital transformation in NAV IT 2016–2020: key factors for the journey of change. In: Digital Transformation in Norwegian Enterprises, 1st edn, pp. 115–134. Springer (2022). https://doi.org/10.1007/978-3-031-05276-7
37. Mohagheghi, P., Lassenius, C.: Organizational implications of agile adoption: a case study from the public sector. In: Proceedings of the 29th ACM Joint Meeting on European Software Engineering Conference and Symposium on the Foundations of Software Engineering, Athens, Greece, pp. 1444–1454. ACM (2021). https://doi.org/10.1145/3468264.3473937
38. Moalagh, M., Mikalsen, M., Farshchian, B.A.: Are team autonomy and flexibility enough for agile transformation? A review of transformed practices in a public sector organization. In: Proceedings of ECSCW 2023, Trondheim, Norway. EUSSET Digital Library (2023). https://doi.org/10.48340/ECSCW2023_EP08
39. Urquhart, C.: Grounded Theory for Qualitative Research: A Practical Guide. SAGE Publications (2022)
40. Strauss, A.L., Corbin, J.: Open coding. Social research methods: a reader. In: Social Research Methods: A Reader, pp. 303–306. Routledge, New York (2004)

Agile Mobile Application Development with Integrated Artificial Intelligence: The Case of Diabetes Patient Support Application

Marks Calderon(✉), Carlos Celi, and Diego La Torre

Esan University, Lima, Peru
mcalderon@esan.edu.pe, {20100177,16100781}@ue.edu.pe

Abstract. Software development in critical healthcare domains presents unique challenges due to the non-deterministic nature of Artificial Intelligence (AI). Traditional agile frameworks often face friction when aligning the exploratory cycles of model training with fixed sprint cadences. This paper presents a case study on the development of a mobile application for diabetes patient support, powered by a specialized Large Language Model (LLM). The project adapted Scrum ceremonies to manage the full AI lifecycle, from corpus preparation to clinical validation. We identify four key challenges, specifically the insufficiency of automated metrics (e.g., BERTScore) to ensure medical safety and the limitations of standard "Definition of Done" (DoD) in experimental contexts. As a solution, we implement "hybrid sprints" incorporating "question stories" and multi-level acceptance criteria that prioritize clinical expert validation over technical scores. The results demonstrate that while standard agile methods provide a foundation, they require pragmatic decoupling of data and model lifecycles to ensure safety-critical value delivery.

Keywords: Agile Software Development · Agile ML · Case Study · Question Stories · Artificial Intelligence · Healthcare Technology · Large Language Models (LLMs) · Clinical Validation

1 Introduction

Diabetes mellitus represents one of the greatest public health challenges of the 21st century, with a global prevalence affecting nearly 589 million adults and a projection exceeding 1.3 billion by 2050 [6]. The effective management of this chronic disease imposes a considerable cognitive load on patients, who must make dozens of daily decisions regarding nutrition, medication, and physical activity, often without the continuous support of a healthcare professional [9]. While mobile applications (mHealth) have emerged as promising tools, many are limited to being passive documentation systems, failing to offer the intelligent interpretation and empathetic support that patients truly need [7].

A. Goldman et al. (Eds.): XP 2026, LNBIP 578, pp. 244–252, 2026.
https://doi.org/10.1007/978-3-032-22375-3_15

The integration of Generative Artificial Intelligence (AI), specifically Large Language Models (LLMs), offers a transformative opportunity to bridge this gap. We selected a layered architecture and LLM fine-tuning to ensure modularity and safety, allowing for independent clinical validation before UI deployment. However, software development in this domain presents a dual problem. On one hand, there is the complexity of the medical domain, which demands high precision, safety, and contextual personalization. On the other hand, the very nature of machine learning engineering introduces a non-deterministic uncertainty: the model training process is exploratory, results are not always predictable, and functional requirements evolve as the model's capacity is better understood. Traditional development lifecycles, such as the waterfall model, are inadequate for handling this double uncertainty, as their rigidity makes adaptation to unexpected discoveries and the incorporation of continuous feedback difficult.

In this context, agile methodologies, with their emphasis on iterative delivery, constant collaboration, and adaptability to change, emerge as a theoretically ideal approach [3]. However, literature and practice show that applying agile frameworks like Scrum to projects with a central machine learning component (Agile ML) is non-trivial. Significant challenges persist in sprint planning, estimating research tasks, defining "Done" for a model, and the mismatch between non-deterministic ML activities and fixed timeboxes [5]. Managing the data lifecycle alongside the product lifecycle remains a major obstacle for a smooth Agile ML implementation.

This article addresses this gap by presenting a case study on the development of a cross-platform mobile application for diabetes patient support, powered by a specialized LLM fine-tuned for the Peruvian context. The project was developed following an iterative and incremental process adapted from Scrum. Through reflexive analysis of this process, we seek to answer the following research questions:

- **RQ1:** What specific challenges arise when integrating the LLM development lifecycle (data preparation, fine-tuning, evaluation) within an iterative agile framework?
- **RQ2:** What methodological adaptations and concrete practices were effective in overcoming these challenges and facilitating continuous, validated value delivery?

By detailing the difficulties encountered and the practical solutions implemented, this work offers a set of learned lessons and actionable strategies. Our contribution is aimed both at professionals facing the growing need to merge agile software development with AI engineering, and researchers exploring the evolution of agile methodologies in high-technology domains.

2 Theoretical Basis

Modern software development faces increasing complexity, especially in domains where requirements are not fully known at the outset and the underlying technology is inherently exploratory. The principles of the Agile Manifesto, such as valuing "responding to change over following a plan" and "customer collaboration over contract negotiation," provide an ideal philosophical framework for navigating this uncertainty [3]. Methodologies like Scrum operationalize these principles through short development cycles (sprints) that allow for continuous inspection and adaptation, ensuring the product evolves in the right direction based on real feedback [11].

However, the application of these frameworks becomes particularly challenging when the "product" to be developed includes a Machine Learning (ML) component. The emerging discipline of Agile ML seeks to reconcile these two worlds, but academic literature and industry reports agree on a series of fundamental frictions.

A recurring challenge is the non-deterministic nature of ML work. Unlike traditional software development, where a task usually has a binary outcome (it works or it doesn't), an ML task, such as fine-tuning a model, is an experiment. Its result can be an improvement, a worsening, or no significant change in model performance [1]. This complicates sprint planning and effort estimation, as the "value" delivered is often a learning that informs the next iteration.

Another friction point is the "Definition of Done" (DoD). While a robust DoD is rarely simple in any software project, it presents unique challenges for AI models [5]. In Scrum, the DoD ensures a product increment is potentially releasable. For an AI model, the friction arises from the duality between quantitative metrics and qualitative validation by a domain expert. This creates a bottleneck in the agile flow, as activities for ML development do not always align with the rigid cadences of regular timeboxes.

Finally, managing dual lifecycles—that of the software product and that of the data/model—is a complex logistical problem. The development of a new feature in the application may depend on a new capability of the model, which in turn may require a long process of data collection, cleaning, and labeling [12]. Coordinating these dependencies within the limits of a 2–4 week sprint is one of the main obstacles to a smooth Agile ML implementation.

3 Methodology

To address our research questions regarding the challenges and adaptations of agile development in an AI project, we adopted a **case study** methodology [10]. This approach is particularly suitable for investigating contemporary phenomena within their real context, allowing for a deep and detailed analysis of complex processes. Our case study focuses on a single software development project, enabling us to observe team dynamics and the evolution of the process longitudinally. The methodology of the fine-tuning and app development is shown in the Fig. 1.

The case study is the development of a mobile application intended to provide support to patients with diabetes in the Peruvian context. The project was carried out by a team composed of two developer-researchers over a period of 16 months (September 2024 – December 2025). The product goal was to offer a

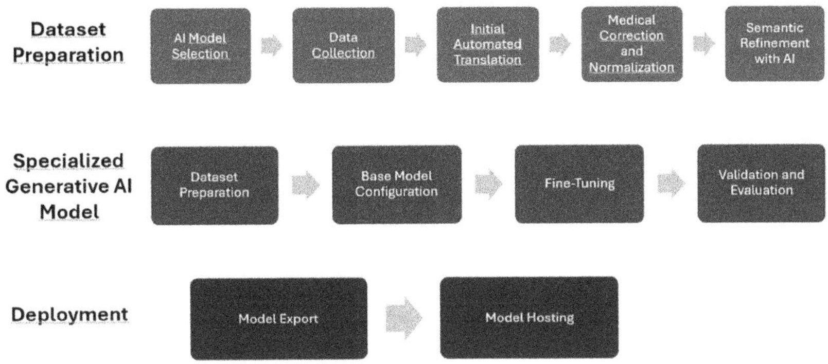

Fig. 1. Methodology of the fine-tuning process.

conversational assistant based on a specialized Large Language Model (LLM), capable of answering queries about diabetes management in an empathetic and contextualized manner. The main technology stack consisted of a model that was specialized using Supervised Fine-Tuning (SFT) and Low-Rank Adaptation (LoRA) techniques.

The project adopted an iterative and incremental agile framework, inspired by Scrum principles [11]. This framework was selected to manage the high uncertainty of both user requirements and AI technology.

- **Roles and Collaboration:** The development team assumed implementation responsibilities, while an academic advisor and a specialist endocrinologist acted as Product Owners. This collaborative structure was designed to ensure that the AI model's outputs were continuously anchored in clinical accuracy and utility, mitigating the risks of non-deterministic behavior.
- **Development Cycles (Sprints):** Development was organized into three-week sprints. Each sprint began with a planning session to select a set of items from the Product Backlog and ended with a Review session where the functional increment was demonstrated to the specialist. This was followed by an internal retrospective to improve the team's process.
- **Backlog Management:** The Product Backlog contained a mix of different types of work items:
  - **User Stories:** For user-visible functionalities (e.g., "As a patient, I want to log my glucose level").
  - **Technical Tasks:** To enable infrastructure (e.g., "Configure REST API for the model").
  - **Research Spikes:** Time-boxed tasks to explore the feasibility of a technical approach, especially for model training and evaluation.

4 Results

The iterative development of our diabetes support application revealed a series of frictions between the principles of a standard agile workflow and the realities of machine learning engineering. This section details the most significant challenges we encountered and the practical adaptations our team implemented to mitigate them.

4.1 Challenges Encountered

Throughout the project, we identified four main challenges that disrupted the rhythm and predictability expected from a Scrum-based process.

Challenge 1: The Experimental Nature of Fine-tuning. The goal of a sprint is to deliver a "Potentially Shippable Value Increment." However, LLM fine-tuning tasks did not guarantee a positive result due to the non-deterministic nature of the training process. In several iterations, a new dataset or hyperparameter adjustment (e.g., learning rate) resulted in a degradation of metrics (e.g., increased Perplexity) or, worse, the appearance of hallucinations.

Challenge 2: Ambiguity of the "Definition of Done" (DoD) for the Model. Initially, we defined the DoD for an AI task quantitatively using metrics like BERTScore or BLEU. However, we quickly realized that automated metrics are at most supplementary and insufficient to ensure medical safety. A model could have excellent scores yet generate a clinically unsafe recommendation. This forced us to redefine the DoD to include manual validation by our endocrinologist expert, a process that could not always be completed within sprint timeboxes, creating a bottleneck.

Challenge 3: Managing Dependencies between Data, Model, and UI. The Product Backlog contained interdependent stories spanning three distinct layers:

1. **Data Layer:** "We need a data corpus on Peruvian nutritional plans."
2. **Model Layer:** "The model must be able to generate a meal plan based on a query."
3. **UI Layer:** "As a user, I want to see my meal plan on a card in the app."

Planning these dependency chains in a single sprint was unfeasible. Data work was a blocking prerequisite, and its duration was difficult to estimate.

Challenge 4: The Hidden Cost of Qualitative Feedback. Expert feedback on model logic (e.g., confusing insulin types) could not be resolved with a simple code change. It required a full cycle of identifying and correcting defective training data, re-training the model (a process taking hours or days), and re-evaluating it. This "AI rework cycle" was much more costly and slow than typical software development, challenging the team's agility.

4.2 Methodological Adaptations

To overcome these challenges, our team evolved its process, adopting the following pragmatic adaptations:

Adaptation 1: Hybrid Sprints with Question Stories. We formalized the use of Research Spikes and **Question Stories** [2]. Each sprint contained a mix of predictable User Stories and AI-focused Question Stories. The goal of the latter was to answer a research question (e.g., "Will performance improve if we double the data?"), and the deliverable was documented learning rather than functional code.

Adaptation 2: Multi-level Acceptance Criteria for AI. We replaced a single DoD with a staged approach for AI tasks:

- **Level 1 (Technically Complete):** The training script runs without errors and the resulting model is saved. Automatic metrics are logged.
- **Level 2 (Functionally Integrated):** The new model is deployed in a staging environment and accessible via API. The application can interact with it.
- **Level 3 (Clinically Validated):** The model has been reviewed by the expert for a predefined set of test cases and approved for use. Only upon reaching this level was the item considered truly "Done."

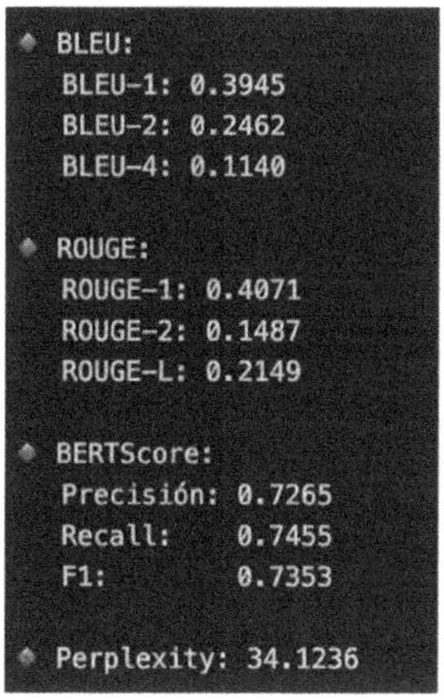

Fig. 2. Automatic metrics of the model.

Adaptation 3: Creation of a "Data Backlog". We separated data management from the Product Backlog. We created a simple artifact (a shared spreadsheet) that functioned as a Data Backlog. Tasks such as "translate dataset from Chinese to Spanish," "validate 500 responses with the expert," or "generate synthetic data" were managed here, allowing data work to be performed in parallel and feed into future training sprints (Figs. 2 and 3).

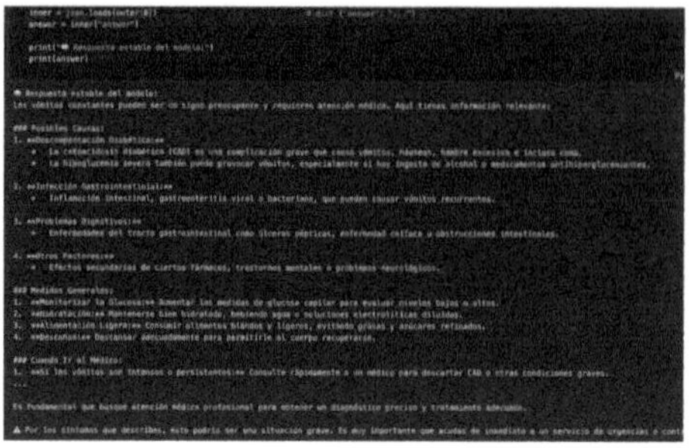

Fig. 3. Endpoint test.

Adaptation 4: API-First as a Decoupling Contract. We adopted a strict **API-first** approach [4]. At the start of a new functionality, we defined the REST API contract (user query and JSON response format) between the model and the application. This allowed UI development and model fine-tuning to progress in parallel. The UI team could work with a mocked API while the model was developed independently, reducing blockages.

The final prototype of the application is shown in the Fig. 4.

Fig. 4. Last Version of DiabeBlue.

5 Conclusions

This study confirms that standard agile frameworks require pragmatic adaptations to manage the non-deterministic uncertainty of AI projects. Through the development of an LLM-based diabetes support application, we identified that the experimental nature of model training and the necessity of clinical validation conflict with the fixed predictability expected in traditional Scrum.

To address these frictions, we validated four effective methodological adaptations: (1) the implementation of **Hybrid Sprints** using *question stories* to manage learning as a tangible outcome [2]; (2) **Multi-level Acceptance Criteria** that formalize the transition from technical completeness to clinical safety; (3) a decoupled **Data Backlog** to handle data preparation in parallel; and (4) an **API-First** strategy [4] to minimize dependencies between the frontend and the AI model.

These findings suggest that practitioners should move away from treating ML tasks as standard user stories and instead embrace artifacts that explicitly account for non-deterministic experimentation. Future work should focus on exploring Lean or Continuous Delivery lifecycles to further reduce the friction of fixed timeboxes in AI development. Ultimately, the successful fusion of Agile and AI relies on intelligent adaptation that prioritizes clinical safety over automated technical metrics.

References

1. Amershi, S., et al.: Software engineering for machine learning: a case study. In: 2019 IEEE/ACM 41st International Conference on Software Engineering: Software Engineering in Practice (ICSE-SEIP), pp. 291–300. IEEE (2019). https://doi.org/10.1109/ICSE-SEIP.2019.00042
2. Ambler, S.W.: The machine learning (ML) lifecycle. Ambysoft (2023). https://ambysoft.com/essays/machine-learning-lifecycle.html
3. Beck, K., et al.: Manifesto for agile software development. Agile Alliance (2001). https://agilemanifesto.org
4. Fielding, R.T.: Architectural Styles and the Design of Network-based Software Architectures. University of California, Irvine (2000)
5. Hohl, P., Gscheidle, C., Ludwigs, K.: Agile meets AI: A practical guide for applying agile frameworks to data science projects. Springer (2018)
6. International Diabetes Federation: IDF Diabetes Atlas, 11th edn. (2025). https://diabetesatlas.org/
7. Joensen, L.E., Fisher, L., Skinner, T., Willaing, I.: Integrating the evidence on social support in diabetes self-management. Diabetes Educ. **45**(4), 346–358 (2019). https://doi.org/10.1177/0145721719853381
8. Oates, B. J.: Researching Information Systems and Computing. SAGE Publications (2022)
9. Pérez-Gandía, C., et al.: Decision support in diabetes care: the challenge of supporting patients in their daily living using a mobile glucose predictor. J. Diabetes Sci. Technol. **12**(2), 243–250 (2018). https://doi.org/10.1177/1932296818758803
10. Runeson, P., Höst, M.: Guidelines for conducting and reporting case study research in software engineering. Empir. Softw. Eng. **14**(2), 131–164 (2009). https://doi.org/10.1007/s10664-008-9102-8
11. Schwaber, K., Sutherland, J.: The Scrum Guide. Scrum.org (2020). https://scrumguides.org
12. Washizaki, H., Uchida, H., Khomh, F., Guéhéneuc, Y.G.: Studying software engineering patterns for machine learning. In: 2019 IEEE 26th International Conference on Software Analysis, Evolution and Reengineering (SANER), pp. 375–385. IEEE (2019)

AI in Agile Teams

Adoption of Large Language Models in Scrum Management: Insights from Brazilian Practitioners

Mirko Perkusich[1(✉)], Danyllo Albuquerque[1], Allysson Allex Araújo[3], Matheus Paixão[2], Rohit Gheyi[1], Marcos Kalinowski[4], and Angelo Perkusich[1]

[1] VIRTUS Research, Development and Innovation Center, UFCG, Campina Grande, Brazil
{mirko,danyllo.albuquerque,rohit,perkusich}@virtus.ufcg.edu.br
[2] State University of Ceará (UECE), Fortaleza, Brazil
matheus.paixao@uece.br
[3] Federal University of Cariri (UFCA), Juazeiro do Norte, Brazil
allysson.araujo@ufca.edu.br
[4] Pontifical Catholic University of Rio de Janeiro (PUC-Rio), Rio de Janeiro, Brazil
kalinowski@inf.puc-rio.br

Abstract. Scrum is widely adopted in software project management due to its adaptability and collaborative nature. The recent emergence of Large Language Models (LLMs) has created new opportunities to support knowledge-intensive Scrum practices. However, existing research has largely focused on technical activities such as coding and testing, with limited evidence on the use of LLMs in management-related Scrum activities. In this study, we investigate the use of LLMs in Scrum management activities through a survey of 70 Brazilian professionals. Among them, 49 actively use Scrum, and 33 reported using LLM-based assistants in their Scrum practices. The results indicate a high level of proficiency and frequent use of LLMs, with 85% of respondents reporting intermediate or advanced proficiency and 52% using them daily. LLM use concentrates on exploring Scrum practices, with artifacts and events receiving targeted yet uneven support, whereas broader management tasks appear to be adopted more cautiously. The main benefits include increased productivity (78%) and reduced manual effort (75%). However, several critical risks remain, as respondents report 'almost correct' outputs (81%), confidentiality concerns (63%), and hallucinations during use (59%). This work provides one of the first empirical characterizations of LLM use in Scrum management, identifying current practices, quantifying benefits and risks, and outlining directions for responsible adoption and integration in Agile environments.

Keywords: Scrum · Large Language Models · Survey · Management Activities · Empirical Study · Agile Projects

A. Goldman et al. (Eds.): XP 2026, LNBIP 578, pp. 255–273, 2026.
https://doi.org/10.1007/978-3-032-22375-3_16

1 Introduction

Agile project management has increasingly shaped contemporary software engineering practices as teams seek ways to handle evolving requirements, coordinate work more effectively, and maintain consistent delivery rhythms [36]. Within this context, Scrum has emerged as the most widely adopted framework, structuring teamwork through artifacts, events, and roles that facilitate coordination and continuous delivery [11,41]. These practices are highly knowledge-intensive, requiring effective communication, documentation, and stakeholder alignment [7]. In particular, the Brazilian software industry has seen a substantial increase in Agile maturity, with companies adopting Scrum to manage increasingly complex, fast-paced projects across sectors such as fintech, e-commerce, and public-sector digital services [5]. This growth intensifies the need for practices that support communication and knowledge work, positioning Brazil as an important context for understanding how LLMs are being incorporated into Scrum management.

At the same time, the rapid evolution of Large Language Models (LLMs)—accessible through platforms such as ChatGPT, Gemini, Claude, and DeepSeek—has introduced new opportunities to support Scrum teams' activities. In fact, LLMs have already demonstrated an impact in technical areas of software engineering, including requirements definition [3], architecture design [21], coding [14], debugging [27], testing [30], and documentation [19]. These capabilities fuel interest in understanding how LLMs may extend their influence to management activities. However, agile management activities (such as refining artifacts, facilitating events, and supporting role-specific responsibilities) pose distinct challenges because they involve ambiguity, negotiation, prioritization, and human dynamics [25]. These dimensions, central to Scrum, demand contextual understanding and shared meaning-making [2]. As Agile practices mature, understanding how LLMs can support the management dimension of Scrum becomes increasingly relevant [23]. However, the literature concentrates on assistance for technical tasks, leaving open questions about how LLMs are being applied to artifact refinement, event preparation, or communication among Scrum roles [10]. In other words, organizations risk adopting these tools based on "hype" rather than evidence. This perspective includes challenges such as over-reliance on AI, propagation of biased outputs, confidentiality risks, and potential erosion of shared team accountability.

To address the aforementioned challenges, this study aims to understand how software professionals are incorporating LLMs into Scrum management activities. In particular, we focus on Brazilian professionals because Brazil hosts one of the largest and fastest-growing software markets in Latin America, where Scrum has become the predominant approach for structuring digital transformation initiatives in both private and public organizations [5,16]. To examine these practices at scale and generate an initial characterization anchored in practitioners' real-world behavior, we adopt a survey as our research method. Surveys enable the identification of broad usage trends, perceived benefits, and concerns across heterogeneous organizational settings, offering the empirical breadth needed to study a phenomenon that is still emerging and scarcely documented in the literature [31].

Regarding the contributions, this study offers three insights into how LLMs are being incorporated into Scrum management activities. First, we map how Brazilian professionals employ LLM-based assistants to support artifacts, events, and role-specific responsibilities. Second, we identify perceived benefits (such as productivity gains, improved documentation, enhanced communication, and support for decision-making) that illustrate where LLMs already add value to Agile work. Finally, we expose the main barriers influencing adoption, including trust issues, confidentiality risks, unreliable outputs, and organizational resistance.

The remainder of this paper is organized as follows. Section 2 reviews related work. Section 3 describes the research design. Section 4 presents the results, and Sect. 5 discusses their implications. Section 6 outlines threats to validity, and Sect. 7 concludes the paper.

2 Related Work

This section briefly reviews prior work across three areas relevant to this study: (i) the use of LLMs in software engineering tasks, including their capabilities and known limitations; (ii) the adoption of Artificial Intelligence (AI) assistants in professional and organizational settings; and (iii) research on Agile management, particularly Scrum. By connecting these strands, we also highlight the current lack of empirical evidence on how LLMs are used in real Scrum management activities, which motivates our investigation.

LLMs in Software Engineering. LLMs have become transformative assets in software engineering, supporting technical activities across the entire development lifecycle, including requirements elicitation, code generation, testing, maintenance, documentation, and analytics [42]. Different surveys already reinforce this rapid expansion: [19] reviewed nearly 400 studies spanning multiple SE phases, while [44] mapped research clusters showing strong growth in LLM-assisted coding, testing, and defect prediction. Despite these advances, significant challenges remain. Reliability issues (such as hallucinations and inconsistent outputs) have been widely documented [17], and the proliferation of benchmarks [20] highlights ongoing difficulties in evaluation and standardization. Beyond code-centric tasks, LLMs have shown promise in supporting complex and knowledge-intensive activities, such as software model evolution [39]. However, their role within broader organizational and managerial settings is still emerging.

LLMs in Professional and Organizational Contexts. LLMs are increasingly integrated into professional environments to enhance productivity, creativity, and decision-making. Studies demonstrate their ability to support workplace choices by providing rationale and recommendations [26], as well as to assist group work by analyzing meeting transcripts and enhancing coordination [29]. They also strengthen information management through more efficient query resolution and document summarization, contributing to higher work productivity [1]. However, their performance varies across cognitive tasks: while LLMs can mimic human-like reasoning [38], they still struggle with creativity and context-sensitive ideation. In specialized domains, professionals find them more effective for translation and review than for planning or generating novel concepts [8]. Broader surveys indicate that knowledge workers mostly rely on LLMs for code generation, refinement, and text improvement, while expecting deeper enterprise integration in the near future [6]. Successful adoption depends on trust, transparency, and skillful prompt engineering [13]. Although these studies highlight the benefits of LLMs in individual and group productivity, their implications for collaborative, knowledge-intensive methods, such as Agile and Scrum, remain insufficiently understood.

Agile Project Management. Agile marked a shift from hierarchical to collaborative and knowledge-intensive practices [15]. Prior studies emphasized that agile teams rely on tacit knowledge exchange and personalization strategies rather than codification, with up to 81% of knowledge-management activities occurring through social interaction [33,40]. Agile practices, such as pair programming, Scrum meetings, and continuous stakeholder involvement, foster transparency, learning, and a shared understanding [37]. Organizational culture is a critical enabler of effective knowledge management within agile teams, shaping collaboration and sustaining productivity [34].

Building on these empirical foundations, emerging research has explored whether LLMs can support or extend these knowledge-intensive dynamics. Early studies experimented with LLMs acting as Scrum Masters in educational settings [9], automating project-planning tasks through systems such as AutoScrum [35], or coordinating software-process simulations via multi-agent models [28]. Other work investigated LLMs' ability to extract domain models from agile backlogs [4]. While these results are promising, they remain largely confined to prototypes and academic scenarios, leaving open the question of how LLMs are actually being adopted in real-world Scrum management activities.

Research Gap. LLMs have demonstrated potential across various software engineering tasks, indicating their value in knowledge-intensive activities. Scrum, as a highly collaborative and adaptive framework, represents promising environment for using such tools, including in backlog refinement, event preparation, and support to role-specific responsibilities. Existing studies have begun to explore these possibilities, but most remain confined to prototypes or educational scenarios, offering limited visibility into professional practice. Despite growing interest, there is still a lack of empirical evidence on how LLMs are being adopted within real Scrum teams, what benefits practitioners perceive, and which challenges or risks emerge. To address this gap, this study examines the use of LLMs in Scrum management activities, aiming to map current practices, benefits, and barriers from the perspective of Brazilian practitioners.

3 Research Design

This study followed a systematic process for conducting a survey in software engineering, drawing on the recommendations of Wagner *et al.* [43]. Figure 1 provides an overview of this process, which was organized into six key steps described below.

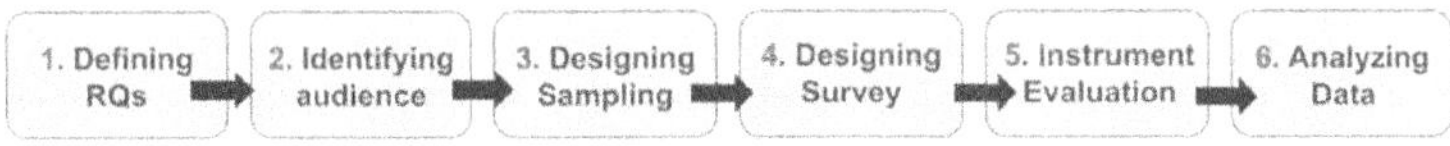

Fig. 1. Methodological workflow of the questionnaire survey.

1) Defining Research Questions (RQs). We followed a *Goal-Question-Metric* (GQM)-driven survey design [22] and defined the RQs to capture different dimensions of how LLMs are being used in Scrum management activities. Each RQ (see Table 1) addresses a specific gap identified in the literature and practice.

These RQs provide a comprehensive framework for investigating the role of LLMs in Scrum management activities. By combining descriptive findings on knowledge and adoption (RQ1), practical applications in Scrum practices (RQ2), perceived benefits (RQ3), and experienced risks and challenges (RQ4), the study aims to build a balanced understanding of both the opportunities and limitations of LLMs.

2) Identifying Target Audience and Sampling Frame. The target audience of this study comprised professionals with practical experience in Scrum-based projects. To ensure respondent eligibility, a screening question required participants to confirm prior or current participation in Scrum projects; those without such experience were automatically redirected and excluded, in accordance with recommended practices for survey validity [24]. The sampling frame was intentionally broad, aiming to capture the diversity of the Scrum community across industries, organizational sizes, and team roles, including Product Owners, Scrum Masters, developers, and testers. Although this heterogeneity enhances ecological validity, it does not yield a statistically representative sample, an inherent limitation of non-probabilistic sampling in surveys [32].

3) Designing Sampling Plan. To operationalize the sampling frame, we employed a non-probabilistic strategy combining convenience and snowball sampling, a common approach in software engineering surveys where practitioner registries are unavailable [12]. Recruitment occurred through multiple channels (e.g., LinkedIn Agile communities, professional mailing lists, and direct invitations to industry and academic contacts), with respondents encouraged to share the survey to broaden reach. Although the initial goal was to obtain at least 70 valid responses for descriptive and comparative analyses [18], participation remained voluntary. Following Dillman's tailored design principles, the invitation emphasized clarity of purpose, approximate completion time, and full anonymity, aiming to reduce response bias and increase engagement [12].

4) Designing Survey Instrument. The instrument was structured into nine sections, each aligned with the study's RQs and grounded in established guidelines for survey-based research [32] [24]. The instrument consisted primarily

Table 1. Research Questions, Descriptions, and Rationales.

RQ	Goal	Motivation
RQ1	What is the current level of knowledge and usage of LLMs among Scrum professionals?	Understanding baseline familiarity and adoption is essential because the diffusion of innovations depends not only on tool availability but also on practitioners' awareness, proficiency, and willingness to integrate them into management-oriented activities.
RQ2	In which Scrum practices (artifacts, events, and roles) are LLMs being adopted, and how helpful are they perceived to be?	Scrum is structured around artifacts, events, and roles. Identifying where LLMs already contribute helps reveal how these tools support real management work, rather than only technical tasks.
RQ3	What benefits do Scrum practitioners perceive from using LLMs?	Industry narratives emphasize the potential of LLMs, but empirical evidence is limited. Mapping perceived benefits clarifies whether LLMs provide tangible value in practice, such as increased productivity, improved documentation quality, or enhanced decision-making support.
RQ4	What risks and challenges are associated with LLM use in Scrum contexts?	LLMs can produce biased or incorrect outputs, creating risks such as over-reliance, privacy concerns, and resistance from team members. Understanding these barriers is crucial to avoiding naïve adoption and to guiding responsible use in Agile environments.

of closed-ended items (multiple-choice questions, Likert scales, and frequency measures) with a small number of open-ended questions to capture qualitative insights and provide illustrative examples. Operationalized in Google Forms, the survey was voluntary, anonymous, and designed to strike a balance between breadth of coverage and ease of completion. Table 2 summarizes the structure of the instrument and its connection to the RQs. The complete questionnaire used in this study is provided in the supplementary material (see Artifacts Availability).

5) Survey Instrument Evaluation. The questionnaire underwent a multi-step evaluation process to ensure clarity, relevance, and alignment with the study objectives, following survey research guidelines in software engineering [18,32]. First, three researchers with expertise in empirical SE, Agile methods, and AI reviewed the initial version of the instrument, refining wording, removing redundancies, harmonizing Scrum terminology, clarifying key concepts (e.g., LLM adoption modes), and reordering sections to improve flow and content validity. Next, the instrument was piloted with five Scrum practitioners (PO, SM, and developers) from different organizations, who completed the form and provided structured feedback on clarity, terminology, layout, and timing; this

Table 2. Survey sections, descriptions, and relation to RQs.

Section	Description	RQs
1–3: Profile definition	Collects demographic and background data about participants (country, age, education), organizational context (industry, size, team), and project characteristics (role, domain, Scrum adoption).	–
4: Knowledge and use of LLMs	Assesses familiarity with LLMs, adoption mode (formal/informal), frequency of use, time spent, and models/versions employed.	RQ1
5: Use in Scrum	Investigates LLM use across Scrum artifacts, events, and roles, including perceived helpfulness and potential role replacement.	RQ2
6: Perceived benefits	Identifies benefits already experienced with LLMs (e.g., productivity, quality, decision-making, and communication) and collects positive examples.	RQ3
7: Difficulties and challenges	Explores encountered difficulties (e.g., bias, privacy, resistance, over-dependence), agreement with risk statements, and negative examples.	RQ4
8: General comments	provides an open space for additional insights, suggestions, or reflections about LLMs in Scrum.	RQ1–RQ4
9: Closure	Final thanks, option for follow-up contact, and confirmation of survey completion.	–

led to minor adjustments such as simplified instructions, reduced scale redundancy, more consistent terminology, and improved sequencing, resulting in an average completion time of about 10 min. To ensure data quality, the questionnaire included simple attention checks and automatic routing that redirected respondents without Scrum or LLM experience to a closure section, minimizing careless responses and enforcing eligibility in line with [12]. Ethical procedures included an informed consent statement describing the study's aims, risks, voluntariness, and anonymity; no identifiable data were collected, and all data were stored securely and accessed only by the research team. Overall, this process enhanced the clarity, reliability, and validity of the instrument, supporting high-quality data collection and future replication.

6) Analyzing Survey Data. The questionnaire was deployed through Google Forms and remained open throughout October and November 2025. Participation was voluntary and anonymous, with informed consent and automated routing to exclude respondents without Scrum experience or prior use of AI chat assistants. The response flow was periodically monitored to ensure accessibility and prevent technical issues, and no personally identifiable information was collected. Because most items were mandatory, the resulting dataset contained no missing values. After collection, all responses were exported to `XLSX` format for further processing.

Data analysis combined quantitative and qualitative techniques. Closed-ended items were examined through descriptive statistics such as frequencies, percentages, and means, while open-ended responses were coded using a mixed deductive–inductive coding approach. To improve the reliability of qualitative interpretations, two researchers independently coded a subset of responses and reconciled discrepancies through discussion. Analyses were explicitly mapped to the research questions: RQ1 addressed participant profiles and familiarity with LLMs; RQ2 examined usage across Scrum artifacts, events, and roles; RQ3 focused on perceived benefits; and RQ4 investigated risks and challenges. All procedures followed established guidelines for survey research in software engineering [12,18,32]. The dataset, survey instrument, and analysis scripts are available as supplementary material (see the Artifacts Availability section).

4 Results and Discussion

This section presents and discusses the survey's results. The first part characterizes the respondents, their organizations, and project contexts. The subsequent subsections integrate findings and interpretative discussion for RQ1–RQ4. Additional breakdowns, supporting tables, and the complete dataset are available in the supplementary material (see the Artifacts Availability section).

Participant, Organizational, and Project Profiles

A total of 70 Brazilian professionals completed the demographic section. Of these, 49 had worked on a Scrum project in the past six months and reported using AI chat assistants in Scrum-related activities; therefore, they completed the full instrument. The analyses presented in the following focus on this sample.

The demographic profile indicates a predominantly young respondent base: 83% are between 20 and 39 years old, 14% fall in the 40–49 range, and only 2% are older than 50. Formal education levels are high, with 63% holding undergraduate degrees or MBAs and 20% reporting a master's or doctoral degree. Regarding Scrum knowledge, 69% classify themselves as "Beginner" (knowledge of the main practical aspects) or "Qualified" (solid conceptual understanding and practical experience), reflecting a population with well-established familiarity with Agile practices. This educational and professional profile aligns with the strong presence of technical roles in the sample.

Respondents work across diverse industries, although technology-oriented sectors dominate. Technology accounts for the largest share (25%), followed by education (18%) and research, development, and innovation (16%). Smaller proportions come from finance, retail, industry, public administration, and consulting. Organizational size also varies substantially: 33% come from companies with more than 1,000 employees, 27% from medium-sized companies (251–1,000 employees), and the remaining 40% from small organizations with up to 250 employees. This distribution indicates that Scrum practices and AI-supported workflows are present in both consolidated enterprises and smaller, fast-moving companies.

Regarding professional roles, developers constitute the largest segment of the sample (47%), followed by Scrum Masters (12%), QA/testers (8%), and Product Owners (6%). In terms of application domains, Web and cross-platform development predominate (66%), with additional representation from education (21%), finance (18%), transport and distribution (16%), and telecommunications (10%). Most initiatives involve small teams of 1–10 members (65%), and over half of the projects (53%) have been running for one to three years.

Knowledge and Usage of LLMs Among Scrum Professionals (RQ1)

RQ1 examined how familiar Brazilian Scrum professionals are with AI chat assistants and how frequently they use them. The results reveal a user base that is already relatively mature in its understanding of LLMs. Among the respondents who use AI assistants, 61% describe themselves as "Qualified" and 21% as "Proficient". Only 15% classify themselves as "beginners". Usage frequency follows a similarly intensive pattern. Daily use is reported by 52% of respondents, weekly use by another 18%, and monthly use by 21%. Only 9% indicate sporadic use, and no respondent reports having abandoned the technology after initial experimentation. Time allocation also reflects sustained integration: among valid answers, 47% use assistants for less than one hour per day, while another 50% use them between one and two hours daily.

The ecosystem of tools and models used by respondents reveals a diversified but strongly centralized pattern. ChatGPT is universally adopted (100%), followed by Gemini (82%) and Copilot Chat (67%). Adoption of Claude and DeepSeek reaches only 27%, while niche tools such as Perplexity, Manus, Qwen, Phind, and Grok appear in less than 12% of responses, reflecting exploratory rather than systematic use. At the model level, references are similarly concentrated: GPT-4o (27%), GPT-5/5o/5.1 reported by 21% when aggregated, Gemini 2.5 Pro (21%), and Gemini 2.5 Flash (15%) were the most cited. Mentions of Claude 4.1, Sonnet, Llama, and Qwen were isolated, showing that advanced model awareness is present but uneven across practitioners.

Interaction patterns emphasize "text" as the default modality (100%), but document-based workflows (76%) and image/screenshot analysis (61%) are already common, highlighting multimodal adoption. More than half the sample

(55%) uses LLMs in technical tasks (debugging, coding, testing), reinforcing the dual role of assistants in both managerial and technical activities within Scrum practitioners. Organizational governance is mixed: 36% report no policy, 36% have formal policies, and 12% rely on informal guidelines, suggesting fragmentation and a lack of institutional standardization. Despite this, 51% use LLMs informally, while 45% follow a prescribed process, reinforcing that adoption is practitioner-driven rather than organizationally mandated.

Summarized Answer - Knowledge and Usage of LLMs (RQ1)

The results indicate that LLM use among Brazilian Scrum practitioners is routine rather than exploratory. Practitioners rely on LLM assistants across multiple modalities, integrating them into both managerial and technical tasks through short, iterative interactions. Adoption is concentrated in major ecosystems (ChatGPT, Gemini, and Copilot), with some experimentation involving smaller models. However, organizational governance has not kept pace: both the presence of formal policies and the complete absence of policies account for 36% of responses, indicating practitioner-driven adoption. Overall, the findings suggest that LLMs are embedded as everyday cognitive aids for reasoning and problem-solving, while core responsibility and decision-making remain human-centered.

Adoption Across Scrum Practices (RQ2)

RQ2 examined where, across Scrum management activities, LLM chat assistants are being used and how helpful practitioners perceive them. To contextualize these results, Fig. 2 first overlays the classical Scrum workflow with the main areas where LLMs support practitioners, such as learning Scrum, refining artifacts, assisting events, and complementing broader management tasks. This figure provides a structural view of how LLM support aligns with the framework's canonical elements.

Across all categories, respondents indicate that LLM assistants are used primarily as supportive cognitive tools rather than as substitutes for human decision-making. Their use clusters around four major areas. As shown in Fig. 3, these domains exhibit distinct adoption profiles, both in terms of current use and

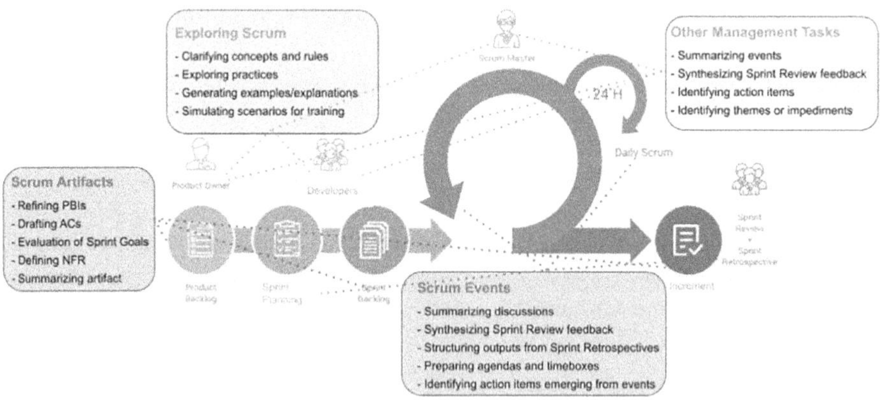

Fig. 2. LLM uses across Scrum activities: learning, artifacts, events, and management tasks.

future intention to use. "Exploring Scrum" dominate the outer rings, reflecting widespread use. "Artifact and event" items cluster in the mid-ring, showing substantial but selective adoption. Finally, "other Management tasks" appear closer to the inner rings, confirming cautious use.

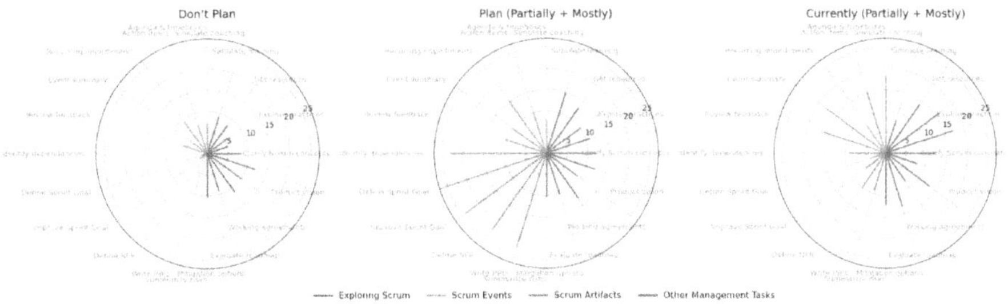

Fig. 3. Non-planned, planned, and current use of LLMs across categories.

Exploring Scrum exhibits the most consistent adoption. For all five exploration activities, the respondents report either "current use" or "plans to use" LLMs. Exploring practices (82% use or plan), practical resources (78% use or plan), and clarifying Scrum concepts (72% use or plan) are the most frequently adopted. In all cases, current partial use is the dominant pattern (22–35%), confirming that LLMs have become a primary cognitive aid for understanding, explaining, and preparing Scrum work.

LLM support for **Scrum Artifacts** also exhibits substantial adoption. Core refinement tasks (writing Product Backlog Items (PBIs), defining Non-Functional Requirements (NFRs), improving Sprint Goals) show 72–87% reported "use or planned use". For instance, 77% intend to or currently use LLMs to improve Sprint Goals (19 "plan mostly", 4 "currently partially", and 2 "currently mostly"), and 76% do so for defining NFRs. These activities align closely with LLMs' strengths in text transformation, summarization, and structured reasoning, which explains their high levels of acceptance.

In **Scrum Events**, adoption is led by summarization and synthesis activities. Summarizing what happened during events reaches 68% combined use/plan (with 36% already using), while synthesizing Sprint Review feedback reaches 64% (with 42% already using). More interpretive tasks show lower adoption: designing agendas/timeboxes (54%) or identifying impediments (48%) involve judgment and contextual nuance, explaining the more cautious uptake. Nonetheless, even these tasks show non-trivial planned adoption, indicating growing trust in LLM-assisted facilitation.

Finally, Adoption for **Other Agile Management Tasks** is more heterogeneous. Moderate levels of "use or planned use" (30–45%) appear in summarizing key risks (47%) and defining mitigation options (43%), reflecting practitioners' interest in LLM-based analytical support. However, alignment-heavy or culturally embedded tasks show clear resistance: improving working agreements

(33% use/plan, 33% don't plan) and describing product vision (29% use/plan, 38% don't plan). These results underscore that practitioners intentionally retain human ownership over value-driven and consensus-sensitive activities.

Overall, Fig. 3 indicates a consistent pattern in which practitioners rely on LLMs for text-heavy, analytical, and exploratory tasks, while responsibilities requiring judgment, collaboration, or strategic reasoning continue to be handled primarily by humans. This finding points to a pragmatic form of hybrid human–AI work within Scrum practitioners.

Summarized Answer - Adoption Across Scrum Practices (RQ2)

The results indicate that Brazilian Scrum practitioners widely use LLM assistants in management activities, primarily as supportive aids rather than substitutes for human judgment. Conceptual exploration is the most common use, while Scrum events mainly involve summarization and synthesis, with planning tasks used more cautiously. Artifact-related work shows the highest acceptance, reflecting strong alignment between LLM capabilities and text-intensive refinement tasks. In broader management activities, adoption is uneven, with summarization and risk-related uses gaining traction, while vision-setting and team alignment face greater resistance.

Perceived Benefits (RQ3)

Figure 4 summarizes the benefits most frequently reported by practitioners. The distribution reveals that AI chat assistants are perceived as highly effective in enhancing individual efficiency, improving artifact quality, and reducing repetitive cognitive load. Productivity and quality improvements (each 78%) and reduced effort in repetitive tasks (75%) form a cluster of strong, text-intensive benefits, suggesting that LLMs have become reliable companions for refinement, rewriting, summarizing, and structuring Scrum-related information.

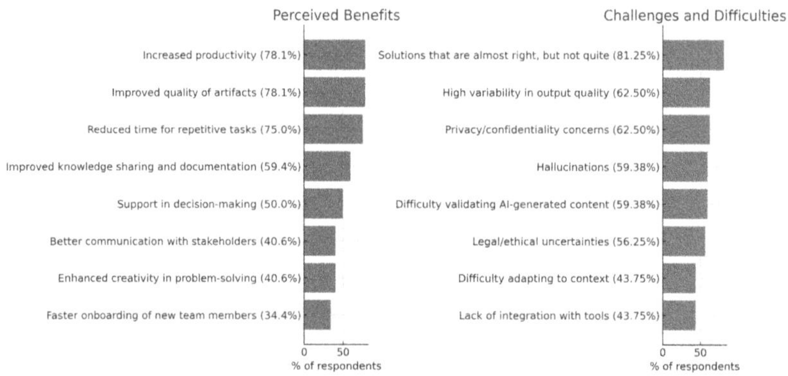

Fig. 4. Perceived benefits and challenges associated with the use of AI-based assistants.

Beyond speed and quality, respondents also highlighted benefits tied to knowledge work. Improved documentation and knowledge sharing (59%) reflect that AI assistance is increasingly embedded in organizational memory practices.

Half of the respondents also report support for decision-making, indicating that LLMs are used not only as writing tools but also as sensemaking partners in everyday reasoning tasks. Collaboration-oriented gains (improved stakeholder communication and enhanced creativity) appear less frequently (≈40%) yet still point to emerging uses where LLMs help practitioners articulate ideas, explore alternative solution paths, and communicate more effectively.

Responses to benefit-oriented statements further reinforce these trends. Most participants agree that AI assistants help them work more efficiently (89%) and reduce cognitive effort in routine activities (85%). Perceived team-level improvements are also strong (83%). However, benefits tied to collaboration (64%) and transparency or traceability (57%) are more modest, suggesting that organizations are still navigating how to consistently integrate AI-generated content into workflows, governance mechanisms, or shared documentation.

We also found that perceived usefulness varies across Scrum roles. Developers report overwhelmingly positive perceptions (84% finding AI useful or very useful), reflecting strong alignment with task-level reasoning, refinement, and technical exploration. Scrum Masters show moderate but steady benefits (56%), consistent with facilitation, coaching, and impediment-resolution tasks that can benefit from AI but remain deeply human-centered. Product Owners display the most heterogeneous perceptions: while some find LLMs useful for prioritization, vision communication, or backlog reasoning, a notable portion reports low applicability, reflecting the strategic nature of PO responsibilities.

Summarized Answer - Perceived Benefits (RQ3)

LLM assistants are widely perceived as valuable aids in Scrum management, particularly for efficiency, quality, and cognitive relief. Practitioners report substantial gains in productivity, artifact refinement, and reduction of repetitive effort, with strong perceptions of improved individual and team performance. Benefits involving collaboration and transparency appear more moderate, reflecting partial and uneven integration into collective workflows. Perceived usefulness differs across roles: Developers report the strongest benefits, Scrum Masters show steady but moderate gains, and Product Owners express mixed views. Overall, LLMs reinforce text-intensive and reasoning-focused tasks, while their impact on coordination or strategic responsibilities remains more situational.

Risks and Challenges (RQ4)

Figure 4 also highlights the challenges and frustrations practitioners face when using AI chat assistants for Scrum work. The most frequently cited difficulty is receiving outputs that are "almost correct but not quite" (81%), which aligns with known limitations of LLMs in precision-required contexts. High variability in output quality (63%) further reinforces the perception that AI responses require continuous monitoring and cannot yet be fully trusted for autonomous use.

In summary, we found that trust-, safety-, and reliability-related issues are central to the reported challenges. Privacy and confidentiality concerns (63%), hallucinations (59%), and difficulty validating AI-generated content (59%) illustrate that practitioners must apply active oversight, especially in contexts involving sensitive information or formal decision-making. Legal and ethical uncertainties (56%) additionally underscore unresolved organizational questions surrounding responsible use, compliance, and governance. Contextual adaptation issues—difficulty tailoring outputs to team or project realities (44%)—and lack of tool integration (44%) reveal frictions in practical adoption. These results show that although LLMs provide substantial value, their usefulness is constrained by organizational readiness, ecosystem integration, and the cognitive costs associated with validating and contextualizing their outputs.

When evaluating potential negative effects of intensive AI use, nearly 30% worry that over-reliance may erode practitioners' understanding of Scrum processes, while concerns about blurred accountability (23%), reduced human connection (26%), and diminished engagement (17%) reflect broader anxieties about the human dimension of Agile work. Neutral responses were relatively common, suggesting that these risks are perceived as contingent: they depend on how the tools are used, by whom, and under which constraints.

Summarized Answer - Risks and Challenges (RQ4)

Although LLM assistants are widely used in Scrum practice, their adoption is accompanied by persistent concerns about reliability and trust. Practitioners report frequent issues with near-correct but flawed outputs, inconsistent response quality, and privacy or confidentiality risks, which reinforce the need for human oversight. Contextual and organizational frictions, such as limited tool integration and challenges in adapting AI outputs to real project settings, further constrain effective use. Overall, the findings indicate that responsible adoption depends not only on individual judgment but also on organizational governance to mitigate risks while preserving accountability and team engagement.

5 Implications

This section presents implications for practice, organizations, and future research on the use of LLMs in Scrum management. For ***practitioners***, the results suggest that LLMs function effectively as cognitive aids for preparing and refining Scrum artifacts, exploring solution alternatives, and structuring reasoning during planning and analysis. However, the high incidence of "almost correct" outputs (81%) and "hallucinations" (59%) highlights that AI-generated content should remain subject to careful review. Teams must preserve human ownership over negotiation, prioritization, and decision-making, ensuring that reliance on assistants does not erode accountability or engagement.

For ***organizations***, the prominence of confidentiality concerns (63%) and legal or ethical doubts (56%) indicates the need for explicit guidelines on the appropriate use of LLM assistants. Policies on data sharing, validation of generated content, and acceptable use would support responsible adoption. Training initiatives focused on prompt articulation and critical evaluation of outputs may further amplify benefits while reducing risks.

Lastly, for the ***researchers***, the findings empirically reinforce the opportunities to investigate how hybrid human–AI workflows reshape collaboration, learning, and knowledge sharing within Agile teams. The results also highlight the importance of studying mechanisms to mitigate reliability issues and to adapt assistant outputs to specific contexts.

6 Threats to Validity

As with any survey-based study, this research is subject to potential threats to validity. We describe these threats below, structured according to the common standards, and outline the measures taken to mitigate them.

Internal Validity. This study relied on self-reported data, which may capture perceptions rather than actual practices, an inherent limitation of surveys. To mitigate this, the instrument emphasized concrete, practice-oriented items (e.g., frequency of LLM use, supported artifacts, impacted roles) to reduce overgeneralized responses. Response bias, including social desirability, was addressed by ensuring anonymity, voluntary participation, and clarifying that responses would not be individually evaluated. Non-response bias may have occurred if professionals less familiar with LLMs chose not to participate; however, the survey was disseminated across diverse channels (professional networks, Agile communities, industry partners) to broaden reach and reduce systematic exclusion.

External Validity. The generalizability of the findings is limited by the use of non-probabilistic sampling strategies (convenience and snowball sampling). While these limitations represent a lack of representativeness, we mitigated the risk by targeting participants from diverse industries, roles, organizational sizes, and regions, thereby increasing heterogeneity. Another concern is temporal validity, as LLM technology evolves rapidly. Since the data were collected in October 2025, future adoption patterns may differ. We therefore clearly report the collection period and technological context to support proper comparison in future studies.

Construct Validity. These threats stem from the difficulty of accurately capturing perceptions of benefits, challenges, and expectations regarding LLM use in Scrum contexts. To strengthen construct validity, the survey design followed established methodological guidelines [32] and prior work on AI adoption. The instrument underwent expert review and pilot testing to refine wording, reduce ambiguity, and ensure alignment with the study objectives. Common method bias was mitigated by combining objective items (e.g., usage frequency, models adopted) with perceptual ones (e.g., benefits, risks) and by incorporating open-ended questions for qualitative triangulation. Because the study relied on a single survey instrument, mono-method bias remains a limitation; to address this, we recommend complementary approaches (such as interviews, focus groups, or case studies) in future work. Finally, potential language and interpretation bias was reduced through clear wording, explicit definitions of technical terms, and pilot validation with practitioners.

Reliability. Reliability threats arise from potential inconsistencies in responses or in the interpretation of open-ended answers. To mitigate the first, all survey items were made mandatory in Google Forms, ensuring complete responses and reducing variability due to missing data. For the qualitative analysis, two researchers independently coded a subset of open-ended responses to strengthen inter-coder agreement, with disagreements resolved by discussion. Additionally, clear coding guidelines were established to minimize interpretive bias.

7 Final Remarks

This study aimed to characterize how Brazilian professionals are integrating LLMs into Scrum management activities. To achieve this objective, we conducted a survey with 70 practitioners, of whom 33 already reported active use of AI chat assistants in Scrum contexts. The findings show that Brazilian Scrum practitioners who use LLMs already demonstrate substantial familiarity with these tools: 85% report intermediate or advanced proficiency and 52% use them daily, typically in short sessions embedded in routine activities (RQ1). Adoption spans four major areas, but with different intensities: Exploring Scrum shows the strongest engagement (65–85% planned or current use), artifact and event tasks form a substantial mid-tier (40–70%), while broader management activities remain more cautious (20–50%), especially in strategic or value-driven work. (RQ2). The main benefits include increased productivity (78%), improved artifact quality (78%), and significant reduction of manual effort (75%), reinforcing the role of LLMs as cognitive and textual accelerators rather than autonomous agents (RQ3). At the same time, serious concerns persist: 81% frequently encounter "almost correct" outputs, 59% report hallucinations, and 63% cite confidentiality risks, indicating that effective use requires careful validation and organizational safeguards (RQ4).

The study highlights important implications. Organizations should establish clear usage policies, foster AI literacy, and ensure that human judgment remains central to negotiation, prioritization, and decision-making processes. Practitioners, in turn, should treat AI outputs as drafts that require verification. As LLMs continue to evolve, balancing efficiency gains with reliability, privacy, and collaboration will be essential for their responsible adoption in Scrum management.

Future research could examine how these hybrid human–AI workflows evolve over time, especially regarding team learning, collaboration, and accountability. Longitudinal studies may reveal whether LLMs shift from preparatory roles to more integrated forms of participation in Agile activities. Additional work is needed to develop mechanisms that mitigate reliability issues, support contextual adaptation, and incorporate organizational knowledge into AI-assisted workflows.

Artifacts Availability Supplementary materials in: https://github.com/Ilusinusmate/surveyxp26.

Acknowledgments. This work has been partially funded by the project "*iSOP Base: Investigação e desenvolvimento de base arquitetural e tecnológica da Intelligent Sensing Operating Platform (SOP)*" supported by CENTRO DE COMPETÊNCIA EMBRAPII VIRTUS EM HARDWARE INTELIGENTE PARA INDÚSTRIA – VIRTUS-CC, with financial resources from the PPI HardwareBR of the MCTI grant number 055/2023, signed with EMBRAPII.

References

1. Agarwal, N.S., Behera, R.K.: Harnessing the power of large language models for effective query resolution and document summarization. 2024 6th International Conference on Computational Intelligence and Networks (CINE) pp. 1–6 (2024)
2. Alami, A., Krancher, O.: How scrum adds value to achieving software quality? Empir. Softw. Eng. **27**(7), 165 (2022)
3. Arora, C., Grundy, J., Abdelrazek, M.: Advancing requirements engineering through generative ai: Assessing the role of llms. In: Generative AI for Effective Software Development, pp. 129–148. Springer (2024)
4. Arulmohan, S., et al.: Extracting domain models from textual requirements in the era of large language models. International Conference on Model Driven Engineering Languages and Systems Companion (MODELS-C) pp. 580–587 (2023)
5. Associação Brasileira das Empresas de Software (ABES): Mercado brasileiro de software: panorama e tendências 2025. Relatório Técnico (2025)
6. Brachman, M., El-Ashry, A., Dugan, C., Geyer, W.: How knowledge workers use and want to use llms in an enterprise context. In: Extended Abstracts of the CHI Conference on Human Factors in Computing Systems. p. 189. Association for Computing Machinery, New York, NY, USA (2024)
7. Burga, R., et al.: Examining the transition to agile practices with information technology projects: Agile teams and their experience of accountability. Int. J. Project Manage. **40**(1), 76–87 (2022)
8. Chakrabarty, T., Padmakumar, V., Brahman, F., Muresan, S.: Creativity support in the age of large language models: An empirical study involving professional writers. Proceedings of the 16th Conference on Creativity & Cognition pp. 132–155 (2024)
9. Couder, J., Ochoa, O.: Large language models, the new scrum masters (2024)
10. Dhruva, G., et al.: Agile project management using large language models. In: 2024 5th International Conference on Innovative Trends in Information Technology (ICITIIT). pp. 1–6. IEEE (2024)
11. Digital.ai: 18th annual state of agile report: The adaptation era (2025), https://digital.ai/resource-center/analyst-reports/18th-state-of-agile-report/, accessed: 2025-11-21
12. Dillman, D.A., Smyth, J.D., Christian, L.M.: Internet, phone, mail, and mixed-mode surveys: The tailored design method. Indianapolis, Indiana **17** (2014)
13. Eigner, E., Händler, T.: Determinants of llm-assisted decision-making. ArXiv **abs/2402.17385** (2024)
14. Fan, L., et al.: Exploring the capabilities of llms for code-change-related tasks. ACM Transactions on Software Engineering and Methodology **34**(6), 1–36 (2025)
15. Fernandez, D.J., Fernandez, J.D.: Agile project management –agilism versus traditional approaches. Journal of Computer Information Systems **49**, 10–17 (2008)
16. Fontana, R.M., Wojciechowski, J., Montaño, R.A.N.R., Marczak, S., Reinehr, S.S., Malucelli, A.: A countrywide descriptive survey of agile software development in brazil. In: XP. pp. 185–202 (2022)
17. Gao, C., et al.: The Current Challenges of Software Engineering in the Era of Large Language Models. ACM Transactions on Software Engineering and Methodology **34**(5), 1–30 (may 27 2025)
18. Graziotin, D., Lenberg, P., Feldt, R., Wagner, S.: Psychometrics in behavioral software engineering: A methodological introduction with guidelines. ACM Transactions on Software Engineering and Methodology (TOSEM) **31**(1), 1–36 (2021)

19. Hou, X., et al.: Large language models for software engineering: A systematic literature review. ACM Transactions on Software Engineering and Methodology **33**(8), 1–79 (2024)
20. Hu, X., Niu, F., Chen, J., Zhou, X., Zhang, J., He, J., Xia, X., Lo, D.: Assessing and advancing benchmarks for evaluating large language models in software engineering tasks. ACM Transactions on Software Engineering and Methodology (2025)
21. Jahić, J., Sami, A.: State of practice: Llms in software engineering and software architecture. In: 2024 IEEE 21st International Conference on Software Architecture Companion (ICSA-C). pp. 311–318. IEEE (2024)
22. Kalinowski, M., Araújo, A.A., Mendez, D.: Teaching survey research in software engineering. In: Handbook on Teaching Empirical Software Engineering, pp. 501–527. Springer (2024)
23. Karnouskos, S.: The relevance of large language models for project management. IEEE Open Journal of the Industrial Electronics Society **5**, 758–768 (2024)
24. Kasunic, M.: Designing an effective survey (2005)
25. Kerzner, H.: Project management: a systems approach to planning, scheduling, and controlling. John Wiley & Sons (2025)
26. Kim, Y., Hsu, C.C.: Leveraging large language models for hybrid workplace decision support. ArXiv **abs/2402.03616** (2024)
27. Lee, J.Y., Kang, S., Yoon, J., Yoo, S.: The github recent bugs dataset for evaluating llm-based debugging applications. In: 2024 IEEE Conference on Software Testing, Verification and Validation (ICST). pp. 442–444. IEEE (2024)
28. Lin, F., Kim, D.J., Chen, T.H.P.: Soen-101: Code generation by emulating software process models using large language model agents p. 1527–1539 (2025), https://doi.org/10.1109/ICSE55347.2025.00140
29. Lubos, S., et al.: Towards group decision support with llm-based meeting analysis. Adjunct Proceedings of the 33rd ACM Conference on User Modeling, Adaptation and Personalization (2025)
30. Mathews, N.S., Nagappan, M.: Test-driven development and llm-based code generation. In: International Conference on Automated Software Engineering. pp. 1583–1594 (2024)
31. Molléri, J.S., Petersen, K., Mendes, E.: Survey guidelines in software engineering: An annotated review. In: Proceedings of the 10th ACM/IEEE international symposium on empirical software engineering and measurement. pp. 1–6 (2016)
32. Molléri, J.S., Petersen, K., Mendes, E.: An empirically evaluated checklist for surveys in software engineering. Inf. Softw. Technol. **119**, 106240 (2020)
33. Ouriques, R.A.B., Wnuk, K., Gorschek, T., Berntsson-Svensson, R.: Knowledge management strategies and processes in agile software development: A systematic literature review. ArXiv **abs/1807.04962** (2018)
34. Paterek, P.: Effective knowledge management in agile project teams - impact and enablers. In: 5th International Scientific Conference on Project Management in the Baltic Countries in the University of Latvia, April. University of Latvia, Faculty of Economics and Management (2016)
35. Schroder, M.: Autoscrum: Automating project planning using large language models (2023)
36. Shastri, Y., Hoda, R., Amor, R.: Spearheading agile: the role of the scrum master in agile projects. Empir. Softw. Eng. **26**(1), 3 (2021)
37. Singh, A., Singh, K., Sharma, N.: Knowledge management: The agile way. In: Communication Systems and Applications (2015)
38. Tang, Z., Kejriwal, M.: Humanlike cognitive patterns as emergent phenomena in large language models. ArXiv **abs/2412.15501** (2024)

39. Tinnes, C., Fuchß, T., Hohenstein, U., Apel, S.: Towards Automatic Support of Software Model Evolution with Large Language Models. arXiv.org (2023)
40. Vasanthapriyan, S.: Knowledge management initiatives in agile software development. Human Factors in Global Software Engineering (2019)
41. Verwijs, C., Russo, D.: A theory of scrum team effectiveness. ACM Transactions on Software Engineering and Methodology **32**(3), 1–51 (2023)
42. Viet, N.V., Vinh, N.T.: Large language models in software engineering. Journal of Education For Sustainable Innovation **2**(2), 146–156 (dec 8 2024)
43. Wagner, S., Mendez, D., Felderer, M., Graziotin, D., Kalinowski, M.: Challenges in survey research. In: Contemporary Empirical Methods in Software Engineering, pp. 93–125. Springer (2020)
44. Zhang, Q., Fang, C., Xie, Y., Zhang, Y., Yang, Y., Sun, W., Yu, S., Chen, Z.: A survey on large language models for software engineering. arXiv preprint arXiv:2312.15223 (2023)

Human-AI Collaboration in Software Development Activities: Perspectives of Agile Practitioners

Daniel Planötscher[1(✉)], Xiaofeng Wang[1,2], Mahum Adil[3], Peggy Gregory[3], and Sepideh Larimian[1]

[1] Free University of Bozen—Bolzano, Bolzano, Italy
{dplanoetscher,xwang,slarimian}@unibz.it
[2] LUT University, Lappeenranta, Finland
[3] University of Glasgow, Glasgow, UK
{mahum.adil,peggy.gregory}@glasgow.ac.uk

Abstract. While Generative AI (GenAI) has rapidly transformed software development and GenAI tools receive widespread adoption, how humans and AI should collaborate has become a focal point for Agile practitioners, whose values emphasise teamwork and collaboration. Yet, despite growing interest, research on human-AI collaboration in software engineering, especially within Agile contexts, remains limited. Our study investigates Agile practitioners' perceptions of collaborating with GenAI in software development activities. We conducted a survey with 73 Agile practitioners, revealing how they currently collaborate with GenAI across various activities and how they expect this collaboration to evolve. Key findings include that GenAI is currently not a substantial part of real-world workflows, being either unused or limited to an assistant role, but that there is a clear tendency towards greater AI involvement in the future, with practitioners increasingly viewing AI as a collaborator rather than merely a tool. These findings advance our understanding of human-AI collaboration in Agile settings and can guide both future research and the practical adoption of GenAI in Agile environments.

Keywords: Human-AI Collaboration · Agile Software Development · Software Development Activities · Generative AI

1 Introduction

In the last few years, generative AI (GenAI) has significantly impacted the field of software development, and an increasing number of practitioners are working with GenAI to create software[1]. GenAI has drastically reshaped how software applications are designed, implemented, and maintained. It is not only used to enhance current practices, for instance, with widely adopted coding assistants

[1] https://survey.stackoverflow.co/2025/ai.

A. Goldman et al. (Eds.): XP 2026, LNBIP 578, pp. 274–289, 2026.
https://doi.org/10.1007/978-3-032-22375-3_17

such as GitHub Copilot[2] and AI features added to popular tools such as Jira[3], but it has also introduced new paradigms of software development, such as vibe coding[4] and spec-driven development[5].

The effective use of GenAI-driven software development tools has been a central theme of debate since their debut. Due to the conversational and interactive nature of these systems, human-AI collaboration has sparked particular interest from both practitioners[6] and researchers [5,6].

Nevertheless, introducing GenAI as a potential team member is a particularly relevant topic for Agile practitioners, whose workflows are based on teamwork and collaborative decision-making. As a result, the growing presence of human-AI collaboration raises questions about how existing Agile practices, roles, and interactions may need to adapt. Understanding how Agile practitioners perceive human-AI collaboration can therefore provide insights into its opportunities, limitations, and practical implications.

Due to the nascent nature of GenAI in the Software Engineering (SE) research area, little is known about human-AI collaboration in software development, let alone Agile practitioners' perceptions of it. Therefore, this study aims to investigate how Agile practitioners, across different roles and backgrounds, currently collaborate with GenAI and how they expect to collaborate with it in the future, to understand their general opinion on human-AI collaboration and its importance. Given that collaboration practices may vary across different software activities, such as requirements gathering and software implementation, this study investigated each activity individually. As a result, we formulated the following two research questions (RQs):

- **RQ1**: How do Agile practitioners currently collaborate with GenAI in different software development activities?
- **RQ2**: How do Agile practitioners expect human-AI collaboration in software development activities to evolve?

A survey study was conducted to answer the research questions. A total of 73 Agile practitioners have responded to the survey questionnaire. The survey's findings reveal that currently, GenAI is still mainly used as an assistant or not used at all. However, in the future, practitioners expect to collaborate more with it. The findings contribute to a better understanding of human-AI collaboration in software development in the Agile context. Researchers can use this to better understand how GenAI is currently being integrated into Agile software development and what barriers exist, and Agile practitioners can use it to see how other teams currently use GenAI and what opportunities may already exist. In the paper, for brevity, the term AI is used interchangeably with GenAI.

[2] https://github.com/features/copilot.
[3] https://www.atlassian.com/software/jira/ai.
[4] https://x.com/karpathy/status/1886192184808149383.
[5] https://github.blog/ai-and-ml/generative-ai/spec-driven-development-with-ai-get-started-with-a-new-open-source-toolkit/.
[6] https://claude.com/blog/how-anthropic-teams-use-claude-code.

The rest of the paper is organised as follows. In Sect. 2, the related work is reviewed, and the conceptual basis that underpins the survey design is introduced. Section 3 elaborates on the survey design and the data analysis process. The findings from the survey are reported in Sect. 4 and discussed in Sect. 5. The limitations of the study are reflected upon in the same section. The paper concludes with Sect. 6, where we lay out interesting future research directions.

2 Human-AI Collaboration in Agile Software Development

Human-AI collaboration is a rapidly expanding area of research as GenAI systems demonstrate increasing capability across knowledge-intensive tasks. Early research in this area primarily examines collaboration at an abstract level, exploring how humans and AI-based systems can work together, how responsibility and decision-making may be shared, and what competencies each party contributes [11]. For example, Bobba [2] conceptualises cognitive partnership through categories such as assistive, advisory, co-creative, and agentic collaboration, while Fragiadakis et al. [4] emphasise the distribution of workload between humans and AI, distinguishing human-centric, symbiotic, and AI-centric modes. These conceptual frameworks illustrate a broad spectrum of possible collaboration arrangements and highlight ongoing uncertainty about how responsibility, autonomy, and trust should evolve as AI capabilities advance.

More recent research highlights the growing integration of GenAI as an active collaborator in human-AI collaboration within software engineering and Agile development. For instance, Hamza et al. [5] highlight that large language models can assist in problem-solving, code optimisation, and collaborative brainstorming. Other studies present activity-specific applications: Cabrero-Daniel et al. [3] investigate LLM-based assistants for facilitating Agile ceremonies, Abbasi et al. [1] explore AI-supported approaches to requirements engineering in AI-native projects, and Zhang et al. [12] introduce AgileGen, a system in which humans and AI iteratively co-develop software prototypes guided by continuous feedback.

Nevertheless, existing research tends to focus on isolated tasks, specific tools, or controlled prototypes. This highlights a gap in understanding how Agile practitioners actually perceive human-AI collaboration across software development activities, which could help clarify the real-world challenges and opportunities for integrating AI into their daily workflows. As such, it might be interesting to investigate how Agile practitioners currently collaborate with AI and how they believe this could evolve in the future.

To address this gap, our study categorises human-AI collaboration from a workload perspective, refining Fragiadakis et al.'s [4] collaboration mode into a human-AI collaboration spectrum. This spectrum introduces five categories: (1) *No AI involvement* where humans complete all tasks without any AI support; (2) *AI as Assistant*, where AI helps with specific, well-defined and limited tasks while the human stays fully in charge of decisions and direction; (3) *AI as Collaborator*, where humans and AI work together and share the workload more evenly; (4) *AI as Lead*, where AI does most of the work and the human mainly delegates high-level tasks and reviews the results; and (5) *No human involvement* where the task is fully automated and carried out by AI alone. These modes form a continuum of human-AI collaboration, ranging from fully human-driven activities to AI-driven or fully automated tasks (see Fig. 1).

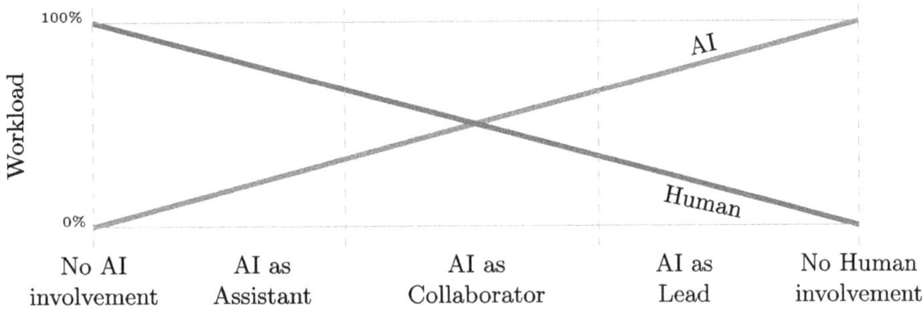

Fig. 1. Human-AI collaboration modes based on [4].

To better investigate the collaboration modes in practice, we decided to examine their application across different software activities. As Agile software development lifecycles vary and teams adopt diverse frameworks and practices, it is difficult to identify a single set of agile-specific activities common to most teams. For instance, while one team might conduct two-week sprints with daily standups, another might use Kanban with continuous flow and weekly check-ins. As a result, this study does not focus on Agile practices but rather on the core software engineering and project activities that together characterise different aspects of software development. These activities, while possibly being practised by agile teams in varying forms, provide a more stable and common basis for analysis.

To this end, seven core software activities were defined that are broadly relevant in Agile methodologies. These activities were selected based on established software engineering and project management literature [9,10] and reflect common tasks performed by Agile teams. The activities include: *Requirements Gathering*, *Requirements Management*, *Planning & Estimation*, *UI/UX Design*, *Software Architecture Design*, *Implementation*, and *Quality Assurance & Testing*. We divided requirements engineering into two distinct activities to capture differences in collaborative dynamics during elicitation versus ongoing prioritisation and coordination. By focusing on these seven activities, our study addresses both technical and managerial aspects of software development, providing a comprehensive view of how humans and AI collaborate across different tasks.

Together, the five collaboration modes and seven activities form the foundation for this study, providing a systematic view of current perceptions and anticipated future changes in human-AI collaboration in Agile software development. This process enables us to generate insights that go beyond individual tools or isolated tasks, providing a holistic understanding of human-AI collaboration in practice.

3 Research Method

We conducted an online survey to capture the perspectives of Agile practitioners on human-AI collaboration in various software development activities. The unit of study is an individual Agile practitioner. The survey design was underpinned by the human-AI collaboration modes and software activities reported in the literature [4,9]. In addition to respondents' demographics, such as their work experience and experience with Agile approaches, we asked which software activities they are involved in, the level of their involvement, which human-AI collaboration mode they currently use and expect to use in the future.

The survey was piloted with three Agile practitioners to ensure the questions were clearly understood and to estimate the time required to complete it. The survey was improved based on the feedback received from the pilot. The final version is shared in the replication package [8]. Eventually, it was published online in late 2025 and remained open for about four weeks. A convenience sampling strategy was employed. Potential respondents were approached through the professional networks of all the authors involved, which proved an effective way to ensure responses from the target population, Agile practitioners. In total, we received 81 responses, of which 73 were valid and included in the data analysis. Reasons for not including survey responses were, for example, if a responder stated they did not have did not use any Agile methodologies in their work.

Since the main variables, human-AI collaboration modes and software development activities, are categorical, and our aim is to understand the evolution of human-AI collaboration across software development activities from current to future, we conducted descriptive and comparative analysis on the quantitative data. For the qualitative data collected through open-ended questions that ask respondents to comment on their views on the evolution of human-AI collaboration across various software development activities, we analysed them alongside the quantitative data to provide richer insights into the results.

4 Results

The 73 respondents come from different countries around the globe, with the most from Italy (32%), the UK (20%), and Austria (17%). Other countries include Germany, Indonesia, Pakistan, India, Australia, France, Poland, South Africa and the UAE.

Almost half (46%) of the respondents are software developers, 15% are product owners, and the rest are in other roles such as managers, software architects, quality assurance (QA) and testers, and scrum masters. They report diverse experiences within the field and in Agile, with the largest group typically having 1–5 years of experience in their roles across both Agile and the software development industry. However, a fair number of respondents have more than

10 years of professional experience. The detailed distribution of the respondents' experience levels is shown in Table 1.

Table 1. Experiences of the respondents (n=73)

Experience Type	<1 year	1–5 years	6–10 years	11–15 years	>15 years
Role Experience	6 (8%)	29 (40%)	16 (22%)	17 (23%)	5 (7%)
Agile Experience	7 (10%)	31 (42%)	19 (26%)	11 (15%)	5 (7%)
Industry Experience	7 (10%)	25 (34%)	22 (30%)	7 (10%)	12 (16%)

Regarding the Agile methods adopted, 56% of the respondents use Scrum, which is hardly surprising, as it is the most common Agile framework[7]. 12% of the respondents use Kanban, and 9.5% use the hybrid ScrumBan. However, other frameworks are also represented in this survey, such as SAFe (Scaled Agile) and Pace. Interestingly, some respondents state that they have not adopted a clearly defined Agile framework but still practice Agile software development.

In general, the responses show a broad adoption of GenAI. Most respondents use generative AI tools, such as Copilot or ChatGPT, daily (60%), while others use them several times a week (27%). Only 3 out of 73 responders use GenAI less than once a month.

Figure 2 is a heatmap that visualises the percentage distribution of selected collaboration modes by the practitioners, contrasting what the respondents report doing now (the upper heatmap) with how they expect to collaborate with GenAI in the future (the lower heatmap).

The transition graph (Fig. 3) illustrates how respondents anticipate changes in collaboration with AI. Each arrow shows how a respondent expects to move from their current collaboration mode to a new one in the future, while percentages indicate how often these shifts occur. In both charts, we provided a number n for each activity, indicating the number of practitioners who are involved in this activity and therefore answered the survey for this part. The following subsections will examine each software activity in detail.

The anonymised survey results are available in our replication package, along with the complete survey design [8].

4.1 Requirements Gathering

Currently, close to half of the respondents (48%) use GenAI as an assistant in *requirements gathering*. According to respondents, GenAI can be used as an assistant to "*set out templates*", for *reviewing <information> to identify potential gaps* or to "*take notes and possibly mention what it thinks about the aspects we should look into*". Around 20% of the respondents use no AI in this activity, whereas a roughly equal percentage claim they use GenAI collaboratively to

[7] https://stateofagile.com/.

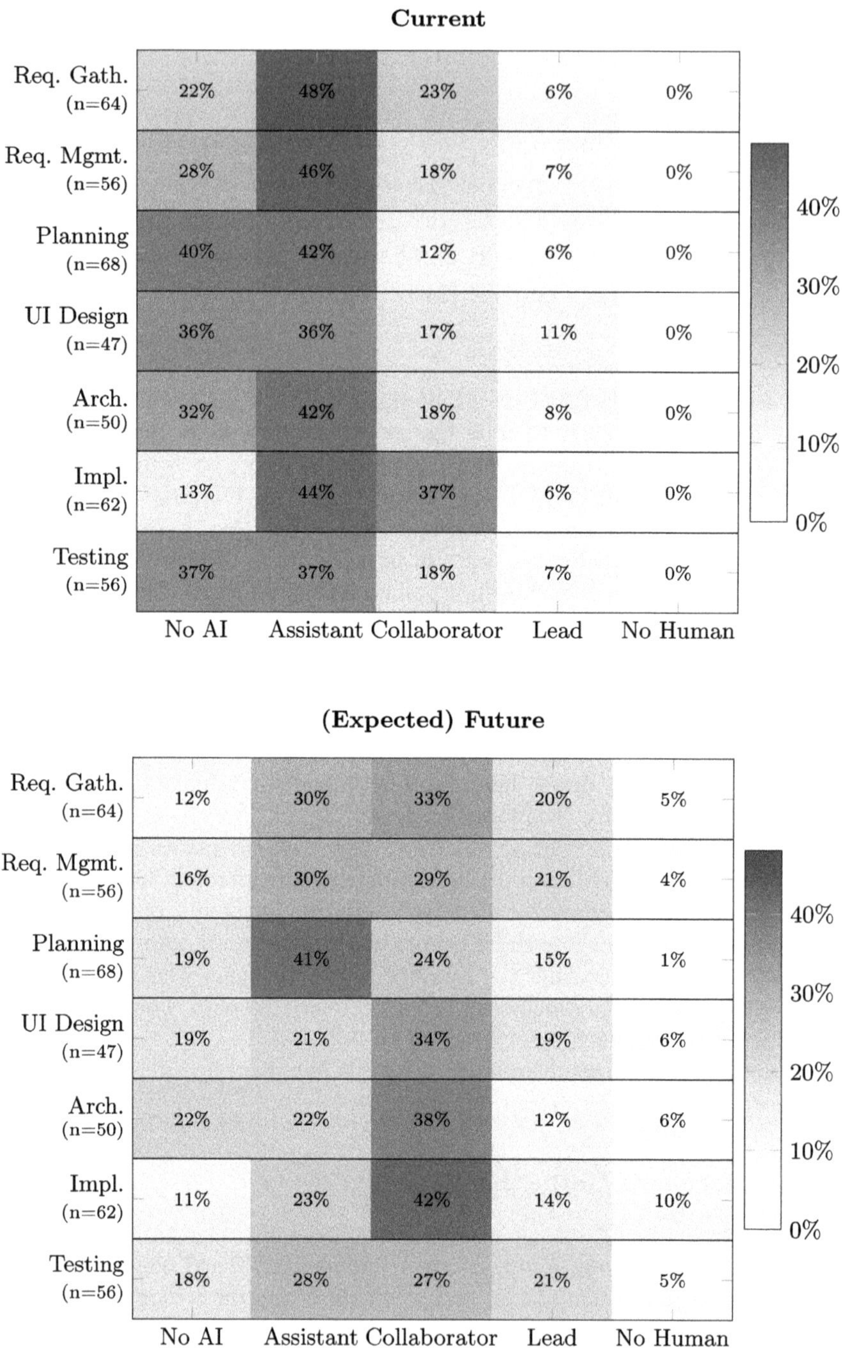

Fig. 2. Distribution of perceived current and future human-AI collaboration mode per software activity

gather requirements, brainstorm, or conduct research alongside AI, which greatly speeds up many work processes. An additional 6% of the respondents allow AI to take a leading role in their current usage mode. Respondents state that they have "*growing trust in AI*" but still would have "*safeguards*" in place and "*review the output of AI to ensure the quality*".

Regarding the future expectations, it is not possible to derive a strong preference for any collaboration modality; the Agile practitioners believe that GenAI will either be used collaboratively (33%) or continue to be used as an assistant (30%). The transition graph (Fig. 3) shows a similar picture, depicting that the leading group of people either continue using AI as an assistant or expect to start using it as a collaborator in the future. 13% of the respondents insisted on no AI usage in the future, with one stating that: "*AI does not know the entire scope; I do not see AI as useful or helpful here*". Another respondent believes that "*requirements gathering needs human interaction - an AI cannot 'ask' a stakeholder about their process*". Similar opinions were expressed by some of the 24% who see no departure from AI as an assistant in the future, saying: "*[Requirements gathering] is more about speaking to users and understanding their needs. That's the source of information, though AI can be useful for formatting and filling out stories.*"

However, it is interesting to note that while no respondents believe AI can currently perform requirements gathering without human involvement, three practitioners believe that, in the future, it might be possible to do so completely autonomously. As one respondent commented, "*I expect models to become far more superior, so expect the work to be fully autonomous, where the review can be super limited/occasionally.*"

4.2 Requirements Management

AI as an assistant is currently the predominant collaboration mode in *requirements management*, according to a large plurality of respondents (46%). One respondent comments that they "*use AI to help structure, document, and manage requirements more efficiently*". The second-largest group stated that they do not use AI at all (28%), with some perceiving that AI is not needed in this activity, stating "*I cannot see AI being helpful here*".

In the future, respondents expect to continue using AI as an assistant or start using it as a collaborator, again, without any strong preference for one modality over the other. Still, the percentage of respondents believing that they will start using AI as a lead increased. One respondent, who is fully responsible for requirements management, is "*learning to trust AI*" and believes that "*with better safeguards, I will be able to let AI take the lead and or even automate some tasks completely*", showing AI might be increasingly involved in this activity in the future.

The transition graph tells a similar story. It shows that practitioners believe that they will likely move from using AI as an assistant to using it more as a collaborator. However, it also shows the opposite. Many respondents do not expect to change their collaboration mode, especially if they currently use it as an assistant or not at all. As one respondent who expects to keep the AI assistant collaboration mode in the future puts it: "*I use AI to help structure, document, and manage requirements more efficiently. However, decisions, prioritisation, and final coordination remain clearly the responsibility of humans, as AI is not yet reliable enough to fully understand complex technical dependencies.*"

4.3 Planning & Estimation

An even distribution of the Agile practitioners currently either do not incorporate AI into these activities (40%) or use it only as an assistant (42%). Those who do not use AI stated that "*planning the timeline and the work involved requires a lot of thought and experience*", and "*[Planning & estimation] depends on team members and team size.*" Interestingly, AI is seen as an additional overhead by one respondent, who believes that "*Following story points should be enough for estimation.*"

In the future, a large plurality of respondents (41%) still believe that AI will only be able to be an assistant in planning and estimation, with only 24% believing it could become a collaborator. In fact, inspecting the transitions between the collaboration modes in Fig. 3, it is noticeable that respondents either continue using AI as an assistant (23%) or start using it only as an assistant (18%).

4.4 UI&UX Design

As with the planning activities, respondents of equally sized groups tend not to use AI at the moment, or use it only as an assistant in *UI&UX design* activities, with 36% of respondents in each group reporting this. As an assistant, AI can help in "*writing CSS or designing basic templates*", according to one respondent. Another mentions that a major reason they have not incorporated GenAI into design activities is that UI design is "*a creativity thing and AI can hardly provide good solutions... there's so much hidden context*".

In the future, however, 38% of the respondents believe AI might be a collaborator, while a smaller percentage (21%) think it might be only an assistant. One respondent would even like to use AI as a lead of the collaboration, believing that: "*On the frontend side I see a lot of improvement on GenAI features, especially the base design.*" Another respondent regularly involved in UI design believes that AI could perform without human involvement and makes an interesting connection between this mode of collaboration and vibe coding.

The transition graph of UI design shows an even distribution of the respondents who would like to remain at their current mode of collaboration with AI and those who would like to collaborate more with AI in the future.

4.5 Software Architecture Design

Again, a similar pattern to the previous activities can be observed in *software architecture design*, where AI is used by respondents either as an assistant (42%)

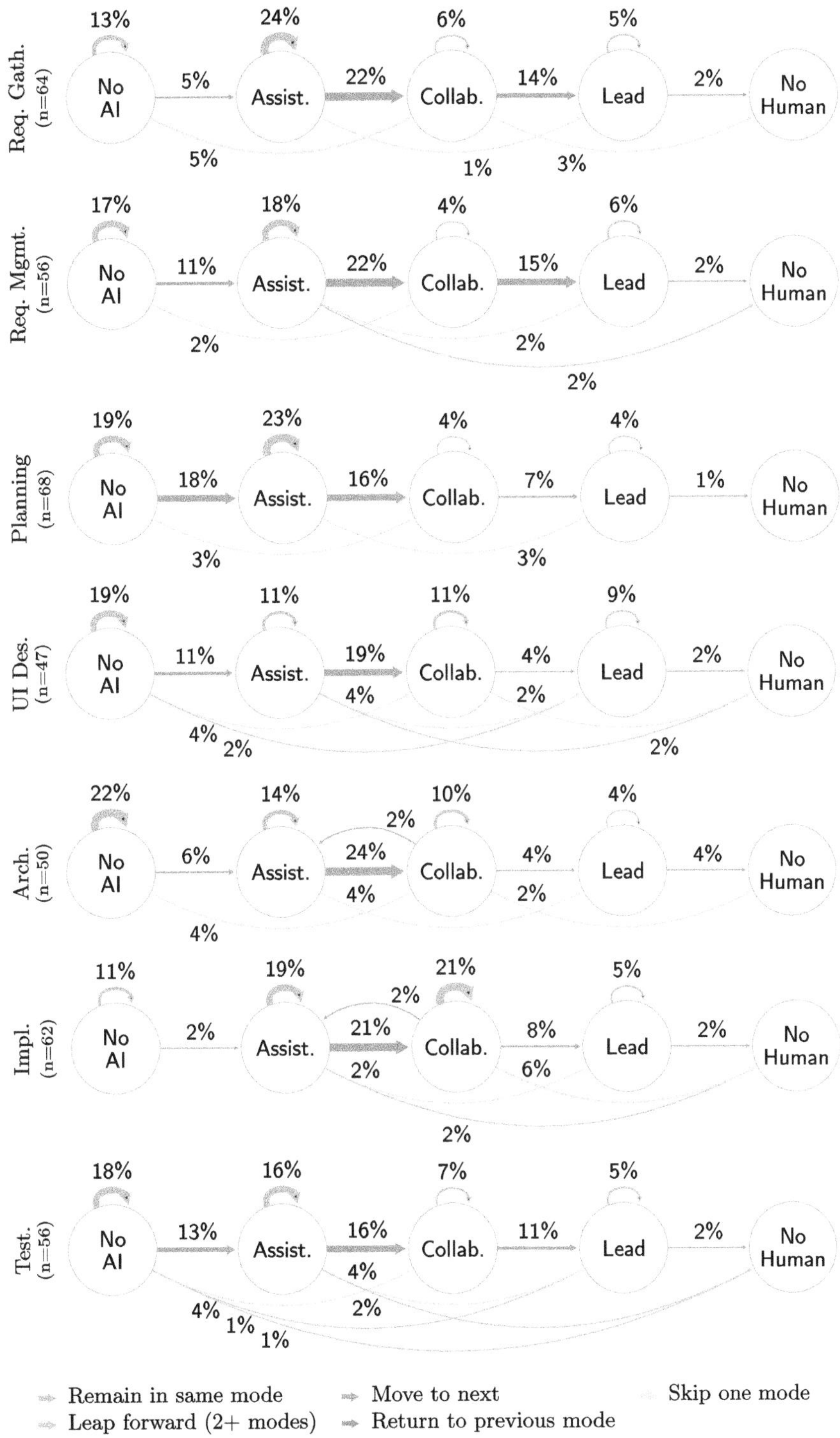

Fig. 3. Perceived evolution of human-AI collaboration mode per activity.

or not at all (32%). A respondent fully responsible for architecture design argues that "*AI cannot (and, in my opinion, never will) replace years of experience and involvement in enormous industrial projects; such projects are not part of the training data.*" Another respondent, who is a software architect, currently uses AI as an assistant and believes that "*AI is good for ideation and validation, but has found that it is often wrong about facts and shouldn't be trusted to lead yet.*"

Nevertheless, in the future, the largest group of respondents (38%) expects to use AI more collaboratively in software architecture design. In fact, 24% of respondents expect to transition from using it as an assistant to using it as a collaborator in the future. Notably, 22% of the respondents said they will not involve AI in software architecture design in the future. One respondent holding full responsibility for architectural design identified an interesting transition: rather than progressing to more intensive collaboration, they expect to revert from using AI as a collaborator back to AI as an assistant. As the respondent explains: "*I'm relatively new to software engineering, so AI helped a lot in gathering information online. But as time goes by, I should rely on my personal judgments more as AI content can be misleading.*"

4.6 Implementation

For software *implementation*, there is already a strong tendency to use AI either as an assistant (44%) to handle *basic tasks and speed up initial implementation*, or as a collaborator (37%), more often called a co-pilot or pair programmer in implementation activities. Only a small proportion of the respondents (13%) do not yet use AI in this activity. One reason holding them back is that AI "*still makes mistakes and is not very secure, so it needs plenty of human intervention for production-ready code*", sometimes to the extent of "*delay[ing] and derail[ing] implementation.*"

Almost half of the respondents believe that in the future, AI might be even more involved in implementation activities than it is now, primarily as a collaborator (42%). A small portion (10%) of the respondents believe that AI might fully autonomously write code in the future, while 14% believe that it might be used as a lead. Looking at the transitions, an equal number of respondents (21%) either shift up to using it as a collaborator or continue using it collaboratively. A developer respondent, who is reluctant to move forward from using AI as an assistant, explains why: "*I mainly delegate annoying/trivial tasks or very specific minor details to save brainpower. AI remains an assistant at best; very rarely can I use an output 1:1. Since I enjoy my job, I don't see any change for me personally in the future.*"

It is also noteworthy that, within implementation activity, one respondent expected they would collaborate less with AI in the future. For this, the respondent states that they are still learning programming and therefore use it more often; however, in the future, they aim to reduce the use of AI in the workflow.

4.7 QA & Testing

For *QA & testing*, an equal number of the survey participants currently either do not use AI or use it only as an assistant, with 37% of the practitioners in each group. One respondent who is regularly involved in testing claims that "*Without contextual knowledge, I don't see any advantage in using AI.*", and therefore decides to stay away from AI. Others say data security is a major reason they do not use AI. When AI is used as an assistant for QA, it is seen as helpful in writing and refining test cases, since "*decent improvement on GenAI*" has been perceived.

When inspecting future predictions, however, no clear pattern emerges in this activity. An almost equal number of practitioners believe that it might be used either as an assistant (28%) or a collaborator (27%). At the same time, a similar number of participants also expect they might be involved as a lead (21%) or not at all (18%). The transition graph shows longer jumps in testing activities than in the graphs of other activities, and the longest jump is from currently no AI usage to future no human involvement.

5 Discussion

5.1 RQ1: Current Extent of Human-AI Collaboration

We observe that for many activities, practitioners either use AI as an assistant or have not yet incorporated it into the specific software activity. For the activities where AI is being incorporated as an assistant, requirements gathering and management are prominent. Here, AI assistants are used to take notes, review information for potential gaps, and structure, document, and manage requirements more efficiently.

Other activities, such as planning, UI design, architecture, and testing, are notable for being areas where many practitioners still do not use AI at all. For this, various reasons are mentioned, such as a lack of trust or past bad experiences with AI systems when performing the task, or a lack of perceived necessity to use AI in the activity.

In contrast, the implementation activity clearly distinguishes itself as one in which practitioners already believe they are using AI as a collaborator. Here, AI is often perceived as a co-pilot or pair programmer that helps create software code, speed up initial implementation, or even handle basic tasks.

It is also interesting to point out that currently, no activity is yet being performed without any human involvement, and only a few respondents believe that they are currently letting the AI lead the collaboration in software activities.

5.2 RQ2: Expected Evolution of Human-AI Collaboration

We observe that, in general, practitioners expect that AI involvement will increase in the future, with most focus on using AI as a collaborator. Even though the distributions differ notably across software activities, there is a tendency for practitioners currently using AI as an assistant to expect to be using it as a collaborator in the future. Respondents often attribute this to their expectation that generative AI will continue to improve, alongside their ongoing efforts to build trust and learn to use AI effectively in specific tasks.

Nevertheless, we can also notice voices that remain reluctant to integrate AI more deeply into their workflow. For this, several reasons are cited, ranging from people not trusting AI to help with the task to the fear of losing the joy of their work as AI becomes a larger part of the workflow. There are even some practitioners who believe they will never use AI in their activities, often citing security restrictions or AI lacking sufficient contextual information or"industry experience" to perform the task. Especially notable are planning & estimation activities, where a plurality of practitioners believe that AI can, at most, be an assistant.

At the other extreme, we can observe some practitioners believing that AI might completely automate certain activities, or at least that AI may take the lead in these tasks. Especially, implementation is an activity that practitioners believe may have even more AI involvement in the future, beyond symbiotic workload-sharing.

Only a few respondents (2), both of whom identified as beginners/juniors in the field, decided they would reduce their AI use over time. According to them, they currently rely on AI while they are still learning and trying to understand the concepts, but later, they want to take more control of their work. This is especially worth highlighting, as research often cites overreliance on AI as a potential challenge in the future, especially for beginners. For instance, [7] highlights concerns that junior developers may not learn to code properly if they rely on it too much. In our study, beginners seem to be aware of this issue; however, they see GenAI as a potential learning assistant that can help them understand core principles more quickly.

Overall, in most activities, such as requirements gathering and management, testing, and UI design, we see no strong tendencies towards a concrete collaboration mode. This is probably because industry is still in the early stages of GenAI adoption. Findings show a wide variety of adoption modes across individuals with different backgrounds and roles, and across activities.

5.3 Insights, Implications, and Limitations

This study complements existing literature on human-AI collaboration in Agile software development by examining practitioners' perspectives on how to perform human-AI collaboration. For this, it first developed a spectrum of human-AI collaboration modes observed in the real world, based on existing literature, and then analysed practitioners' opinions from a survey. These results provide a fine-grained yet sufficiently comprehensive overview of how human-AI collaboration can look across different software activities. It also shows where transitions between collaboration modes are more likely, and where practitioners still show scepticism about involving AI more intensively.

The findings from RQ1 and RQ2 have implications for both researchers and practitioners. For researchers, it shows that even as AI involvement is expected to increase in the future, however, some practitioners remain reluctant to use it. Research could focus on better understanding the barriers these practitioners face and why human-AI collaboration modes differ across activities. For practitioners, it provides an overview of how human-AI collaboration currently manifests across different teams, showing that for some, the future expectations of the human-AI collaboration mode are already the current reality, suggesting there may be an opportunity to introduce AI more deeply into the workflow.

While this study provides valuable insights into perceived and practised human-AI in Agile software development, several limitations must be noted to contextualise these results. The study is constrained by its relatively small sample size, despite respondents being globally distributed and representing diverse experience levels. Moreover, a more detailed examination of demographic data could reveal a richer understanding of human-AI collaboration, particularly in relation to respondents' roles and experience. Nevertheless, the small sample size limited the depth of the analysis. As such, it was decided to keep the survey ongoing and conduct the study with a larger sample. In addition, various inferential rather than descriptive statistics could be conducted. It is also important to note that the survey does not cover every software activity in detail. To keep the survey brief and applicable to most respondents, the most important and widely practised activities were objectively identified from the literature. Similarly, the collaboration modes were kept general to make it easier for participants to answer the survey.

6 Conclusion

GenAI, as a disruptive force, has transformed, maybe permanently, how software is developed and will be developed, as well as our understanding of how software development activities are conducted. Agile practitioners, more than others, are confronted with such a force and sense the strong need to respond and adapt. Our study, through a global survey, investigates Agile practitioners' perspectives on the extent to which humans and AI collaborate across various software development activities. The findings demonstrate that there is no consensual understanding among Agile practitioners on how humans and AI could collaborate in software development. This is not surprising since we are still in the initial phase of GenAI adoption in the workplace. However, some early patterns were observed: currently, AI is used more as an assistant or not at all, while in the future, practitioners expect to collaborate more closely with AI, with some even believing that more workload can be shifted to AI.

With this, our study contributes to a refined understanding of human-AI collaboration through the perspectives of Agile practitioners by providing a comprehensive yet nuanced overview of the human-AI collaboration mode across different activities, showing where practitioners are still reluctant to use AI and where they believe more AI collaboration is possible.

Our findings have implications for research on practitioners' scepticism and uncertainties about collaborating with AI in activities such as requirements gathering, management, planning, and so on. Our findings are also relevant to practice because they reveal different realities of human-AI collaboration, suggesting that for some, future expectations are already reality.

Future work will comprise conducting a more elaborated and focused analysis of the chosen collaboration modes in relation to the respondents' demographics. After that, we also plan to conduct follow-up interviews with participants and more in-depth case studies to better understand the challenges, opportunities, as well as the deeper implications of human-AI collaboration in Agile software development. Through this, we aim to examine how human-AI collaboration might change Agile roles, practices and workflows.

References

1. Abbasi, M.A., Ihantola, P., Mikkonen, T., Mäkitalo, N.: Reconsidering requirements engineering: Human–ai collaboration in ai-native software development. In: Taibi, D., Smite, D. (eds.) Euromicro Conference on Software Engineering and Advanced Applications, pp. 164–180. Springer, Cham (2025). https://doi.org/10.1007/978-3-032-04190-6_11
2. Bobba, A.R.: The evolution of cognitive partnership: a taxonomic framework for human-ai collaboration modalities. J. Comput. Sci. Technol. Stud. **7**(8), 992–1005 (2025)
3. Cabrero-Daniel, B., Herda, T., Pichler, V., Eder, M.: Exploring human-ai collaboration in agile: customised llm meeting assistants. In: Šmite, D., Guerra, E., Wang, X., Marchesi, M., Gregory, P. (eds.) International Conference on Agile Software Development, pp. 163–178. Springer, Cham (2024). https://doi.org/10.1007/978-3-031-61154-4_11
4. Fragiadakis, G., Diou, C., Kousiouris, G., Nikolaidou, M.: Evaluating human-ai collaboration: a review and methodological framework. arXiv preprint arXiv:2407.19098 (2024)
5. Hamza, M., Siemon, D., Akbar, M.A., Rahman, T.: Human-ai collaboration in software engineering: Lessons learned from a hands-on workshop. In: Proceedings of the 7th ACM/IEEE International Workshop on Software-intensive Business, pp. 7–14 (2024)
6. Mseer, I., Ali Samhan, A.A.: Collaboration between humans and ai. In: Alaali, M., Musleh Al-Sartawi, A.M.A., Aydiner, A.S. (eds.) The Paradigm Shift from a Linear Economy to a Smart Circular Economy: The Role of Artificial Intelligence-Enabled Systems, Solutions and Legislations, pp. 1299–1308. Springer, Cham (2025). https://doi.org/10.1007/978-3-031-87550-2_83
7. Pereira, G.V., et al.: Exploring genai in software development: Insights from a case study in a large brazilian company. In: 2025 IEEE/ACM 47th International Conference on Software Engineering: Software Engineering in Practice (ICSE-SEIP), pp. 330–341. IEEE (2025)
8. Planötscher, D., wang, X., Adil, M., Gregory, P.: Human-ai collaboration in agile environments: Survey results (2026). https://doi.org/10.5281/zenodo.18504873
9. Sommerville, I.: Software engineering (ed.). America: Pearson Education Inc (2011)

10. Stellman, A., Greene, J.: Applied Software Project Management. O'Reilly Media, Sebastopol, CA (2005)
11. Wang, D., et al.: From human-human collaboration to human-ai collaboration: Designing ai systems that can work together with people. In: Extended abstracts of the 2020 CHI conference on human factors in computing systems, pp. 1–6 (2020)
12. Zhang, S., et al.: Empowering agile-based generative software development through human-ai teamwork. ACM Trans. Softw. Eng. Methodol. (2025)

Between Policy and Practice: GenAI Adoption in Agile Software Development Teams

Michael Neumann[1], Lasse Bischof[2], Nic Elias Hinz[1], Abdullah Altun[1], Luca Stockmann[1], Dennis Schrader[1], Ana Carolina Ahaus[1], Erim Can Demirci[1], Benjamin Gabel[1], Maria Rauschenberger[2], Philipp Diebold[3,4](✉), Henning Fritzemeier[5], and Adam Przybyłek[6]

[1] University of Applied Sciences and Arts Hannover, Hannover, Germany
michael.neumann@hs-hannover.de
[2] University of Applied Sciences Emden/Leer, Emden/Leer, Germany
maria.rauschenberger@hs-emden-leer.de
[3] Bagilstein GmbH, Mainz, Germany
philipp.diebold@bagilstein.de
[4] IU International University, Erfurt, Germany
philipp.diebold@iu.org
[5] Volkswagen AG, Wolfsburg, Germany
henning.fritzemeier@volkswagen.de
[6] University of Galway, Galway, Ireland

Abstract. *Context:* The rapid emergence of generative AI (GenAI) tools has begun to reshape software engineering practice. Yet, their adoption within agile environments remains underexplored. *Objective:* This study investigates how agile practitioners adopt GenAI tools in real-world organizational contexts, focusing on regulatory conditions, role-specific use cases, benefits, and barriers. *Method:* An exploratory multiple case study was conducted in three German organizations, involving 17 semi-structured interviews and document analysis. A cross-case thematic analysis was applied to identify GenAI adoption patterns. *Results:* Findings reveal that GenAI is primarily used for creative tasks, documentation, and code assistance. Benefits include efficiency gains and enhanced creativity, while barriers relate to data privacy, validation effort, and lack of governance. Using the Technology-Organization-Environment (TOE) framework, we find that these barriers stem from misalignments across the three dimensions. Regulatory pressures are often translated into policies without accounting for actual usage patterns or organizational constraints, leading to systematic policy-practice gaps and shadow IT behavior. *Conclusion:* GenAI offers significant potential to augment agile roles but requires alignment across TOE dimensions, including pragmatic policies, data protection measures, and user training to ensure responsible and effective integration.

Keywords: Agile Methods · generative AI · generative AI adoption · multiple case study

A. Goldman et al. (Eds.): XP 2026, LNBIP 578, pp. 290–308, 2026.
https://doi.org/10.1007/978-3-032-22375-3_18

1 Introduction

The rapid advancement of generative artificial intelligence (GenAI) has catalyzed profound transformation across diverse economic and technological domains. While impacts are evident in institutional contexts such as higher education [21] and public administration [28], the proliferation of GenAI since the release of ChatGPT in November 2022 has significantly reshaped daily work across industries [11,22].

Currently, GenAI tools such as ChatGPT or GitHub Copilot are pervasive in software engineering [4], fundamentally altering how software development teams operate [26]. Professionals now routinely apply GenAI for tasks ranging from code generation [18] and test case creation [2,10] to requirements elicitation and analysis [29,39]. While the literature highlights benefits such as increased team performance, it simultaneously warns of risks [30,31], *e.g.*, on source code quality [23,33]. Consequently, scholars emphasize the importance of human-integration [24], exemplified by the ethical guidelines proposed in the Copenhagen Manifesto [27].

Within agile software development (ASD), GenAI tools promise to automate routine tasks, foster creativity, and enhance the productivity of software developers and project stakeholders [38]. Agile methods, characterized by iterative development cycles, cross-functional collaboration, and continuous feedback, provide a conducive environment for the piloting and integration of GenAI tools into established workflows [9]. However, deploying these tools also introduces a range of new challenges. According to Bahi et al. [3], practitioners are confronted with critical questions such as: "Is the use of such tools permissible?" and "Can sensitive data be safely disclosed to GenAI services?".

As agile methods focus strongly on social interaction and communication, one may assume that various agile related practices with a strong emphasis on social interaction such as pair programming are affected [32] when specific tasks are performed with GenAI support instead of humans [1]. Despite this potential disruption, empirical research on how agile teams specifically adopt GenAI tools in their practice remains underrepresented in the literature.

Thus, in this study, we address the following research questions:

- **RQ 1:** What organizational and regulatory conditions shape GenAI adoption in practice?
- **RQ 2:** Which use cases of GenAI tools are adopted in agile software development teams?
- **RQ 3:** What benefits and barriers do agile team members associate with GenAI adoption?

The paper is structured as follows: Sect. 2 reviews related work and outlines our contributions. In Sect. 3, we explain how we applied the multiple case study. Next, we present our results and answer the research questions in Sect. 4. The paper concludes in Sect. 6.

2 Literature Review

The study most closely related to ours is by Kemell et al. [15], who conducted a multiple case study across seven companies to examine GenAI adoption, identifying relevant use cases and challenges. They identified six organizational barriers, including data privacy and legacy system concerns, as well as issues related to the black-box nature of LLMs. From a user perspective, they reported four further challenges, notably the complexity of learning to apply GenAI tools, particularly regarding prompt formulation in daily work. Our work builds on this by shifting the analytical lens from their broad categorization of "individual users", primarily focused on coding tasks, to a granular analysis of agile-specific roles. This reveals distinct adoption patterns where GenAI extends beyond technical assistance to support agile ceremonies and soft skills. Furthermore, while Kemell et al. document data privacy and legislative concerns as adoption barriers, we extend this by examining their behavioral consequences, showing how rigid policies drive practitioners to circumvent compliance to maintain agile velocity. Consequently, we reframe validation not merely as a user capability challenge, but as a systematic process bottleneck.

Karlovs-Karlovskis [14] corroborates the technical emphasis in current research: among 117 studies reviewed, about 65% focus on GenAI-based code generation, revealing major gaps in empirical research on real-world integration and a lack of studies in other domains with potential for cost reduction, innovation, and optimization.

A recent research agenda by Nguyen-Duc et al. [22] provides broader theoretical grounding, identifying 78 open research questions across 11 knowledge areas. While implementation and testing dominate current discourse, significant potential exists in requirements engineering, software design, and engineering management. The authors note persistent challenges including reliability of GenAI outputs, data privacy and accessibility, transparency in AI-assisted decision-making, and sustainability. Critically, they observe that managerial, organizational, and socio-technical dimensions of GenAI adoption remain significantly underrepresented compared to purely technical considerations, a gap our study addresses within agile contexts.

Overall, existing research on GenAI in software engineering especially within ASD remains limited. While some studies (*e.g.*, Ulfsnes et al. [35]; Coutinho et al. [7]) highlight productivity gains and tool versatility, they also point to persistent issues in knowledge sharing, reliability, and security. Bahi et al. [3] similarly show that GenAI can support Scrum practices but emphasize ongoing challenges across the development lifecycle, underscoring the paucity of empirical evidence from real-world agile environments.

Recent XP conference editions also hosted two workshops on GenAI and Agile (2024; 2025), producing exploratory papers on GenAI use in specific agile practices, such as Test-Driven Development [19], and broader topics like responsibility [34] and teamwork effects [17]. While informative, their exploratory nature and workshop format limit their applicability to our research questions.

To address the identified gaps, our study examines GenAI adoption within agile software teams. It explores how GenAI is applied in practice, the organizational implications of its adoption, and relevant use cases along with associated benefits and barriers. By grounding the investigation in a real-world agile setting, this study provides empirical insights into how GenAI is reshaping software development dynamics in mid-sized enterprises.

3 Research Design

Guided by Runeson and Höst's guidelines [25], this study adopts an exploratory qualitative multiple-case design to investigate how GenAI is embedded, applied, and experienced within the various roles operating in agile software-development teams. Case studies are well-suited for examining modern software engineering practices in real-world contexts, especially when the phenomenon cannot be easily separated from its context. For this study, the units of analysis are the employees operating in the agile software development teams.

3.1 Case Selection and Context

Our study was conducted across three German organizations, selected to capture diversity in roles, agile methods, experience levels, and expertise. All identifying information—including company, site, and team names has been anonymized for confidentiality. The three cases are described below:
Case 1: Dinoco is one of the world's largest automobile manufacturers, operating more than nine vehicle brands and producing automobiles, motorcycles, and trucks worldwide. Our study took place at one of its German software development sites, the Dinoco Software Development Expertise Site (DSDES), which spans multiple locations and employs around 450 people. As part of Dinoco's digitization strategy, DSDES develops strategic software products such as cockpit software and over-the-air update processes across more than ten agile teams. These teams follow eXtreme Programming principles within the Scaled Agile Framework (SAFe).

Case 2: Gray Matter Technologies (GMT) is a medium-sized company in Germany and Austria with around 150 employees across three sites. GMT develops software products for external clients, including an ERP system and web shop applications. Its software development division consists of four agile teams, each dedicated to specific customer projects and working with an adapted Scrum approach. GMT's clients range from large retail and manufacturing companies to medium-sized craft businesses.

Case 3: Insight Inc. is a small, fully remote consulting company in Germany with eight employees. It provides agile coaching and training and offers interim roles in which staff embed within client teams for six months to two years, typically as Scrum Masters and occasionally as Product Owners. Insight Inc.'s clients span various industries; for the employees involved in this study, the relevant clients were in the banking sector.

Table 1. Interviewee profiles

ID	Role	Exp. with Agile Methods	Case
P01	Agile Coach	10 years	Dinoco
P02	Product Owner	13 years	Dinoco
P03	Software Developer	8 years	Dinoco
P04	Software Developer	10 years	Dinoco
P05	Software Developer	8 years	GMT
P06	Software Developer	30 years	GMT
P07	Software Developer	18 years	GMT
P08	Product Owner	15 years	GMT
P09	Software Developer	25 years	GMT
P10	Product Owner	11 years	GMT
P11	Agile Coach	5 years	Insight Inc.
P12	Lean Coach	10 years	Insight Inc.
P13	Agile Coach	10 years	Insight Inc.
P14	Agile Coach	5 years	Insight Inc.
P15	Junior Agile Coach	3 years	Insight Inc.
P16	Agile Coach	13 years	Insight Inc.
P17	Agile Coach	5 years	Insight Inc.

3.2 Data Collection

Runeson & Höst [25] emphasize that case studies must combine direct, indirect, and independent data sources so that weaknesses inherent in a single method can be counterbalanced through data source triangulation. Our data collection comprised two primary data sources:

Semi-structured Interviews: We conducted 17 semi-structured interviews across all three cases; interviewee profiles are summarized in Table 1. The interviews were conducted using an interview guideline which we created based on the Goal-Question-Metric (GQM) approach [5]. The interview guide consists of four core clusters considering the personal background of the interviewee and the three main themes among the research questions: GenAI-related contextual information, use cases of GenAI adoption, and barriers/benefits of the daily use of GenAI. The interview guide is available in our research protocol [20]. All interviews were held online using Microsoft Teams between March and May 2025 and have been recorded. The interviews lasted around 30 min for Dinoco, between 30 and 45 min for Insight Inc. and Gray Matter Technologies. To increase the quality, we performed a pre-test to verify the structure of the interview guide. The interviews were conducted by two researchers, while one researcher performed the interview based on the interview guide and the other researcher took an observing role during the interview and made notes.

Document Analysis: We supplemented the interviews with analysis of internal documents, particularly, GenAI usage guidelines for software development processes. Notably, only GMT maintains a formalized internal GenAI guideline; the other organizations provide informal guidance, functioning as living artifacts (Fig. 1).

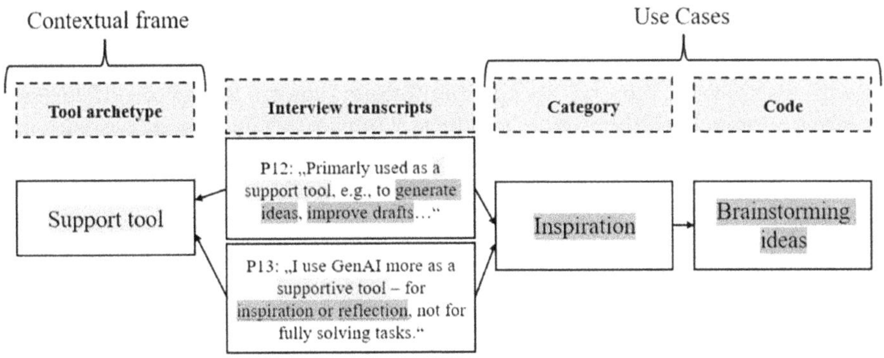

Fig. 1. Example of the coding process.

3.3 Data Extraction and Analysis

Thematic Analysis and Coding: Recorded interviews were transcribed using Microsoft Teams and Whisper AI. The resulting transcripts were subsequently reviewed and edited by the second and third authors to ensure accuracy and completeness. These validated transcripts formed the basis for thematic analysis following Braun and Clarke [6] to identify adoption patterns. The process involved six phases: familiarization, initial coding, theme identification, theme review, theme definition, and reporting.

In order to establish a reliable and consistent coding process, multiple authors (authors 24 for the Dinoco case; 57 for GMT; and author 8 for Insight Inc.) independently coded a subset of the material. Their coding outputs were then compared and discussed with the first author. Any divergences were resolved through collaborative deliberation, fostering a shared understanding of the data and enhancing the stability of the thematic structure. This iterative procedure ensured that the resulting themes were both empirically grounded and aligned with the overall aims of the study.

Cross-Case Analysis: To strengthen the results of the multiple-case study, we conducted a cross-case analysis following Yin [37]. For each case, the data were transferred into Microsoft Excel and examined for thematic overlaps, using separate sheets for contextual information, role-specific use cases, and identified barriers and benefits. We first compared context-related information (*e.g.*, licensed GenAI tools or usage guidelines) across all three cases. Second, we analyzed the use cases, all of which appeared in at least two cases, meaning no borderline cases occurred. Third, we compared categories and codes from the interviews to identify overlaps in reported barriers and benefits. The analysis was carried out by the first author and validated by one additional researcher (the second author), with no discrepancies identified.

3.4 Threats to Validity

As with every study, ours has specific limitations that are inherent to the chosen research approach. Although we conducted our study in accordance with the relevant guidelines, we acknowledge the limitations and explain the actions we took to mitigate their impact. To do so, we used the Threats to Validity schema according to Wohlin et al. [36] and Runeson and Höst [25]. Due to space limitations, we focus on the most important aspects here. A detailed explanation of the limitations of this study can be found in our research protocol [20].

Construct Validity: Our interview participants may have interpreted specific terms related to GenAI (LLM or GPT) differently or assigned varying meanings to key concepts such as prompting strategies and "guidelines". To address this, we provided clarification and used "such as Github CoPilot" or asked participants for specific examples to clarify their understanding and ensure consistency across responses.

Internal Validity: We took specific actions to follow the same approach in conducting the interviews to mitigate potential bias. First, the interview guideline was composed of neutral, non-leading questions. Additionally, the interviews were semi-structured, allowing us to explore topics in depth based on the interviewee's responses. Each interview was conducted by two researchers, ensuring rigor. Furthermore, we used different data sources to strengthen the internal validity of our findings.

External Validity: Our findings are constrained by the context of three German organizations operating under similar regulatory conditions. While the cases differ in size and structure, they do not represent the full range of software development environments. To support transferability, we provided detailed case descriptions and contextual information, enabling readers to assess the applicability of findings to their own settings.

4 Results

4.1 Contextual Information on GenAI Adoption

This section addresses RQ1: *What organizational and regulatory conditions shape GenAI adoption in practice?*

Organizational conditions cover both licensing of GenAI tools and training or coaching for professional use of GenAI in practice. Notably, none of the three cases offers training or coaching for GenAI usage in their software development teams. Interestingly, at GMT, while company policy mandates at least two annual training sessions on AI applications and legal frameworks, interviewees were either unaware of these offerings or reported that the training focused exclusively on explaining the AI guideline itself rather than developing practical skills. This reveals a substantial gap between formal policy and practitioner needs.

Table 2. Overview of licensed GenAI tools

Tool	Dinoco	GMT	Insight Inc.
ChatGPT	no	no	yes
ChatGPT Pro Version	no	no	yes
GitHub Co-Pilot	yes	yes	no
Microsoft Co-Pilot	yes	yes	no

Regarding licensing, an overview is provided in Table 2. The governance mechanisms for tool selection differ markedly across cases. At Dinoco, licensing decisions are led by compliance and top management, following a risk-averse strategy that favors established vendors; for instance, Co-Pilot was licensed through existing Office 365 agreements. GMT, by contrast, follows a formal company guideline that classifies tools according to the EU AI Act's risk pyramid (Minimal, Limited, High Risk) [12], maintains an official whitelist, requires management approval, and involves an internal expert group for validating newly requested tools. Key criteria include customer data protection, legal compliance, data-leakage prevention, and control over tools transmitting usage data externally. At Insight Inc., no comparable governance structure exists.

A gap exists between sanctioned and actual tool usage. Tools such as DeepL Write, Gemini, and NotebookLM are not licensed in any of the three cases, yet unsanctioned tool usage is common. At both Dinoco and GMT, ChatGPT functions as a form of "shadow IT," despite lacking approval. At Dinoco, an informal agreement permits developers to use ChatGPT during "private time." At GMT, survey and interview data confirm ChatGPT as the most frequently used tool. In contrast, Insight Inc. licenses ChatGPT, though employees occasionally rely on private accounts for sensitive topics to ensure data separation.

Internal guidelines for GenAI use constitute a critical regulatory dimension. At Dinoco, the use of ChatGPT is not explicitly regulated, whereas clear policies exist for GitHub Co-Pilot and Microsoft Co-Pilot. Nevertheless, several interviewees reported using the Pro version of ChatGPT for work-related tasks. The specific use of these tools varies considerably across roles: while Agile Coaches and Product Owners use ChatGPT frequently, developers rely on it less often. Due to the integration of Co-Pilot tools into the IDE, their use is more seamless and compliance can be more easily monitored. Furthermore, regulatory aspects also include data protection, which is explicitly governed through agreements between Dinoco and the respective tool providers. For instance, P03 stated: "Dinoco [...] *has made an agreement with Copilot that the data may not be used to evaluate or train the model.*"

At GMT, several interviewees highlighted concerns that certain GenAI tools or models may not ensure sufficient data sovereignty, as user inputs and the information they contain can be used for model training. Given the opaque nature of AI model operations, it cannot always be determined how such data are further processed. Consequently, GenAI tools cannot be applied to code segments involving sensitive information, such as encryption keys or personal data. Without formal guidelines, users "[...] *often rely on personal judgement, experience or informal principles*" (P11). While this approach allows for flexibility, it also entails risks related to consistency, legal certainty, and accountability. P14 emphasized that formal frameworks are frequently missing within organizations, resulting in uncertainty, inconsistent implementation, and highly individualized approaches. At the same time, there is a strong demand for clear, pragmatic and legally sound guidance. Such guidelines are particularly essential for fostering acceptance of the technology among less experienced users.

Concluding our findings for RQ1, we observe that while ChatGPT emerges as the most frequently used tool across all three cases, the organizational conditions governing GenAI adoption differ considerably. Licensing arrangements vary, with Insight Inc. providing company-licensed ChatGPT accounts while Dinoco and GMT license Co-Pilot tools instead. Governance mechanisms range from formalized approval processes with internal expert groups (GMT) to compliance-driven top-level decisions (Dinoco) to largely absent formal frameworks (Insight Inc.). Crucially, even where policies exist, adherence is inconsistent; some employees circumvent regulations by using private accounts for work-related tasks.

4.2 Applied GenAI Use-Cases in Agile Software Development

This section addresses RQ2: *Which use cases of GenAI tools are adopted in agile software development teams?*

The cross-case analysis revealed three clusters of use cases and three roles applying in total 21 use cases. We categorized these use cases thematically, identifying 6 as creative tasks, 7 as documentation-related tasks, and 8 as coding-related tasks.

Use case adoption varies substantially by role and experience level. Product Owners and Agile Coaches reported higher-intensity usage, particularly for text-based creative tasks, while developers' adoption ranged from minimal to moderate depending on codebase characteristics. At GMT, one senior developer with 15 years' experience self-rated usage intensity at 1 out of 4, attributing low adoption to established workflows and extensive domain knowledge that reduced perceived need for AI assistance. Conversely, newer team members and those in product-focused roles reported more extensive integration of GenAI into daily work.

Figure 2 depicts the identified use cases by role. The complete cross-case analysis including a detailed overview per role and case, as well as systematic

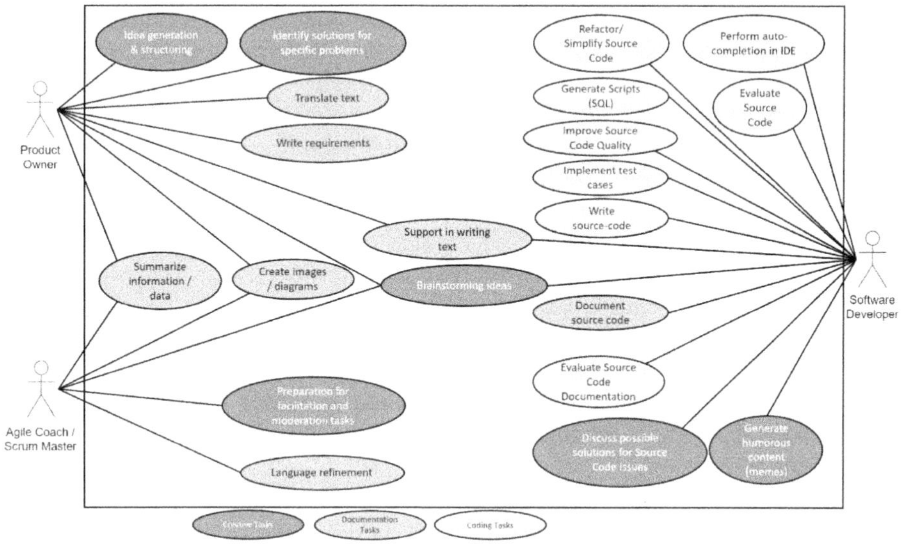

Fig. 2. Visualization of the identified use cases.

use case descriptions following a structured schema is available in our research protocol [20].

Across all three organizations, GenAI is primarily leveraged as a personal productivity assistant, augmenting individual tasks rather than transforming team collaboration. As shown in Fig. 2, we identified a clear pattern of role-specific adoption, with Product Owners, Agile Coaches/Scrum Masters, and Developers applying the tools to distinct aspects of their work. We characterize these patterns through three archetypes: the *Research Assistant* for creative and conceptual tasks, the *Virtual Tutor* for documentation and communication, and the *Pair Software Developer* for coding and technical activities.

Research Assistant: At Dinoco, GenAI is used specifically to support creative processes. P02 uses GenAI tools for brainstorming and idea validation: "*A lot for brainstorming, to have a practical communication partner and to validate a few ideas.*" P1 also reports typical use cases in which GenAI helps to structure thoughts: "*But then you often have these thought blocks: How do I get this into sensible words now*?". In these use cases, GenAI serves less as a pure source of information, but is seen as a discursive partner that provides impulses and removes creative blocks. A particularly prevalent use case across all roles and organizations is GenAI as an enhanced search mechanism, effectively replacing traditional web searches and Stack Overflow queries. Multiple developers characterized ChatGPT as their "first point of contact" for technical questions, valuing consolidated answers over navigating multiple search results.

Virtual Tutor: Product Owners use GenAI to formulate requirements faster. P01 describes this succinctly: "[...] *writing features and stories*". This example shows that GenAI is primarily used here to elaborate the content of user stories and thus simplifies writing work. From an Agile Coach/Scrum Master perspective, tools like ChatGPT were frequently mentioned as primary assistants for content generation, including drafting texts, brainstorming ideas, and refining formulations. P12 described GenAI as a "*very helpful sparring partner*" when initiating tasks or formulating complex content. P11 noted that while the tool does not necessarily complete tasks for them, it significantly accelerates their work by "*kicking off ideas faster*". Furthermore, several Agile Coaches/Scrum Masters (P01, P12, P14) mentioned that they use GenAI to prepare for retrospectives by generating creative formats or by refining formulations in team surveys. Others highlighted that it helps them organize thoughts when faced with a blank page, particularly for internal presentations or training materials (e.g., P13). These scenarios suggest that GenAI is mainly used to support the early phases of cognitive work (ideation, structuring, and polishing) rather than full automation.

Beyond agile artifacts, Product Owners and coaches employ GenAI extensively for stakeholder communication. At GMT, one Product Owner (P8) reported using Microsoft Copilot daily to formulate customer emails, particularly for business English communication where uncertainty about professional phrasing exists. The tool serves as both translator and style consultant. At Dinoco, similar patterns emerge for refining internal communications and ensuring professional tone in external correspondence. This communication support function operates largely invisibly improving message quality without transforming the underlying work process.

Pair Software Developer: For developers, GenAI primarily simplifies standard tasks. Its most valued contributions include generating "*boilerplate code*" (P03), writing repetitive unit tests (P03), and providing "*auto-completion within the IDE*" (P04). Beyond code generation, a common use case is understanding existing code; developers frequently ask the AI to explain complex snippets, especially when working with large, legacy codebases. Most interviewees reported using GenAI as a "pair programmer" to improve, refactor, or get a "*second opinion*" on code segments (P04). This interaction sometimes evolves into a collaborative problem-solving dialogue. Documentation, a notoriously time-consuming task is another key application, used for generating both inline comments and commit messages. One GMT developer noted documenting more because AI makes it faster. These findings confirm that GenAI's value in development lies in automating routine work and augmenting the developer's understanding, allowing them to focus on more complex problem-solving.

Interestingly, none of the interviewees reported using GenAI for decision-making or for directly facilitating meetings, citing concerns about quality, ethics, and team acceptance. Instead, this technology is viewed as a background tool that empowers but does not replace the human element of agile ways of working. Overall, GenAI tools appear to be most effective when they are seamlessly integrated into existing processes and support specific tasks. Perceived value largely depends on the user's role, the specific use case, and individual approaches to the technology.

4.3 Benefits & Barriers of GenAI Adoption

This section addresses RQ3: *What benefits and barriers do agile team members associate with GenAI adoption?*

Benefits can be grouped into three categories: 1) efficiency gains in coding, 2) overall task efficiency through automation, and 3) enhanced creativity in early project phases.

First, GenAI enables efficiency gains in coding by simplifying or optimizing code segments through access to a broader knowledge base than individual developers possess. Developers reported reduced time for boilerplate code generation, faster prototyping for customer requests, and accelerated resolution of unfamiliar technical challenges. GMT developers also reported learning new language features, design patterns, and optimization techniques from AI suggestions. Second, GenAI enhances overall task efficiency by automating routine activities and generating code skeletons, thereby accelerating development processes. It can also handle tedious tasks such as documentation, allowing developers to focus more on value-adding activities. Beyond efficiency gains, GenAI tools also foster creativity, particularly in early project phases such as requirements definition and concept development. They provide inspiration, structure, and support out-of-the-box thinking. Some interviewees also mentioned the use of prompt templates to streamline their work. These insights suggest that GenAI contributes not only to implementation but also to ideation and conceptual design.

Perceived benefits, however, vary by role. While Product Owners and Requirements Engineers described GenAI as a valuable support tool, developers expressed more reserved attitudes, indicating that the impact of GenAI depends strongly on professional role and context of use. This divergence is particularly pronounced at Dinoco, where developers characterized productivity gains as "*modest or even neutral*", with one senior developer (P04) asserting that "*productivity cannot meaningfully be measured*" calling into question the empirical basis for claimed efficiency improvements.

Alongside these benefits, three clusters of barriers emerged: 1) validation and quality assurance effort, 2) effort required to effectively use and integrate GenAI tools, and 3) bureaucratic and governance-related barriers.

The first concerns the effort required to validate GenAI outputs and the risk of uncritically adopting generated results. At GMT, this validation burden is formalized through the AI guideline, which mandates that AI-generated content may only be used after two independent, authorized persons have reviewed and approved it via email. However, this rule is unworkable in practice, as the overhead of a two-person review for every AI-generated snippet would create unsustainable bottlenecks. Several interviewees perceived this as problematic, noting that hidden code dependencies demand a thorough understanding of functionality for correct operation and debugging. As GenAI occasionally produces inaccurate outputs, critical evaluation remains essential.

The second cluster relates to the effort involved in effectively using GenAI. Interviewees emphasized that meaningful results often require substantial input and context, yet the outcome may still lack value. Developers at Dinoco stressed that supplying sufficient context is time-consuming, and incomplete prompts frequently lead to generic or unusable responses. Enhancing usability, by simplifying interaction and reducing reliance on prompt engineering, was seen as crucial. Better integration into existing tools, such as Copilot in Visual Studio Code, was cited as an effective solution, as it allows suggestions directly within the IDE.

The third cluster involves bureaucratic challenges, primarily stemming from GMT's AI guidelines. The mandatory evaluation of GenAI models prior to use was perceived as a barrier to experimentation. Additionally, employees at Dinoco and GMT must manage their own accounts without centralized support, requiring them to independently identify suitable models and verify approval status. Some interviewees also expressed concern that GenAI use might prompt uncomfortable questions or require justification to supervisors, particularly when no tangible results are achieved. For larger organizations, a central obstacle lies in the organizational restrictive attitude towards GenAI tools. This was addressed by several respondents. P01 emphasized: "*My experience with* [Dinoco] *- or with other companies - is that everything is always so restrictive and hostile to innovation.*" This points to structural hurdles that can slow innovation due to safety concerns or bureaucratic processes. At Dinoco, the compliance department's approval requirement acts as a bottleneck; ChatGPT's non-approved status leads developers to use it anyway, reframed as "private time" usage. Although official regulations exist, the actual implementation is often left to the employees themselves. Responsibility for compliant behavior thus becomes highly individualized, while organizational support remains limited. The barrier, therefore, is not merely bureaucratic friction, but the lack of organizational pathways to reconcile security requirements with practical needs forcing employees to choose between compliance and productivity.

In summary, interviewees reported time savings, enhanced creativity, and support for routine tasks as major benefits, but also concerns about data privacy, dependency on AI-generated output, and lack of transparency. These mixed perceptions underscore the importance of context-sensitive implementation and support mechanisms.

5 Discussion

Our findings contribute to the growing body of empirical research on GenAI adoption in software development by offering a practice-centered perspective from within agile teams. To systematically interpret and extend these insights, we employ the Technology-Organization-Environment (TOE) framework [8] as a theoretical lens. The TOE framework posits that technology adoption is shaped by three interrelated contextual dimensions: (1) the technological context, including characteristics of available and internal technologies; (2) the organizational context, encompassing structural attributes, resources, and human capital; and (3) the environmental context, referring to external pressures such as industry conditions and regulatory requirements. By applying this lens, we structure our discussion around how each dimension influences GenAI adoption in agile settings and how tensions across these dimensions give rise to the compliance gaps observed in our study.

Technology Context: The technological dimension centers on tool capabilities and limitations. In line with Kemell et al. [15], we observe that GenAI is predominantly used as a personal productivity assistant, augmenting individual performance rather than fundamentally altering team-level processes. Recent studies by Russo [26] and Banh et al. [4] highlight the importance of seamless workflow integration as a prerequisite for sustained GenAI adoption. Our findings corroborate this, demonstrating that tools embedded into existing development environments, such as Copilot in VS Code, facilitate coding tasks with minimal workflow disruption. However, whereas Kemell et al. [15] limit their scope predominantly to GenAI as a programming assistant, we find that the technological context extends to conversational tools leveraged for communicative and facilitation tasks including retrospective preparation and team alignment.

The technological context also reveals critical limitations regarding validation. The validation burden associated with AI-generated outputs represents a fundamental technological constraint, current GenAI tools cannot guarantee accuracy, necessitating human review that partially offsets efficiency gains. While Kemell et al. [15] frame this primarily as a user capability issue (evaluation difficulty), our findings suggest validation becomes a process bottleneck when organizations impose rigid review procedures that conflict with agile velocity. This constraint is thus not merely technological or individual, but emerges from the interaction between tool limitations and organizational policy responses. Furthermore, interviewees emphasized that meaningful results require substantial context, yet supplying it is time-consuming, and incomplete prompts frequently lead to generic or unusable responses.

Our results further indicate that perceived benefits vary substantially by experience level and organizational context. Senior developers working with legacy systems reported minimal productivity gains, challenging universal efficiency narratives. This suggests that GenAI's value is contingent on factors including domain expertise, codebase maturity, and established workflow efficiency rather than being universally transformative.

Organization Context: The organizational dimension encompasses role structures, internal capabilities, and the cultural readiness of teams to adopt GenAI. While Kemell et al. [15] broadly distinguish between"individual users" and "management" and emphasize governance mechanisms, our explicit focus on agile roles (Product Owners, Agile Coaches/Scrum Masters, and Developers) highlights how role-specific affordances and agile values shape GenAI usage. Based on our analysis, we identify three archetypes that characterize how GenAI is appropriated across agile teams: (1) the *Research Assistant*, where GenAI supports creative and conceptual tasks such as brainstorming, idea validation, and strategic exploration; (2) the *Virtual Tutor*, where GenAI aids documentation, communication refinement, user story formulation, and stakeholder correspondence; and (3) the *Pair Software Developer*, where GenAI assists with code generation, code explanation, debugging, and technical problem-solving. These archetypes reveal that GenAI adoption in agile contexts varies systematically by role, with Product Owners and Agile Coaches leveraging GenAI primarily as Research Assistants and Virtual Tutors, while Developers engage it predominantly as a Pair Software Developer.

The alignment between these archetypes and role-specific task demands determines adoption intensity and perceived value. Crucially, teams appropriate GenAI to align with agile values. Rather than automating core processes, the technology supports—but does not substitute, activities like requirement elicitation and team facilitation. This subtly reshapes work to amplify efficiency while preserving underlying social dynamics. However, organizational readiness remains limited; the absence of adequate training across all cases forces practitioners to develop competencies independently, creating a significant capability gap. This finding resonates with Kucharski's [16] observation that agile mindset leadership is critical for developing dynamic capabilities, particularly "sensing" (identifying technological opportunities) and "reconfiguring" (adapting processes to integrate innovations). Our cases suggest that organizations are failing to sense GenAI's potential systematically or to reconfigure learning pathways accordingly, leaving adoption dependent on individual initiative rather than organizational strategy.

Environment Context: The environmental dimension captures external regulatory pressures, industry norms, and competitive dynamics that shape GenAI adoption. Our findings reveal that data protection requirements constitute the most significant environmental constraints on adoption. Across all roles, GenAI remains subordinate to human judgment, reflecting both epistemic caution and adherence to human accountability. This is not merely a practitioner preference but, in some cases, an institutional mandate, at GMT, internal policies explicitly frame AI outputs as "recommendations" requiring human review, institutionalizing a human-in-the-loop practice. These institutional requirements reflect broader environmental pressures stemming from the EU AI Act's risk classification framework, data protection regulations (GDPR), and sector-specific compliance mandates. While this formalized response creates structured pathways for adoption, it simultaneously introduces bureaucratic friction.

Cross-Dimensional Tensions and the Compliance Gap: A central contribution of our study is identifying systematic tensions across TOE dimensions that manifest as compliance gaps. While Kemell et al. [15] document data privacy and regulatory concerns as adoption barriers, their analysis focuses on describing these challenges rather than examining their behavioral consequences. We extend this by revealing how practitioners systematically respond to and circumvent restrictive policies when compliance conflicts with productivity demands. Viewed through the TOE lens, this gap arises when environmental pressures (regulatory compliance) are translated into organizational policies without adequate consideration of technological characteristics and organizational constraints.

Our analysis reveals that a misalignment between top-down governance and bottom-up work practices creates systemic friction and leads to specific forms of Shadow IT. When organizational policies, designed to mitigate risk, fail to account for the day-to-day productivity needs of practitioners, they are often perceived as impractical and are informally bypassed [13]. This policy-practice gap manifests in distinct ways across our cases, but consistently leads to subversive adoption practices. For instance, GMT's mandatory two-person review for all AI outputs illustrates how strict compliance can conflict with the need for agile velocity. At Dinoco, developers reframe unapproved ChatGPT usage as "private time", an adaptive response that bypasses official regulations to resolve the conflict between policy and productivity. Furthermore, even where organizations provide licensed tools, we found that data protection constraints prohibiting realistic work content can render them impractical, driving practitioners toward unlicensed alternatives for convenience.

Ultimately, when tools offer substantial productivity benefits, prohibition without practical alternatives merely shifts usage into informal arrangements that may increase organizational risk. This challenges the assumption that restrictive policies alone ensure compliance, suggesting that effective governance requires creating frameworks practitioners can and will actually follow.

6 Conclusion and Future Work

This multiple-case study investigates how agile practitioners employ GenAI tools in organizational settings. The findings show that GenAI is already integrated across a wide range of agile practices from repetitive tasks such as code implementation and user-story writing to more strategic activities like team facilitation and reflection. Yet its adoption also presents challenges, including legal ambiguities, the need for governance frameworks, and concerns about data security and trust. Overall, while GenAI offers considerable potential to strengthen agile roles, its integration must be carefully managed to align with organizational structures and policies.

Given that GenAI is already used by software development teams across various organizations, several further questions arise: Do other organizations employ GenAI in similar ways, and does access to adequate training improve team effectiveness? Addressing these questions requires broader empirical research that compares current practices across the wider industry. Future studies could, for example, examine additional organizations across different countries and regulatory regimes to contrast their approaches and outcomes.

Acknowledgements % Final Remark. A. Przybylek's contribution was funded by Taighde Éireann—Research Ireland (Grant No.13/RC/2094_2). Co-funded by the European Union (SyMeCo, Grant No.101081459). The views expressed are solely those of the author(s). Neither the European Union nor the European Research Executive Agency can be held responsible for them.

As a final note, we acknowledge that the text of this paper was refined with the assistance of LLMs. The authors reviewed and edited all content generated using this service and take full responsibility for the published article.

References

1. Alami, A., Ernst, N.: Human and machine: how software engineers perceive and engage with ai-assisted code reviews compared to their peers. In: Proceedings of the 18th International Conference on Cooperative and Human Aspects of Software Engineering, pp. 63–74 (2025)
2. Arora, C., Herda, T., Homm, V.: Generating test scenarios from nl requirements using retrieval-augmented LLMs: an industrial study. In: Proceedings of the 32nd International Requirements Engineering Conference, pp. 240–251 (2024)
3. Bahi, A., Gharib, J., Gahi, Y.: Integrating generative AI for advancing agile software development and mitigating project management challenges. Int. J. Adv. Comput. Sci. Appl. **15**(3) (2024)
4. Banh, L., Holldack, F., Strobel, G.: Copiloting the future: how generative ai transforms software engineering. Inf. Softw. Technol. **183**, 107751 (2025)
5. Basili, V., Caldiera, G., Rombach, D.: The goal question metric approach, pp. 528–532 (1994)
6. Braun, V., Clarke, V.: Using thematic analysis in psychology. Qual. Res. Psychol. **3**(2), 77–101 (2006)
7. Coutinho, M., Marques, L., Santos, A., Dahia, M., França, C., Souza Santos, R.: The role of generative ai in software development productivity: A pilot case study. In: Proceedings of the 1st ACM International Conference on AI-Powered Software, pp. 131–138 (2024)
8. Depietro, R., Wiarda, E., Fleischer, M.: The context for change: organization, technology and environment. Process. Technol. Innov. **199**, 151–175 (1990)
9. Diebold, P.: From backlogs to bots: generative ai's impact on agile role evolution. J. Softw. Evol. Process **37**(1), e2740 (2025)
10. Dong, C., Jiang, Y., Zhang, Y., Zhang, Y., Liu, H.: Chatgpt-based test generation for refactoring engines enhanced by feature analysis on examples. In: Proceedings of the 47th International Conference on Software Engineering, pp. 2714–2725 (2025)
11. Ebert, C., Louridas, P.: Generative ai for software practitioners. IEEE Softw. **40**(4), 30–38 (2023)
12. European Union: Regulation (EU) 2024/1689 on harmonised rules on artificial intelligence . https://eur-lex.europa.eu/legal-content/EN/TXT/?uri=CELEX:32024R1689 (2024), Accessed 29 Nov 2025
13. Jarzebowicz, A., Ślesiński, W.: Assessing effectiveness of recommendations to requirements-related problems through interviews with experts. In: 2018 Federated Conference on Computer Science and Information Systems (FedCSIS), pp. 959–968. IEEE (2018)
14. Karlovs-Karlovskis, U.: Generative artificial intelligence use in optimising software engineering process: a systematic literature review. Appl. Comput. Syst. **29**(1), 68–77 (2024)
15. Kemell, K.K., Saarikallio, M., Nguyen-Duc, A., Abrahamsson, P.: Still just personal assistants? – a multiple case study of generative ai adoption in software organizations. Inf. Softw. Technol. **186**, 107805 (2025)

16. Kucharski, M., Kucharska, W., Jussila, J.: Impact of agile software development team leaders' mindset on dynamic capabilities for achieving organizational agility. In: Luković, I., et al. (eds.) Empowering the Interdisciplinary Role of ISD in Addressing Contemporary Issues in Digital Transformation (ISD2025 Proceedings) (2025)
17. Kwok, Y.T.C., Adil, M.: Ai and teamwork in agile software development: a systematic mapping study. In: Agile Processes in Software Engineering and Extreme Programming – Workshops, pp. 32–40. Springer Nature Switzerland, Cham (2026)
18. Mendes, W., Souza, S., De Souza, C.: You're on a bicycle with a little motor: benefits and challenges of using ai code assistants. In: Proceedings of the 17th International Conference on Cooperative and Human Aspects of Software Engineering, pp. 144–152 (2024)
19. Mock, M., Melegati, J., Russo, B.: Generative ai for test driven development: preliminary results. In: Agile Processes in Software Engineering and Extreme Programming – Workshops, pp. 24–32. Springer, Cham (2025)
20. Neumann, M., et al.: Research protocol (2025). https://doi.org/10.5281/zenodo.18520760
21. Neumann, M., Rauschenberger, M., Schön, E.M.: We need to talk about chatgpt': the future of ai and higher education. In: Proceedings of the 5th International Workshop on Software Engineering Education for the Next Generation, pp. 29–32 (2023)
22. Nguyen-Duc, A., et al.: Generative artificial intelligence for software engineering—a research agenda. Softw. Pract. Experience **55**(11), 1806–1843 (2025)
23. Oertel, J., Klünder, J., Hebig, R.: Don't settle for the first! how many github copilot solutions should you check? Inf. Softw. Technol. **183**, 107737 (2025)
24. Rauf, I., Sharp, H., Lopez, T., Wermelinger, M.: Human-machine teaming and team effectiveness in ai tools for software engineering. In: Proceedings of the 18th International Conference on Cooperative and Human Aspects of Software Engineering, pp. 75–80 (2025)
25. Runeson, P., Höst, M.: Guidelines for conducting and reporting case study research in software engineering. Empir. Softw. Eng. **14**(2), 131–164 (2009)
26. Russo, D.: Navigating the complexity of generative ai adoption in software engineering. ACM Trans. Softw. Eng. Methodol. **33**(5) (2024)
27. Russo, D., et al.: Generative ai in software engineering must be human-centered: the copenhagen manifesto. J. Syst. Softw. **216** (2024)
28. Salah, M., Abdelfattah, F., Halbusi, H.A.: Generative artificial intelligence (chatgpt & bard) in public administration research: a double-edged sword for street-level bureaucracy studies. Int. J. Public Adm. **0**(0), 1–7 (2023)
29. Sami, M.A., et al.: A multi-agent llm system for automated requirements analysis: A study on user story generation and prioritization. In: Proceedings of the 51st Euromicro Conference on Software Engineering and Advanced Applications, pp. 178–187 (2025)
30. Santos, I., Felizardo, K.R., Steinmacher, I., Gerosa, M.A.: Great power brings great responsibility: Personalizing conversational ai for diverse problem-solvers. In: Proceedings of the 18th International Conference on Cooperative and Human Aspects of Software Engineering, pp. 93–95 (2025)
31. Sauvola, J., Tarkoma, S., Klemettinen, M., Riekki, J., Doermann, D.: Future of software development with generative ai. Autom. Softw. Eng. **31**(26) (2024)
32. Stray, V., Moe, N., Ganeshan, N., Kobbenes, S.: Generative ai and developer workflows: how github copilot and chatgpt influence solo and pair programming. In: Proceedings of the 58th Hawaii International Conference on System Sciences (2025)

33. Tanzil, M.H., Khan, J.Y., Uddin, G.: Chatgpt incorrectness detection in software reviews. In: Proceedings of the 46th International Conference on Software Engineering (2024)
34. Ulfsnes, R., et al: Responsible ai in agile software engineering - an industry perspective. In: Marchesi, L., et al. (eds.) Agile Processes in Software Engineering and Extreme Programming – Workshops. pp, 33–41. Springer, Cham (2025). https://doi.org/10.1007/978-3-031-72781-8_4
35. Ulfsnes, R., Moe, N.B., Stray, V., Skarpen, M.: Transforming Software Development with Generative AI: Empirical Insights on Collaboration and Workflow, pp. 219–234 (2024)
36. Wohlin, C., et al.: The success factors powering industry-academia collaboration. IEEE Softw. **29**(2), 67–73 (2012). https://doi.org/10.1109/MS.2011.92
37. Yin, R.K.: Case study research: Design and methods, applied social research methods series, vol. 5. Sage, Los Angeles, 4. ed. edn. (2009)
38. Zhang, S., et al.: Empowering agile-based generative software development through human-ai teamwork. ACM Trans. Softw. Eng. Methodol. **34**(6) (2025)
39. Zhang, Z., Rayhan, M., Herda, T., Goisauf, M., Abrahamsson, P.: LLm-based agents for automating the enhancement of user story quality: an early report. In: Proceedings of the 25th International Conference on Agile Software Development, pp. 117–126. Springer, Cham (2024)

Author Index

A. Goldman et al. (Eds.): XP 2026, LNBIP 578, pp. 309–310, 2026.
https://doi.org/10.1007/978-3-032-22375-3

www.ingramcontent.com/pod-product-compliance
Ingram Content Group UK Ltd.
Pitfield, Milton Keynes, MK11 3LW, UK
UKHW020953220926
475831UK00001B/56

* 9 7 8 3 0 3 2 2 2 3 7 4 6 *